crypto

also by steven levy

Insanely Great: The Life and Times of Macintosh,
 the Computer That Changed Everything

Artificial Life: How Computers Are Transforming Our
 Understanding of Evolution and the Future of Life

The Unicorn's Secret: Murder in the Age of Aquarius

Hackers: Heroes of the Computer Revolution

how the code rebels beat the government—
saving privacy in the digital age

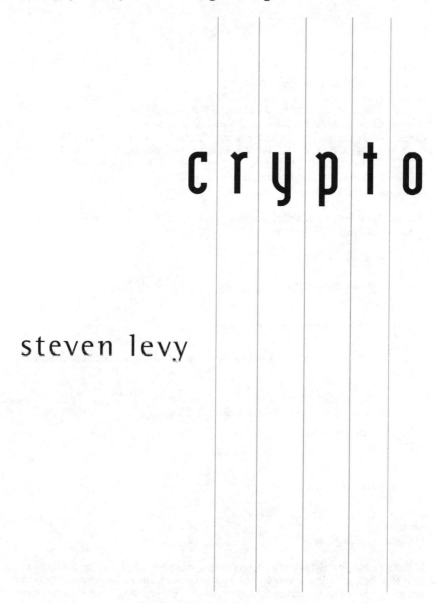

crypto

steven levy

viking

VIKING
Published by the Penguin Group
Penguin Putnam Inc., 375 Hudson Street, New York, New York 10014, U.S.A.
Penguin Books Ltd, 27 Wrights Lane, London W8 5TZ, England
Penguin Books Australia Ltd, Ringwood, Victoria, Australia
Penguin Books Canada Ltd, 10 Alcorn Avenue, Toronto, Ontario, Canada M4V 3B2
Penguin Books (N.Z.) Ltd, 182–190 Wairau Road, Auckland 10, New Zealand

Penguin Books Ltd, Registered Offices:
Harmondsworth, Middlesex, England

First published in 2001 by Viking Penguin,
a member of Penguin Putnam Inc.

10 9 8 7 6 5 4 3

Library of Congress Cataloging-in-Publication Data

Levy, Steven.
    Crypto : how the code rebels beat the government, saving privacy in the digital age /
Steven Levy.
        p.   cm.
    ISBN 0-670-85950-8
    1. Computer security.   2. Cryptography.   I. Title.

QA76.9.A25 L49 2001
005.8—dc21

                                                                          00-043809

This book is printed on acid-free paper. ∞

Printed in the United States of America
Set in Life
Designed by Nancy Resnick

To Teresa and Andrew

acknowledgments

The backbone of *Crypto* is a series of interviews conducted over the past decade with the people who populate, or have had an impact on, the world of cryptography. Obviously, my deepest thanks go to those who have given time and attention to an outsider who wanted to tell a good story. I hope that none of those who cooperated with me will take offense if I single out a few for duty above and beyond: Len Adleman, Jim Bidzos, David Chaum, Whitfield Diffie, Mary Fischer, Eric Hughes, Tim May, Ray Ozzie, Ron Rivest, and Phil Zimmermann.

From September 1994 to June 1995, I was a Fellow at the Freedom Forum Media Studies Center, then located on the Columbia University campus. I enthusiastically acknowledge the kindness of the Freedom Forum, the accommodations and assistance of the Media Studies Center staff, and the terrific company and well-timed wisdom of my fellow Fellows. My researcher there, Kaushik Arunagiri, dug out innumerable documents and also walked me through some math. John Kasdan kindly allowed me to audit his cyberlaw course and Matt Blaze and Joan Feigenbaum welcomed me to their computer science course on cryptography.

Mark Rotenberg, David Banisar, and David Sobel of the Electronic Privacy Information Center gave me access to the astounding documents coughed up by the government under their skillful use of the Freedom of Information Act. John Gilmore and his lawyer Lee Tien also provided me with armloads of declassified materials. Roger Schlafly sent me a huge pack of documents related to RSA and Cylink. Simpson Garfinkel e-mailed me notes of interviews he did for his book, *PGP.* (Other suppliers will remain nameless, but thanks to them, too.)

During the past eight years, I wrote a number of magazine articles on crypto, and some of these are reflected in this book, particularly those I wrote for *Wired,* beginning with the cover story on cypherpunks in its second issue and winding up with the first detailed account of nonsecret encryption in 1999. Thanks to all my editors there, especially Kevin Kelly. I also wrote crypto-related stories for *The New York Times Sunday Magazine, Macworld,* and *Newsweek.* The latter has been my professional home for the past five years, and I am grateful to everyone there for providing an inveterate freelance writer with a reason to actually hold a job. Thanks to Mark Whitaker, Jon Meacham, and the editor who suffers most with me, George Hackett. I also owe a large debt to the late Maynard Parker.

At Viking, editor Pam Dorman hung tough throughout the marathon. Ann Mah kept the bits flowing. Victoria Wright was both a master transcriber and sharp observer. My agent, Flip Brophy, was once again a flawless advisor and facilitator. And some early readers caught mistakes and offered great suggestions (I won't cite them by name because any errors are solely mine). Those who discover more are encouraged to get in touch with me through my Web site (www.steven levy.com), where I will post corrections and updates.

Words, even in plaintext, can't express what I owe my family, Andrew and Teresa.

Steven Levy, September 2000

contents

Acknowledgments | vii

Preface | 1

The Loner | 3

The Standard | 37

Public Key | 66

Prime Time | 90

Selling Crypto | 125

Patents and Keys | 155

Crypto Anarchy | 187

The Clipper Chip | 226

Slouching Toward Crypto | 269

Epilogue: The Open Secret | 313

Notes | 331

Bibliography | 343

Glossary | 345

Index | 349

crypto

preface

The telegraph, telephone, radio, and especially the computer have put everyone on the globe within earshot—at the price of our privacy. It may feel like we're performing an intimate act when, sequestered in our rooms and cubicles, we casually use our cell phones and computers to transmit our thoughts, confidences, business plans, and even our money. But clever eavesdroppers, and sometimes even not-so-clever ones, can hear it all. We think we're whispering, but we're really broadcasting.

A potential antidote exists: cryptography, the use of secret codes and ciphers to scramble information so that it's worthless to anyone but the intended recipients. And it's through the magic of cryptography that many communications conventions of the real world—such as signatures, contracts, receipts, and even poker games—will find their way to the ubiquitous electronic commons. But as recently as the early 1970s, a deafening silence prevailed over this amazing technology. Governments, particularly that of the United States, managed to stifle open discussion on any aspect of the subject that ventured beyond schoolboy science. Anyone who pursued the fundamental issues about crypto, or, worse, attempted to create new codes or crack old ones, was doomed to a solitary quest that typically led to closed doors, suddenly terminated phone connections, or even subtle warnings to think about something else.

The crypto embargo had a sound rationale: the very essence of cryptography is obscurity, and the exposure that comes from the dimmest ray of sunlight illuminating the working of a government cipher could result in catastrophic damage. An outsider who knew how our encryption worked could make his or her own codes; a foe who learned what codes we could break would shun those codes thereafter.

But what if governments were not the only potential beneficiaries of cryptography? What if the people themselves needed it, to protect their communications and personal data from any and all intruders, including the government itself? Isn't everybody entitled to privacy? Doesn't the advent of computer communications mean that everyone should have access to the sophisticated tools that allow the exchange of words with lawyers and lovers, coworkers and customers, physicians and priests with the same confidence granted face-to-face conversations behind closed doors?

This book tells the story of the people who asked those questions and created a revolution in the field that is destined to change all our lives. It is also the story of those who did their best to make the questions go away. The former were nobodies: computer hackers, academics, and policy wonks. The latter were the most powerful people in the world: spies, and generals, and presidents. Guess who won.

the loner

Mary Fischer loathed Whitfield Diffie on sight. He was a type she knew all too well, an MIT brainiac whose arrogance was a smoke screen for a massive personality disorder. The year of the meeting was 1969; the location a hardware store near Central Square in Cambridge, Massachusetts. Over his shoulder he carried a length of wire apparently destined for service as caging material for some sort of pet. This was a typical purchase for Diffie, whose exotic animal collection included a nine-foot python, a skunk, and a rare *genetta genetta,* a furry mongooselike creature whose gland secretions commonly evoked severe allergic reactions in people. It lived on a diet of live rats and at unpredictable moments would nip startled human admirers with needlelike fangs. An owner of such a creature would normally be of interest to Mary Fischer, an animal lover who at that very moment had a squirrel in her pocket. At home she also had a skunk as well as two dogs, a fox, a white-wing trumpeter bird, and two South American kinkajous. Diffie saw that she was buying some cage clips and abruptly focused his attention on her.

In future years, Whit Diffie would be known—extraordinarily well known—as the codiscoverer of public key cryptography, an iconographic figure with his shoulder-length blond hair, Buffalo Bill beard, and his bespoke suits cut by London tailors. But back in those days he was a wiry, crew-cut youth with "the angriest face I'd ever seen," Fischer says, and he immediately began peppering Mary Fischer with questions. *You keep exotic animals? Then you'll need this, and this, and this.* He took things out of her hands and put other things in as he lectured. His rudeness appalled Mary. But she hadn't yet cracked his code.

Mary Fischer didn't know that Diffie was spending prodigious amounts of time thinking about problems in computer security and their mathematical implications. She had no idea that he was casting about for a new way to preserve secrets. All she knew was that Whit Diffie was unappetizing and he loved animals. But animals meant a lot to her, and soon Diffie and his girlfriend began visiting Mary and her husband, sometimes accompanied by their creatures. The skunks got along, some ferrets were exchanged, and Diffie's visits to her home became routine.

Mary began to reconsider her initial repulsion to Diffie. But, in his failure to decode her, he seemed generally oblivious to her. On his visits he interacted only with the man of the house. After Mary and her husband moved to New Jersey, where he started veterinary school, she would sometimes pick up the ringing phone and hear Diffie's cuttingly precise voice brusquely ask for her spouse, as if she were an answering service. One day she made her feelings plain. "Look," she said, "I understand I'm not as bright as you and some of your friends, and I understand your friendship is primarily with my husband. But I don't really think it would kill you to say hello."

The message got through. Diffie's demeanor toward Mary dramatically improved, and she was not just startled but saddened when one day in 1971 he told her that he was going to travel for a while. Mary didn't know yet that Whit Diffie was preparing himself for a solitary—and romantic—quest, looking for answers to questions that the United States government didn't want asked. The odds against his success were astronomical, because he was confronting a near complete blockade of relevant information on a subject that, on its most sophisticated levels, was almost unspeakably obscure. What were the odds against such an unheralded outsider's transforming an entire field with an original discovery that would redefine the ground rules for personal privacy in the computer era?

The length of those odds would shorten with the role of Diffie's courtship of Mary Fischer in overcoming them—and a scientific breakthrough would result that affects every citizen in the digital age. "The discovery of public key," says Fischer, "was a romance."

Bailey Whitfield Diffie was born on the eve of D-Day, June 5, 1944. His professor father had just completed a wartime sabbatical in government service. (Though he disliked Communists—more for their humorless single-mindedness than their ideology—Whit Diffie's father was a passionate antifascist and often lectured against the repressive movement in Europe.) Both of Whit's parents were educated people. Bailey Wallace Diffie taught Iberian history and culture at City College in New York. Diffie's mother was the former Justine Louise Whitfield, a stockbroker's daughter from Tennessee who met her husband while working in the foreign service in Spain. She was a writer and scholar who studied Madame de Sévigné, a figure in the court of Louis XIII and Louis XIV.

Whit Diffie was always an independent sort. As one early friend remarked, "That kid had an alternative lifestyle at age five." Diffie didn't learn to read until he was ten years old. There was no question of disability; he simply preferred that his parents read to him, which seemingly they did, quite patiently. Apparently both parents understood that their son was extremely intelligent and obstinately contrarian, so they didn't press him. Finally, in the fifth grade, Diffie spontaneously worked his way through a tome called *The Space Cat*, and immediately progressed to the Oz books.

Later that year his teacher at P.S. 178—"Her name was Mary Collins, and if she is still alive I'd like to find her," Diffie would say decades later—spent an afternoon explaining something that would stick with him for a very long time: the basics of cryptography. Specifically, she described how one would go about solving something known as a substitution cipher.

Diffie found cryptography a delightfully conspiratorial means of expression. Its users collaborate to keep secrets in a world of prying eyes. A sender attempts this by transforming a private message to an altered state, a sort of mystery language: *encryption*. Once the message is transformed into a cacophonous babble, potential eavesdroppers are foiled. Only those in possession of the rules of transformation can restore the disorder back to the harmony of the message as it was first inscribed: *decryption*. Those who don't have that knowledge and try to decrypt messages without the secret "keys" are practicing "cryptanalysis."

A substitution cipher is one where someone creates *ciphertext* (the scrambled message) by switching the letters of the original message, or *plaintext,* with other letters according to a prearranged plan. The most basic of these has come to be known as the Caesar cipher, supposedly used by Julius Caesar himself. This system simply moved every character in the plaintext to the letter that occurs three notches later in the alphabet. (For instance, a Caesar cipher with its "key" of three would change A to D, B to E, and so on.) Slightly more challenging to an armchair cryptanalyst is a cryptosystem that matches every letter in the alphabet to one in a second, randomly rearranged alphabet. Newspaper pages often feature a daily "cryptogram" that encodes an aphorism or pithy quote in such a manner. These are by and large easy to crack because of the identifiable frequency of certain letters and the all-too-often predictable way they are distributed in words.

Like countless other curious young boys before him, Whit Diffie was thrilled by the process. In his history of cryptography, *The Codebreakers*, author David Kahn probes the emotional lures of secret writing, citing Freud's theory that the child's impulse to learn is tied to the desire to view the forbidden. "If you're a guy, you're trying to look up women's skirts," says Kahn. "When you get down to it basically, that's what it is, an urge to learn." For many, the fascination of crypto also deals with the thrill that comes from cracking encoded messages. Every intercepted ciphertext is, in effect, an invitation to assume the role of eavesdropper, intruder, voyeur. In any case, it wasn't the prospect of breaking codes that excited Whit Diffie but the more subtle pursuit of *creating* codes to *protect* information. "I never became a very good puzzle solver, and I never worked on solving codes very much then or later," he now says. He would always prefer keeping secrets to violating the secrets of others.

Diffie's response to Miss Collins's cryptography lesson was characteristic. He ignored her homework assignment, but independently pursued the subject in his own methodical, relentless fashion. He was particularly interested in her off-the-cuff remark that there were more complicated ciphers, including a foolproof "U.S. Code." He begged his father to check out all the books in the City College library that dealt with cryptography. Bailey Diffie promptly returned with an armload of books. Two of them were written for children; Diffie quickly devoured those. But then he got bogged down in Helen Forché Gaines's *Cryptanalysis*, a rather sophisticated 1939 tome.

Gaines offered a well-organized set of challenges that would provide hardworking amateurs an education in classical cryptographic systems. Many of these were refinements of advances made centuries ago, which in turn were more complicated variations of the earlier substitution ciphers. The best known were the polyalphabetic systems, first hatched in Vatican catacombs and later revealed in the early 1500s by a German monk named Johannes Trithemius. Published in 1518—two years after his death—Trithemius's *Polygraphia* introduced the use of tables, or tableaux, wherein each line was a separate, reshuffled alphabet. When you encoded your message, you transformed the first character of the text using the alphabet on the first line of the tableau. For the second character of your message you'd repeat the process with the scrambled alphabet on the second line, and so on.

On the heels of Trithemius came the innovations of a sixteenth-century French diplomat named Blaise de Vigenére. Here was a man who had penetrated the soul of crypto. "All things in the world constitute a cipher," he once observed. "All nature is merely a cipher and a secret writing." In the most famous of almost two dozen books he produced after his retirement from the diplomatic service, Vigenère produced devastating variations on previous polyalphabetic systems, adding complexity with a less predictable tableaux and "autokeys" that made use of the plaintext itself as a streaming key. The Vigenère system won a lasting reputation for security—it was known as *le chiffre indéchiffrable*—so much so that until almost the twentieth century, some armchair cryptographers believed that a certain streamlined version of the system was the sine qua non of cryptosystems.

Actually, by the time Diffie encountered them, the cryptologic arts had progressed dramatically since Vigenère. Still, Diffie's juvenile inquiries led him to think that Vigenère was the endpoint of the subject. Bored by the thought that cryptography was a problem already solved, he didn't delve too deeply into Gaines's book. His obsession with codes faded. At the time, he also felt that *everybody* was interested in codes, and, as a dogged contrarian, "this made it seem vulgar to me," he later recalled. "Instead, I learned about ancient fortifications, military maps, camouflage, poison gas, and germ warfare." He came to share his interests with a small group of teenage friends, and even considered pursuing a career in the armed forces, checking out the ROTC programs of universities he was interested in. But only one of Diffie's militia-minded clique actually enlisted in one of the armed services—and died in Vietnam.

Ultimately it was mathematics, not munitions, which dictated Diffie's choice of college. Math offered one thing that history did not: a sense of absolute truth. "I think that one of the central dilemmas of Whit's life has been to figure out what is really true," explains Mary Fischer, who says that early in the boy's life, Diffie's father was called to school and told that his son was a genius. As Fischer tells it, Bailey Diffie's reaction was to offer a ruse, in hopes that it would provoke discipline. He told Diffie that he wasn't as bright as other boys, but if he worked harder than those favored with high intelligence and applied himself, he might be able to achieve something. "With some children that might have worked," says Fischer, "but with Whit it was a bad tactic. It shook him for years, and I think it gave Whit a real hunger for what was ground-zero truth."

Though Diffie performed competently in school, he never did apply himself to the degree his father hoped. He was sometimes unruly in class; he worked best with material untainted by the stigma of having been assigned. Once a calculus teacher, fed up with Whit's noise-making, remarked, "One day you'll be roasting marshmallows in here!" and sure enough, the next class Diffie brought a Sterno can to toast the marshmallows a friend smuggled into school. He failed to fulfill the requirements for a full academic diploma, settling for a minimal distinction known as a general diploma. Nor did he attend graduation; he left with his father on a European trip. (The great tragedy of Diffie's high school years was the death of his mother; he still avoids talking about it.) Only stratospheric scores on standardized tests enabled him to enter the Massachusetts Institute of Technology in 1961.

"I wasn't a very good student there, either," Diffie admits. He was, however, dazzled by the brainpower of the student body, a collection of incandescent outcasts, visionaries, and prodigies, some of whom could solve in a minute problems that would take Diffie a day to complete. Of these mental luminaries, Whitfield Diffie might have seemed the least likely to produce a world-changing breakthrough. But since his brilliant friends were human beings and not high-powered automata, their trajectories proved far from predictable. Some of the very brightest wound up cycling through esoteric computer simulations, or proselytizing smart drugs, or teaching Transcendental Meditation.

Contemporaries from MIT recall Diffie vividly as a quirky teenager with blond hair sticking out from his head by two inches ("You wanted to take a lawn mower to it," says a friend). He bounded through campus on tiptoe, a weird walk that became an unmistakable signature in motion. But he was noted for his deep understanding of numbers as well.

He also took up computer programming—at first, Diffie now says, to get out of the draft. "I thought of computers as very low class," he says. "I thought of myself as a pure mathematician and was interested in partial differential equations and topology and things like that." But by 1965, when Diffie graduated from MIT, the Vietnam War was raging and he found himself deeply disenchanted with the trappings of armed conflict. "I had become a peacenik," he says. Not to mention a full-blown eccentric. He and his girlfriend lived in a small Cambridge apartment that eventually became packed with glass-walled tanks to hold their prodigious collection of exotic fauna. An aficionado of Chinese food, Diffie was also known for carrying around a pair of elegant chopsticks, much the way a serious billiard player totes his favorite cue.

To avoid the draft, Diffie accepted a job at the Mitre Corporation, which, as a defense contractor, could shelter its young employees from military service. His work had no direct connection to the war effort: he worked under a mathematician named Roland Silver, teaming up with another colleague to write a software package called Mathlab, which later evolved into a well-known symbolic mathematical manipulation system called Macsyma. (Though few knew of the nature of his contribution, the nerd cognoscenti understood that Diffie's work here involved a virtuosic mastery of arithmetic, numbers theory, and computer programming.)

Best of all, Diffie's team did not have to work at the Mitre offices but, in 1966, became a resident guest of the esteemed Marvin Minsky in the MIT artificial intelligence lab. During the three years he worked there, Diffie became part of this storied experiment in making machines smart, in pushing the frontiers of computer programming and in establishing an information-sharing ethos as the ground zero of computer culture. One aspect of this hacker-oriented society would turn out to be particularly relevant to the direction that Diffie's interests were heading. Just as some words in various languages have no meaning to drastically different civilizations (why would a tropical society need to speak of "snow"?), the AI lab had no technological equivalent for a term like "proprietary." Information was assumed to be as accessible as the air itself. As a consequence, there were no software locks on the operating system written by the MIT wizards.

Unlike his peers, however, Diffie believed that technology should offer a sense of privacy. And unlike some of his hacker colleagues, whose greatest kick came from playing in forbidden computer playgrounds, Diffie was drawn to questions of what software could be written to ensure that someone's files could not be accessed by intruders. To be sure, he participated in the literal safecracking that was a standard hobby in the AI lab: a favorite hacker pastime involved discovering new ways of opening government-approved secure safes. But Diffie got more of a kick from the protection of a strongly built safe than the rush of breaking a poorly designed system of locks and tumblers. He liked to keep his things in high-security filing cabinets and military safes.

In the information age, however, the ultimate information stronghold resides in software, not hardware: virtual safes protecting precious data. Information, after all, represents the treasure of the modern age, as valuable as all the doubloons and bangles of previous eras. The field charged with this responsibility back then was computer security, then in a nascent stage. Not many people bothered to discuss its philosophical underpinnings. But Diffie would often engage his boss in conversations on security. Inevitably, cryptography entered into their discussions.

Silver had some knowledge in the field, and the elder man opened Diffie's eyes to things unimaginable in his fifth-grade independent study. One day the pair sat in the cafeteria at Tech Square, the boxy nine-story building whose upper levels housed the AI lab, and Silver carefully explained to Diffie how modern cryptosystems worked.

Naturally, they depended on machinery. The machines that did the work—whether electromechanical devices like the Enigma cipher machines used by the Germans in World War II, or a contemporary computer-driven system—scrambled messages and documents by applying a unique recipe that would change the message, character by character. (The recipe for those transformations would be a set of complicated mathematical formulas or algorithms.) Only someone who had an identical machine or software program could reverse the process and divine the plaintext, with use of the special numerical key that had helped encrypt it.

In the case of the Enigma machines, that key involved "settings," the positions of the various code wheels that determined how each letter would be changed. Each day the encrypters would reset the wheels in a different way; those receiving the message would already have been informed of what those settings should be on that given day. That's why the Allied coup of recovering live Enigma machines—the key intelligence breakthrough of World War II—was only part of the elaborate codebreaking process that took place at Bletchley Park in England. The cryptanalysts also had to learn the process by which the Axis foes made their settings; then they could conduct what was known as a "brute force" attack that required going through all the possible combinations of settings. This could be efficiently done only by creating machines that were the forerunners of modern computers.

With computers, the equivalent of Enigma settings would become a *digital* key, a long string of numbers that would help determine how the system would transform the original message. Of course, the intended recipient of the message had to have not only the same computer program, but also that same key. But both mechanical and digital systems had two components: a so-called black box with the rules of transformation and a key that you'd feed into the black box along with your everyday message in plain English. Such was the background for what Silver talked about to Diffie that day—but not being privy to government secrets, he actually knew few of the details. He was able to explain, however, how computer cryptosystems generated a series of digits that represented a keystream, and how that would be "xor-ed" with the plaintext stream to get a ciphertext. (As any computer scientist knows, an xor operation involves pairing a digital bit with another bit, and generating a one or zero depending on whether they match.) If the key is suitably unpredictable, your output would be the most imponderable string of gibberish imaginable, recoverable (one hoped) only by using that same key to reverse the process.

Imponderable, of course, is a relative term, but those who devised cryptosystems had a standard to live up to: randomness. The idea was to create ciphertext that appeared to be as close to a random string of characters as possible. Otherwise, a smart, dedicated, and resourceful codebreaker could seize upon even the most subtle of patterns and eventually reconstruct the original message. A totally random stream could produce uncrackable code—this essentially represented the most secure form of encryption possible, the so-called one-time pad, a system that provided a truly randomly chosen substitute for every letter in the plaintext. One-time pads were the only cryptographic solution that was mathematically certain to be impervious to cryptanalysis.

The problem with one-time pads, however, was that for every character in the message, you needed a different number in the "key material" that originally transformed readable plaintext into jumbled ciphertext. In other words, a key for a one-time pad system had to be at least as long as the message and couldn't be used more than once. The unwieldiness of the process made it difficult to implement in the field. Even serious attempts to deploy one-time pads were commonly undermined by those tempted to save time and energy by reusing a pad.

His conversations with Silver excited Diffie. The subject of "pseudo-randomness" was clearly of importance to both the mathematical and real worlds, where security and privacy depended on the effectiveness of those codes. How close to randomness could we go? Obviously, there was a lot of work going on to discover the answer to that question—but the work was going on behind steep barriers erected and maintained by the government's intelligence agencies.

In fact, just about all the news about modern cryptography was behind that barrier. Everyone else had to rely on the same texts Whitfield Diffie had encountered in the fifth grade. And they didn't talk about how one went about changing the orderly procession of ones and zeros in a computer message to a different set of totally inscrutable ones and zeros using state-of-the-art stuff like Fibonacci generators, shift registers, or nonlinear feedback logic. Diffie resented this. "A well-developed technology is being kept secret!" he thought. He began to stew over this injustice. One day, walking with Silver along Mass Avenue near the railroad tracks, he spilled his concerns. *Cryptography is vital to human privacy!* he railed. Maybe, he suggested, passionate researchers in the public sector should attempt to liberate the subject. "If we put our minds to it," he told Silver, "we could rediscover a lot of that material." That is, they could virtually declassify it.

Silver was skeptical. "A lot of very smart people work at the NSA," he said, referring to the National Security Agency, the U.S. government's citadel of cryptography. After all, Silver explained, this organization had not only some of the best brains in the country, but billions of dollars in support. Its workers had years of experience and full access to recent cryptographic discoveries and techniques unknown to the hoi polloi—however intelligent—without high security clearances. The agency had supercomputers in its basement that made even MIT's state-of-the-art mainframe computers look like pocket calculators. How could outsiders like Diffie and Silver hope to match that?

Silver also told Diffie a story about his own NSA experience years earlier while writing a random number generator for the Digital Equipment Corporation's PDP-1 machine. He needed some information: his reasons were noncryptographic; he simply had a certain mathematical need, a polynomial number with some particular properties. He was sure that a friend of his at the NSA would know the answer instantly, and he put in a call. "Yes, I do know," said the friend. What *was* it? After a very long silence, during which Silver assumed that the friend was asking permission, the NSA scientist returned to the phone. Silver heard, in a conspiratorial whisper, "x to the twenty-fifth, plus x to the seventh, plus one."

Diffie was outraged at this secretiveness. He'd heard about the NSA, of course, but hadn't known that much about it. Just what *was* this organization, which acted as if it actually owned mathematical truths?

Created by President Truman's top-secret order in the fall of 1952, the National Security Agency was a multibillion-dollar organization that operated totally in the "black" region of government, where only those who could prove a "need to know" were entitled to knowledge. (It was not until five years after its founding that a government document even acknowledged its existence.) The NSA's cryptographic mission is twofold: to maintain the security of government information and to gather foreign intelligence. The double-sided nature of its duty led the NSA to organize itself into two major divisions: Communications Security, or COMSEC, which tries to devise codes that cannot be broken, and Communications Intelligence, or COMINT, which collects and decodes information from around the world. (Since the latter function most often involves intercepting and interpreting electronic information, it is more broadly referred to as signals intelligence, or SIGINT.) Over the years the NSA has established a vast network of listening devices and sensors to gather signals from even the most obscure reaches of the globe, an operation that expanded beyond the planetary atmosphere when the satellite era began in the 1960s.

In the early 1970s, none of this was discussed publicly. Within the Beltway, people in the know jokingly referred to the organizational acronym as No Such Agency. Those very few members of Congress who had oversight responsibility for intelligence funding would learn what had to be conveyed only in shielded rooms, swept for listening devices.

Access to the organization's headquarters at Fort George Meade, Maryland, was, as one might imagine, severely limited. A triple-barbed-wired and electrified fence kept outsiders at bay. To work within the gates, of course, one had to survive a rigid vetting.

"By joining NSA," reads the introduction to a handbook presented to new hires, "you have been given an opportunity to participate in the activities of one of the most important intelligence organizations of the United States government. At the same time you have assumed a trust which carries with it a most important individual responsibility— the safeguarding of sensitive information vital to the security of our nation."

Since all the salient information about modern crypto was withheld from public view, outsiders could only guess at what happened in "The Fort." The NSA undoubtedly operated the most sophisticated snooping operation in the world. It was universally assumed (though never admitted) that no foreign phone call, radio broadcast, or telegraph transmission was safe from the agency's global vacuum cleaner. Signals were sucked up and the content analyzed with multi-MIPS computers, combing the text for anything of value. (These suspicions were later confirmed with leaks of Project Echelon, the NSA's ambitious program to monitor foreign communications.) Were the results worth the billions of dollars and the questionable morality of the effort itself? This was something known only to the very few government officials who received briefings on the fabled intercepts—and even they were dependent on the quality of information that came from the agency itself.

What's more, the NSA considered itself the sole repository of cryptographic information in the country—not just that used by the civilian government and all the armed forces, as the law dictated, but that used by the private sector as well. Ultimately, the triple-depth electrified and barbed-wire fence surrounding its headquarters was not only a physical barrier but a metaphor for the NSA's near-fanatical drive to hide information about itself and its activities. In the United States of America, serious crypto existed only behind the Triple Fence.

Every day the NSA pored over new ideas for cryptographic systems submitted by would-be innovators in the field. "Their ideas disappear into the black maw of the NSA, and may see service in American cryptography," wrote David Kahn, "but security prevents the inventor from ever knowing this—and may enable the agency or its employees to utilize his ideas without compensation." But even those who did not submit ideas were not free of the NSA's stranglehold. The agency monitored all patent requests concerning cryptography and had the legal power to classify any of those it deemed too powerful to fall into the public domain.

As he learned more about the NSA, Whit Diffie came to feel a bit foolish that despite his having heard of the agency, the extent of its power had only belatedly dawned on him. Diffie had actually visited the Institute for Defense Analysis (IDA) at Princeton, a quasi-private outpost of the NSA, but he'd had only the vaguest idea about the organization's mission at the time. Not that it would have helped him get information from those crypto illuminati. One may socialize and even exchange thoughts with those who had ventured behind the Triple Fence, but only as long as those thoughts did not involve the forbidden subject of cryptography.

Cryptography, however, was exactly what Diffie wanted to talk about. He wanted to learn as much as he could, to have far-ranging conversations with the leaders in the field. Even the *foot soldiers* in the field would do. But he quickly became frustrated with those who would not, or could not, talk about it.

For instance, Diffie quizzed an MIT colleague named Dan Edwards, who would join the NSA after graduating. "He was extremely unhelpful," Diffie later reported, "failing to reveal things which were certainly not classified and which I later saw in the bibliography of his thesis." And when a colleague at Mitre went to work at IDA, Diffie asked him if he could share anything about his work. After a tantalizing pause: no.

Perhaps the idea of pursuing the forbidden was simply irresistible to a contrarian like Diffie. He kept thinking about crypto and the silent embargo against it. And the more he thought about the problem, the more he came to understand how deeply, deeply important the issue was. Especially in what he saw as the coming era of computational ubiquity. As more people used computers, wireless telephones, and other electronic devices, they would *demand* cryptography. Just as the invention of the telegraph upped the cryptographic ante by moving messages thousands of miles in the open, presenting a ripe opportunity for eavesdroppers of every stripe, the computer age would be moving billions of messages previously committed to paper into the realm of bits. Unencrypted, those bits were low-hanging fruit for snoopers. Could cryptography, that science kept intentionally opaque by the forces of government, help out? The answer was as clear as plaintext. Of course it could!

Right at MIT there was an excellent example of a need for a cryptographic solution to a big problem. The main computer system there was called Compatible Time Sharing System (CTSS). It was one of the first that used time-sharing, an arrangement by which several users could work on the machine simultaneously. Obviously, the use of a shared computer required some protocols to protect the privacy of each person's information. CTSS performed this by assigning a password to each user; his or her files would be in the equivalent of a locked mini-storage space, and each password would be the equivalent of the key that unlocked the door to that area. Passwords were distributed and maintained by a human being, the system operator. This central authority figure in essence controlled the privacy of every user.

Even if he or she were scrupulously honest about protecting the passwords, the very fact that they existed within a centralized system provided an opportunity for compromise. Outside authorities had a clear shot at that information: simply present the system operator with a subpoena. "That person would sell you out," says Diffie, "because he had no interest in defying the order and going to jail to protect *your* data."

Diffie believed in what he called "a decentralized view of authority." By creating the proper cryptographic tools, he felt, you could solve the problem—by transferring the data protection from a disinterested third party to the actual user, the one whose privacy was actually at risk. He fantasized about a company that would invent and implement such tools. He even had a name for this imaginary concern: Privacy Protection, Incorporated.

But in Diffie's fantasy, it was someone else who devised the solution, someone else who founded the company—not him. Though he was becoming absolutely sure that the problems of maintaining privacy in a non-crypto-protected world were insurmountable, he assumed that others would be better qualified, better motivated, more practically oriented than he to create the crypto to tackle such problems. So he tried to convince others to work on the solution. With little success. "None of the people I tried to get interested in the subject did anything," he recalls.

So Diffie kept working on his main interest, which lay in a mathematical problem called "proof of correctness." But he kept researching what he could on crypto, though at this point his efforts were far from methodical. One day at the Cambridge Public Library, Diffie was browsing the recent acquisitions and came across *The Broken Seal* by Ladislas Farago, a book about the pre–Pearl Harbor codebreaking efforts. He read a bit of it right there, and he certainly thought it worth reading further. But he never did. (Worse, he came to confuse this book with another book published at that time, David Kahn's *The Codebreakers*, which delayed his reading of the more important work.)

Similarly, one day at Mitre, a colleague moving out of his office gave Diffie a 1949 paper by Claude Shannon. The legendary father of information theory had been teaching at MIT since 1956, but Diffie had never met him, a slight, introverted professor who lived a quiet family life, pursuing a variety of interests from reading science fiction to listening to jazz. (Presumably, by the time Shannon had reached his sixties, he had put aside the unicycle he had once mastered.)

Shannon's impact on cryptography was considerable. After receiving an MIT doctorate in 1940, he had worked for Bell Telephone Laboratories during the war, specializing in secrecy systems. The work was classified, of course, but in the late part of the decade the two key papers in Shannon's wartime work found their way into the public domain. In 1948, Shannon's seminal article on information, "Mathematical Theory of Communication," ran in the *Bell System Technical Journal*, and subtly set the stage for the digital epoch. A year later, "Communication Theory of Secrecy Systems" appeared in the same journal.

Both efforts were highly technical; those without advanced math degrees could barely venture a few paragraphs without being snared in a thicket of thorny equations and formulas. But Shannon had a sense of clarity that enabled him to send a clear signal through the noise of high-level math. In the latter paper, he clearly and concisely examined the basic cryptographic relationship from scratch, addressing the "general mathematical structure and properties of secrecy systems." He even provided a diagram of the classic cryptanalytic situation, beginning with a box representing the original message. This was transformed by an "encipherer" with access to a "key source." The message would move to the "decipherer," who'd use the same key source to return the message to its original form. But there was another line branching out from the cryptogram. It led to the "enemy cryptanalyst," who might be able to intercept the encrypted message. That third party was always to be assumed. The challenge was to make it impossible for that enemy to crack the cryptogram.

The concepts of *signal* and *noise* loomed large in Shannon's view of cryptology. He saw crypto as a high-stakes zero-sum game between secret keeper and foe, where a successful secret was a signal that could not be teased out of the apparent noise. In his sixty-page discussion of the matter, he masterfully clarified the dilemma of both encrypter and enemy. The gift of the Shannon paper was undoubtedly one of the most valuable that a prospective cryptographer like Diffie could hope for in the late 1960s. Diffie himself would later consider it the last worthwhile unclassified paper published for over twenty years.

Too bad that Whit Diffie, still pursuing knowledge in a scattershot manner, waited several years before actually reading it.

In 1969, Diffie finally left Mitre. His funding had run out, and now that he was approaching the draft cutoff age, he had the freedom to leave. He had never really liked Cambridge very much. In high school, Diffie had hung out with the left-liberal and even the red diaper set, and led a full social life, with folk-singing parties and lots of friendly girls. Though similar scenes undoubtedly existed in Cambridge, "I just didn't find them," Diffie now moans. But at the University of California at Berkeley, where he spent a summer after his freshman year, Diffie found a place among the left-leaning protest crowd. "I really believe in the radical viewpoint," he says. "And I have always believed that one's politics and the character of his particular work are inseparable."

So Diffie and his girlfriend moved west, and Diffie went to work at John McCarthy's Stanford Artificial Intelligence Lab. Supposedly, he would continue working on proof of correctness and other mathematical problems that applied to computer science. But in conversations with McCarthy, Diffie was led into a deeper consideration of privacy concerns. A pioneer in time-sharing, McCarthy understood that soon computer terminals would find their way into the home. Inevitably, he believed, the nature of work itself would change, as the electronic office became something that moved out of the cloistered world of computer scientists and hackers and deep into the mainstream. This would open up not only a thicket of security problems, but also a host of novel challenges that almost no one was thinking about in 1969: If work products became electronic—produced on computer and sent over digital networks—how would people duplicate the customary forms of authentication (the means to verify that the author of a document was actually the person he or she claimed to be)? What would be the computerized version of a receipt? How could you get a computer-generated equivalent of a signed contract? Even if people were given unique "digital signatures"—say, a long, randomly generated number bequeathed to a single person—the nature of digital media, in which something can be copied in milliseconds, would seem to make such an identifier pointless. If you "signed" such a number to a contract, what would stop someone from simply scooping up the signature, making a perfect copy, and affixing it to other documents, contracts, and bank checks? If even the *possibility* of such unauthorized signed copies existed, the signature would be worthless. "I didn't sign this," someone could say. "Someone copied my signature!" Diffie began to wonder how one could begin to fix this apparently inherent flaw in the concept of digital commerce.

Diffie and McCarthy spent hours in rambling discussions on issues like authentication and the problems of distributing electronic keys. But Diffie still was more interested in letting others create the solution. In the summer of 1972, however, machinations in Washington, D.C., indirectly changed his course.

The government, under the aegis of the Defense Department's Advanced Research Projects Agency (ARPA), had recently begun a program to link major research institutions. This was known as the ARPAnet, a system that would one day transmogrify into today's Internet. ARPA's director of information-processing techniques, Larry Roberts, realized that such a computer network, the first computer net to link multiple sites and handle hundreds if not thousands of users, would need a way to keep messages secure, and the obvious way of doing that was to devise new crypto solutions. But when Roberts approached the NSA, he got a quick brush-off. Ultimately, he enlisted the help of Bolt Baranek Newman, the Boston-based company that helped set up ARPAnet in the first place. In the meantime, he mentioned the problem to his friend John McCarthy, who encouraged people at Stanford to concoct some crypto programs. They began working on what Diffie later called "a very complicated system combining the effects of several linear congruential random number generators."

Since Diffie's girlfriend was on that team, he also was drawn into the effort. Naturally, his curiosity led him to study the system closely. As he came to understand it, he found himself dissatisfied with its lack of efficiency. Diffie believed that if cryptography were to be used in a computer system, it was essential that users not have to suffer performance lags. Ideally, encryption should add but a tiny—or imperceptible—increment to the time it took to perform a function like copying a file. Diffie went over the group's basic encoding algorithm and eventually wrote a routine that ran much faster. In the process—now that he was actually doing some cryptography—he began to spend even more time thinking about the larger issue of how to advance the field. Later that year he went to Cambridge and saw Roland Silver again; Diffie now had much more hands-on expertise to bring to a discussion of crypto, and their rich exchange fueled his interest even more.

By now Diffie had finally gotten around to reading David Kahn's *The Codebreakers*. Since Diffie was a very slow, methodical reader, tackling a book of a thousand densely packed pages was a major undertaking for him. "He traveled everywhere with that book in hand," says his friend Harriet Fell. "If you invited him to dinner, he'd come with *The Codebreakers*." But Diffie found the hundreds of hours he spent on the book to be well worth the trouble.

Indeed, *The Codebreakers* was a landmark work—and one that the government had not wanted to see published. Kahn was a *Newsday* reporter who, as a twelve-year-old, had been thrilled, like Diffie and countless other boys, with his first exposure to the mysteries of secret writing. That moment first came on a visit to the local Great Neck (Long Island, New York) library, where the cover to a potboiler history called *Secret and Urgent*, by Fletcher Pratt, was on display. "This was about 1942 or '43," recalls Kahn. "That dust jacket was terrific; it had letters and numbers swirling out of the cosmos. I was hooked." The hook sank deeper when he actually read the book and learned about how ciphers worked. The youngster joined what was then probably the most sophisticated cryptography organization outside the government, the American Cryptogram Association. Which wasn't saying much. "It was a bunch of amateurs," he says. "They solved cryptograms as puzzles, and used a little publication with articles on how to solve them." Many of the members were elderly, or at least had time on their hands. There was even an offshoot called the Bed-warmers. "These were people with polio, or were in some sort of clinic, or were paralyzed," says Kahn. "They couldn't move around very well so they solved puzzles." Such was the scope of crypto work outside the government.

Unlike Diffie, however, Kahn loved to solve the puzzles himself, and kept his interest into adulthood. He discussed some sophisticated schemes with some fellow Cryptogram Association members. "Other-wise, you were totally isolated," he says. "This was an unknown field; nobody knew anything about it." But he didn't detect a more general interest in cryptography until 1961, when two NSA cryptographers defected to the USSR and held a press conference about their experience. This was revelatory to Kahn; despite diligently monitoring all the public literature about cryptography, he had hardly known that the NSA existed! Still, since he knew something about crypto, he dared to ask editors at the *New York Times Magazine* if they would like a backgrounder on the subject. They did, and he produced it.

The day after the story's publication, Kahn received three book contract offers. He turned them down since they were from paperback publishers and he wanted his work between boards. He got his wish a week later when an editor named Peter Ritner asked him to do a hardcover for Macmillan. Kahn wrote up an outline for a general book about codes, and received a $2000 advance. But as he began working on the introductory section, his research efforts kept kicking up more and more interesting stories from disparate sources. By the time he reached page 250 of his "preliminary chapter"—he had barely gotten to the Renaissance—he realized that he was really writing the comprehensive history of cryptology.

Two years into the project, Kahn quit his job to focus his efforts full time on the book. He lived off his savings, bunking at his parents' house and eating meals cooked by his grandmother. He wrote hundreds of letters, spent days in the New York Public Library, and, most important, connected with people who had never previously told their stories. A high-ranking Department of Defense official allowed him access to two important World War II codebreakers—an astonishing event given how Cold War politics decreed that revealing any information of this sort was virtually treason—if he agreed to submit his notes from the interviews to the government. "I guess the [Defense official] didn't know what he was getting into," reasons Kahn, "and when the notes got submitted to the NSA, the government panicked, and said I had to [disregard the information]. I respectfully declined."

Kahn also constructed, with the help of an important confidential source, the first public account of the extent of the NSA's power, constructing it from the bits and pieces that had dribbled out over the years. But the most explosive details of Kahn's book lay in its methodical explanation of how cryptography works, and how the NSA used it. When *The Codebreakers* was finished in 1965, it contained the most complete description of the operations of Fort Meade that had ever been compiled without an EYES-ONLY stamp on each page.

Quite correctly, officials at the National Security Agency had come to view Kahn's book as a literary hand grenade, with the potential for serious damage to the government's carefully maintained ramparts of secrecy. In his NSA exposé *The Puzzle Palace*, author James Bamford wrote that "innumerable hours of meetings and discussions, involving the highest levels of the agency, including the director, were spent in an attempt to sandbag the book." Countermeasures considered behind the Triple Fence ranged from outright purchase of the copyright to a break-in at Kahn's home. Kahn, who had moved to Paris to work for the *Herald Tribune*, was placed on the NSA's "watch list," enabling eavesdroppers to read his mail and monitor his conversations.

To Kahn's dismay, in March 1966 his editor sent the manuscript off to the Pentagon for its scrutiny and comments. Of course, it was then shipped to Fort Meade. The Defense Department wrote Macmillan's chairman that publishing *The Codebreakers* "would not be in the national interest." But Macmillan didn't bend, less because of backbone, Kahn guesses, than the fact that by that point in the production process "they had too much money put into it."

So the NSA took an extraordinary step. In July 1966, its director, Lt. Gen. Marshall S. Carter—a man so secretive that his name never appeared in newspapers—flew to New York City and met with the chairman of the publishing company, its legal counsel, and Kahn's editor, Peter Ritner. After attacking Kahn's reputation and expertise, Carter finally made a personal appeal for three specific deletions. A few days later, Ritner presented Kahn with the request. The actual deletions struck Kahn as surprisingly inconsequential. "It didn't really hurt the book, so I took the three things out," Kahn says. "But I insisted that we put in a statement to the effect that the book had been submitted to the Department of Defense. In the end that had a good effect, because right-wing reviewers could otherwise have said the book was destroying the republic. Now they couldn't."

While *The Codebreakers* never made the *New York Times* bestseller list, it became a steady seller, going through dozens of printings. And it did not, as the NSA had hysterically predicted, bring an abrupt close to the American century. It did, however, enlighten a new generation of cryptographers who would dare to work outside of the government's wall of secrecy. And its prime student was Whitfield Diffie.

"I read it more carefully than *anyone* had ever read it. . . . Kahn's book to me is like the Vedas," he explains, citing the centuries-old Indian text. "There's an expression I learned: 'If a man loses his cow, he looks for it in the Vedas.' "

By the time Whitfield Diffie finished *The Codebreakers*, he was no longer depending on others to tackle the great problems of cryptography. He was personally, passionately engaged in them himself. They consumed his waking dreams. They were now his obsession.

Why had Diffie's once-intermittent interest become such a consuming passion? Behind every great cryptographer, it seems, there is a driving pathology. Though Diffie's quest was basically an intellectual challenge, he had come to take it very personally. Beneath his casual attire and streaming blond hair, Diffie was a proud and determined man. He had an unusual drive for getting at what he considered the bedrock truth of any issue. This led to a fascination with protecting and uncovering secrets, especially important secrets that were desperately held. "Ostensibly, my reason for getting interested in this was its importance to personal privacy," he now says. "But I was also fascinated with investigating this business that people wouldn't tell you about." It was as if solving this conundrum would provide a more general meaning to the world at large. "I guess in a very real sense I'm a Gnostic," he says. "I had been looking all my life for some great mystery. . . . I think somewhere deep in my mind is the notion that if I could learn just the right thing, I would be saved."

And then, Diffie's quest to discover truths in cryptography became intertwined with another sort of romance: his courtship of Mary Fischer.

It had not been Whit Diffie's original intention to fall in love with a Jewish Brooklyn-born animal trainer who was already married. Up to the day when she upbraided him on the phone for ignoring her, he had in fact hardly thought of her. But her outburst struck a nerve, perhaps more so because his own longtime relationship was on the wane. When he bid goodbye to Mary on his way across the country, and told her he'd see her in a year, he meant it. With about $12,000 he had saved from his salary at Mitre and an intention to live "low on the hog," as he later put it, he was out to learn all he could about crypto— and maybe do something about it. That seemed like a solitary mission.

But in August 1973, when he stopped by Fischer's New Jersey house for a visit, he found that her marriage was falling apart and that she was finding relief by going to charismatic prayer meetings. It was not the type of thing she felt comfortable talking about to mathematical types like Diffie, but when she came out with it, his reaction took her aback. "You know, Mary," he said, "I've always had a soft spot for mystics." They began to spend time together. Fischer didn't drive, and Diffie fell into the habit of escorting her to zoos—especially to locate a King cobra—and then on longer trips to view architecturally interesting churches. At one point, on a Massachusetts road, Diffie impulsively pulled the car over and very quietly told Mary he loved her. She said she loved him back. And that was that. Though it was painful for Fischer to acknowledge the end of her marriage, Diffie hastened the process by daring her to join him on a sojourn to Florida to watch a launch of the Skylab mission. They drove straight through and arrived at Cape Canaveral at three in the morning. Some hours later, they watched together as the big rocket blew fire on its jump toward the cosmos.

From that point, Mary Fischer was Diffie's companion, and eventually his wife, as he drove thousands of miles in his search for an answer to the riddle of cryptography. They would pass the hours talking, or, more often, singing popular tunes. The National Security Agency had no clue that the man who was about to make life infinitely more difficult for them was spending endless hours in a Datsun 510, crooning "Sweet Caroline" with his new girlfriend. Though Fischer had little understanding of the technologies and mathematics that drove Diffie, she became his partner in the quest. His cryptographic muse.

"I was terrified all the time because I'd abandoned everything that was familiar to me," she recalls of those days. "Every now and then he'd stop off at a library, or see somebody, and it was really cloak and dagger—people who didn't want to talk to him, people who put their coats over their faces, people who wanted to know how the hell he'd found out their names, people who had secrets, clearly, and were not about to share them. And Whit was trying to ferret those secrets out.

It was a perpetual kind of voyage of discovery because he kept checking out these people. And sometimes he'd say, 'I want you to stand
here to listen. I don't want anybody to see you but I just want you to
listen.' So I went on some of these encounters. But basically I didn't
have a clue what he was up to."

Sometimes Diffie would try to explain his motivations to her. The
computer age, he told Mary, held terrible implications for privacy. As
these machines become ascendant, and we use them for everyday
communication, he warned, we may never experience privacy as we
know it today. His apocalyptic tone unsettled Mary, but she wanted to
hear more.

Eventually, Mary understood how Diffie's mission mixed the political with the personal. Devising a way to wedge open the NSA's grip on
crypto would satisfy not only Diffie's sixties-style rebelliousness, but
also what would later be identified as a strongly libertarian ethic in
him. "Whit wants to uncover secrets," she says. "Anything that's
secret is something that Whit has to know. When we first got together
I couldn't believe it. He was doing things like going through my
garbage bags. He didn't trust anything. He feels as though what ordinary people take for granted is just too simple and there must be
more under the surface there. And he builds up terrible complications
that way."

Of course, the most significant complication was his seemingly
quixotic mission to discover something under the nose of the National
Security Agency. He wondered whether he was putting himself at risk,
and indeed, because of this, "my attitude was to keep my head down
for the first couple of years," he says. Ultimately, though, the length of
the odds stacked against him only made the quest more attractive to
Diffie.

One thing Diffie did trust during this period was the Datsun 510
automobile. He kept buying and rebuilding them, even though the evidence indicates that the cars were far from immortal. "I was stubborn," he explains, adding that "most of what I do is characterized by
the fact that I'm stubborn." Mary Fischer puts it differently. "When
Whit decides he wants something, he'll research it thoroughly, fix on
the best idea of its kind, and from then on he is married to that thing."
His Datsun broke down in Nebraska, whereupon Diffie rented a truck
and transported the car to the West Coast. He then purchased a sec-

ond 510, a black junker with about 100,000 miles on it. "It had a fine set of insides in it," Diffie recalls fondly. This took him and Mary on their second continental crossing. The car took sick in La Mesilla, New Mexico, emitting an ominous *chink-chink-chink* sound, but it got Whit and Mary back to California, only to go dead in a Redwood City parking space two days later. Diffie then purchased more Datsuns, initiating an elaborate process of vehicular organ transplants. "At one point we had five Datsuns," recalls Mary Fischer. "Whit would work on them himself; he didn't trust mechanics. He is not an utterly trusting soul."

What did Diffie encounter during his cross-country journeys? Many people who refused him. But a few helped, providing him with hints of contemporary crypto techniques, or even unpublished works. Among those helpers was Diffie's personal Mao, David Kahn, who invited Diffie for pizza at his Long Island home after Diffie had cold-called to introduce himself. Though taken aback by Diffie's appearance—an abundance of hair and ultracasual attire—*The Codebreakers'* author was impressed with his knowledge. He agreed to provide Diffie with some crypto documents from his research.

One important cache of papers dealt with William Friedman, the acknowledged godfather of the government's cryptographic efforts. A naturalized American born in Russia late in the nineteenth century, Friedman had become interested in cryptography while researching the possibility that Francis Bacon was the true author of Shakespeare's plays. (Many years later Friedman and his wife Elizabeth would authoritatively debunk this notion in their book, *The Shakespearean Ciphers Examined*.) During World War I, Friedman became involved in the U.S. government's codebreaking efforts and developed a series of courses to train prospective cryptanalysts. Within the closed community, his works became classics, particularly those on his use of statistics to crack codes. Friedman's World War II work was instrumental in breaking the Japanese cipher PURPLE, and he was an important figure in the early NSA, remaining active as a consultant long after his retirement in 1955. Throughout, virtually all his critical work was top-secret, so when Kahn offered Diffie a look at some rare, recently declassified materials, Diffie treated them like the original copies of the Constitution. Instead of handing the bound books over to attendants at a photocopying center, he lovingly photographed each page with a 35mm camera. This meticulousness proved prescient, as the NSA hadn't yet realized that copies of these papers had slipped underneath the Triple Fence; when it did, the agency would attempt to retroactively classify the material, thus making criminals of those who did not immediately turn them over to the proper authorities.

In the summer of 1974, Diffie heard that Jim Reeds, a Harvard doctoral student in statistics he had met a year earlier, was leading a seminar in cryptography there. Diffie headed back to Cambridge and sat in. Also attending was Bill Mann, a friend who was working on the ARPA security plan. At one point Diffie was trying to explain to Mann the meaning of something called a one-way function. This was a mathematical oddity that he had come across and couldn't stop thinking about. A true one-way function is something that can be calculated easily in one direction but not easily reversed—a mathematical Humpty-Dumpty. One cryptographer would later explain that when you broke a dinner plate, you were using a one-way function: "It is easy to smash a dinner plate," he wrote. "However, it's not easy to put all of those tiny pieces back together again into a plate."

Diffie was increasingly convinced that one-way functions could figure into a new kind of cryptographic approach, but he wasn't sure how. He couldn't even explain what it was clearly enough for Mann to understand it. But Mann misunderstood it rather creatively. He came away with the impression that a one-way function was something that not only could be quickly computed in one direction but could be calculated in reverse as well—if you had the proper information. Using the plate analogy, Mann said it was as if the guy who broke the plate had some magic way to *un*-break it, like a film running backward showing those tiny shards of broken china fusing back into a pristine dinner plate. As he laid out his conception to Diffie, Mann was envisioning what one day would be called a "trapdoor one-way function." It would prove to be a prescient misunderstanding.

Also in Cambridge, Diffie talked about crypto with Richard Schroeppel. He was a former MIT hacker who had a reputation as a math wizard. Schroeppel had been thinking about the idea of electronic commerce, and was beginning to grapple with the same sorts of problems that Diffie and McCarthy had discussed: What if Company A wanted to place an electronic order with some Company B and no preexisting relationship existed? How could they secure their communications?

Schroeppel was impressed that Diffie had done a lot of thinking about such problems. And he certainly respected Diffie, who had done great, though unheralded, work at MIT's AI lab, building Macsyma. Schroeppel also knew that Diffie had written the complicated routines to handle large numbers in the Stanford version of the computer language LISP. "To my mind, writing a set of big number routines crosses you over a threshold," says Schroeppel. "It's like passing the Bar [exam]; it means you really know how to use a computer and you really know how to do arithmetic."

Over lunch one day Diffie floated the idea that perhaps there was a way to get around the electronic commerce problem. What about a one-way function, he suggested—a *reversible* one-way function, like the one Bill Mann had unwittingly suggested? Could that possibly be part of a solution? They talked about it for a while, but Schroeppel was skeptical. "Actually, you probably can't find any of those functions," he warned Diffie. "They probably don't exist."

Undaunted, Diffie kept on, desperate for someone who could provide him with more clues. He and Fischer went to see a friend in Cambridge who mentioned a fellow named Alan Tritter. Tritter supposedly had done work in cryptography. He now worked for IBM. So during that same summer of 1974, Diffie tracked him down at the major center of cryptographic activity outside the government, IBM's T. J. Watson Labs, in Westchester County, New York.

Even in a field littered with brilliant oddballs, Tritter stood out. Due to a rare disease that generated a massive volume of body fat, he weighed what friends estimated as a minimum of 400 pounds. Rumor had it that his grandfather had been a wealthy man who had left Tritter only enough money to attend school. Though some regarded him as a mathematical genius, others felt that his reputation was unearned. "Immediately after he was hired, it was regretted, but IBM wouldn't admit its error," complained one former IBM colleague. "I don't really think he did anything there." On the other hand, Tritter was ahead of his time by acquiring an early mastery of telephone hacking. He would die young.

Diffie was immediately gratified to learn that Tritter was knowledgeable about Identification Friend or Foe (IFF) devices. Reading Kahn's book, Diffie had been intrigued by its mention of these systems, which are communications devices that essentially quiz each other to authenticate one's identity. As Tritter explained it to Diffie, an IFF device works by issuing a cryptographic "challenge," one that can be successfully met only by use of secret information to precisely solve the problem. The canonical IFF situation is a fighter plane encountering another airborne craft during a period of hostilities. If the intruder is a foe, it must be shot down, but it's obviously unwise to fire before determining if the target might be an ally. The IFF process is an electronic equivalent to a sentry's question to an approaching foot soldier: "What's the password?" Of course, IFF systems relied on more complicated protocols than passwords. Since such communications were generally conducted by radio, it was assumed that enemies could listen in, and if a general password were issued to the forces of one side, a foe could easily discover the magic utterance that would enable its own planes to pose as friends.

It turned out that one of Tritter's colleagues at IBM, a German-born scientist named Horst Feistel, had performed crucial work in the field. (Unfortunately, Feistel had left for a Cape Cod weekend, and Diffie could not meet him then.) Tritter explained to Diffie how Feistel's IFF system got around the eavesdropping problem: when confronting an as-yet-unidentified aircraft, an American plane could send a radio signal containing a challenge randomly selected from a large number of possible alternatives. Other U.S. planes would be supplied with the means to encrypt that signal in the correct manner and send that scrambled response back to the questioner. The questioner would validate the response by decrypting it. If this process yielded the original signal, the second craft was definitely a fellow American. If enemy planes were listening in, it would do them no good simply to copy the friendly response and use it as a response to a later challenge, because in any subsequent encounter, the American planes would choose a different signal, one that would be transformed to a different encrypted transmission.

Tritter's information was exciting to Diffie. By that explanation, IFFs worked in somewhat the same way that a one-way function might. He hoped for similarly helpful clues when he wangled an audience with the head of the mathematical group at IBM, Alan Konheim. He didn't get any. "He was very secretive," complains Diffie. Konheim, now a professor at the University of California at Santa Barbara, was one of those mathematicians who had taken several NSA-sponsored courses and had signed the fatal document that bound them to submit their future cryptographic works to the agency. "You sign it once and it's forever," he later explained.

There was no way that Konheim was going to give any crucial information to the stranger who sat in his office along the curved-glass walls of the Watson research building. However, Diffie says that Konheim did give him one critical piece of information. "He only told me one thing, and since then, he's wished he'd never said that," crows Diffie. That datum was not a cryptographic tip but a referral, the name of someone who had been asking the same kinds of questions as Diffie had, a guy who had briefly worked at the lab and was now an assistant professor at Stanford. His name was Martin Hellman. Maybe, Konheim suggested, two people can work on a problem better than one.

When Diffie and Mary next drove whichever Datsun 510 was running at that time to the West Coast for a stint of house-sitting for John McCarthy, one of the first things that Diffie did was phone this young professor of electrical engineering. "I arranged a half-hour meeting at my office at Stanford," Marty Hellman now recalls, "figuring it's just not going to go anywhere, but what the heck." Thus was made the match that, in the world of crypto, would later attain the resonance of famous pairings elsewhere: Woodward-Bernstein. Lennon-McCartney. Watson-Crick.

Diffie-Hellman.

Though he lived in California, Marty Hellman was pure Big Apple: pugilistic, in-your-face New York City. With his dark hair, beard, and intense stare, he resembled a Semitic version of Martin Scorsese. Born in 1945, he grew up Jewish in a tough Catholic neighborhood and learned to take an outsider's view. He also took refuge in science. His father and uncle both taught physics in the public schools. Young Hellman had always been turned on by explorers and new frontiers, whether it was Magellan charting the New World or Einstein on redefining the way we understand the universe. He was accepted into the Bronx High School of Science; his avocation was ham radio. "That probably pulled me into electrical engineering," he said. "It's a very broad area; you can move from theoretical physics through solid-state physics and math." He got his doctorate from Stanford in

1969, and his first job was at IBM research in Yorktown Heights, New York.

Not long after he was hired, Hellman gave a paper at an information theory symposium held at the Neville hotel and resort, the headquarters of the Catskills' Borscht Belt. The banquet speaker was David Kahn. Hellman had always believed that there was something kind of sexy about cryptography, but Kahn's appearance got him thinking about it as a serious scientific pursuit, and those thoughts got stronger when he discovered that his new employer was already working in that field. Surely commercial applications existed, he figured. Though Hellman didn't work directly with Horst Feistel, the German-born cryptographer worked nearby in the building, and sometimes the two of them would sit together at lunch, where the older man would describe some of the classical cryptosystems and some of the means of breaking them.

Hellman left IBM in 1970, accepting a post as assistant professor at MIT. At that time Peter Elias, who had worked closely with Claude Shannon, was just stepping down as the head of the electronic engineering department. Elias's talks with Hellman drew the young academic deeper into crypto, and for the first time he began thinking about making it the focus of his research. "Partially, it was the magician aspect, being able to impress people with magic tricks," he now explains. "Also, the potential to make a real impact, and advance my career by doing it."

He resisted the temptation to do what the vast majority of scientists and academics in his field had already done: work within NSA strictures. "From the very beginning, once someone heard I had an interest in cryptography, the people from NSA would come at me," he says. Hellman would profess interest in hearing what they knew, but only if he would remain free to publish his own findings. The officials would warn him he was wasting his time, and that by depriving himself of the research performed at The Fort, he'd never come up with anything worthwhile. But Hellman, brimming with chutzpah in those days, said, in effect, *To hell with you, I'm doing it anyway!* He figured that even if he wound up rediscovering something that was already in the classified literature, his feat would not be redundant, because his findings could be exploited for commercial use. "It was hard," he says. "But it was also doing something exciting that no one else was doing."

Enter Whit Diffie.

"It was a meeting of the minds," says Hellman. It came at a propitious time: though Hellman had recently published his first paper in the field of cryptography—a gloss on Shannon's work—he'd been stuck for a follow-up, and longed for a kindred ear. "I'd been working in a vacuum," he says, "and was feeling, 'Is this really worth it?' I was really getting concerned about whether this was going to lead anywhere."

Showing up wearing what Hellman called "the AI uniform"—black chinos, white socks, white shirt, and tennis shoes—Diffie was undoubtedly quirky. But he knew his stuff. He knew *volumes*. Only someone like Hellman, who had banged his own head against the ramparts of crypto secrecy, could appreciate how well spent were Diffie's months and years traveling, talking to anyone he could find, burrowing in libraries for forgotten books like Luigi Sacco's 1938 treatise on cryptography, and poring over obscure texts like the Friedman papers that NSA had later tried to reclassify. "He'd dug up everything I had never seen or had the energy to dig up," says Hellman. Finally, someone with whom he could toss ideas back and forth; it was like an elegant game of hard catch between two professional ballplayers.

The half-hour meeting went on for an hour, two hours, longer. Hellman simply didn't want it to end, and Diffie, too, seemed eager to continue for as long as possible. Hellman had promised his wife he'd be home by late afternoon to watch their two small children while she went off, so finally he asked Diffie back to his house. No problem! Diffie called Mary and she came over to have dinner with Whit and all the Hellmans, and it wasn't until 11:00 or so that night that the dialogue broke up.

Not surprisingly, the two decided to continue the conversation. "It was very nebulous," says Hellman. "He had some great ideas, I had some great ideas, and there was some overlap. We just loved talking to each other. It wasn't that we had a goal of doing this or a goal of doing that—we just wanted to go further down the path we had each gone down, without finding someone at the end of the path telling us what everybody else was telling us: that we were wasting our time."

Both Diffie and Hellman firmly believed that the advent of digital communications made commercial cryptography absolutely essential. All of these huge computer and telephone networks made life incredibly easy for eavesdroppers—it was going to be possible to fully automate spying. At least with radio broadcasts, snoopers had to monitor numerous points in the channel band; with a network, it was as if everyone were broadcasting on the same channel. A spy agency like the NSA could—and would—simply turn on the Hoover and inhale gigabytes of data. "Ninety-nine percent of what they suck up gets blasted out as hot air," says Hellman. "But by combing the data for key words, key phrases, key names and addresses, one percent gets caught in the bag as dirt."

The antidote for this would amount to, in essence, a cryptographic revolution, which would allow ordinary people to encrypt the stuff they sent over the network. The big problem, as Diffie had discussed with McCarthy and Schroeppel, was scaling crypto for more users, and making it easier to use. Something had to replace, or at least augment, the old-style, classical form of symmetrical-key crypto (where the same key that scrambles the messages can unscramble it, too), because it was totally unfit for the massive numbers of private conversations and digital transactions that people would require. The problem was that in order to have those private conversations, *both* parties had to arrange in advance what the key would be, and then somehow use that key without exposing it to eavesdroppers or intruders. This was a fairly straightforward act for a military organization, but an absolute nightmare in a bustling marketplace. What were you going to do—send millions of bonded couriers out into the streets to personally hand someone a new key every time he wanted to start up a phone conversation or file a purchase order? The only feasible approach seemed to be an infrastructure of key distribution centers that would generate a key every time two people requested one for a private conversation. But Hellman shared Diffie's deep-seated suspicion of such a centralized system.

"I knew he'd be around for a couple of months, but I also had the feeling that he might pick up and leave, and I was really anxious to see him stay here," says Hellman. So Hellman called his grant monitor in the National Science Foundation (NSF) and wheedled some more funds to spend working on cryptography. There was enough to hire Whit Diffie as a part-time researcher. "It might have been for ten to twenty hours a week, or about a quarter to a half of what a working person would normally make," says Hellman, who also suggested that while they were at it, why not have Diffie enroll as a graduate student and get a doctorate in the process?

That part of the arrangement didn't work out. "Whit is a truly free spirit," was Hellman's postmortem. "When he's interested in something for himself and no one's making him do it, he will spend unbelievable hours a day, get by with little sleep. But [not] when he has homework assignments and the structure." Ultimately, Diffie dropped out of the graduate program when the administrators noticed that he hadn't taken the requisite physical examination. "I didn't feel like doing it; I didn't get around to it," says Diffie. Though he finessed the matter for some months, ultimately, when the Stanford bureaucrats refused to register him without proof he had taken the physical, Diffie told them to go to hell.

"I used to think of it as a handicap on Whit's part," says Marty Hellman, "but maybe he was just mature at an earlier age, thinking, Damned-if-I'll-follow-some-of-your-stupid-rules. Because some of them *are* stupid."

Ultimately, it was only by questioning the conventional rules of cryptography and finding some of them "stupid" that Diffie made his breakthroughs. A case in point: the belief that the workings of a secure cryptosystem had to be treated with utmost secrecy. That might have held true for military organizations, but in the computer age, that didn't make sense. There would be unlimited users who needed a system for privacy; obviously, such a system would have to be distributed so widely that potential crackers would have no trouble getting their hands on it and would have plenty of opportunity to practice attacking it. Instead, the secrecy had to rest somewhere else in the system. Maybe those one-way functions that obsessed Diffie could be involved in such a system.

In the months that followed, they became close colleagues and friends. Mary and Whit often hung out at the Hellmans'. Marty's wife Dorothy was an enthusiast of purebred dogs—obviously something Mary was interested in—and Mary got one of Hellman's daughters interested in playing the harp. Whit and Marty would usually be off in a corner, talking cryptography.

Between Whit and Mary there was now an understanding that the traveling was over. They began their Palo Alto house-sitting stint for John McCarthy, watching his teenage daughter Sarah while the AI pioneer was on a Japanese sabbatical. Meanwhile, they started looking for a place of their own in Berkeley. Mary took a job with British Petroleum in San Francisco. Whit had the house to himself all day, and he would clean and cook. Mainly, he would work with Marty, hoping against hope that his years of didactic study would bear fruit and he would make a contribution, however slender, to the maddingly secretive field of cryptography.

His years of obsession had not decreased his passion for the subject. Nor had his deep affection for Mary Fischer—his other romance—distracted him. On the contrary, their relationship had only intensified his hunger for privacy, and the quest for a technology to provide it. His epic quest had begun from a lack of trust in computer systems and their keepers. Now it was about maintaining a valuable personal connection, too. "When he felt he'd finally found a trustworthy person," as Mary Fischer later explained, "the question became, 'How do you deal with a trustworthy person in the midst of a world full of untrustworthy people?' "

the standard

O n March 17, 1975, a dry government document produced a shock wave that just about tore the plaster off the walls of Martin Hellman's little cipher operation at Stanford University. It was a *Federal Register* posting from the National Bureau of Standards (NBS), ostensibly one of countless protocols proposed by that agency that, if adopted, would become the officially endorsed means of doing things for the federal government. By extension, it would become the no-brainer choice for private industry and just plain folks as well. This proposal involved something seldom ventured in the public literature: a brand-new encryption algorithm. And a strong one to boot. It was to be called the Data Encryption Standard, or DES.

The Stanford team had known that the unprecedented move was in the offing—the NBS had been issuing requests for such a standard—and Hellman knew that his old and trusted colleagues at IBM had been cooking up a system designed to satisfy the government's criteria. So at first they welcomed the announcement. "This was big news," recalls Hellman. "We were happy to see a standard. We thought it was a wonderful thing."

Then they began to actually examine the DES system—and learned that the National Security Agency apparently had a hand in its development. And their enthusiasm turned to dismay. Right away, it was glaringly obvious that the flaw in the DES was the size of the encryption key, a metric that directly determines the strength of a cryptographic system. It was 56 bits long. That's a binary number of 56 places. You could envision this as a string of 56 switches, each of which could be on or off. Though 2 to the 56th power was a hell of a big number in most circumstances—it meant that there were 2^{56} possible keys, or about 70 quadrillion—Hellman and Diffie believed that it was too small for high-grade encryption. Sophisticated computers, they insisted, could eventually work hard enough to find solutions to such encrypted messages by "exhaustive search": trying out billions of key combinations at lightning speed until the proper key was discovered and the message suddenly resolved itself into the orderly realm of plaintext. This would be a classic "brute-force" attack. "A large key is not a guarantee of security," says Hellman, "but a small key is a guarantee of insecurity."

Diffie wrote as much in an otherwise respectful initial analysis of the standard, submitted in May 1975 as part of the NBS's public comment process. "The key size is at best barely adequate. Even today, hardware capable of defeating the system by exhaustive search would strain but probably not exceed the budget of a large intelligence organization." He postulated that a free-spending agency could feasibly build a customized machine that would crack such a key within a day. "Although cryptanalysis by exhaustive search is far from cheap, it is also far from impossible," he wrote, "and even a small improvement in cryptanalytic technique could dramatically improve the cost performance picture. We suggest doubling the size of the key space to preclude searching."

Naively, the Stanford duo believed that such advice might be heeded by the United States government: *Well, damn, you guys are right! Let's double that silly key size!* Instead, the government's response was sufficiently evasive for Hellman to suspect that a smoke screen lay behind the NBS's actions. In subsequent months, in fact, Hellman would publicly begin to question whether the DES algorithm might have been a daring ruse on the government's part to lull citizens and perhaps even foreign foes into an illusion that they were protecting information—while that supposedly secure data was easily accessible to the NSA. At his most paranoid, Hellman wondered whether the

DES had a "back door" implanted in it by Fort Meade's clever cryptographers. While there was no direct proof of that, there *was* reason for suspicion. If everything was on the up-and-up, Hellman wanted to know, why was it that the design principles of the algorithm, as well as its inner workings, were being treated as government secrets? If the government had nothing to hide, why were they hiding something?

Diffie and Hellman were only the first to question the murky origins of the Data Encryption Standard. The debate would continue even as the DES became a kind of gold standard for strong commercial cryptography—and an object of continued suspicion among the outsiders of the crypto and civil liberties world. Only with the passage of time would it become clear that the development and certification of DES was in a sense an inspiring story of its own, one that had elements in common with the quest of Diffie and Hellman themselves.

The story began with one of IBM's most enigmatic researchers, Horst Feistel. He was the German-born cryptographer who had done the work on Identification Friend or Foe protocols that Whit Diffie had learned from Alan Tritter. Feistel had been working at IBM's research division in Yorktown Heights since the late sixties. It was one of the few jobs in the private sector that involved work in cryptographic research.

In fact, some of his colleagues suspected that Feistel had been in the NSA's employ and was somehow still hooked up with it, even while working for IBM. In any case, his biography is somewhat sketchy. Born in 1914, he had left Germany as a young man. His aunt had married a Swiss Jew living in Zurich, and on the concocted pretext of tending to his aunt's illness, Feistel joined them just before the Third Reich began a military conscription that would have prevented his escape. After studying in Zurich, Feistel came to the United States in 1934. He was about to become a naturalized citizen when America was thrust into World War II. Feistel was put under what he once described as "house arrest," his movements restricted to the Boston area where he was living. But in January 1944, Feistel's circumstances changed abruptly. He was not only granted citizenship but also given a security clearance and a job at a highly sensitive facility: the Air Force Cambridge Research Center.

What he did there is unclear. Codes had fascinated him since his boyhood, but in the early 1990s he told Whit Diffie that while crypto work was indeed his desire, he was informed that this was not suitable wartime work for a German-born engineer. On the other hand, in a 1976 interview with David Kahn, Feistel said that during the war he had worked on Identification of Friend or Foe systems—not cryptography per se at that time, but close.

There are other contradictions in Feistel's various accounts of his activities. He told Diffie that before he was granted U.S. citizenship, he had to report to authorities every time he left Boston to visit his mother in New York. But he once told a coworker that his mother didn't emigrate until the Cold War began. The U.S. had spirited her out of East Berlin, he reportedly said, just in case the Soviets discovered that Feistel was doing crypto and decided to pressure her.

There was no doubt, however, that after the war, Feistel began to specialize in IFF. He headed a crypto group at the Cambridge Research Center, and part of his job was testing an advanced IFF system that depended on an amazing new invention, the transistor. This tiny marvel would enable an IFF system to be built so compactly that it could fit into the nose of a fighter plane. Another important project of Feistel's was a longtime passion: constructing a strong cryptosystem based on block ciphers. (This kind of system encrypted messages by processing them in chunks, or "blocks," as opposed to stream ciphers, which did their scrambling on text as it flowed, or "streamed," by.)

Did the NSA embrace Feistel's work, or did it see his work as a threat, and try to stifle it? According to what Feistel told Diffie, the people at The Fort had closely monitored his air force work and used the NSA's power to influence the direction Feistel's work took. But the agency also regarded the project as a threat and eventually managed to kill the entire crypto effort at the Cambridge lab. When Feistel left for another job in the mid-1960s at Mitre (the same military contractor that would later put Whit Diffie on its payroll), he unsuccessfully tried to organize a group there that would resume his crypto work. He blamed the failure on more NSA pressure.

So Feistel took the advice of his friend, A. Adrian Albert, and went to work for IBM, which seemed more open to such pursuits. (Albert was a mathematician, a onetime head of the American Mathematical Society, who had himself done extensive cryptography work for the government.) IBM was an amazingly rich company with little competition, and its research division was an intellectual playground where incredibly bright scientists were encouraged to explore whatever interested them. "If they hired you at Yorktown, you'd do what you wanted, as long as you did something," says Alan Konheim, who became Feistel's boss in 1971. "And Feistel did something—he formalized this idea for a cryptosystem."

The most remarkable aspect of Feistel's creation was not its mathematics or its technology—or even its resistance to codebreakers—but the motivation behind it. His superstrong cipher wasn't intended to defend government secrets or diplomatic dispatches, but to protect people's privacy—specifically, to protect databases of personal information from intruders who might steal the contents to create detailed dossiers on individuals. "Computers," wrote Feistel in a 1973 article for *Scientific American,* "now constitute, or will soon constitute, a dangerous threat to individual privacy. . . . It will soon be feasible to compile dossiers in depth on an entire citizenry." Feistel declared that the antidote was cryptography, traditionally the domain "of military men and diplomats." He proposed that computer systems be adapted "to guard [their] contents from anyone but authorized individuals by enciphering the material in forms highly resistant to cipher-breaking." Considering Feistel's familiarity with the government's zeal for keeping cryptography to itself, this was a significant position to take. So important was privacy in the computer era, Feistel believed, that the knee-jerk national security arguments would have to be shelved.

Meanwhile, Feistel was concocting a system that would grant people that privacy.

The system was called Demon, so dubbed because file names in the computer language he used (APL) could not handle a word as long as his unimaginative choice for the first version, "Demonstration." Later, in a burst of inspiration, an IBM colleague would change the name, carrying over the satanic theme from Demon, to "Lucifer," thus containing a cryptographic pun.

As a block cipher, Lucifer was a virtual machine that sucked in blocks of plaintext data and spit out blocks of ciphertext. Feistel created several versions; the best known used a digital key of 128 bits, an enormously tough target for a brute-force attack. *Impossibly* tough. Of course, the issue of key length would be of little importance if a codebreaker could quickly crack the system by detecting and exploiting structural weaknesses that would recover plaintext without having to bother with brute-force attacks. If even the most subtle pattern could be discernible in ciphertext, a codebreaker would be on his way to breaking the system. Lucifer's strength, like that of any other cipher, depended on denying potential foes any such shortcuts. Feistel's cipher avoided telltale patterns by subjecting the plaintext characters to a tortuous mathematical journey, leading them through a complicated whirl of substitutions. Ultimately, after sixteen "rounds" of furious swapping with other letters in the alphabet, the actual plaintext words and sentences would appear only as a block of seemingly random letters: an oblique ciphertext.

The crucial rules of substitution took place by means of two substitution boxes, or "S-boxes." These, of course, were not physical boxes, but sets of byzantine nonlinear equations dictating the ways that letters should be shifted. (At least one colleague of Feistel's, Alan Konheim, believes that the idea of S-boxes had been given to Feistel by the NSA at a summer workshop, supposedly to get a technology well understood by Fort Meade into the mainstream. "Horst is a very clever guy, but my guess is he was given guidance," says Konheim.)

The S-boxes did not merely initiate a set of predictable substitutions in the letters; they used information drawn from a series of numbers that comprised a secret key to vary the sequence as the bits passed through the boxes. The security of the system ultimately rested with this key. Without knowing this key, even a foe who understood all the rules of Lucifer would have no advantage in transforming ciphertext into plaintext by some reverse-engineering technique.

Such knowledge of the rules was to be assumed; the nuts and bolts of a well-distributed commercial cipher were much more likely to be accessible to eavesdroppers than the workings of military codes, which could be more tightly controlled. A cryptanalyst trying to crack an army code would often have no clue as to the system used to produce the ciphertext, a problem that required not only plenty of extra time to break the code, but also a huge amount of resources in the black art of undercover intelligence. Huge spy networks devoted themselves to learning the sorts of codes the enemy used. On the other hand, if Chase Manhattan Bank decided to use IBM's brand-name code to encrypt its financial transactions, a potential crook would find it relatively simple to discover what cryptosystem the bank used. Since IBM might license the cryptosystem to others, the rules of that system would probably be circulated fairly widely. So in this new era of non-military crypto, all the secrecy would rely on the key.

IBM applied for, and received, several patents for Lucifer. As an innovation of its Watson Research Lab, Lucifer fell into the research category. But unlike some blue-sky schemes at Watson that were way ahead of their time, an invention that provided an instant answer to a pressing problem—data security in the communications age—was naturally positioned on a fast-track to commercialization. Lucifer's first serious implementation came quickly, in Lloyds of London's Cash-point system, a means for distributing hard currency to bank customers. Undoubtedly, this was a harbinger of bigger things to come for both IBM and crypto. It was only a matter of time before Horst Feistel's baby would no longer be a research project; it would be a major IBM initiative. And that would change everything.

As Feistel was refining Lucifer, a thirty-eight-year-old engineer named Walter Tuchman was working at IBM's Kingston, New York, division. He was a Big Blue lifer, having first gotten his feet wet during a three-month period at IBM in 1957 between college and the army. When he finished his stint, IBM not only rehired him but sent him off to Syracuse to pursue a doctorate in information theory. Most of his classmates remained in academia, but Tuchman wanted to use his knowledge to actually create sophisticated technology, so he stuck with IBM and wound up heading product groups.

Tuchman's most recent IBM task involved an odd sort of computer security vulnerability. When computer terminals are in operation, they leak out faint electronic impressions that a sophisticated eavesdropper can use to reconstruct the information being shown on the screen. In effect, those blips represent an unauthorized computer-data wiretap. The government wanted a special means to shield its computers from such potential leaks, and IBM responded by devising what came to be known as Tempest technology. It was considered a big win, and when Tuchman's team finished its work around 1971, people in the group wanted to stay together rather than disperse to other projects, a routine known internally as "volkerwanderung." To do this, they needed a new mission. Tuchman's boss knew there were some interesting things going on in the banking division that might require innovative advances in computer security, and suggested Tuchman and his team look into it.

IBM's banking division was fortuitously located just across the road from Tuchman's offices in Kingston. He quickly found that his boss's instinct was sound in sending him there. Building on the Lloyd's project, IBM had decided to advance the idea of cash-issuing terminals, where bank customers could get money from their accounts without having to see a teller. The first cash-issuing machines had been giant safes that held not only the money but also all the electronic and computer equipment necessary to process the transaction. This was both costly and unwieldy. The better solution would be to spread the computer application between a terminal and the bank's mainframe computer, which could do all the heavy-duty processing. This solution was not only efficient, but hewed to IBM's recent, painful realization that the standard model of computing was headed to the junkyard. "Before then, data processing was all done on the mainframe. The security model was that you locked your door, you locked your desk, and you had a guy with a gun guarding the building," explains Tuchman. But now, even the most tradition-bound minds in Armonk understood that in the future, as Tuchman puts it, "data processing was leaving the building." And since a guard with a gun couldn't be everywhere, the security model would have to change.

Of course, a system that actually doled out cash would represent a trial by fire for whatever new type of security IBM employed. The crucial commands that flashed a green light to spit out twenty-dollar bills would be sent over the phone line. Tuchman was quick to understand how precarious this could be. Imagine if some techno-crook managed to elbow his way on to the phone line and mimic the messages that said, "Lay on the twenties!"

The answer was cryptography. Though Tuchman had a background in information theory, he had never specifically done any crypto work. But he soon found out about the system that the guys in IBM research at Yorktown Heights had cooked up. He ventured down to Watson Labs one day and heard Feistel speak about Lucifer. He immediately set up a lunch with Feistel and Alan Konheim. The first thing Tuchman asked Feistel was where he had gotten the ideas for Lucifer. Feistel, in his distinctive German accent, mentioned the early papers of Claude Shannon. "The Shannon paper reveals all," he said.

Meanwhile, Tuchman's colleague Karl Meyer was exploring whether Lucifer might be a good fit for an expanded version of the Lloyd's Cashpoint system. Ultimately he and Tuchman concluded that it would probably need a number of modifications before it was strong enough to rely upon. But it would be a fine beginning. And so, they made an arrangement with Alan Konheim and his Information Theory Group. Tuchman and Meyer's team at Kingston would build a revised algorithm for Lucifer. Then they would send it to Yorktown for evaluation and testing.

The internal name for the cipher was the DSD-1.

Before this arrangement was approved, however, a top IBM executive demanded to know why they were even bothering with Lucifer when he knew of a cheaper, faster algorithm. Tuchman took this supposedly superior algorithm home and broke it over the course of a weekend. (He and Meyer eventually published the break in the trade magazine *Datamation*.) Tuchman would often cite this triumph as proof that his team knew what it was doing—and to ensure that the work wouldn't be disrupted by clueless interference from upstairs. "We can't deal with amateurs in the field," he remembers telling the muckety-mucks high on the corporate food chain. "There's no cheap way out of doing a crypto algorithm. You've gotta work, work, work. Qualify, qualify, qualify. It's going to take a long time."

This was a fairly difficult process because, as Whit Diffie could have told the Kingston group, there was pathetically little information available on how one could construct a modern, military-strength cryptosystem. "All of it was classified," sighs Tuchman. "But we understood from our mathematics classes what makes a cipher hard to solve." His group read everything they could in the library, and, as Feistel had predicted, the most helpful papers were those of Shannon. And they talked a lot to Feistel himself. But mainly they reinvented a lot of what must have been common knowledge among the algorithm weavers at Fort George Meade. "We sat around in our conference rooms working on the blackboard, teaching ourselves," says Tuchman.

Ideally, Feistel himself would have been recruited to temporarily move to Kingston. Tuchman kept asking Konheim, "What does Horst want to do? I'll give him a nice desk and his own office, and he can come up here."

And Konheim would say, "Nah, I don't think it'll work out."

Tuchman eventually came to understand why. "Horst was like a European version of James Stewart in the movie *Harvey*," he later said. "He was sort of living in a little magical world between what happens in a commercial business like IBM and his hobbies. I never quite felt that Horst understood what the business world—especially the high-tech business world—was all about. He was cloistered in research in Yorktown, and here we were, these crazy guys from Kingston who were actually willing to make *products,* to see if we could do something that made *money.*"

Konheim agrees that Feistel was oddly misplaced in the corporate world and, as time went on, even in the research division of that universe. According to Konheim, as Lucifer became less and less Feistel's invention and more the commercial product of an IBM division, Feistel would arrive at Yorktown later and later in the day. And even then, he wouldn't seem to be working on the project, but rather spending a lot of time on the phone speaking German. Konheim says that Feistel's elderly aunt had promised him a considerable inheritance, and a lot of that phone time was spent cultivating her almost fanatically. (According to Konheim, it was a bitter disappointment years later when she died and left him nothing.)

And Feistel's 1973 article for *Scientific American*—one of the most explicit scientific descriptions of crypto presented to the public in years—could have been interpreted as a rebellion of sorts. Certainly in some quarters such frankness about the cryptographic innards of a potential IBM product could have more than raised an eyebrow. Apparently, the NSA itself objected to the article; years later, Feistel would allude to the agency's unhappiness with it, also remarking that if it hadn't been for the Watergate scandal then turning Washington upside down, the NSA might have tried to shut down the entire Lucifer project, as it had with his previous ventures.

The Kingston group was blissfully unaware of such intrigues. To them, the Lucifer effort was simply a product ramp-up. They focused on their goal of modifying the system, of increasing its complexity and difficulty so that its ciphertext would pass the Shannon tests for apparent information randomness. The first step was to set up a list of what they called "heuristic qualifiers," a series of mathematical tests that would evaluate the cryptosystem's output—the scrambled message—so that it bore no apparent relationship to the original message, appearing to be a random collection of letters. In Claude Shannon's terminology, the apparent information content would be zero.

Feistel's version of Lucifer certainly attempted to reach this ideal but didn't go far enough. Its strongest feature was its two S-boxes, where the trickiest substitutions took place—the nonlinear transformations designed to drive cryptanalysts batty. So the Kingston team decided that the new, improved Lucifer—DSD-1—would have even more devious S-boxes. And the number of those would increase from Lucifer's two to a much more formidable eight.

Complicating that effort were the requirements for compactness and speed: "It had to be cheap and it had to work fast," says Tuchman. To fulfill those needs, the entire algorithm had to fit on a single chip. So another part of the team was a VLSI (Very Large Scale Integration) group, split between Kingston and IBM's Burlington, Vermont, labs, whose job was to put the entire scrambling system on a 3-micron, single wiring layer chip. If everything worked out, IBM would have the tiniest strong-encryption machine ever known.

Working under those constraints, the Kingston team constructed the complicated DSD-1, still informally referred to as Lucifer. If all went well, their new Lucifer would take a 64-bit block of plaintext, submit those bits through a torturous process of permutation, blocking, expansion, blocking, bonding, and substitution involving a digital key, and then repeat the process fifteen times more, for a total of sixteen rounds. The result would be 64 bits of what appeared to be total digital anarchy, a Babel that could only be returned to order by someone reversing the encryption process by using the digital key that determined how the scrambling had been done.

Then the Watson Lab team would try to attack it, to see if things really had gone well.

Though Horst Feistel was not involved in the actual reconstruction of DSD-1, he did help bring his colleagues in research up to speed for the testing process. On January 11, 1973, he gathered five fellow members of the Data Security Group at Yorktown Heights and gave them their first exposure to the Lucifer cipher. One of the group, Alan Tritter (the same eccentric computer scientist who had told Whit Diffie about IFF protocols), raised questions as to the wisdom of the entire enterprise. Was IBM putting itself at risk by vying to be a power in the new world of commercial cryptography? What if Lucifer could be cracked?

Tritter's comments drew interest because they seemed to echo some remarks made, but not proven, by a professor at Case Western Reserve University named Edward Glaser. A blind man who was one of the endless consultants IBM routinely hired with its bottomless budget, Glaser, according to Konheim, had blustered that if he were given twenty examples of ciphertext, along with the original plaintext (this is known as a chosen plaintext attack), he could break Lucifer's system. (It turned out to be a specious claim.)

But the point was well taken, and Tritter repeated it in a memo written later that year. "We were/are in an unusually exposed position," he wrote. Noting that the first use of Lucifer was already implemented in a Lloyd's cash terminal, he ticked off the consequences that could come if the system, like so many seemingly "unbreakable" ones before it, was somehow compromised. If someone was able to produce a valid key for a Lucifer cipher, he wrote, "a clever, resourceful, highly organized attempt to remove illicitly but without the use of force the entire cash contents of all the terminals in the 'Cashpoint' system, say over a single bank holiday weekend, would certainly succeed."

But such a possible loss was only the beginning of the sorts of perils IBM was courting by drawing on crypto's implicit promise of security. With Big Blue's fat cash reserves, it would be no problem replacing even a steep stack of twenties to reimburse Lloyd's. More troublesome would be restoring public confidence. And then would come the lawsuits.

"Were the security of [Lucifer] *or of any other crypto product we may subsequently field* to be breached publicly, the harm it would do us in the marketplace would be incalculable," wrote Tritter. "And this is in addition to actual damages and the very real possibility of exemplary damages awarded against us in a lawsuit which would give the press, the industry, and the public a field day."

On the other hand, how could IBM *not* pursue cryptography? Its business was the information age, and without a means of protecting data as they moved from one computer to another, IBM would not sell nearly as many computers. The lack of cryptography was a potential roadblock to the computerization of America—and the computerization of the world itself. So on February 5, 1973, a high-level meeting was held to review "the status and plans of cryptography within the entire IBM corporation." As Tritter later summarized the meeting, "It appeared to be broadly agreed . . . that IBM was apparently in the crypto business for keeps, and would have to acquire a corporate expertise in the area. In the meanwhile, attacks on Lucifer were to be intensified."

An outside expert, Jim Simons of the math department at the State University of New York at Stony Brook—who had also practiced cryptography at the Institute for Defense Analysis, the NSA satellite in Princeton—was recruited to organize a concentrated attack on Lucifer. He worked with three researchers from Yorktown Heights for about seven weeks in the late spring of 1973. Even before he issued his report, IBMers were buzzing with the good news: Simons and his team hadn't cracked it.

"The Lucifer machine is certainly stronger than I had originally thought," Simons wrote in his report of August 18, 1973. But he didn't exactly bestow a crypto seal of approval on it. "It seems highly improbable that Lucifer will be broken by two high school students as part of their science fair project," concluded Simons. "On the other hand, there isn't nearly enough evidence to feel confident that it won't succumb to sophisticated attacks by a professional cryptanalyst." Simons worried that if Lucifer, as currently constituted, was put into commercial use, it would almost inevitably be used to protect "traffic of genuine importance" (like money, or trade secrets), providing the incentive to encourage an intense, ultimately successful effort to break it. So while Lucifer seemed to be a good start for IBM, Simons warned, the company should work harder to come up with an improved product. "There really is no choice," he concluded.

Meanwhile, IBM itself kept wondering if Lucifer was up to the task. In a confidential memo in May 1973, its chief scientist Lewis Branscombe, summarizing the consensus of the firm's Scientific Advisory Committee, emphasized the need for the company to "establish a single cryptographic architecture, technology and product strategy." Lucifer, he wrote, was not the only candidate. But later in the month, another memo deemed the Kingston scheme superior, with one caveat: "Unless there is a clear evidence of a significant threshold of vulnerability."

The tests continued for months, conducted by private-sector researchers hired by IBM. "Alan would give them the algorithm and say, 'Break it. Just go break it.' And Alan kept reporting back that nobody could find a shortcut," says Tuchman. "Finally I reached that magical psychological place where I figured this thing doesn't have a shortcut, so there is just no shortcut solution. Forget it, guys, let's concentrate on implementing the product now."

Still, compared to the world-class codebreakers behind the Triple Fence, most of the math professors hired to bang their heads against Lucifer were Little Leaguers. How could IBM be sure the scheme was *really* sound? They certainly didn't want to find out its vulnerabilities by discovering that one day some former KGB cryptanalyst hired by the Mafia had cleaned out their virtual cash vault.

At the beginning of 1974, Tuchman figured his team was about halfway through its work. "We had a pretty good idea how much algorithm we could get on a single chip," he says. And much of that algorithm was written. But two things happened that year that would profoundly affect the project. The first would throw it open to the public. The second would cast a clandestine shadow over it that would last for a generation.

IBM was not the only institution aware of the vital need for cryptographic protection in the computer age. That view was also shared at the National Bureau of Standards, the government agency in charge of establishing commonly accepted industry standards for a wide variety of commercial purposes. The bureaucrats and scientists there believed that digital protection should be centered in a single system, one well-tested means of encrypting information that would be accessible by all. So NBS decided to solicit proposals for a standard cryptographic algorithm. (The NSA declined to submit one of its own ciphers, since allowing outsiders to examine its work was unthinkable.) In the May 15, 1973, *Federal Register*, the NBS listed a number of exacting criteria that such a standard should meet.

Not surprisingly, the NBS received no submissions at that time that even vaguely met the criteria. By and large the only cryptographers in this country who had the wherewithal and expertise to meet this challenge were working behind the Triple Fence. And the work done there was never published, never revealed.

But there was one cryptosystem in development that seemed to fit a lot of the government's needs: Lucifer, the DSD-1. Lewis Branscombe, IBM's chief scientist—who, not coincidentally, was himself a former head of the NBS—in particular felt that this work in progress might be an excellent candidate for the encryption standard for the next generation.

Walt Tuchman was against the idea, primarily because of the trade-off involved in submitting the revised Lucifer as a federal standard: IBM would be required to relinquish its patent rights, essentially giving—not selling—the algorithm to the world. "I was this typical capitalistic product manager," he explains. "I'm in this thing to make money, not to foster some great social improvement." He argued his point before IBM's high-level executive Paul Rizzo, who was then Big Blue's number two. Branscombe presented the other point of view: make it public. Finally, Rizzo weighed in. Lucifer, he argued, was like a safety component that benefited all of society. If the Ford Motor Company came up with a seat belt superior to those of its competitors, one that saved the lives of moms and dads, would they allow General Motors to use it? *You better believe they would, because it was the right thing to do.* Jimmy Stewart couldn't have topped that homily. You could almost hear the violins playing. The speech convinced not only the IBM board, but Tuchman himself, who called a staff meeting when he returned to Kingston. "Well, guys," he said, "we're going to give the stuff away."

Not completely, of course. The ways they built Lucifer into a chip, the ways they would implement it within a full-featured solution, the little tricks to get the most of it . . . these would be great selling points for IBM-created versions of the DSD-1. Other companies would get access just to the algorithm itself. So maybe it wasn't such a bad idea from a business perspective to give the thing away.

The feeling at IBM was that merely submitting its work to the NBS was sufficient to fast-track DSD-1 toward a coronation as the standard. Even though the response date for the NBS's request for crypto algorithms in 1973 had long expired, Branscombe wrote to his NBS successor Ruth Davis in July 1974, offering what he described as the "Key-Controlled Cryptographic Algorithm," developed at Kingston, as a candidate. With this favored new candidate already in hand, the NBS, somewhat superfluously reissued its request for crypto algorithms in the August 27, 1974, *Federal Register*. No serious competitor emerged. And thus the revised Lucifer, a.k.a. DSD-1, was destined to be known by a lofty, though generic, moniker: the Data Encryption Standard. The title would eventually become so familiar among the digital cognoscenti that it would be pronounced not as an acronym but as a single phoneme: *Dez.*

By then, the *other* crucial process in Lucifer's transformation was well under way. It had been fairly early in 1974 when Walt Tuchman received what he later would refer to as "that deadly phone call." It was his boss, telling him he had to take a trip down to the National Security Agency to cool them down about Lucifer.

Tuchman didn't like it. But he understood the importance of playing ball with Uncle Sam. By creating a cryptographic product for the commercial sector, IBM was treading on strange turf. If the company didn't get export clearance to send its crypto chip to its international customers, the whole product might as well be scrapped. What good was a product for a global company like IBM if you couldn't sell it to the global market?

So Tuchman went on his first visit to The Fort. He eyeballed the Triple Fence, contemplated the armed marine guards, parked in the visitors' lot, and entered the small concrete building where outsiders lacking previous clearance fill in a stack of papers and wait to be called. Then an elderly woman appeared and guided him through a labyrinth of hallways to the second-level manager assigned to the case, a guy just below the deputy-director level. He was not in a military uniform or even in a suit. And he quickly proposed a quid pro quo: *We want to control the implementation of this system. You will develop it in secret, and we will monitor your progress and suggest changes. We don't want it shipped in software code—just chips. Furthermore, we don't want it shipped to certain countries at all, and we will allow you to ship it to countries on the approved list only if you obtain a license to do so. That license will be dependent on customers we approve sign-*

*ing a document vowing that they will not subsequently ship the product
to anyone else.*

This went on for a while, until Tuchman finally had a chance to
speak. "What's the pro quo of the quid pro quo?" he asked. After all,
the NSA man had focused entirely on restrictions and conditions, and
had neglected to mention what IBM would receive for its troubles.

"The pro quo will be something very useful to you," said the NSA
man. The agency itself would qualify the algorithm. Their all-star
cryptanalysts would analyze it and bang away at it. If there was a
weakness, it could be noted and corrected. And when the mathematical dust settled, IBM would have a priceless imprimatur, one that
would assure the instant confidence of its customers: the National
Security Agency Good Secret-Keeping Seal.

This was a powerful offer. It spoke directly to Tuchman's greatest
fear—that outlaw codebreakers would discover a shortcut solution
that would allow them to steal secrets and even money from IBM customers, thus exposing the fabled computer giant to international
embarrassment and a legal Armageddon. Instead of having to rely on
the smart but inexperienced amateurs at Yorktown and the random
consultants they hired, IBM would have the ultimate in due diligence:
the cryptanalysis gold standard. As soon as he returned from Fort
Meade, he went to see his boss and urged him, "Let's do it. Let's work
with these guys." It was a solution that felt good to the top IBMers,
who, after all, were virtually synonymous with the "Establishment." So,
just like that, the country's single most important cryptographic effort
in the private sector—save for that of Whit Diffie, still in obscurity
struggling at Stanford with his weird ideas about one-way functions—
came under the friendly but firm embrace of the National Security
Agency.

Unspoken was the question as to whether the NSA—which after all
was not an arm of the Commerce Department but an intelligence
agency, the ultimate spook palace—might discover a gaping weakness
in DES but keep its collective mouth shut, smug in the knowledge that
it could use that shortcut to quickly break messages encrypted in the
IBM code. Tuchman understood the risk of this. As the development
process unfolded over the next few months and years, he watched for
signs that this might be happening. Ultimately, he was convinced of
the NSA's sincerity. "If they fooled me," he says, "I will go to my grave

being fooled. I looked at those guys eyeball to eyeball. I'm a bit of a film buff, and I've seen good acting and poor acting. And if the NSA people fooled me, they missed their profession. They should've gone to Hollywood and become actors."

From that point on, DES's development process became, for all practical purposes, a virtual annex within the Triple Fence. The government issued a secrecy order on Horst Feistel's Lucifer patent, known as "Variant Key Matrix Cipher System." On April 17, 1974, an IBM patent attorney sent a memo to the crypto teams at Yorktown Heights and Kingston explaining that this meant there would be not only no publishing on the subject, but no public discussion whatsoever without the written consent of the Commissioner of Patents. Even the fact that a secrecy order existed was itself considered a secret, and talking about that was just as serious a crime as handing out encryption algorithms in the departure lounge at Kennedy Airport. A loose lip could result in a $10,000 fine, two years in prison, or both. Fortunately, the memo explained, "IBM has been granted a special permit which allows the disclosure of the subject matter in the application to the minimum necessary number of persons of known loyalty and discretion, employed by or working with IBM, whose duties involve cooperation in the development, manufacture, or use of the subject matter." Without that exemption, of course, IBM could not have continued its effort, because of the obvious difficulty of collaborating on a project when one risked a jail term for admitting its existence to a co-worker.

The NSA's demands for secrecy were particularly rigid concerning the agency's cryptanalysis of DES. Anything—*anything*—that shed light on the way that The Fort's codebreakers went about their business was regarded as the blackest of black information. The agreement drawn between the agency and the corporation clearly outlined the limited nature of what IBM's scientists could glean from the collaboration. IBM was strictly required to limit those who were involved in the evaluation, and to keep up-to-date lists of those people. Any contact between Big Blue and Big Snoop would come at a series of briefings with rules as circumscribed as a Kabuki performance: IBM would essentially present information, and the NSA people would silently evaluate it. No geeky chatter: the NSA people were formally prohibited "from entering into technical discussions with IBM representatives in regard to the information presented." Afterward, the NSA folks would hold postmortems to determine whether the IBM scientists might have stumbled on information or techniques "of a sensitive nature." In that case NSA would then formally notify the company, and IBM would keep the information under wraps.

The NSA certainly did know its stuff. It was particularly interested in a technique discovered by the IBM researchers that was referred to at Watson labs as the "T Attack." Later it would be known as "differential cryptanalysis." This was a complicated series of mathematical assaults that required lots of chosen plaintext (meaning that the attacker needed to have matched sets of original dispatches and encrypted output). Sometime that year, the Watson researchers had discovered that, under certain conditions, the IBM cipher could fall prey to a T Attack—a successful foray could actually allow a foe to divine the bits of the key. To prevent such an assault, the IBM team had redesigned the S-boxes. After the redesign, under even the most favorable conditions, a T Attack would provide a cracker only a slight, virtually insignificant advantage.

Hearing about this unhinged the NSA crowd. Apparently, the T Attack was very well known—and highly classified—behind the Triple Fence. So imagine the agency's dismay when the IBM team not only discovered the trick (which, presumably, the NSA had been merrily employing to crack enemy codes) but had created a set of design principles to defend against it. The crypto soldiers at Fort Meade could not tolerate the possibility that such information might leak into the general literature. And so the NSA put its secrecy clamp down harder on IBM.

"They asked us to stamp all our documents confidential," says Tuchman. "We actually put a number on each one and locked them up in safes, because they were considered U.S. government classified. They said do it. So I did it."

The man who probably did the most work for IBM on the T Attack, Don Coppersmith, would not discuss the issue for twenty years. It was not until 1994, long after other researchers had independently discovered and described the technique, that he divulged the S-box design principles. "After discussions with the NSA," he explained in a technical article for the *IBM Research Journal*, "it was decided that the disclosure of the design considerations would reveal the technique of differential cryptanalysis, a powerful technique that can be used against many ciphers. This in turn would weaken the competitive advantage the United States enjoyed over other countries in the field of cryptography."

Ultimately, IBM got what it wanted for DES—a clean bill of health from the NSA. (This was also a crucial factor in the process by which the National Bureau of Standards would place its imprimatur on DES as a federal standard.) But IBM paid a steep price for adhering to the NSA's demands to keep its S-box design principles secret. The behavior of the S-boxes in the DES system involved complicated substitutions and permutations that put Rube Goldberg to shame. The best way that outsiders could evaluate whether those bizarre transformations were done simply to produce a tougher cipher—or were clandestinely jimmied to put in a back door by which the NSA could secretly get a head-start on codebreaking—was to know why the designers chose their formulas. So IBM's refusal to explain the logic behind the S-box design encouraged critics like Diffie and Hellman to let their suspicions run wild and entertain all sorts of theories about secret back doors.

Telling people that a presumably public algorithm was based on secret designs was a recipe for paranoia, and indeed, the resulting dish nourished critics for years. But to the NSA, this point was non-negotiable. The Fort Meade brain trust might have considered it a necessary evil to allow a strong crypto algorithm into the world of banks and corporations. But permitting the release of sophisticated techniques that might encourage outsiders to bulletproof their own codes . . . well, that was quite unacceptable.

The whole episode turned out to embody in a nutshell a dilemma that the NSA had yet to acknowledge, even to itself. For years, people at The Fort could be reasonably confident that when they devised a breakthrough technique like differential cryptanalysis, such information would be unlikely to tumble into the public domain. Those days were over. Consider that the IBM group had come across the T Attack *on its own,* without the help of government. Differential cryptanalysis was ultimately a mathematical technique just waiting to be rediscovered by someone outside the Triple Fence interested in sophisticated codes. The NSA couldn't hold on to such mathematical machinations any more than an astronomer discovering a previously unknown nebula could cover up the skies to mask its presence to future stargazers.

This was to be the reality of the dawning era of public crypto: whether the NSA liked it or not, bright minds were inevitably going to reinvent the techniques and ideas that had been formerly quarantined at Fort Meade—and maybe come up with some ideas never contemplated even by the elite cryptographers behind the Triple Fence.

S-boxes aside, the most controversial feature of DES would be its key length. Horst Feistel's Lucifer specified a 128-bit key. But clearly the National Security Agency did not want the national encryption standard—even if it were used only by financial institutions and corporations—to lock information within such a mighty safe. By the time the algorithm had threaded its way through the Triple Fence and was released as a potential NBS standard, the key length had been cut in half, and then cut some more, down to the relatively paltry 56 bits.

It's hard to exaggerate the difference this makes. Assume that a codebreaker trying to crack DES is unable to discover any shortcuts to cracking. The only way that an intruder can recover an encrypted message, then, is to launch a brute-force attack, experimenting with every possible key combination until he finds the one that was used to scramble the original. Such a search is the equivalent of a safecracker painstakingly twisting the dial to stumble upon the exact series of numbers that would align the tumblers. Even with a computer twisting the virtual dials at high speed, a very large "keyspace" (a numerical range that contains all possible key combinations) can make such a search impossible to pull off. A 128-bit key is very, very large. If a computer tried one million keys every second—a million different combinations of the numbers on the safe dial—it would take aeons to try every possible key.

So what would be the effect of cutting the key size in half? To assess this, you have to keep in mind the nature of digital numbers. Each bit in a binary key is like a fork in the road that a codebreaker must negotiate in order to get to the destination of the correct combination of ones and zeros. Every fork presents a random choice between the correct turn and the wrong turn; a 128-bit key means that you have to guess the correct way to turn 128 times in a row. To make the course twice as difficult, you simply have to add one more fork; then you've created twice as many possible paths to negotiate, but still only one is correct. But to make the course half as difficult, you don't divide the number of forks by two, but simply remove one.

That's why removing a single bit from the key size means that the encrypted message is only half as safe as it was before. Switching from a 128-bit key to a 127-bit key means you're cutting by half the work factor to break it. If you cut the key size one more bit, to 126 bits, then you've halved *that* key. And so on.

According to Tuchman, the Kingston group figured that a 128-bit key was not only overkill but would require too much chip space and computation. "We had to fit the whole algorithm on there," says Tuchman. "The S-boxes, everything. We were using two-micron CMOS chips, and the data coming in could only be 8 bytes wide [one byte equals eight bits]. So our first key length was 64 bits." Sixty-four bits was a good fit for a chip, a number divisible by the eight-bit bytes.

This was quite a dramatic reduction. It cut down the time required for a full search on the theoretical million-keys-a-second computer from billions of years to around 300,000. Still, a 64-bit key length was considerable in the mid-1970s, especially since it was agreed that computer technology would not be sufficiently advanced to conduct searches at such speeds for the next couple of decades.

But then the Kingston group made a seemingly inexplicable second cut, to the mathematically awkward key length of 56 bits. And suddenly, the possibility of a brute-force attack was smack in the picture. Why did a lousy eight bits make such a difference? Remember, every time the key is reduced by a single bit, it becomes twice as easy to crack. So this eight-bit loss made the cipher 256 times easier to crack: from 300,000 years to a little over a thousand. Put another way: the percentage of key space that formerly would have occupied a foe's computers from January to August could now be scanned in less than a day.

What was IBM's explanation for this? According to Tuchman, it was standard company practice in hardware design to allow a certain number of extra bits for "parity checks," a sort of synchronization to make sure that the electronic signals were being properly read. "It was an IBM internal spec," he says, at the same time admitting that it was a "foolish" requirement. "We don't do that anymore, but at the time we had a standard—so I had to reduce the key size [to accommodate the extra bits]."

Tuchman didn't think that this further cut really compromised DES. (Privately disagreeing with this was Horst Feistel, who still preferred a 128-bit key. But he was no longer actively involved with the project and would soon be quietly eased out of IBM itself.) Tuchman and his colleague Karl Meyer believed that a 56-bit key, with its 70 quadrillion variations, was more than sufficient for the commercial, even the financial, secrets that DES would protect. The idea of DES, Tuchman would argue, was to provide computer networks the level of security that people had in their physical workplaces: "locked desk drawers, locked doors on computer rooms, and loyal, well-behaved employees." Not the military secrets customarily transported in exploding briefcases handcuffed to couriers or entrusted to spies who were taught to ingest poison pills upon capture.

Others, however, have always believed that the reduction was caused by NSA pressure. This even included skeptics inside IBM, like Alan Konheim, who headed the mathematical team on the DES project. "Fifty-six bits is very unnatural," says Konheim, obviously disregarding Tuchman's "parity check" explanation. "The government [must have] said, 'Listen, 64 bits is too much—make it 56.' " Why would IBM go along with it? "You see, IBM does business all over the world. It can't send a pencil outside the United States without an export license. Not only that, when [the NSA invokes] patriotism and national security, well, these are not things you can argue about."

To outsiders like Martin Hellman and Whit Diffie, of course, the key size was a smoking gun that proved the NSA had weakened the standard for its own nefarious purposes. In the months after the standard was first announced, the Stanford cryptographers wrote a steady stream of suggestions and objections to their contact at the National Bureau of Standards—and became increasingly frustrated that the officials kept insisting that there was no problem. Hellman came to believe that the NBS wasn't speaking for itself but was acting as a stooge for Fort Meade.

To prove his point about the weakness of the key size, Hellman challenged an executive he knew at IBM to contradict his and Diffie's contention that this DES key could actually fall in a day to a sophisticated, high-powered machine. At this point, the Stanford researchers were postulating that such a machine could be built for $20 million. Thus, if one key were broken each day, over a five-year period the price of breaking each key would be around $10,000. Not a bad investment if some of the broken messages included precious data like oil reserve locations and corporate merger plans—such information was worth millions. "But even if we were off by a whole order of magnitude, and it would cost $100,000, that wouldn't matter," says Hellman. "Because in five years computers would be ten times faster, and the solution would cost only a tenth as much as it would now." According to Hellman, the IBM executive ordered his own researchers to investigate. "He called me back and said that their numbers were in the same ballpark as ours," says Hellman. "That was his exact word, the 'ballpark.' But he told me that the key size was set by the NBS, not IBM."

Meanwhile, officials at the NBS were assuring Hellman, in their responses to his frequent, increasingly pointed letters, that their own studies showed that a machine like the one envisioned by Hellman would take all of ninety-one years to search through a DES keyspace. Obviously, they were not playing in the same ballpark.

Hellman believed that all of this was bald evidence that the Data Encryption Standard was a swindle from the start. It was all the NSA's master plan. The supposedly benign NBS—acting as the NSA's public face—allowed IBM to construct its algorithm independently. This gave it deniability: *Hey, it wasn't us spooks who cooked it up, Big Blue did.* But by getting IBM to cut the key size to an infuriatingly puny 56 bits, the spooks got what they wanted anyway. "They knew they could control the key size, which would ultimately control the strength of the standard," complains Hellman.

And that was the kindest interpretation. If you wanted to be skeptical—and like any good cryptographer, Hellman and his colleagues were plenty skeptical—you'd still wonder about the possibility of an actual trapdoor that would allow the Fort Meade tricksters to decode a DES message within seconds. Why else were they keeping the design principles a secret?

In any case Hellman rejected the government's ninety-one-year estimate and decided to go over the heads of the NBS functionaries with whom he was corresponding. On February 23, 1976, Hellman stated his complaints in a letter to Elliot Richardson, who, as secretary of commerce, was the ultimate boss of the NBS:

I am writing to you because I am very worried that the National Security Agency has surreptitiously influenced the National Bureau of Standards in a way which seriously limited the value of a proposed standard, and which may pose a threat to individual privacy. I refer to the proposed Data Encryption Standard, intended for protecting confidential or private data used by non-military federal agencies. It will also undoubtedly become a de facto standard in the commercial world.

 . . . I am convinced that NSA in its role of helping NBS design and evaluate possible standards has ensured that the proposed standard is breakable by NSA.

The response Hellman received from Ernest Ambler, the acting director of the NBS, did little to cool him down. Instead of answering Hellman's charges directly, Ambler gave some general comments defending DES, and praised the NSA for its contributions in certifying the algorithm. He helpfully attached an executive order which outlined "the functions and responsibilities of NSA." Monkeying with private-sector algorithms didn't make the list.

That summer, Hellman, Diffie, and five other academics took a month to bang on the system and produced a paper called "Results of an Initial Attempt to Cryptanalyze the NBS Data Encryption Standard." They were straightforward about their concerns: any algorithm approved by the NSA was "mildly suspect a priori" because "the NSA does not want a genuinely strong system to frustrate its cryptanalytic intelligence operations." It was not surprising, then, that while falling far short of actually breaking a DES key, they concluded that the system could not be trusted. Besides the key strength, they found what they considered a "suspicious structure" in the S-boxes—possibly, they wrote, "the result of a . . . deliberately set trapdoor."

To IBM's Walt Tuchman, though, the Diffie-Hellman complaints were a travesty born of paranoia and ignorance. He was no secret agent—he was a *product guy*—and to the best of his ability, he'd led a team to create a good product! It had been a happy day for his team when the first two DES devices were completed. They were shoe-box-sized metal cases stuffed with chips that went between a mainframe computer and a modem. Such a device on each end of a data transfer would allow two computers to communicate in a secret stream, impervious to eavesdroppers—no matter *what* Marty Hellman said. One box was sent to IBM's Paris headquarters, the other to Lew Branscombe's office in Armonk. Then they made some history. The Paris office sent off an encrypted message to the Armonk machine. The Armonk machine, having been previously fed the symmetrical key that performed both encryption and decryption, deciphered the message back to its original form. "It went to a little printer and the message was printed in all the IBM newspapers," recalls Tuchman. "It was some innocuous little message, of course, because everybody knew it was going to be published in the clear."

All that happiness, though, was tempered by the attacks that came from Hellman and friends. Tuchman and his colleague Karl Meyer had to defend themselves at two public workshops sponsored by the NBS. The second, held in September 1976 at the NBS's Gaithersburg, Maryland, headquarters, was the most contentious. *I didn't do anything wrong!* insisted Tuchman. The key size was plenty big enough, and building a machine to crack DES would not take Hellman's low-seven-figure pricetag, but a cool *$200 million.* And if that key size wasn't large enough, people could design devices to run DES through its paces twice, with two different keys. Though such a process might be difficult to set up, this would effectively double the key size to 112 bits—enough keyspace to confound every damned computer on the planet for the next gajillion years. (Eventually, a process would emerge called "Triple DES," which would use *three* keys and rule out even the most extravagantly brutish of attacks. But all of this was a moot point because the version of DES with the allegedly hobbled 56 bits was the one proposed for the standard.)

Tuchman's appeal failed to quiet the critics. *Why didn't you publish the design heuristics?* they wanted to know. *Did you put a trapdoor in DES?*

Then came the newspapers. "Those professors told the *New York Times* and the *Washington Post*," Tuchman complains. The next thing he knew, at IBM's request, Tuchman himself was being interviewed. After taking a gander at the newly famous desks of Woodward and Bernstein, he told the *Post* reporter the same thing he told the *Times* reporter: *The NSA didn't modify the algorithm. They didn't put a trap-*

door in. Look, you guys, it's ridiculous; we're not going to risk the entire IBM company by putting a trapdoor in its product.

Even so, the publicity took its toll. It was bad enough that the *Times*, the *Post*, and the *Wall Street Journal* were listening to Hellman and the critics. Worse came when Tuchman's own mother called him from her retirement home in Florida, concerned with what friends had been telling her after reading the New York papers. She pleaded with her son, who had started life so wonderfully as a whip-smart college boy from Brooklyn: *Please, Walter, leave IBM and stop hanging around with those bad people.* Tuchman had to explain to her that he wasn't going to wind up in a jail cell with Ehrlichman and Haldeman—he was a good guy!

After the publicity came hearings by the Senate Intelligence Committee. These top-secret sessions were closed, and the final report was classified. But a summary was issued for the general public, too. Its contents provided ammunition to both sides.

On one hand, Hellman was proved correct in asserting who the power was that dictated the 56-bit key: "The NSA convinced IBM that a reduced key size was sufficient," the report read. The reduction wasn't, as Tuchman still insists, due to the rigor of chip design or the need for parity checks: it was the fact that the government wouldn't tolerate anything more. IBM knew that it would need export licenses for approved customers. But the NSA, which had been charged to collaborate with the National Bureau of Standards in evaluating DES as a government standard, certainly was not going to rubber-stamp an algorithm that used, in its view, too long a key. Apparently, the 56-bit key length provided the NSA a certain comfort level. Though the work factor to break a cipher of that length seemed dauntingly high, it was clear that if anyone could contemplate a brute-force attack on DES, it was the National Security Agency itself, with what were assumed to be literally acres of computers in its top-secret basement. Obviously, while an ideal code for users was the strongest one possible, the ideal code for the NSA's purposes would be one that was too powerful for criminals and other foes to break, but just weak enough to be broken by the billions of subterranean computer cycles at Fort Meade. Did a 56-bit key fit into that sweet spot? The NSA didn't say. And never would.

Despite its conclusion that the key size was a result of NSA demands, the committee concluded that there was no wrongdoing by either IBM or the government. The Data Encryption Standard had been determined fairly. Like it or not, this was something that Marty Hellman and his friends would have to accept.

It took years, but eventually they not only accepted it, but came to eat some crow. As Walt Tuchman proudly notes, for more than two decades after the algorithm was formally accepted as a standard in 1977, no one had been successful at finding a significant shortcut to cracking a DES-encrypted message. (Of course, if the NSA had done so, it would never have admitted it.)

In 1990, outside cryptanalysts revealed the technique of what was called differential cryptanalysis, proving that under certain (admittedly rare) conditions, one could crack a DES key using slightly less computation than a brute-force attack would require. But this was essentially the "T Attack," discovered by IBM during the development process in time to fortify the algorithm against such assault. And kept confidential at the NSA's request. (A different group of researchers introduced another theoretical attack on DES, linear cryptanalysis, in 1993—but neither did it truly compromise the cipher.)

So if the key size was indeed the only point of attack in DES—if one had to devote massive computational resources to breaking a single message and then wait for days, weeks, or months for the cipher to crumble—then the National Security Agency had certified what could be an extraordinarily powerful tool for the spread of strong encryption throughout the land, and maybe even the world. It had always been the impression of the folks behind the Triple Fence that the users of DES would be conservative, trustworthy institutions like banks and financial clearinghouses. They misjudged the situation. Instead, the development of DES marked the beginning of a new era of cheap, effective means of using computer power to keep personal information private. It was used not only in banks but in all sorts of commercial communications, and was widely available to private communications, too. Though the NSA still controlled its export, it quickly grew unfettered within U.S. borders. And while U.S. producers could not market DES overseas, the algorithm itself would find its way overseas, allowing foreign developers to make their own versions.

The dawning of this era of increased protection might have pleased some of the people in the communications security branch of the

NSA, which was in charge of securing American data as they moved around the globe. But it was already causing conniptions among those in the signals intelligence area, the people whose job it is to make sure that our guys can quickly intercept and circulate all the rich and fascinating information buzzing around the globe as electronic blips. If those blips were encrypted, and thus not easily read, well, then, that would be a problem. Making things even worse were the faster and cheaper computer technologies that made it feasible—made it the rule, in fact—for DES users to switch keys not every few months as the NSA assumed they might, but on a daily basis or even more often than that.

Yes, the Data Encryption Standard *was* a problem for The Fort. Years later even Martin Hellman came to realize that his attacks sometimes were based more on bravado than substance. "They were Darth Vader and I was Luke Skywalker," he says. "I was bearding the NSA, and that's a pretty heady thing for a young guy to be involved in." Now, however, he admits that there were two sides to the issue: that DES, despite its key size, was strong enough to provide a measure of security to people, and that even though the NSA could presumably marshal the resources to brute-force a DES key into submission, the process was certainly more cumbersome and costly than simply reading an unencrypted intercept. DES was the NSA's first lesson that the new age of computer security was going to complicate its life considerably—perhaps even to the point of shaking the entire institution.

Alan Konheim thinks that the bottom line on DES came from Howard Rosenblum. He was the deputy director for research and development at the NSA, where football fields of mainframe computers cracked the codes of the country's friends and enemies and tested the codes that potentially protected our own secrets. One day, Rosenblum and Konheim were talking about DES, and the NSA official made an off-the-cuff remark that stayed with Konheim for years. "You did too good a job," he said.

"It was not," Konheim says delightedly, "a comment of flattery."

public key

Though Whit Diffie and Marty Hellman regarded the Data Encryption Standard as a tainted and possibly fraudulent gambit by IBM and the United States government, its introduction was in a strange way an important gift to the Stanford researchers. By combing through the available technical data on the proposed standard—and speculating on what was not made public—Diffie and Hellman had a new prism through which to consider their own efforts. Ever since Diffie had heard the first reports of the government standard, at a 1974 chowdown at Louie's, the Chinese restaurant where Stanford geeks congregated, he had wondered about the possibility of an NSA trapdoor. This led him to a deeper consideration of the concept of trapdoors. Could an entire crypto scheme be built around one?

Designing such a system would present considerable challenges, because it would have to resolve a fundamental contradiction. A trapdoor provides a means for those with proper knowledge to bypass security measures and get quick access to encrypted messages, something that seems efficient. But the very thought of using a trapdoor in a security system seems like a nutty risk, precisely because crafty intruders might find a way to exploit it. It's the same problem posed by a physical trapdoor: if your enemies can't find it, you can use it to hide. But if they do, they'll know exactly where to look for you.

This contradiction made the prospect of designing a trapdoor scheme incredibly daunting. After all, the strongest cryptosystems were finely tuned in every aspect to *prevent* their contents from leaking. Tampering with their innards to insert a back door—a leak!—could easily produce any number of unintended weaknesses. When Diffie explained this to Hellman, both of them concluded that such a system would probably be impractical. But Diffie still thought it was interesting enough to add to a list he was compiling entitled "Problems for an Ambitious Theory of Cryptography."

Still, in early 1975, for all of Diffie's Sisyphean labors, even with the fruitful collaboration with Hellman, weeks were going by and he didn't seem to be getting anywhere. Was all his work at learning crypto against terrific odds going to lead to nothing? Hellman at least had a job. But Diffie had nothing. Though his house-sitting stint for John McCarthy was pleasant enough, he was now over thirty years old, making peanuts at his research job, and it was clear that he could never cope with the nit-picking hurdles one had to jump before earning a doctorate. Though Diffie was by nature cheerful, these ruminations were bringing him down.

Mary Fischer recalls the lowest point. One day she walked into the McCarthys' bedroom and found Diffie with his head in his hands, weeping. "I asked him what was wrong," she says, "and he told me he was never going to amount to anything, that I should find someone else, that he was—and I remember this exact term—a broken-down old researcher."

She tried to comfort him. She told him that the world didn't know it yet, but he was a great man. Mary had been studying Egyptology, and she explained that the ancient Egyptians made a distinction between acquired and innate characteristics. She believed "greatness" must be one of those traits that were not acquired—it was just there, and one could see it in such a person. "I know what I'm looking at," she told him, "and I know you're a great man."

Whit Diffie did not feel like a great man. He felt like a failure.

One day Diffie and Hellman brought in a Berkeley computer scientist named Peter Blatman to attend one of the informal seminars on crypto they had been convening on campus. Afterward, as Diffie drove him to the Stanford AI lab a few miles away, Blatman mentioned that a friend of his named Ralph Merkle was working on an interesting problem: how can you get a secure conversation over an insecure line when the two people in the conversation have never had previous contact? Obviously, if the two people hadn't known each other previously they would have had no opportunity to exchange secret keys before a private conversation.

This was, in effect, a different formulation of the big question that had been bugging Diffie for years: was it possible to use cryptography to protect a huge network against eavesdroppers, and wiretappers to boot? (More subtly, it reflected Mary's observation of his dilemma: in a world of untrustworthy people, how do you maintain intimate contact with the one person you trust?) Because Diffie had enjoyed so little success at attacking that problem, he argued to Blatman that his friend's scheme was in fact impossible. Diffie thinks that his outburst even convinced Blatman. But even as Diffie passionately argued the impossibility of such a feat, he secretly believed otherwise, and his mind was racing to figure it out. It was almost as if he *needed* there to be such a solution.

How *could* you create a system where people who had never met could speak securely? Where all conversations could be conducted with high-tech efficiency—but be protected by cryptography? Where you could get an electronic message from someone and be sure it came from the person whose return address appeared?

During his quest, Diffie had struggled to gather information in an atmosphere where almost all of it was classified. And he had wound up with more than anyone could have expected: one-way functions. Password protections. Identification Friend or Foe. Trapdoors. Somewhere in all of that *had* to be an answer to privacy. Diffie knew that reconciling the different protections offered by these disparate systems was crucial to his quest. As he thought more, he began to understand how you might be able to use some of those techniques to verify someone's identity. He began mentally constructing a means by which this could be done by one-way functions, the mathematical phenomenon where something easily calculated could not easily be reversed. Such a scheme would be, as he later wrote, "a challenge which could only be answered by one person but whose response could be recognized

by many as genuine." In other words, a system of "one-way authentication," which used the creative misunderstanding of his friend Bill
Mann some years earlier: a trapdoor one-way function where the difficult reversal of a calculation could be performed if someone had a
crucial bit of information on how the original figuring had been done.

This addressed a key issue that Diffie had discussed in his conversations with McCarthy about electronic commerce. But that was only
half the problem. What about privacy? Could the idea of a trapdoor
one-way function work in a system that solved two problems—first,
the authentication necessary for computer passwords and similar cre-
dentials, and, second, secret communication?

That spring, Diffie had settled into a routine at the McCarthy
house. Every morning he would make breakfast for Mary and Sarah,
McCarthy's fourteen-year-old daughter. Then Mary would go off to
work, Sarah would go off to school, and Diffie would stay home. One
day in May 1975, he spent the morning hours thinking. After a lunch
break, he returned to his mental work. For the umpteenth time, he had
been thinking about the problem of establishing a secure log-in password on a computer network. Again, there was that old problem of
having to trust the administrator with the secret password. How could
you shut that third party out of the scheme entirely? Sometime in the
afternoon, things suddenly became clear to Diffie: devise a system
that could not only provide everything in Diffie's recently envisioned
one-way authentication scheme but could also deliver encryption and
decryption in a novel manner. It would solve the untrustworthy administrator problem, and much, much more.

He would split the key.

Diffie's breakthrough itself involved something that, in the context of
the history of cryptography, seemed an absolute heresy: a *public* key.
Until that point, there was a set of seemingly inviolable rules when it
came to encryption, a virtual dogma that one ignored at the risk of
consignment to crypto hell. One of those was that the same key that
scrambled a message would also be the instrument that descrambled
it. This is why keys were referred to as symmetrical. That is why keeping those keys secret was so difficult: the very tools that eavesdroppers
lusted after, the decryption keys, had to be passed from one person to

another, and then existed in two places, dramatically increasing the chances of compromise. But Diffie, his brain infused with the information so painstakingly collected and considered over the past half decade, now envisioned the possibility for a different approach. Instead of using one single secret key, you could use a key *pair*. The tried-and-true symmetrical key would be replaced by a dynamic duo. One would be able to do the job of scrambling a plaintext message—performing the task in such a way that outsiders couldn't read it—but a secret trapdoor would be built into the message. The other portion of the key pair was like a latch that could spring open that trapdoor and let its holder read the message. And here was the beauty of the scheme: yes, that second key—the one that flipped open the trapdoor—was of course something that had to be kept under wraps, safe from the prying hands of potential eavesdroppers. But its mate, the key that actually performed the encryption, didn't have to be a secret at all. In fact, you wouldn't *want* it to be a secret. You'd be happy to see it distributed far and wide.

Now, the idea of ensuring privacy by using keys that were exchanged totally in the open was completely nonintuitive, and on the face of it, bizarre. But using the mathematics of one-way functions, it could work. Diffie knew it, and for an illuminating instant, he knew how to do it using one-way functions.

It was the answer. From that moment, everything was different in the world of cryptography.

First, by presenting an alternative to systems that worked with a single, symmetrical key, Diffie had solved a problem that had become so embedded in cryptographic systems that it had occurred to almost no one that it could be solved: the difficulty of distributing those secret keys to future recipients of secret messages. If you were a military organization, you might be able to protect the distribution centers that handled symmetrical keys (though God knows there were lapses even in the most vital operations). But if such centers moved into the private sector, and masses of people needed to use them, there would not only be inevitable bureaucratic pile-ups but also a constant threat of compromise. Figure it this way: if you needed to crack an encrypted message, wouldn't the very existence of a place that stored all the secret keys present an opportunity for some creep to get the keys by theft, bribery, or some other form of coercion?

But with a public key system, every person could generate a unique key pair on his or her own, a pair consisting of a public key and a private key, and no outsider would have access to the secret key parts. Then private communication could begin.

Here's how it would work: say that Alice wants to communicate with Bob. Using Diffie's concept, she needs only Bob's public key. She could get this by asking him for it, or she might get it from some phone-book-type index of public keys. But it has to be Bob's personal public key, a very long string of bits that could only have been generated by only one person in the world . . . Bob. Then, by way of a one-way function, she uses that public key to scramble the message in such a way that only the private key—the other half of that unique key pair—performs the decrypting calculation. (Thus the secret key is the "trapdoor" in the trapdoor one-way function Diffie was thinking about.)

So when Alice sends the scrambled message off, only one person in the world has the information necessary to reverse the calculation and decipher it: Bob, the holder of the private key. Say that the scrambled message gets intercepted by someone desperate to know what Alice had to say to Bob. Who cares? Unless the snooper has access to the unique partner of Bob's public key—the instrument Alice used to convert the message to seeming mush—the snoop would get no more than that mush. Without that private key, reversing the mathematical encryption process is too damn difficult. Remember, going the wrong way in a one-way function is like trying to put together a pulverized dinner plate.

Bob, of course, has no problem reading the message intended for his eyes only. He possesses the secret part of the key pair, and he can use that private key to decipher the message in a jiffy.

In short, Bob is able to read the message because he is the only person in possession of *both* sides of the key pair. Those who obtain the public key have *no advantage* in attempting to break the message. When it comes to encrypted messages, the only value of having Bob's public key is to, in effect, change the message to Bob-speak, the language that only Bob can read (by virtue of having the secret half of the key pair).

This encryption function was only part of Diffie's revolutionary concept, and not necessarily its most important feature. Public key crypto also provided the first effective means of truly *authenticating* the sender of an electronic message. As Diffie conceived it, the trap-door works in two directions. Yes, if a sender scrambles a message with someone's public key, only the intended recipient can read it. But if the process is inverted—if someone scrambles some text with his or her own *private* key—the resulting ciphertext can be unscrambled only by using the single *public* key that matches its mate. What's the point of that? Well, if you got such a message from someone claiming to be Albert Einstein, and wondered if it was *really* Albert Einstein, you now had a way to prove it—a mathematical litmus test. You'd look up Einstein's public key and apply it to the scrambled ciphertext. If the result was plaintext and not gibberish, you'd know for certain that it was Einstein's message—because he holds the world's only private key that could produce a message that his matching public key could unscramble.

In other words, applying one's secret key to a message is equivalent to signing your name: a digital signature. But unlike the sorts of sig-natures that are penned on bank checks, divorce papers, and baseballs, a digital John Hancock cannot be forged by anyone with the minimal skills required to replicate the original signer's lines and loops. With-out a secret key, the would-be identity thief has scant hope of pro-ducing a counterfeit signature.

Nor could a would-be forger hope to monitor a phone line, wait until his prey's digital signature appears, and then snatch it, with the intention of reusing the signature to create faked documents or to intercept future messages. In practice, a digital signature is not applied as an appendage to the document or letter to which it is affixed. Instead it is deeply interwoven with the digits that make up the actual content of the entire message. So if the document is intercepted, the eavesdropper cannot extract from it the tools to stamp the sender's signature on some other document.

This technique also assures the authenticity of an entire document. A foe cannot hope to change a small but crucial portion of a digitally signed document (like switching the statement "I am not responsible for my spouse's debts" to "I take full responsibility for my spouse's debts," all the while maintaining the signature of the unwitting sender). If the message was digitally signed with a private key but unencrypted, such a rogue could intercept it, use the sender's well-distributed public key to descramble it, and then make the change in the plaintext. But what then? In order to resend the text with the proper signature, our forger would require the private key to fix the signature on the entire document. That secret key, of course, would be unobtainable, remaining in the sole possession of the original signer.

If someone sending a signed message wanted secrecy in addition to a signature, that's easy, too. If Mark wanted to send an order to his banker, Lenore, he'd first sign the request with his private key, then encrypt that signed message with Lenore's public key. Lenore would receive a *twice*-scrambled message: shaken for privacy, stirred for authentication. She would first apply her secret key, unlocking a message that no one's eyes but hers could read. Then she would use Mark's public key, unlocking a message that she now knows only he could have sent.

Digital signatures offer another advantage. Since it is impossible for a digitally signed message to be produced by anyone but the person who holds the private key that scrambles it, a signer cannot reasonably deny his or her role in producing the document. This *nonrepudiation* feature is the electronic equivalent of a notary public seal.

For the first time, it became possible to conceive of all sorts of official transactions—contracts, receipts, and the like—to be performed over computer networks, with no need for one's physical presence.

In short, Diffie had not only figured out a way to assure privacy in an age of digital communications, but he had enabled an entirely new form of commerce, an electronic commerce that had the potential not only to match but to exceed the current protocols in commercial transactions. Even more impressive, his breakthrough had been performed completely outside the purview of government agencies in close possession of even the most trivial details of the most obscure cryptographic system.

What a triumph for Whit Diffie! And what a panic he had when, scant moments after hatching one of the most important breakthroughs in cryptographic history, *Whit Diffie almost forgot the whole thing.* He went downstairs to get a Coke and for one horrible moment the idea simply fell out of his head. He stepped back around the kitchen counter, and, just like that, he got it back. This time, it stuck. Still, he didn't write it down; suddenly, he was hyperaware that the computer on which he kept his notes was not secure. There was no way to encrypt his thoughts so that intruders could not steal them. He would have to tell Marty Hellman about it face-to-face.

But first he waited until Mary got home from work.

When Mary Fischer came home from British Petroleum that day, she found her husband waiting for her at the door. This was not usual. He had a strange look on his face, and he told her to come to him, that he wanted to talk to her.

"I think," said Whit Diffie, "I've made a great discovery."

He explained his idea to her. Though the mathematics of the procedure were beyond her, the concept rang true. What's more, from Mary's close observation of her husband during the years he had wrestled with the problem, she found the solution to be not just fitting, but poetic. "Whit has always been a dualistic individual," she says of her husband, born under the sign of Gemini, "and I think that the notion of splitting the key emerged from that tension."

He was not a broken-down old researcher after all.

That night Diffie walked down the hill to Hellman's house to tell him, for the first time, about public key cryptography. It took a bit of explaining, but Hellman quickly understood the significance of Diffie's brainstorm. It remained, however, for them to formalize it, to put it into scientific context, and to publish it. Marty Hellman had just the place for it; he had been invited to write a paper for the journal *IEEE Transactions on Information Theory*, and he broached this idea to his editor, who enthusiastically endorsed his suggestion that he and Diffie collaborate on developing this concept. (The IEEE, or Institute of Electrical and Electronic Engineers, was a prominent academic engineering society which published a variety of journals, some the most influential in their disciplines.) They set about working on it immediately, squarely facing the fact that while Diffie had successfully envisioned a system that could catapult cryptography into a new era, his vision was all they had.

Even to Hellman, the concept, he later recalled, sometimes "sounded a little crazy." One day he decided to run it past his former IBM colleague Horst Feistel. It was a weird conversation. Hellman had barely begun talking when Feistel told him that they could only talk for twenty minutes or so because he was on his way to a doctor's appointment. So Hellman hastily explained how he and Diffie had gotten around the key distribution problem by postulating a trapdoor one-way function that allowed you to use a public key. Feistel didn't buy it at all. "You can't do that!" he admonished Hellman, lecturing to him that the great Flemish cryptologist Auguste Kerckhoffs, in his landmark 1881 work *La cryptographie militaire*, had laid out six iron-clad commandments for producing secure ciphers, and one of them was that all secrecy must reside not in the system but in the keys. How, then, concluded the IBM genius behind the Lucifer cipher, could you even *think* of making a key public? (Had Feistel not been in such a hurry to make his doctor's appointment, perhaps he would have understood that Diffie and Hellman's idea quite elegantly conformed to Kerckhoffs's stringent requirements, that the security of public key systems lay in the fact that a *private* key was never accessible to anyone but its owner.)

Feistel was right on one count: Diffie's concept was a heresy. But "heresy is the way changes begin," says Hellman. For the next few weeks the pair worked intensely on creating the mathematical basis for the theory of public key cryptography. Hellman by then had figured out how his collaboration with his mercurial partner would work: "Whit often, playing with ideas, sees something first in an embryonic form," he says, "and then I take it to a more polished result."

In this case, the result was a paper called "Multiuser Cryptographic Techniques." In a sense, the work was a placeholder—something that would express the public key idea while its authors burned brain cells attempting to find a way to actually execute the concept. "At present," they admitted in the paper, "we have neither a proof that public key systems exist, nor a demonstration system." While they had laid out the mathematical basis for such a system, they were still groping for the precise functions—particularly the trapdoor one-way functions—that would make it happen. Still, those who received early drafts of the paper found it an astounding twist on the conventional cryptographic wisdom, a foray into territory where no one, from Trithemius to Turing, had dared venture.

Or had they? Of course, if someone had come up with this behind the Triple Fence or any of its foreign cousins, Diffie and Hellman wouldn't have known it. Certainly, if anyone had actually *published* anything about it, Diffie would probably have discovered the paper in his extensive research of the past few years.

As it turned out, there had been at least one outsider who had been thinking along the same lines as Diffie and Hellman.

In early February 1976, Marty Hellman received an intriguing letter from a graduate student at the University of California at Berkeley:

> Dear Dr. Hellman,
>
> About three days ago, a copy of your working paper, "Multiuser Cryptographic Techniques," fell into my hands. Just prior to this, I had finished revising a paper on the same subject, which will shortly be re-submitted to the *Communications of the ACM* [Association of Computing Machinery]. (Original submission was in August 1975.) I enclose a copy of it in the hopes that you'll find it interesting. Actually, I'm glad to know there's someone else who's interested in the problem. The people with whom I try and discuss it either fail completely to understand what's going on, or regard any attempt at solution as impossible. Fortunately the (partial) solution described in the enclosed paper demonstrated that it is possible. Now, if only we can do better! . . .

The letter ended with a proposal: "The possibility arises of doing joint work, and I would be interested in this possibility. I hope to hear from you, and wish you the best of luck in the hunt."

It was signed Ralph C. Merkle. The return address, in Berkeley, seemed to coincidentally reflect the speed with which things were now moving: Haste Street.

Merkle's name had actually come up some months before: he was the Berkeley student whose work had been mentioned to Diffie by mutual friend Peter Blatman, a mention that led Diffie to unkink his thought process and make the crucial public key connection. Now it appeared that, working totally independently and with no more equipment than his own brain, Merkle had already made a breakthrough similar to Diffie's. What's more, according to the unpublished paper he enclosed, he had actually turned the trick that Hellman and Diffie were still fumbling to perform: he'd created a public-private key scheme.

Like Marty Hellman and Whit Diffie, Merkle was the son of an educated man; his father had been the associate director of the Lawrence Livermore Laboratory, one of the nation's top military research facilities, until he died of colon cancer in 1966. (The illustrious nature of Merkle's family extends to his great-uncle Fred, a professional ballplayer who made the famous omission of not touching second base in a game that ultimately decided the 1908 National League pennant race.) Young Ralph Merkle was, understandably, a science buff, a math whiz, and, by the time he enrolled as an undergraduate at Berkeley, a computer enthusiast. As for cryptography, "I had not displayed any noticeable high interest in the subject area," he says. This changed during the fall 1974 semester, when Merkle, in his last term as an undergrad, took a class known as CS 244, on computer security. Taught by Lance Hoffman, an assistant professor in the department of electrical engineering and computer sciences, the course's key requirement, besides a November midterm, was a term project. "Grading is done on a curve," wrote Hoffman on the syllabus, "but if you do excellent work in a class full of geniuses, fear not! You'll still get your A."

Hoffman included cryptography in CS 244 but not at a particularly sophisticated level. Since the varieties of crypto deployed by the government were classified, those used in the private sector, even in academia, were relatively rudimentary. "We didn't get into the details," admits Hoffman now. "I'm sure I would teach the Caesar cipher and things like that. Don't forget, all you really had back then were substitution ciphers and transposition ciphers and combinations."

But almost from the moment the class first met on October 1, convening twice a week until December 5, when final papers were due, Ralph Merkle began thinking more ambitiously. Hearing about the way cryptography operated—as a means to protect information that might be exposed to eavesdroppers—he hardly paused to concentrate on what everybody since Caesar had considered the main problem: coming up with stronger, less crackable cryptosystems that would be encoded and decoded by a symmetrical key.

Instead, for reasons that remain unclear but are probably related to

Merkle's unconventional mind, he fixated on what struck him as a weird, somewhat challenging aspect of a more basic dilemma. The essential cryptographic scenario assumed that the channel of communication was vulnerable. This was certainly the case in telegraph transmission, radio broadcasts, and the subject of Hoffman's course, open computer networks. But what measures could you exploit if you wanted to communicate with someone who wasn't already in possession of a prearranged, secure symmetrical key? Was there a way in which those two people could spontaneously engage in a conversation that would be clear to both of them but opaque to whoever was listening? As Diffie and Hellman now understood, this was a problem no one else had tackled, undoubtedly because it defied solution.

Merkle, unpolluted with knowledge about the theory or history of crypto, was unaware of the apparent impossibility of his mission. He simply tried to solve the problem. The crucial aspect of the situation, he figured, lay in the different circumstances of two people who wished to privately communicate and a potential interloper. The pair were actively involved in a conversation, while the interloper was a passive listener. He sensed that his solution lay in exploiting the conspiracy of the private communicators, creating a situation where, says Merkle, "the active participants can confuse the heck out of the passive listener, even though the listener hears everything." Merkle began thinking about this almost obsessively. And one night, in October 1974, sitting in bed in his small apartment staring at the ceiling, Merkle figured out a way this might be done.

Puzzles.

Here's the scheme that Merkle conceived in the dark. The situation is classic: Bob and Alice want to communicate. Bob is a sender and Alice is the intended recipient of a secret message. Unfortunately, there exists an unwanted eavesdropper, Eve, who has access to anything that passes between those two parties. How can Bob send a message that Alice can read and Eve can't? First, he creates puzzles. Each puzzle is an encrypted message scrambled by a relatively small key—something solvable with a modicum amount of brute-force effort, a challenging yet feasible task for Alice's computer. "That's why it's a puzzle," says Merkle. "It's hard to solve but it's solvable, by searching through all the combinations of the keyspace." With the use of his own computer, Bob creates not one puzzle, but thousands, maybe millions, of these puzzles. All of these are sent off to Alice.

Alice, in effect, spreads these puzzles on the floor and chooses one at random. (Eve, of course, is capable of intercepting all those puzzles—but she would not know which particular one Alice chose.) Then Alice attacks her chosen puzzle by having her computer search through the keyspace until the solution is revealed. That solution includes a string of numbers: it's the decrypted message of that puzzle. At this point both Alice and Bob have the solution to that particular puzzle. Bob, of course, knows the solution because it's his own puzzle—he has the answers to all the puzzles he's sent off. But Eve doesn't have that solution. Even though she may have intercepted Bob's massive transmission to Alice, she doesn't have the time or computer power to find the answer to all the puzzles—and she doesn't know which one Alice selected.

The next step requires Alice to inform Bob which puzzle was chosen. That's easy; among the contents of the encrypted puzzle would be an identifier (something that says, for instance, "Hey! I'm Puzzle No. 3!") and a long digital key. So when Alice ships back the message, "Puzzle No. 3," Bob can look up which key is stored in that puzzle. At this point, they would both be in possession of a shared secret key they could use to conduct further secret communications. Eve may even hear that it's Puzzle No. 3, but she would have no clue which one of the millions of puzzles that refers to. Remember, she has to crack all the puzzles in order to get the keys. While this might be a feasible task with the help of some extremely super computer, it would always require much more effort than it took Bob and Alice. Maybe millions of times more. But the amount of effort wasn't the point.

Here was the point: Ralph Merkle, in a tiny Berkeley apartment, totally off the National Security Agency's radar screen, had figured out a way in which two people, with no prior agreement on a secret key, could send a secret message that would frustrate the cracking efforts of a diligent eavesdropper.

What goes through the mind of someone who comes up with a totally novel concept of cryptography, something that confounds what has been the mainstream thought in this field for over a thousand years? "My first response was, 'Gee this looks neat; I ought to be able to get a quarter project out of it.' " says Merkle. If that seemed like an understatement, it was nevertheless an overly optimistic one. The protocol for the research paper, or the "quarter project," was to submit a proposal to Professor Hoffman, and Merkle promptly wrote up a description of what he wanted to do. Of necessity, it was skimpy and vague. "I couldn't cite any previous literature saying this is an important problem because I'd never seen any literature saying this was an important problem," explains Merkle. "I suspected [correctly] that there was no previous literature. So I basically wrote up a little thing about it." As a backup, he also mentioned that he was also thinking about a paper on data compression.

After reading the proposal, Lance Hoffman told his student he'd be better off writing about the data compression problem.

Merkle tried to persuade his professor otherwise, recasting his proposal several times in an attempt to get Hoffman to concede that it was at least interesting enough to pursue further. But Hoffman wouldn't even toss him that harmless bone. Why not? "Let me be polite and simply say he did not appear to understand what I was saying at the time," says Merkle. "So I dropped the course."

Years later, Hoffman, now a Georgetown professor who has become an expert on issues of cryptographic policy, would ruefully recall the incident, attributing the rejection to a combination of Merkle's abstruse writing style and his own failings as a mathematician. "Merkle struck me as a young sort of pimply faced kid who might have a good idea, but it wasn't clear to me that I had the time to extract it out of him, or that he had the communication skills to deliver it in a way I could at least understand," he says. "I've got a math degree from Carnegie Tech, but I'm not a mathematician, and so he probably needed somebody like Marty Hellman to really sit down with it."

Merkle, of course, did not know about Marty Hellman yet. He just wanted someone, anyone, to assure him that his instincts were correct, that he had stumbled on something significant. But the usual reaction of the Berkeleyites he asked was similar to Hoffman's. "Basically people sort of stared at me and were utterly baffled by what I was talking about," Merkle says, "on the grounds that it was obviously something very strange." Finally, one of Merkle's professors, Robert Fabry, offered some encouragement. This is a good idea, he told Merkle— you should try to get it published. So Merkle rewrote the paper more formally, hoping to publish it in the prestigious *Communications of the ACM*. He entitled it "Secure Communications Over Insecure Channels," and in August 1975 formally submitted it to Sue Graham, the journal's editor.

On October 22, 1975, Graham wrote to Merkle. An "experienced cryptography expert" had gone over his paper, she explained, and found the article unworthy of publication. In the words of the reader (due to the practice of "blind refereeing," his or her name was withheld, but typically such readers were the illuminati in a given field), the gaping flaw in the paper was its very premise: assuming that a cryptosystem could work without the secure delivery of keys. What made Merkle's idea revolutionary also made it unacceptable. "I am sorry to have to inform you that the paper is not in the mainstream of present cryptography thinking," said the reader. "Experience shows that it is extremely dangerous to transmit key information in the clear." Sue Graham herself took pains to emphasize that she agreed with the referee. "I read the report myself and was particularly bothered by the fact that there are no references to the literature," she wrote. "Has anyone else ever investigated this approach[?]"

The answer, as far as published work was concerned, was no.

Merkle was disappointed, but not defeated. His mien may not have been as swashbuckling as that of his father, who was once referred to as a "perfect combination of physicist and pitchman" and was known for blasting through the Livermore Lab parking lot at high speeds in a beat-up Packard convertible. But he did inherit a dogged perseverance. So he kept revising and rerevising his paper, despite a series of further rejections. "What was striking," he said later, "was how the publication process was tuned to incremental improvements, but was very bad at handling something that is fundamentally different." He just *knew*, though, that the idea was worth pursuing. "It couldn't be wrong because it was simple," he says. "It was unclear exactly what it would lead to, but it was pretty obvious it should be made available. I basically wanted to publish that idea and say, 'Here is a neat idea—it clarifies what this problem is, it clarifies the fact that a solution is feasible, and it is now a well-defined research problem. Now let's get some other folks in there and see what else we can find.' "

In early 1976, just as Merkle was beginning to lose faith, a colleague told him that he knew some people who talked just the way he did, notably a guy named Marty Hellman. Coincidentally, one of Hellman's courses was being carried on a closed-circuit broadcast line between Stanford and Berkeley. Merkle managed to tune into the audio portion of one of the sessions and immediately realized that Marty Hellman was indeed thinking the same things he was. By that time, a draft of Diffie and Hellman's "Multiuser Techniques" paper was being privately distributed, and Merkle managed to get hold of a copy. Instead of grinding his teeth at seeing that someone else had published first, Merkle became excited at the idea that work on "his" concept was actually being done. His immediate instinct was to team up with the Stanford researchers. Thus his letter to Hellman of February 7, where he proposed a collaboration and included a draft of his paper in place of a vitae.

Merkle's work was a revelation to Diffie and Hellman, neither of whom had really thought that they would see a possible implementation of their idea for some time. Merkle's puzzle concept, though it still had problems, was a definite advance. Soon Merkle became part of Hellman's discussions with Diffie on implementing public key cryptography. Merkle wondered how his puzzle scheme could be jiggered to work within the kind of public key cryptosystem that Diffie and Hellman had suggested. In a letter dated April 2, 1976, he proposed a system in which each user would have a unique arrangement of puzzles—and that itself would be the public key. "Thus," he wrote, "if anyone wishes to send a message to A, then all they have to do is select one of A's puzzles at random. They then encrypt their message, and send it to A. A looks up the puzzle key using the puzzle ID on the front of the message. Anyone else is up shit's creek, because they can't figure out the puzzle key."

Merkle also speculated on how puzzles, integrated into a public key system, could also provide a way to get receipts to prove that messages had been delivered. With that as a lure, he confided that he was looking for a summer job. His concluding sentence referred to the main practical flaw of his system—that the level of security provided by puzzles was merely at the mathematically polynomial level, not the more rigorous exponential level. An eavesdropper would have to perform a lot of work in order to crack the puzzles, but that work factor was limited by the number of puzzles. Say that in the puzzle cryptosystem, Alice sent Bob a million puzzles to choose from, but intruder

Eve had a computer that was a thousand times faster than Bob's. (Not a wild assumption if you figure that wealthy governments with huge computational resources might want to break somebody's message code.) Then, in the time it took Bob to solve a single randomly chosen puzzle, Eve would be able to solve a thousand puzzles. If it took Bob a minute to solve his puzzle, Eve would solve the entire set of one million puzzles in about sixteen hours—a totally intolerable situation for those needing strong protection. Even if Eve's computer was no more powerful than Bob's she could crack all the puzzles in less than two years. If maintaining secrecy was essential, that wasn't very desirable, either. (On the other hand, such a spread was sufficient for authentication, since breaking a signature key a year after it was used wouldn't give a foe any appreciable advantage.) Any decent encryption system had to assure that whatever one-way function was used, a mathematically *exponential* relation would exist between the easy calculation of the communicator and the more difficult task posed to the cracker. Ideally, this should jack up a foe's work factor to a task requiring thousands, millions, or even billions or trillions of years of crunching. Merkle was hopeful that he could figure out a way for his system to satisfy these conditions. "Perhaps," he wrote Hellman, "we can get exponential by the end of the summer."

While Merkle was figuring out how to get exponential, Diffie and Hellman focused on finding their own means of implementing a public key cryptosystem. Without some way of actually putting their ideas into action—or at least proving that some feasible scheme could exist—the whole concept of public key cryptography would be merely a mathematical mind-trick.

One path was suggested by Stanford computer scientist Donald Knuth, whose encyclopedic series of books in progress, *The Art of Computer Programming*, would earn him the reputation as the high guru of algorithms. Knuth reminded them of an interesting mathematical phenomenon: while it is child's play to multiply a pair of prime numbers, reversing the process—a task known as factoring—is an assignment that could confound the devil himself. Could this phenomenon be the basis for a devilishly challenging one-way function? Though Diffie and Hellman did not choose to pursue this idea, others would.

Another alternative involved computational complexity, and Diffie pored over a book on the subject, particularly a chapter on what was known as NP-complete functions. The class of NP-complete problems, Diffie later wrote, are "problems thought not to be solvable in polynomial time on any deterministic computer." This meant that they were so hard that you could set your Macintosh, or even your Cray supercomputer (if you were the NSA), to work on the problem and when you checked the results a few trillion years later, you wouldn't even be in the general neighborhood of solving it. But though Diffie did have some ideas on using complexity to create a formula for a one-way cryptographic function, he never found a way to do it with trapdoors.

It was a suggestion by one of Hellman's colleagues in Stanford's electrical engineering department, John Gill, that proved most promising. Gill pointed to a mathematical process known as "discrete exponentiation" as a potential function. Since the inverse of this process, known as discrete logarithm, was extremely difficult, this had the potential to fulfill the basic criterion of a one-way function: easy numbers for the good guys to crunch, and computational hell for the bad guys to reverse-calculate.

Diffie was working at the Stanford AI lab one day in May 1976, rewriting the public key cryptography paper that he and Marty were planning to publish later that year in the major IEEE journal, when Hellman called, excitement in his voice. He'd been working on discrete exponentiation, and *had actually cooked up a workable system.* When he explained it, Diffie instantly realized that Hellman had tied up the tangled threads of a theory that had been swirling around in his own mind for weeks.

The scheme would come to be known as the Diffie-Hellman algorithm. It presupposes two parties who want to communicate in secret; by using one-way functions, these parties can jointly generate a shared key, one that an eavesdropper listening in on the session cannot intercept. Here's how it works.

The two parties first choose two numbers. This is done openly, since knowing these numbers will not help an eavesdropper. Each party then selects his or her own secret number, which will *not* be revealed or sent to anyone else. Then, using a mathematical formula that involves exponentiation, each party takes his or her own secret number and performs a calculation that involves both that secret number and the two previously chosen public numbers. After this brief number crunching, each person has a transformed secret number that is then sent to his or her counterpart. There's no problem in sending this number over an open channel because, in effect, it's an *encrypted* secret number, scrambled by means of a one-way function that was easy to perform but extremely hard to reverse. (How hard? Undoing the process would, in theory at least, be as difficult as solving what is known as the discrete logarithm problem. This requires performing about a million million quadrillion more operations than the exponentiation used to transform the numbers. *That's* a one-way function!)

You can think of this second pair of numbers as sort of an offspring of the openly agreed-upon public numbers and the closely held secret numbers. Trying to figure out the secret number from the figure passed over the clear channel would be like examining the DNA in a human cell and trying to figure out which parent was the contributor of each individual gene. You couldn't do it unless you had access to DNA from either the sperm or egg cells.

That leads to the third and final step of the Diffie-Hellman algorithm. Both parties separately use a related mathematical formula that combines those transformed numbers, *in conjunction with his or her original secret numbers* (the source DNA!), to arrive at yet another number. The formula works in such a way that both parties, despite the fact that their original numbers are different, will get the identical final number, which can be called K, as in key. Thus both people will now have possession of an identical numerical key—calculated in such a way so that *only* someone who has one of the original secret numbers can get K. An eavesdropper, of course, never had a chance to get hold of the secret numbers; that foe would be holding only the nearly-impossible-to-convert transformed variations.

The Diffie-Hellman algorithm was both more efficient and secure than Merkle's puzzle system. But it was not even close to a complete implementation of the sort of public key cryptosystem that the two were envisioning. Diffie-Hellman did not provide for digital signatures and didn't even supply a means to encrypt messages. But it did provide a method for two people who have had no prior communication to use an open channel and arrive at a secret key. That key could then be used with a conventional encryption system like DES to scramble messages and unscramble them. (This double-barreled approach—

one method to find a key without a prior arrangement and another method to actually communicate in secret—would be called a *hybrid system*.)

Including their new algorithm in the revision of "Multiuser Techniques" would make it a much more powerful document. The new paper, "New Directions in Cryptography," was submitted on June 3, 1976. Later that month, they presented some of their ideas at conferences in Lenox, Massachusetts, and Ronneby, Sweden—appearances that would prove to have unintended patent implications. But thoughts about exploiting intellectual property were the furthest thing from the minds of these information scientists. In contrast to what struck them as a government refusal to provide all the details of the Data Encryption Standard, they were creating a fully open alternative to conventional cryptography itself.

Meanwhile, Ralph Merkle, who was now well along in the graduate computer science program at Berkeley, was finally reconciled to the fact that his puzzles scheme wasn't likely to overcome its work-factor flaw. He began casting about for another public key approach. "I had various schemes involving circuits and complicated fiddling around with subsets of various types," he said. None seemed to work. Merkle was further handicapped by his chronic difficulty in expressing complex ideas clearly; this made it difficult for colleagues to suggest modifications to his schemes. "You're stretching your mind, and sometimes you get bizarre, baroque things," he says in his defense. "It's only after you've cooked up the idea that you start simplifying to the point where it's clean and easy and straightforward to present."

Hellman took Merkle up on his offer to work together, giving him a summer research job. It would be exhilarating to work with the two people in the world who best understood the problem. "I was basically isolated until I met Whit and Marty," he says. "I was ready to keep banging away until I got some response, but there was no one else who was interested in pursuing this." Merkle arrived at Stanford convinced that his most promising idea revolved around a scheme built around finding trapdoor one-way functions involving the NP-complete problem. The system was built around a mathematical problem known as knapsacks. To understand his scheme, picture, naturally, a knapsack. "The idea is to put things into this knapsack, to exactly fill it to the brim without going either over or under," he says. Diffie would later describe the problem as that of a shipping clerk faced with a collection of packages of various sizes and shapes who had to find the absolute best way to stuff the packages in the mailbag. The perfect solution is one that fills every cubic inch of space. Actually, in Merkle's scheme, it would be more accurate to say that the shipping clerk must know the proper combination of packages that will precisely meet the weight limit of a given knapsack. With only a few packages to choose from, the optimal solution isn't that tough to find, but if there are plenty of packages, it gets much harder.

Since Merkle wanted these knapsacks to act as trapdoor one-way functions—something that would be easy for the right person to solve but nearly impossible for everyone else to crack—he needed to figure out a way to tame this difficult problem for the proper keyholder. He did this by first using a much easier variation of the knapsack problem called a superincreasing knapsack. In these problems, the list of weights is ordered in such a way that discovering the solution is a breeze. Merkle then figured out a way to transform that easy process to the far knottier problem that comes with figuring out the solution to a normal knapsack, where the weights aren't so helpfully arranged.

It was a complicated but logical process. Someone who wished to receive a private message would begin with her own superincreasing knapsack, which would essentially be her secret key. Then she'd use that key to create a hard-to-solve normal knapsack to act as a public key. With the formula Merkle devised (working with Marty Hellman), that second knapsack could act as an encrypting function, scrambling messages in such a way that they could be unscrambled only by someone who had the ability to solve the problem of that normal knapsack. In a practical sense, there would be only one way to do that—by using the secret key, which was the related superincreasing (easy-to-solve) knapsack.

The impractical way would be to spend a few billion years trying to solve the problem by brute force.

Was there a simpler way to break the system than using megacomputers for a brute-force attack, hoping to get the keys sometime before the sun went dead? In other words, could cryptanalysts find a shortcut, a flaw? Merkle was supremely confident that no such flaw existed and posted a challenge on his office door. "I'm offering $100 to the first person to break it," he wrote to Hellman. "I've discreetly shown it to a few people here, and after listening to the resulting silence, I've concluded that the solution, if it exists, is at least not embarrassingly simple." To be sporting about it, he made the task immeasurably easier, asking potential crackers to solve the problem with the difficulty of the knapsack problem set at a level so low that Merkle knew that there was at least a remote chance that someone might collect the reward. After that, he figured, he could raise the stakes and offer a higher bounty if someone cracked the real thing. "The point was that no one gave a damn about this stuff," he says. "I figured that if I offered money for the [possibly unbreakable] knapsack, people would just throw in the towel. So I offered money for the [easier problem], because somebody might actually break that, or at least think they have a chance at breaking that." (He would publish a paper on knapsacks with Hellman in 1978.)

In November, Diffie and Hellman's IEEE paper came out. "New Directions in Cryptography" was a revelation, a true blow against the empire. (The title itself drew upon the authors' generational roots by evoking the mind-blowing paperbacks of the New Directions publishing house—ground-shifting beatnik bibles like *Waiting for Godot*, *Siddhartha*, and *In the American Grain*.) "We stand today," their article began with a fanfare, "on the brink of a revolution in cryptography." The computer age allows for dramatically cheaper implementations of scrambling devices, they explained, necessary tools for a world that features "effortless and inexpensive contact between people or computers on opposite sides of the world." But because of the key distribution problem and the lack of a digital signature component, conventional cryptography is unable to handle those challenges: "Its use would impose such severe inconveniences on the system users as to eliminate many of the benefits of teleprocessing." Thus, there is the need for something new, a means by which private conversations can actually be conducted without prior acquaintance, messages can be authenticated to guarantee that the actual senders and recipients are involved, and a true digital signature can be contemplated. Not only were Diffie and Hellman the first to articulate these problems in an open forum, but in the succeeding breath they proposed to solve them with their original creation, public key cryptosystems.

Once, Diffie had harbored dreams of writing up any great crypto-graphic discovery he made, not as an academic paper but as an espio-nage novel. He had been disappointed in books of that genre that included great technical discoveries in their plot lines, because the fic-tional breakthroughs weren't convincing; they had "feet of clay," he complained. "Unfortunately," he would note, "once I had the required technical discovery, I still did not know how to write a novel and had to content myself with publication in the professional journals like everyone else." But he could take comfort in the fact that the paper he published with Marty Hellman was in many ways as enthralling as any page-turner that ever hit the bestseller list. This was science that broke the ground that science fiction had not yet contemplated; within its mathematical formulas lay a blueprint for twenty-first-century communications.

Diffie and Hellman ended their paper with the observation that throughout the history of codes, it had often been amateurs who came up with the innovations in cryptography. They cited Thomas Jefferson, whose code wheel system was used two centuries after its invention, and also mentioned the four amateurs who independently came up with the implementations of electronic rotor machines that character-ized Enigma-style crypto during World War II. Then they concluded with a wish that their efforts would be only the beginning of an effort to change the landscape of modern cryptography: "We hope this will inspire others to work in this fascinating area in which participation has been discouraged in the recent past by a nearly total government monopoly."

That monopoly had just been smashed open by a long-haired for-mer MIT hacker and his passionate Stanford graduate school advisor.

prime time

"**h**ere's something interesting. . . ."

A casual handoff of an academic paper from a graduate student to a professor. Ron Rivest, a twenty-nine-year-old assistant professor at the Massachusetts Institute of Technology, had no reason to believe that this paper was any more interesting than the hundreds of papers, articles in journals, and technical memos he had already seen in his nascent career in academia. One of its authors, Whit Diffie, had worked in the same building—Tech Square in Cambridge, where the AI lab was one floor above Rivest's office at the Laboratory for Computer Science. But neither that name nor that of the coauthor, Martin Hellman, was familiar to him. And actually, Rivest knew very little about encryption and virtually nothing about how sensitive a topic it was. Nor did the paper contain any breakthroughs in mathematical reasoning; the spirit of Fermat was nowhere to be found in its equations.

Even so, "New Directions in Cryptography" turned out to be more than interesting to Rivest: it thrilled him. Ultimately, it changed his life.

The paper appealed to Rivest's heart as well as his head. Rivest was a theoretician, but one for whom simple abstractions were not enough. The ideal for him was actually putting the ethereal mechanics of math to work, of making a tangible difference in the world of flesh and dirt.

Diffie and Hellman's breakthrough wedded the spheres of abstraction and reality, applying an original mathematical formula to meet a need in society. Ron Rivest wanted to spend his time in the neighborhood where those two realms met.

Despite a prodigious talent for math, Rivest did not grow up as a classic numbers nerd. His father had been an electrical engineer at the General Electric lab at Schenectady, New York, and Rivest had taken advantage of the strong science programs in the public high school there. For one summer, he'd attended a special math program at Clarkson College. But as high school graduation loomed, he mulled over careers in psychology or law. He wound up majoring in mathematics at Yale but only, he remembers, because "it had the fewest course requirements, and it allowed me to take a lot of other courses." These included plenty of classes in psychology, history, and other sojourns sans slide rule. Mathematics, he says, was "just one of many things I was doing."

He speaks of this in his characteristic soft, thoughtful cadence, a ruminative mumbling that draws a listener closer. Rivest is a balding man with pleasantly plump cheeks, neatly bearded. He certainly does not appear to be the sort of man who poses a threat to national security. While at Yale, Rivest attended a few marches protesting the Vietnam conflict, but he was far from a flaming activist. Thoughts of sedition had never truly crossed his mind.

At Yale, Rivest discovered computer science. While taking courses offered by the engineering department, he realized that programming offered an opportunity to merge theory with tangible effect, and he fell in love with that form of instant karma. He used his programming skills in a part-time job for an economics professor. Working on a huge punch-card-munching IBM mainframe, Rivest hacked away at arcane subjects like price indices in Latin America or New Zealand— and felt just as powerful as if he were moving mountains. If Yale had offered a computer science major back then, Rivest would have signed up in a minute. In any case, after graduating from Yale in 1969 with a math degree, he went on to graduate school at Stanford, in the four-year-old computer science department.

Rivest spent much of his time at Stanford's cutting-edge artificial intelligence lab, helping with a fairly quixotic project involving an autonomous robot rover. The idea was to get the electronic beast to roam the parking lot with no human intervention, a typical overly optimistic task for AI workers in the 1960s. He had terrific fun with this, and was fascinated with the idea of making computers "smart." But the problems of making robots behave forced him to concentrate on hard-core engineering problems, and he didn't want to get *too* far from theory. He increasingly became drawn to understanding the mathematics of computation itself. His guru was not the AI elder John McCarthy but Don Knuth, Stanford's Jedi Master of algorithms. But Rivest's goal was always *applying* theory.

"Artificial intelligence gets to be a bit mushy—it's hard to tell what it is you're doing, and hard to tell when you've done something right," Rivest explains. "But with theory you can make a crisp model and say, '*This* is what I want to do and *here's* the solution to it.' " There was nothing like using the beauty of mathematics to solve a problem. Not only was it possible to pull a cerebral arrow from your quiver and hit the bull's-eye dead center, but you had the equivalent of a celestial arbiter—your proof—ringing the buzzer to let you know you'd scored. So while Rivest enjoyed writing AI software programs, his doctoral thesis involved database retrieval algorithm and research techniques. Very Knuth-ish. And in a yearlong postdoc at the Institut National de Recherche en Informatique et en Automatique (INRIA) outside Paris, he concentrated on other theoretical problems.

In the fall of 1974, Rivest accepted his post as an assistant professor on a tenure track at MIT. It was an ideal job, one that would enable him to pursue his theoretical interests in a department that also allowed him the freedom to work on programming problems as well. Rivest had been married since graduating from Yale. At twenty-seven, he seemed poised to begin a productive yet quiet life as an academic in one of America's best scientific institutions. From his eighth-floor window in the boxlike Tech Square building in Cambridge, he would watch the gorgeous campus sunsets, their drama enhanced by pollution spewed out by Boston-area industry. And then he would return to his algorithms.

In December 1976, and throughout that entire winter, the algorithms Rivest grappled with were the ones suggested by Diffie and Hellman's "interesting" paper. It might be more accurate to say that he was consumed by the formulas *missing* from that cryptologic manifesto. While the two Stanford researchers had indeed presented a mathematical outline for a new way of passing secret messages—and also digitally "signing" messages so that a communication could be definitively associated with its author—when it came to an implementation that one could really use, they'd come up dry. The Diffie-Hellman key exchange approach allowed two parties to set up a common key, but there was no obvious way that it could be extended to signatures. (Merkle's not-yet-published knapsack solution also fell short of this.) Diffie and Hellman had speculated on various ways that one might eventually come up with a workable system where each individual could have his or her own key pair, one public and one kept secretly. But without the proper mathematical scaffolding, it was really nothing more than a suggestion. It all hinged on finding sufficiently powerful one-way functions. Was there indeed a set of these that could stand as the reliable scaffolding of a *volks*-cryptosystem? A set of functions so sound that the system based on them would be impervious to all sorts of eavesdroppers and codebreakers, even highly motivated ones equipped with high-speed computers, deep cryptographic experience, and a touch of genius themselves?

Answering those questions became Rivest's obsession. Though the mathematical component of the quest was exciting in itself, the process was charged with a thrilling frisson, in that a successful solution could potentially kick off an entirely new kind of commerce—business done over computer networks. *This is important,* Rivest thought, and immediately began evangelizing the challenge to his colleagues.

Leonard Adleman was the first one to fall victim to Rivest's exhortations. He was a young mathematician who also split his time between the computer science lab and the math department. One day that December, he recalls, he walked into Rivest's office just a few doors down from his own at Tech Square. "Did you see this paper?" Rivest asked. "It shows how you can build this secret code, where if I wanted to send you something and we wanted it to be secret, and somebody was listening . . ."

As Rivest gushed about the workings of public key, Adleman asked himself, *Do I care about this?* Unlike Rivest, Leonard Adleman worshipped theory, pure and simple. He often thought about Gauss, Euler, Fermat . . . giants of previous centuries who had discovered the foundations of mathematical truth, blue-sky brainiacs without regard for any practical applications their constructs may have had. These geniuses were as gods to Adleman, and he longed for nothing less than to play in the same arenas of pure mind. This stuff about cryptography that so excited Rivest sounded to Adleman like some problem about how to build a better automobile or something. Not the sort of intellectual gauntlet that a math god like Carl Friedrich Gauss would have jumped at. So Adleman waited patiently until Rivest was finished, then remarked, "That's very interesting, Ron." And changed the subject.

Rivest had more luck with another recent addition to MIT's computer faculty. Just that month, Adi Shamir, a rail-thin, witty Israeli, had arrived at MIT for a visiting professorship in the Laboratory for Computer Science. Shamir was having a hectic time. Though he was a world-class mathematician, he had yet to learn much about computer algorithms. So he had been unhappily surprised when, several weeks earlier, Rivest had sent him a letter "to discuss the contents of the advanced algorithm course you will teach this spring term." Shamir winced: bad enough an algorithm course—but an *advanced* one? To *doctoral* candidates? Fortunately, Shamir was a lightning-quick study. As soon as he arrived at Tech Square he zoomed to the library and checked out a shelf full of books on the subject; in the next two weeks, he learned everything he needed to know about algorithms. It was sometime during that remedial reading period that his new colleague, Ron Rivest, popped into his office and enlisted him in the effort to implement public key cryptography.

Once he got a look at it, Shamir agreed with Rivest that the Diffie-Hellman paper was significant. Not that it was groundbreaking from a mathematical point of view. He figured that if you took anyone experienced in number theory and tried to explain the Diffie-Hellman scheme to him, it would have taken exactly two minutes. The novelty was how the Stanford guys took something that had absolutely no relation to cryptography in the past and suddenly applied it to a new field. Shamir quickly became Rivest's partner in the search for the perfect mix of one-way functions.

As the winter progressed, Rivest and Shamir became friends; with Adleman they formed a jolly threesome. Adleman, at first almost as a social concession, joined in the algorithmic hunt. "We were roughly the same age, we were all in the same discipline, and we liked each other, so we became not only colleagues and collaborators but hung out all the time," Adleman says. Adleman and Shamir were bachelors, and Rivest's more domestic existence served as a sort of anchor to the group, both at work and in his home in Belmont, a warm, open apartment with access to a nice yard. (Adleman lived in an apartment in Arlington and Shamir had a place in Cambridge.) As the weeks progressed, the young men, with adjoining offices on the eighth floor of Tech Square, began working seriously on their quest.

Not surprisingly, Rivest was the most focused of the group. Though he taught classes during this period, his mental efforts never strayed far from crypto. "Whatever Ron decides to do, he does extremely well," says Adleman. "If he decided, say, to start building rocket ships, I'd put my money on it that in five years he'd be one of the five best rocket builders on earth." Shamir was similarly dogged. "Adi's like an intellectual lion; you just throw some meat in front of him and he'll chew it up," says Adleman.

Adleman himself acted as more of a foil. Of the three, he was the one who most looked and acted like a classic, dreamy mathematician—the kind of shaggy-haired young guy who would be the helpless prey of a wacky heroine in a screwball comedy (by the end of the movie, though, we'd learn that he had his own devilish streak). Perhaps once or twice a week, Rivest and Shamir would come up with a scheme, and then present it to Adleman, the group's Mr. Theory, who would then set about to identify its flaws and break the scheme, sending the other two mathematicians back to the blackboard. To Adleman the exercise was like swatting flies, and not much more intriguing. Even weeks into the project, he was convinced that the whole project was not really worth his effort—it was too grounded in the real world. He understood that both his friends had this sense that the potential practical applications made the quest desirable. That didn't matter to Adleman. He loved math because its beauty transcended earthly concerns.

At first, every scheme they came up with was easily obliterated by an Adleman attack. Frustratingly so. "We experimented with a lot of different approaches, including variations on things that Diffie and Hellman suggested," says Rivest. "We weren't happy with the approaches we came up with." At one point, they got so discouraged that they wondered whether an answer existed at all. Maybe Diffie and Hellman's apparent breakthrough was a dud. So for a little while, they switched gears and attacked the problem from the opposite end, trying to come up with a proof to show that public key cryptography was impossible. "We didn't get very far at that," says Rivest.

In February, the three MIT mathematicians went to the Killington ski resort in Vermont. It was definitely a working holiday. Even as the three computer scientists tried to teach themselves to ski, their minds were never far from the problem. For Shamir, and even more for Rivest, it was almost a biological drive; Adleman was literally along for the ride. "All the way up in the car, around the fire, riding the ski lifts, that's what they were talking about, so that's what I was talking about," he says. Of course, when actually schussing down a mountain on skis, they couldn't continue the discussion—so they *thought* about it. Shamir later recalled, only half facetiously, that they settled into a routine of each racing down the hill for a half hour devising a new public key cryptography scheme. And then the others would break the scheme. On only the second day that the Israeli had ever been on skis, he felt he'd cracked the problem. "I was going downhill and all of a sudden I had the most remarkable new scheme," he later recalled. "I was so excited that I left my skis behind as I went downhill. Then I left my pole. And suddenly . . . *I couldn't remember what the scheme was.*" To this day he does not know if a brilliant, still-undiscovered crypto-system was abandoned at Killington.

In a way, their difficulties were only to be expected. Why would anyone think that three young computer science assistant professors could ever come up with a sound cryptosystem, let alone a bulletproof scheme that for the first time in history allowed people to communicate with each other in total secrecy without having to make arrangements beforehand? A reasonable mind would conclude that this could only be done by someone intimately familiar with the field. If you had a magical instrument that measured cryptographic knowledge, the combined experience of the MIT Three wouldn't have moved the needle even a tickle.

But such ignorance was perhaps their most valuable asset. "We were extremely lucky," Shamir later said. "If we'd known anything about cryptography and known about differential sequences and Lucifer and DES we probably would have been misled into expanding those ideas and using them for public key cryptography. But we were rank amateurs—we knew nothing about cryptography. And as a result we were just exploring the ideas we were taught at university."

These ideas were a mathematical grab bag that suggested all sorts of possibilities—everything from linear algebra to equation sets. And they went through them all. Generally they'd meet in Rivest's office, scrawling equations on the blackboard. Someone would come up with an idea and they'd think about it for a while, and then maybe they'd see a flaw with it. "Sometimes I would break my own scheme, or Adi would break his, or I would break Adi's," says Rivest. The more promising possibilities would go to Adleman, who, despite his initial lack of interest, was developing quite a talent for locating, then tugging at, the threads that would unravel a given scheme.

Eventually, they found a system that looked like it might fly. It was about the thirty-second candidate. Adleman immediately thought this one looked more interesting than the predecessors. He pulled an all-nighter before he broke it—"It took real research to break it, as opposed to observation," he says—and discovered that he had mixed feelings about his success. He was now hooked, too. (Several years later, some researchers published a paper proposing an almost identical scheme, only to be embarrassed when other mathematicians rediscovered Adleman's "scheme 32" attack.)

By then their solutions were beginning to utilize the idea of a promising one-way function: factoring. Though Knuth had suggested this to Diffie and Hellman, the Stanford researchers hadn't followed up on it; by coincidence, Rivest was settling on his former mentor's hunch.

Once again, factoring is a mathematical problem tied to the use of prime numbers. A prime number, of course, is one that cannot be arrived at by multiplying two numbers together (the lone exception being the prime itself and the number one). If you multiply two large primes together, then, you get a much larger number that *isn't* a prime. To factor that number, you have to somehow reverse the process, identifying the two original seeds that produced it. This had been understood as a hard problem ever since a few years before Christ's birth, when Eratosthenes of Alexandria devised a mathematical process called a "sieve" to try to perform this task. At that time, people considered factoring to be virtually the same problem as trying to figure out whether a number was a prime or not. Twelve hundred or so years later, Fibonacci improved the method somewhat, but by no means did he offer a way to reasonably break down a large product into its two parent primes. When Gauss in 1801 recognized that factoring and finding primality were two different problems, he identified the former conundrum as a vexing but critical challenge:

> The problem of distinguishing prime numbers from com-
> posite numbers and of resolving the latter into their prime
> factors is known to be one of the most important and use-
> ful in arithmetic. . . . The dignity of the science itself seems
> to require that every possible means be explored for the
> solution of a problem so elegant and celebrated.

Gauss never did find an efficient solution to the factoring problem, and no one else did either, though no proof existed that a solution was impossible. Not that it was a very hot topic in the mid-1970s. "Factoring at the time was not a problem that people cared about very much," Rivest says. "Publications were few and far between."

Still, as the MIT Three continued trying different variations of schemes to implement the Diffie-Hellman concept, they became increasingly drawn to using factoring in their system.

On April 3, 1977, a graduate student named Anni Bruce held a Passover seder at her home. Rivest was there, and Shamir, and Adleman. For several hours ideas of mathematical formulas and factoring were put aside for a recapitulation of the escape of the Jewish people from Egypt. As is customary with seders, people downed a lot of wine. It was nearly midnight when Rivest and his wife returned home. While Gail Rivest got ready for bed, Ron stretched out on the couch and began thinking about the problem that had consumed him and his colleagues for months. He would often do that—lie flat on the sofa with his eyes closed, as if he were deep in sleep. Sometimes he'd sit up and flip through the pages of a book, not really looking, but reworking the numbers. He had a computer terminal at home, but that night he left it off. "I was just thinking," he says.

That was when it came to him—the cognitive lightning bolt known as the Eureka Moment. He had a scheme! It was similar to some of their more recent attempts in that it used number theory and factoring. But this was simpler, more elegant. Warning himself not to get overexcited—Shamir and Adleman, after all, had broken many of his previous proposals—he jotted down some notes. He did allow himself the luxury of saying to his wife that he'd come up with an idea that just might work. He doesn't remember phoning the guys that night. Adleman, though, insists that he received a call sometime after midnight.

"I've got a new idea," Rivest announced, and explained it.

Essentially, Rivest's idea was to strip the factoring problem down to almost naked essentials. A public key is generated by multiplying two large (over 100 digits), randomly chosen prime numbers. Easy. Then another simple step (if you have a computer): randomly choose yet another large number, one that had certain easy-to-calculate specified properties. This would be known as the encryption key. The complete public key consists of both that encryption key and the product of those two primes.

Rivest then provided a simple formula by which someone who wanted to scramble a message could use that public key to do so. The plaintext would now be ciphertext, profoundly transformed by an equation that included that large product. Finally, using an algorithm drawn from the work of the great Euclid, Rivest provided for a decryption key—one that could only be calculated by using the two original prime numbers. Using the decryption key, one could easily revert the ciphertext to the plaintext message.

Thinking of it another way, on its way to ciphertext, the original message was intimately intertwined with the product of the two primes. What made the information in the plaintext unreadable was a mathematical transformation involving that large product—a transformation that could only be reversed if you knew what those two primes were. Then everything would become clear.

Some of the mathematics of the decryption key—which works as the private key in this system—was derived from the work of another legendary mathematician, Leonhard Euler, who in 1763 devised an equation that dealt in the remainders of numbers obtained after dividing whole numbers. Almost two hundred years after its Swiss inventor first conceived it, an idea that had been deemed valuable only in theoretical math had found an application in the real-world mechanics of codemaking.

The scheme satisfied all of Diffie and Hellman's requirements. A user could confidently broadcast a public key, because its essential component was only the product of the two primes. If snoops wanted to unscramble an intercepted message that had been encrypted with the public key, that information would be useless. In order to cook up a decryption key, they'd need the original primes. How could they do that? Only by factoring, and even Gauss couldn't crack that nut. This was the beauty of the one-way function: easy to do if you're going in the right direction, next to impossible if you approach it from the wrong end. If the people using the system used primes as big as Rivest was specifying, factoring that product would require hunkering down with some supercomputers for a long winter—and for some billions of winters thereafter. As long as factoring remained difficult, this new scheme was secure.

The scheme wasn't limited to encryption, either. If you used the decryption (private) key to scramble a number, that jumbled result could be unscrambled by using the encryption key and the product of the primes—the public key. Since only the owner of the closely held private key could do this, this process would reliably authenticate the source of the message. What Diffie and Hellman had first imagined now seemed real: a solid formula for digital signatures, the enabler for new kinds of commerce, and a means to establish trust on an electronic network.

The formulas sounded beautiful to Adleman. It was a much less messy system than any they'd been dealing with. Others had used relatively convoluted schemes involving multiplication, division, addition. But Rivest had hit the target dead on. "I think that's it, Ron," said Adleman. "I think that's going to work." But Adleman, too, held off on popping a champagne cork. Too often, midnight excitement dissipates when a scheme is examined in cold morning light.

When morning broke, though, the elegance of Rivest's solution hadn't dimmed. When the three researchers convened in Tech Square as usual, a flushed and breathless Rivest presented a manuscript to his colleagues with the whole shebang written out in a near-publishable format. It was signed Adleman, Rivest, Shamir. "I looked at this," said Adleman, "and it was the description of what he'd said the night before." He felt it was Rivest's breakthrough, not his.

"Take my name off," he said. "It's your work."

Rivest insisted that it was a joint project, that Shamir's and Adleman's contributions were crucial, that the scheme was the final point in an evolutionary process. To Rivest, it was as if the three of them had been in a boat together, all taking turns rowing and navigating in search of a new land. Rivest might have stepped out of the boat first, but they all deserved credit for the discovery. Still, Adleman objected again. Maybe Shamir had contributed conceptually, but Adleman had mostly stuck pins in various algorithmic trial balloons. No way he could take credit.

Rivest urged Adleman to reconsider overnight. "So I went home and thought about it," said Adleman. He was, after all, a logical man. Though he felt in his bones that he didn't deserve to share credit, he knew that as an aspiring academic, any publication credit might help when he came up for tenure. And after all, breaking their "Scheme 32" hadn't been trivial. What if he hadn't been around to break it, and Rivest and Shamir had gone on to publish a faulty paper—they certainly would have looked like morons if some pimply grad student cracked their scheme. Given that he had made a contribution, why fight Ron on the matter? After all, Adleman thought, it wasn't as if this was a paper anyone would actually *see*. "I thought that this would be the least important paper my name would ever appear on," he recalls. So Adleman agreed to keep his name on it, if it were listed last. Meanwhile, Adi Shamir agreed with Adleman that Rivest's name should go first. This order determined the name of the algorithm itself: RSA.

With input from his collaborators, Rivest quickly turned his original draft into MIT/Laboratory for Computer Sciences Technical Memo Number 82: "A Method for Obtaining Digital Signatures and Public Key Cryptosystems." It was dated April 4, 1977. Though Adleman might still have dismissed the outcome as mathematically unimportant, a quick glance at the "key words and phrases" offered for indexing purposes demonstrated that this was at the least an unusual effort for three number crunchers from MIT. In fact, the words offered a remarkable blueprint for a network society that would not be widely discussed for twenty years:

> . . . digital signatures, public key cryptosystems, privacy, authentication, security, factorization, prime number, electronic mail, message-passing, electronic funds transfer, cryptography.

With fanfare reminiscent of the Diffie-Hellman work that had first triggered the project, the paper's first words proclaimed, "The era of electronic mail may soon be upon us; we must insure that two important properties of the current 'paper mail' system are preserved."

These properties were that messages remain *private* and able to be *signed*. And then the authors promised to unveil a means by which these characteristics, long accepted as only the domain of hard copy, could be used in the coming, networked era.

The paper was also notable for a more whimsical touch. Instead of what had been the standard form of delineating the recipient and sender of a message by alphabetic notation—A for the sender, B for the recipient, for instance—Rivest personified them by giving them gender and identity. Thus the RSA paper marks the first appearance of a fictional "Bob" who wants to send a message to "Alice." As trivial as this sounds, these names actually became a de facto standard in future papers outlining cryptologic advances, and the cast of characters in such previously depopulated mathematical papers would eventually be widened to include an eavesdropper dubbed Eve and a host of supporting actors including Carol, Trent, Wiry, and Dave. The appearance of these dramatis personae, however nerdly, would be symbolic of the iconoclastic personality of a brand-new community of independent cryptographers, working outside of government and its secrecy clamps.

Despite their confident language, Rivest wasn't sure how significant the discovery was. "It was unclear at the time whether [the scheme] would be broken within a few months," he says. "It was also unclear whether there were better approaches." Still, he initiated a journal publication process, with an eye to the *Communications of the ACM,* where he was a contributing editor. He sent copies to colleagues for peer review. One to Don Knuth. And, in his first contact with the authors of "New Directions in Cryptography," on whose system his own was built (a connection made explicit in his paper), he sent one to Whitfield Diffie and Martin Hellman. (Rivest later explained that among researchers it is not particularly unusual for a group of academics to build upon previous work without notifying the original team until a result is obtained.)

There were still some things that needed to be nailed down before the paper was submitted to a journal. One of them was definitively pinpointing the current state of factoring—the system, after all, relied on the difficulty of extracting two long primes from their product. Through Marty Hellman, they got in touch with Rich Schroeppel, the former MIT hacker whom Diffie had visited on his transcontinental crypto adventure. (Ironically, Schroeppel had been pessimistic about the prospect of cryptosystems based on one-way functions.) Schroeppel was among the few people on earth still doing very serious thinking on factoring.

Schroeppel now was ready to discard his skepticism of one-way functions and was eager to contribute. After reading what Don Knuth had offered as the best available formula for factoring, Schroeppel had done a timing analysis of it and had a deep realization of how truly knotty the problem was: no matter how you tackled it, it seemed that the work required to factor something was many, many times larger than the effort expended on the initial multiplication. "I think it was the first time anybody had looked at how hard it was to factor," he says. Schroeppel was impressed with the RSA paper and sent some suggestions, including an analysis of how long it would take the fastest factoring scheme (an unpublished one by Schroeppel himself) to crack keys. Conclusion: plenty long enough for a good cryptosystem.

Rivest also sent a paper to Martin Gardner, who wrote the "Mathematical Recreations" column for *Scientific American*. "He was always writing these columns about big numbers, and looking for primes," says Rivest. Gardner had a loyal following among both amateur figure twiddlers and serious mathematicians: it was not unusual for one of his monthly dispatches to catapult a hitherto obscure problem into an international obsession.

On April 10, 1977, less than a week after Rivest's breakthrough had occurred, Gardner wrote back. "Your digital signature scheme is indeed fascinating," he wrote. "The whole idea behind it is new to me, and I think a very interesting column could be written around it." He invited Rivest to explain the scheme to him personally.

An excited Rivest headed out to Gardner's home in Hudson, New York. Gardner was an old-school gentleman and something of a scamp. The columnist performed a few card tricks; years later Rivest was still wondering how the hell he did them. The magic show completed, Gardner asked for examples of how the RSA system worked, and it was Rivest's turn to produce magic. Eventually they decided to offer a challenge to readers of the column. Rivest would generate a public key of 129 digits and use it to encode a secret message. If the system worked as promised, no one in the world would be able to read that message, with two exceptions. One would be someone who had both a powerful computer set to break the message with brute force and a very large amount of time on his hands: if the computer was, for instance, a million-dollar PDP-10, the effort would take somewhere in the neighborhood of a quadrillion years. (This estimate, provided by Rivest on an apparent misinterpretation of Schroppel's factoring time analysis, was an error on his part; what he meant to say was that it would take merely hundreds of millions of years to crack the code by calculation. Still not an undertaking for mortals.) The other exception, of course, was the person holding the private key match to that particular 129-digit public key. That person could decode the message in a few seconds.

And if the RSA system didn't work as promised? Then some bright, motivated reader might figure it out. In that case, Rivest, Shamir, and Adleman would present that person a $100 prize. And the RSA system would be given a quick funeral, as it would be useless for protecting people's privacy and authenticating their identities.

Gardner's column appeared in the August 1977 edition of *Scientific American*. It was spiked throughout with enthusiasm for the achievement of the three young MIT scientists. Gardner, in fact, predicted that the breakthroughs by Diffie-Hellman, and then RSA, meant an end to an entire era of codebreaking: "[They are] so revolutionary," he wrote, "that all previous ciphers, together with the techniques for cracking them, may soon fade into oblivion." From now on, he wrote, armed with RSA and similar systems, we would enter a golden age of secure electronic communications, where all messages could be secure, unreadable even by the masters of cryptanalysis. In fact, Gardner used the moment to declare void Edgar Allan Poe's contention that "human ingenuity cannot concoct a cipher which human ingenuity cannot resolve." In Gardner's view, the ingenuity of the Stanford and MIT "outsiders" had concocted that very cipher. The columnist, while excited by the discovery, confessed to a wistfulness at the new reality, where the spy vs. spy aspects of encryption would be relegated to antiquity. "All over the world there are clever men and women, some of them geniuses, who have devoted their lives to the mastery of modern cryptanalysis. . . ." he wrote. "Now these people are standing on trapdoors that are about to spring open and possibly drop them completely from sight."

Gardner completed the column by printing the message encoded by Rivest with the RSA system using a 129-digit key, inviting anyone to try his or her luck, skill, and cryptanalytic prowess at breaking the code. Readers were invited to begin the process, or simply learn more about the system, by sending a self-addressed, stamped envelope to MIT and requesting a copy of the technical paper.

Though the three professors were all on summer break, the secretaries at Tech Square could attest to the instant impact of Gardner's column—thousands of letters began pouring in. When Shamir finally returned to Cambridge after spending the summer backpacking in Alaska, he encountered a near avalanche as the stacks of envelopes that had been stored in his office engulfed him on his way to his desk.

But that was only the first indication of the excitement that Gardner's column inspired. This was the first public notice of the movement that began with Whit Diffie's iconoclastic quest, and it seemed to have unleashed all the pent-up frustrations of anyone who once had been temporarily obsessed with the dark art of codes, only to have sublimated that attention elsewhere, since all the good stuff in the crypto world existed only behind the Triple Fence or, perhaps, its international counterparts. Reading Gardner's account of what seemed like a turning point in this history of cryptography—not only in terms of what the tools were but who had forged them—was like the sun breaking through after decades of gray gloom.

Len Adleman first saw the evidence of this that August, when he was browsing in a bookstore in Berkeley. Waiting to pay for his purchase, he overheard a conversation between a clerk and a customer buying a new copy of *Scientific American*. "Did you see the thing in here about this new code system?" asked the customer.

"Yeah, I read about it," said the clerk. "Isn't it wild?"

Adleman could not contain himself. "That's the stuff *we* did," he exclaimed, identifying himself as one of the three MIT professors in Gardner's column. When the magazine buyer understood that Adleman was on the level, he held out the issue. "Would you sign this for me?" he asked.

As an instrument of crypto's liberation, Len Adleman was suddenly being asked for autographs à la Tom Cruise. Even Fermat hadn't gotten that kind of treatment!

And what about the people who were supposedly standing on those trapdoors Gardner mentioned—namely, the codemakers, codebreakers, analysts, and outright spooks who disappeared each day into the Cone of Silence at Fort George Meade? How did they view the work of Rivest, Shamir, and Adleman and the advances of Diffie and Hellman?

As one might expect: with sheer horror.

The midseventies had already been traumatic for the NSA. For twenty-five years, its relationship with Congress had proceeded with nary a legislative speed bump. The agency addressed only the few representatives who sat on classified intelligence oversight committees. After briefing sessions held in shielded rooms swept for bugs, the legislators routinely rubber-stamped all of The Fort's requests. But in 1975 and 1976, the NSA found itself the focus of a fearlessly insolent investigation of its eavesdropping practices by Senator Frank Church's Intelligence Committee. The committee was shocked to discover the extent of the NSA's snooping efforts, particularly a strategy called Project Shamrock that included surveillance of American citizens. Church was incensed at the agency's blithe insistence that such eavesdropping, performed without benefit of warrants, was still within its authority. The senator's final report concluded with an almost biblical admonition on what could happen if the agency continued on its course without restraint, warning that its monitoring capabilities "could at any time be turned around on the American people and no American would have any privacy left, such [is] the capability to monitor everything. . . . There would be no place to hide." While the NSA avoided any serious repercussions, this "indecent exposure" (as described by an NSA official in an internal memo) was sobering.

The wiser heads of the NSA obviously knew that if there was ever a time to lie low, this was it. Still, Diffie-Hellman's work, and its alarmingly practical follow-ups, represented an encroachment into what the NSA had regarded as its birthright: the domination of cryptography. This was something that the agency could not ignore. After all, if people had access to the means to encrypt their private communications, there *could* be a place a hide—and a universal means to privacy was exactly what an agency charged with eavesdropping is hell-bent to prevent. Though the realization of a such a threat to its mission was slow to filter through the complex bureaucracy at Fort Meade, clearly some officials recognized the problem. As early as 1975 the NSA began to work behind the scenes (where else?) to restrict the nascent academic field.

Its first efforts were directed at the National Science Foundation. The NSF was an independent government agency designed to foster research into all sorts of scientific inquiries; it was extremely common for mathematicians and computer scientists to have work funded, at least in part, by NSF grants. (These would come to include Diffie, Hellman, and the RSA team.) In June 1975, the NSF official in charge of monitoring such grants, Fred Weingarten, was warned that the NSA was the only government agency with the authority to fund research on cryptology. Weingarten was alarmed that he may have been breaking the law. So he held off awarding any new grants while he sought to clarify the matter.

What he found was interesting. Neither the NSF lawyers nor the National Security Agency itself, when pressed for documentation, could come up with any statutory justification for the agency's claim. So Weingarten felt free to ignore the warnings and resume his grants.

Marty Hellman, for one, always appreciated Weingarten's backbone. "When the NSA told him that he couldn't fund cryptography, that the NSA had a monopoly on that funding, Fred not only was courageous but he handled it very well," says Hellman. "He didn't say, 'You're full of shit,' but asked them to put it in writing so he could take it to his counsel for an opinion."

But then came the Diffie-Hellman paper, followed by the RSA discovery. Together, of course, these created the underpinnings for the NSA's worst fear: a communications systems where *everyone* used a secure code. So it seemed hardly a coincidence that on April 20, 1977—barely three weeks after Rivest dashed off his MIT technical memo—the NSA's assistant deputy director for communications security, Cecil C. Corry, ventured from Fort Meade to the capital to meet with Weingarten. He was accompanied by a colleague. Once again the officials attempted to ax any NSF grants that might involve crypto, invoking what they portrayed as a presidential directive giving them "control" over such research. Weingarten reminded them of his previous experience, which established that no such directive was ever issued. While he did agree to forward relevant proposals to the NSA so that the security agency could offer a technical evaluation to use in considering the grant, he insisted that the process be conducted openly, with no decisions made under the shroud of silence.

The NSA people weren't happy with that compromise, offhandedly remarking to Weingarten that "they would have to get a law passed"—presumably to ban such academic research unless the Diffies, Hellmans, and Rivests of the world were willing to deep-six their work under the classified seal. Later, Corry wrote to John R. Pasta, Weingarten's boss, thanking him for a concession that the NSF never made—agreeing to consider "security implications" when evaluating grant proposals. Pasta made it clear that the NSF made no such promise.

In a memo he wrote at the time, Fred Weingarten summarized his views of the agency's motives:

> NSA is in a bureaucratic bind. In the past the only communications with heavy security demands were military and diplomatic. Now, with the marriage of computer applications with telecommunications . . . the need for highly secure digital processing has hit the civilian sector. NSA is worried, of course, that public domain security research will compromise some of their work. However, even further, they seem to want to maintain their control and corner a bureaucratic expertise in this field. . . .
>
> It seems clear that turning such a huge domestic responsibility, potentially involving such organizations as banking, the U.S. mail, and cable televisions, to an organization such as NSA should be done only after the most serious debate at higher levels of government than represented by peanuts like me.

Clearly, NSA wasn't going to slink away.

As the skies darkened inside the Beltway, the MIT professors, crypto virgins all, were unaware of anything but sunshine. They certainly didn't know of anything in the nation's export laws and agreements that could conceivably affect the dissemination of their work. They had no idea that while the first half of 1977 was marked by their major contribution to the field of cryptography, the latter portion of that year would be marked by the government's efforts to stop people from knowing about such work.

That summer a letter dated July 7, 1977, arrived at the New York offices of the IEEE, addressed to E. K. Gannett, the staff director of the organization's publications board. "I have noticed in the past months," the correspondent began, "that various IEEE groups have been publishing and exporting technical articles on encryption and cryptology— a technical field which is covered by federal regulations. . . ." There followed detailed citations, down to the proper subsections of individual regulations that may have already been violated, not only by the publishing of certain articles in IEEE publications, but at various symposia sponsored by the group, including the event in Ronneby, Sweden, where Hellman had first presented public key crypto. As further documentation, the letter writer included photocopies of "a few pages of the relevant law," namely the International Traffic in Arms Regulation (ITAR) code. These regulations were drawn to "control the import and export of defense articles and defense services." While people like Ron Rivest had always assumed that defense articles were things like nuclear detonating devices, Stinger missiles, and aircraft carriers, it turned out that these "instruments of war" were joined on the United States munitions list by "privacy devices [and] cryptographic devices." None of these was allowed to be shipped overseas without specific permission from the State Department. Furthermore, these restrictions did not cover merely the actual devices, but any "technical data" covering these "weapons." This was defined as "any unclassified information that can be used . . . in the design, production . . . or operation" of a restricted weapon. If you disseminated that information to a foreign national, or even allowed such a person to get his or her hands on your matériel (so to speak), you were in violation of the law—an enemy of the state.

The letter writer noted that in October the IEEE planned an International Symposium on Information Theory at Cornell that would include papers on encryption. Under current law, he warned, such presentations or publications were restricted, and if preprints were sent abroad, "a difficulty could arise, because, according to ITAR, an export license is required." His implication seemed to be that such a violation of the law could lead to fines, arrests, and even jail terms. At the Ronneby conference, the letter darkly noted, "this formality was skipped."

The message was clear: *You academic cryptographers may believe that your ideas were conceived under the protection of academic free-dom and that your mathematical formulas belonged to no one but per-haps the God who first crunched them . . . but that is not the case when it comes to ideas and algorithms that can be used to encrypt informa-tion. Those ideas should be kept under close watch—and government control.* Clearly, the letter implied, by allowing the Cornell conference to proceed, the IEEE would be illegally providing the equivalent of heavy-duty military equipment to our nation's foes. "As an IEEE mem-ber," the writer concluded, "I suggest that IEEE might wish to review this situation, for these modern weapons technologies, uncontrollably disseminated, could have more than academic effect."

The letter was signed by a J. A. Meyer, who identified himself only by his home address in Bethesda, Maryland, and his IEEE member-ship number.

Who was this concerned member? It turns out that in January 1971 this same Joseph A. Meyer had written an article for an IEEE publica-tion called *Transactions on Aerospace and Electronics Systems,* a paper so unusual that the editors felt compelled to include an introductory note on its controversial nature. Entitled "Crime Deterrent Transpon-der System," it proposed a system whereby "small radio transponders would be attached to criminal recidivists, parollees, and bailees to identify them and detect their whereabouts." By tagging likely law-breakers, Meyer claimed, we could create "an electronic surveillance and command-control system to make crime pointless." The bio-graphical material described Meyer as a New Jersey native born in 1929 who got a math degree from Rutgers, spent two years in the air force in the early 1950s, and, from that point, "joined the Depart-ment of Defense, where he has worked primarily in the field of mathe-matics, computers, and communications in the United States and overseas."

Even a moderately seasoned observer could guess that the unspo-ken branch of the Defense Department was a three-letter agency whose name seldom appeared in print in 1971. Indeed, several weeks after the Meyer letter was received, *Science* magazine confirmed the rumors: Joseph A. Meyer worked at the National Security Agency.

The timing of Meyer's missive aroused deep suspicions about the NSA's involvement in crushing independent work on crypto. It was sent almost at the moment that Vice Admiral Bobby Inman assumed the NSA directorship and began waging the very war that Meyer had declared against academic cryptographers. In the succeeding years, however, nothing has emerged to contradict Meyer's claim (vociferously seconded by the NSA) that he had received no orders from Inman or anybody else to send his notorious letter. (Inman now says that on the day Meyer was writing his letter, he was getting a "turnover" briefing from the outgoing director, Lewis Allen—and the topic of public cryptography never even came up.) The Senate Intelligence Committee, looking into the matter, came to that same conclusion in 1978, and now even Marty Hellman believes that it's probable that Meyer was simply a loose cannon. On the other hand, the NSA conspicuously refused to repudiate the letter, and Inman later asserted to Congress that he believed that Meyer's comments were valid ones.

In any case, the Meyer letter had an immediate effect. Certainly, the organizers of the Cornell conference took the letter seriously—after all, if Meyer was right, they and the speakers at their conference could wind up in jail for simply presenting their research! It turned out, however, that the issue of technical data and the export regulations had come up a decade before at the society, and, as E. K. Gannett, the recipient of the letter, wrote back to Meyer in a fawning letter dated July 20, 1977, "All IEEE conference publications and journals are exempted from export license requirements under [ITAR] Section 125.11 (a) (1)." He went on to cite a footnote to that section that "places the burden of obtaining any required government approval for publication of technical data on the person or company seeking publication." In other words, he was saying, *it's not our problem—it's the problem of those members who dare perform research in the field.* He expressed his gratitude to Meyer for "bringing this potentially important question to our attention," and promised to bring the problem to the attention of "potentially interested parties." Sure enough, on the same day, Gannett wrote a memo to Dr. Narenda P. Dwivedi, the organization's director of technical activities, suggesting that the IEEE should perhaps ensure that the researchers "are aware of the rules of the game."

On August 20, Dwivedi wrote to researchers at six institutions. "A concerned and good-meaning member has drawn our attention to a possible violation by authors of ITAR regulations. . . . It appears that

IEEE and its groups/societies/councils are exempt but the individuals (and/or their employers) have to watch out." Dwivedi then offered some advice for the new brccd of researchers in cryptography: they "should refer the paper to the Office of Munitions Control, Dept. of State, Washington, D. C., for their ruling."

What Dwivedi was suggesting was neatly in line with J. A. Meyer's wishes. But if a researcher submitted a paper to the State Department, he or she would effectively yield control of the work to the government. As far as the MIT researchers were concerned, there would be, as *Science* put it, "a censorship system by the NSA over the research of the MIT Information Theory Group."

One of the recipients of Dwivedi's letter was Marty Hellman. He quickly showed it to Ron Rivest, who was spending his summer break at Xerox PARC in Palo Alto, just down the road from Stanford. "It was probably my first realization that our work might involve sensitivities," he says. As soon as he got back to MIT, a worried Rivest consulted the institution's lawyers.

Rivest, of course, was concerned about the legal implications of stuffing copies of Technical Memo Number 82 into the self-addressed letters with 35-cent stamps as part of the *Scientific American* "contest." Was distribution of the RSA paper to the publication's readers an illegal act? Could MIT be held at fault? Could Rivest and Adleman be jailed? And what about Shamir—he wasn't even a U.S. citizen! Could MIT be cited for distributing a paper to one of its coauthors?

"The requests for our paper were from all over the world," says Rivest. "Some were from foreign governments. It wasn't clear to me what we should do. When you receive this sort of ominous note from the NSA that this stuff is illegal, you want to be conservative and get it checked out." Rivest even considered the possibility that some of the foreign requests for the memo might have been planted to entrap him under the export regulations, making him a poster boy for mathematicians who ventured too deeply into the forbidden turf of spy agencies.

An answer came back quickly from the MIT administration—*don't send out those papers until this mess is resolved*. To their credit, however, the heads of the university, sensitive to principles of academic freedom, worked diligently to clear the path for a free distribution of the tech memo. Despite MIT's long history of working with national security agencies, often in top-secret research, this wasn't easy. This time it was dealing with the National Security Agency—and at least some NSA officials, now face-to-face with an open challenge to their crypto monopoly, were themselves running scared. But this time, they had clear-eyed foes who believed that intellectual freedom should not be compromised on the basis of unproved claims of national security. In this new academic research area, new ground rules would be laid and most of the major decisions would be made in the early days. After setting the precedents, the MIT researchers believed, it would be much harder to change things in a fundamental way.

At Stanford, Marty Hellman also wasted no time getting an opinion from the university lawyers. On October 7, university counsel John J. Schwartz assured him that "it is our opinion that the dissemination of the results of the research you describe is not unlawful." Of course there was the danger that the lawyers were wrong, and the views of J. A. Meyer reflected those of the federal government; if so, Hellman might be prosecuted for delivering his paper. Schwartz promised that if that were the case, the university would defend him. "Nevertheless," he added, "there would always remain a risk to you personally of fine or imprisonment if the government prevailed in such a case."

In the end, the Cornell conference—the ostensible focus of Meyer's letter—went on as scheduled, including the very talks that Meyer had tagged as potential violations of the export rules and a threat to national security. It turned out that the professors had more backbone than the IEEE, which had urged them to vet their papers with the government. When two of Hellman's graduate students fretted over the implications of getting cited by the government in the tender beginnings of their careers, he volunteered to read their papers himself. "I have tenure at Stanford," Hellman told the *New York Times*, "and if the NSA should decide to push us in court, Stanford would back me. But for a student hoping to begin a career, it would not be so pleasant to go job hunting with three years of litigation hanging over his head."

Ralph Merkle spoke at a panel discussion, too. And Whit Diffie, who was not scheduled to speak at the conference, went out of his way to give a presentation at an informal session. "There was no trouble at the meeting," he says. "My attitude was that the Meyer letter should be ignored."

Meanwhile, MIT's lawyers were still wrangling with the National Security Agency over the legality of stuffing Tech Memo No. 82 into the 7000 self-addressed, stamped envelopes moldering in Shamir's office and dropping them off at the post office. The academics had pointed out that a clause in the ITAR rules put them in the clear: a specific exemption on "published materials." What did The Fort say to *that*?

"As usual with NSA, it was hard to get any complete answer from them," Shamir later recalled. More to the point, it became increasingly clear that the NSA could not come up with a legal rationale for its actions. So MIT allowed its professors to proceed. In December 1977, half a year after Gardner's column appeared and the requests began tumbling in, the namesakes of the RSA algorithm invited grad students to a pizza and envelope-stuffing party. And then the papers were mailed. The RSA algorithm had gone global.

Perhaps the existence of these thousands of papers circulating around the world, in addition to thousands of reprints and photocopies of the Diffie-Hellman papers, should have been a signal to the NSA that the crypto toothpaste was out of the tube, and no decrees or scare tactics could generate the requisite physics to squeeze it back in. But for the next few years the agency, perhaps more from reflex than an expectation of success, kept trying to suppress the intellectual activity in the crypto world that now seemed to be exploding outside the Triple Fence.

In retrospect, the institutional behavior seems strange and conflicted. But what else could the NSA do? The CIA may have had a rich and sordid history of bag jobs, honey traps, and other nut-squeezing enterprises, but the Fort Meade culture was dramatically different. Though the agency had certainly stepped over the line at times (as the Church committee documented), the organizational ethos always seemed to regard heroism in terms of the highly intellectual tasks of sucking up signals, concocting ciphers, and cracking codes. During the years that Whit Diffie crisscrossed the nation seeking guidance in his crypto efforts, there hadn't been even a veiled threat against him, and certainly no indication that anyone would sneak up behind him in a Palo Alto coffeehouse and quietly use the end of a doctored umbrella to inject him with some exotic, slow-acting poison. That just wasn't the NSA's style.

A better question would be, "Given that the law might not back up the agency, why bother to fight the movement toward research in crypto?" Surely some of the smarter strategists within the Triple Fence recognized that, in some ways at least, an independent crypto movement would not be so bad for Fort Meade. Who was better positioned to exploit the revolutionary advances in cryptography than the NSA, whose expertise and knowledge of the field was infinitely ahead of anything resembling competition in either the private or public sectors?

This was the dilemma facing Vice Admiral Bobby Inman literally within days after he took his post as director in July 1977. Though he had considerable experience with crypto as the director of naval intelligence—and years before that as a military recipient of signals intelligence—the idea of outsiders making important cryptologic advances was new to him. He had believed, along with most of his peers in the intelligence community, that "the NSA had a monopoly on talent," he now says. "If there were incredibly bright people who wanted to work on cryptographic problems, the odds were high that they either worked inside the NSA, or worked with one of the scientific advisory groups [whose work was classified]." This insurgent revolt hit him like a fighter sucker punched at the instant the bell rang to begin the fight—especially since the furor over Meyer's letter drew articles in the *New York Times* and the *Washington Post*. Inman understood immediately that not only was this a new sort of threat to his agency, but that new, perhaps unprecedented, responses were called for.

Nonetheless, during the first few months of Inman's tenure, the NSA kept acting as if the rules had not changed. In October 1977, an electrical engineering professor at the University of Wisconsin named George Davida applied for a patent for a device that used mathematical techniques to produce stream ciphers. He had produced the plans for this invention without any access to classified information, and his funding from the National Science Foundation had no strings attached to require him to clear his work with any defense agency. The patent itself was filed in the name of the university's Alumni Research Foundation, conforming to a process whereby the university community retains the bulk of any invention profits by Wisconsin professors funded by the NSF. Davida next heard from the government on

April 28, 1978, not with a patent approval but with a piece of paper marked SECRECY ORDER. The National Security Agency had declared his invention classified material.

It was bad enough that the NSA had banned production of his device. Worse was the dilemma in which Davida found himself. The order put a clamp of secrecy not only over his device, but over the intellectual material behind the patent application as well. In effect, the NSA regarded Davida's actual ideas as a sort of poison, a forbidden substance he was banned from circulating. Davida had little guidance as to how he might adhere to the ban, since his materials had already been well distributed. Was he really expected to follow the requirement to report all the people who might have seen his work—in effect, to drag his colleagues into this kafkaesque realm of ideas too dangerous to share? On the other hand, if he refused to comply with the secrecy order, he was subject to a $10,000 fine and two years in the pokey.

Davida was not alone. On that same day in April, the NSA had slapped a secrecy order on the "Phasorphone," a voice-scrambling device created by a team of scientists led by thirty-five-year-old Seattle technician Carl Nicolai. Five months after applying for a patent for an invention that he hoped would make him a fortune, Nicolai was not only prevented from selling his invention, but also from even using it.

In spook parlance, Davida and Nicolai had become "John Does," stripped not only of their work but of the credit due to them. As James Bamford explained in *The Puzzle Palace*, theirs were the relatively rare cases in which objectionable inventions were not independently discovered duplications of devices that already existed behind the Triple Fence but original creations that the government unilaterally regarded as too dangerous to be produced.

But as the NSA was to learn, the days were gone when it could casually apply a secrecy order to the work of an academic or entrepreneur and have the matter closed. Davida and Nicolai went public, organizing well-placed letter-writing campaigns, educating their representatives in Congress, and spilling the story to the press. Davida, in particular, a compact, scrappy man who was disinclined to take the U.S. government at its word, was strident in his own defense. In his case, a quick meeting of university officials led the chancellor to write a furious letter to the NSF, demanding due process. The chancellor also brought the matter before Commerce Secretary Juanita Kreps, who was apparently dismayed at how easily her patent office could become an instrument of censorship. Meanwhile, Davida raged to *Science* magazine that the NSA's actions were a form of academic McCarthyism.

The NSA backed down. On June 13, it rescinded the order. Vice Admiral Inman's later explanation, offered during a House hearing on "The Government's Classification of Private Ideas," was that the Davida decision was a mistake by a middle-level employee.

Several months later, the restrictions on the Nicolai patent were also reversed. Since Inman himself had signed off on *that* secrecy order, he later offered a "heat of battle" excuse to the House subcommittee. "From dealing day to day with the Invention Secrecy Act, you have to make snap decisions," he explained. Overall, he insisted that the problem with those two orders was "not a faulty law but inadequate government attention to its application." Still, that double rebuke made it clear that the NSA no longer had free rein in using the law to keep crypto in government-approved sealed containers.

By then Inman had decided to take his concerns directly to the institutions he was worried about. In what David Kahn called a "soft sell" attempt to quash work in cryptography, he embarked on a tour of research institutions. One memorable session occurred in the faculty club at the UC Berkeley campus, where Inman's attempts at explaining his point of view were met by relentless, hostile questioning. "It was a dialogue of the deaf," he says. Still, some comments made at the session led him to believe that a more productive relationship was possible. In an extraordinary move for an NSA director, he phoned Marty Hellman and asked for a meeting. "I liked him," says Inman of the coinventor of public key crypto and DES's most virulent critic. "I think he was impressed that I had driven down to see him, so his answer [to the request to begin a dialogue on how public crypto should be handled] was a tentative yes."

Inman tried to diffuse the most blatant of the NSA's restrictive acts against researchers, many of whom believed that, more than ever, the NSA was trying to lure them behind the Triple Fence, where their findings could be restricted. One of those who learned this firsthand was Len Adleman, the once-reluctant "A" in the RSA algorithm. For years Adleman had been receiving research funds from the NSF, routinely renewing his grants every three years. In the first proposal he filed after being involved with the RSA algorithm, he included a section outlining some work involving mathematics that might apply to cryptography. After fielding the normal questions on such a proposal—budget questions and the like—Adleman was startled by a phone call from an NSF official informing him there would be additional changes. Specifically, the portion of the work that involved crypto would be funded by the National Security Agency.

"I didn't submit a proposal to the NSA," Adleman told him. "I submitted it to the NSF, right?"

The official conceded that this was so. But, he said, "It's an interagency matter," and ended the conversation.

Adleman was incensed. He understood that there might be legitimate national security concerns about the direction of academic cryptography. (What if someone suddenly released a means to crack an important code?) But this was over the line. It meant that the country's most secretive intelligence agency was influencing the premier scientific funding agency. "In my mind this threatened the whole mission of a university, and its place in society," he says. Adleman decided to go public with his concerns. He called Gina Kolata, the reporter for *Science* who had been covering the conflict, and told her the story.

Not long afterward, Adleman got another call—from Bobby Inman himself. The whole thing, explained the director of the National Security Agency, was a misunderstanding. "He was very nice," recalls Adleman. The researcher wound up getting his entire grant funded by the NSF.

For Inman, such compromises were in the service of eventually reaching some sort of détente with the academics that would satisfy both national security concerns and the researchers' insistence on academic freedom. He believed that, ultimately, he held the trump card—one that would not only force the academics to play ball but also actually stem the potential tide of actual crypto implementations from covering the world. This winning hand lay in the laws known as the International Traffic in Arms Regulation. When Inman first arrived at The Fort, he told Congress at a hearing some years later, "I didn't even know what an ITAR was." But, he added, "my education went at a pretty fast pace."

Specifically, he now says, he came to realize that when it came to controlling crypto late in the twentieth century, "the whole issue is export." Those laws were all that prevented a disastrous free-for-all in the distribution of cryptography—the equivalent of a national security meltdown. Inman recognized that restrictions on what could be shipped overseas, and the threat of prosecution if those laws were broken, would force people to deal with the NSA not only in what they were permitted to export, but in what they produced for domestic use. Those regulations would become the linchpin of the agency's efforts to stop worldwide communications from becoming ciphertext.

Ironically, the NSA's own attempts to control private research about cryptography had set events in motion that threatened to thwart those regulations. The then–White House science advisor was a man named Frank Press. The controversy over public crypto had piqued his interest, and he asked the Justice Department to provide a legal opinion as to whether the ITAR laws violated First Amendment free-speech protections. The job fell to an assistant attorney general named John Harmon, who carefully analyzed the way the regulations were drafted. He discovered that ITAR required a license not only from arms dealers, but also from "virtually any person involved in a presentation or discussion, here or abroad, in which technical data could reach a foreign national." Presentations and discussions? That was the First Amendment turf! On May 11, 1978, the Office of the General Counsel issued its opinion. It was a bombshell:

> It is our view that the existing provisions of the ITAR are unconstitutional insofar as they establish a prior restraint on disclosure of cryptographic ideas and information developed by scientists and mathematicians in the private sector.

Inman was furious at this analysis, and he set about to fight it. He recruited "a brilliant new lawyer that I had persuaded to come work for NSA" to argue against the opinion. One gambit was to claim that a recent legal precedent had rendered the Harmon opinion moot. But a Justice official rebuffed that interpretation. "We do not believe that [the precedent] either resolves the First Amendment issues presented by restrictions of the export of cryptographic ideas or eliminates the need to reexamine the ITAR," wrote deputy assistant attorney general Larry Hammond.

Meanwhile, the NSA was treading a fine line. It was attempting to threaten crypto researchers who circulated their findings and ideas while it was fully aware that the Justice Department had concluded that such threats violated the Constitution.

All of this wrangling was conducted out of the public eye. And none of it seemed to have affected the way that the NSA chose to interpret the export laws. So even though Vice Admiral Inman's sharp young counsel was legally unable to overturn John Harmon's findings, the attack against his opinion was effective. Because by not circulating its judgment in the matter, the Justice Department was effectively colluding with the NSA to ignore the possibility that its enforcement of the ITAR regulations violated the Bill of Rights.

All of this came out in 1980, when the government operations subcommittee of the House of Representatives held hearings on "The Government's Classification of Private Ideas." At one point, the committee staff director, Tim Ingram, posed a pretty good question. "How would I know, as a private litigant somehow ensnarled in the ITAR regulations, that I am being involved in a matter that the Justice Department, two years previously, has declared unconstitutional?" he asked. A Justice official explained that the opinion hadn't been offered for the benefit of such citizens, but simply as advice to the department itself.

This was not acceptable to Ingram. Perhaps thinking of the Rivests and Hellmans who had been threatened with jail for presenting their papers, or the Davidas and Nicolais who had been confronted with secrecy orders, or all the current researchers like Adleman who were now encountering more subtle pressures, Ingram had another question to ask:

> You have this two-year-old opinion finding the regulation unconstitutional. There has been no change in the regulations. Is there any obligation on the department at some point to go to the president and force the issue and to tell the president that one of his executive agencies is currently in violation of the Constitution?

No satisfactory answer was forthcoming. In any case, Bobby Inman was worried about the new movement in cryptography and his limited power to stem it. His worst fear was that public adoption of encryption "would very directly impact on the ability of the NSA to deliver critical information." He became convinced the agency needed a more formal authority to regain the controls over crypto. In his attempt to obtain this, he did something no one in his place had ever done. He went public.

His chosen venue for this debut was *Science* magazine, the most aggressive press watchdog over the past few years. Of course, the very fact that the interview was granted was news in itself. The article quoted F. A. O. Schwarz, who had been chief counsel in the Church investigation, as saying, "I'm flabbergasted. Back when we dealt with the NSA, they considered it dangerous to have even senators questioning them in closed session." But there was news in Inman's message, too—the NSA director was now openly extending his invitation for researchers to engage in "dialogue" with him and his people. "One motive I have in this first public interview," he said, "is to find a way into some thoughtful discussion of what can be done between the two extremes of 'that's classified' and 'that's academic freedom.' " But in almost the next breath, he conceded that if he got his way—and was able to censor academic research that involved national security—his proposed "thoughtful discussion" would probably end in "a debate between the Administration and the academic community" (one in which presumably the pissed-off college professors wouldn't have much of an impact on making the government change its national security policy).

A few weeks later, Inman made an even more extraordinary break with the NSA's tradition of secrecy. He actually delivered a public speech in defense of his agency. True, the venue wasn't exactly hostile—it was the January 1979 gathering of a trade association of electronics manufacturers who dealt largely in defense contracts. Yet the very fact that he was doing it represented a sea change that could provoke vertigo in even a vice admiral like Bobby Inman. He acknowledged this in his very first words: "A public address by an incumbent director of the National Security Agency on a subject relating to the agency's mission," he said, "is an event which—if not of historic proportions—is, at least to my knowledge, unprecedented." In fact, just a few years previous, merely uttering the *name* of the agency would have been unprecedented.

Now Inman was frankly admitting that the world had changed, and not by his choice. He referred wistfully to the days, only now gone, when his people "enjoyed the luxury of relative obscurity," remaining closemouthed about their work to spouses and even office mates . . . the days when NSA "could perform its vital functions without reason for public scrutiny or public dialogue." But now, in what he called "the encounter between the NSA and the rest of the world," a new era had begun, where the NSA's happy life spent "entirely in the shadows" was replaced by an era of "complex tensions" between the government and those wishing to communicate securely. Inman's hope for his talk was to explain the NSA's point of view on those tensions, the better for people to understand why it was, well, necessary to do things his way.

Trust the NSA? *Yes,* said Inman. His people had gotten a bad rap recently, and he wanted to set the record straight. Did his agency cook the specifications for DES, perhaps inserting a trapdoor? *No way.* Did the NSA use export regulations to suppress scholarly work? *Uh-uh.* Exert influence to quash research grants? *Please.* The NSA, he insisted, was anything but "some kind of all-powerful secret influence." In fact, *that was the problem:* while outsiders griped about a mighty spy agency with too much power over cryptography, "My concern," said Bobby Inman, "is that the government has too little."

In a way, Inman had an excellent point; despite being the richest intelligence agency on the planet, the NSA was relatively toothless. But for its first decades of existence, the agency hadn't needed laws of its own. Its advantages included not only the force of law but the fact that sophisticated cryptography was a devilishly specialized field, one that few people attempted to engage in, and even fewer could gain sufficient knowledge in to be a player. It was nearly inconceivable that outsiders, or even small governments, could compete with its fire-breathing computers, its world-class mathematicians, its unparalleled experience, its understanding of crypto history. But then came the Whit Diffies of the world—mathematically knowledgeable, with access to computers, and knowledge gleaned from books like David Kahn's, books that the NSA had failed to suppress. Now there were dozens of them, academics like Ron Rivest and potential entrepreneurs like Carl Nicolai. These outsiders were backed by a cadre of civil libertarians, screeching that crypto breakthroughs could strike a blow to Big Brother. And suddenly, even the weak-hearted attempts of the NSA to stop the tide were being demonized on the front page of the *New York Times*. In Inman's view, the victim was not free speech, but national security.

But Inman's proposed solution—a national sacrifice of free speech to preserve the national security—was doomed. He wanted trust. If he were to get academics to consciously forgo their freedom of speech, he *needed* trust. If trust were currency, though, the NSA's balance would be roughly zero. It had never even bothered to open a bank account! It would take more than historic speeches by a sitting director for the NSA to figure out how to manipulate the increasingly out-of-control beast of nongovernmental crypto.

As far as stopping academic research in cryptography, Inman lost that round. Despite his attempts to get Congress to grant the NSA legal authority to suppress publications, the First Amendment prevailed. Most impressively, the exemption in the ITAR for "technical publications" was clarified to the point that even a Fort Meade apparatchik couldn't call it ambiguous. "Provision has been added," went a 1980 revision of the rules, "to make it clear that the export of technical data does not purport to interfere with the First Amendment rights of individuals."

Bob Inman ultimately did forge a sort of compromise with the research community. At the NSA's request, the American Council on Education organized a Cryptography Study Group to seek common ground. The group, which included both the NSA's general counsel and a host of academics, including critics Marty Hellman and George Davida, held its first meeting in March 1980 to consider Inman's proposal that some sort of statutory review process be imposed on private crypto researchers. The group rejected the idea, citing First Amendment considerations and the NSA's inability to show evidence that such laws were absolutely necessary to defend the nation. The group's alternative solution was a two-year experimental process by which those publishing work with relevance to cryptography could voluntarily submit papers to the NSA for review. If the NSA read the paper and felt that the information would somehow compromise national security, the researcher could consider such warnings and decide for himself whether or not to publish. Meanwhile, the agency would continue to fund the research of professionals willing to follow its rules, while allowing others to pursue funding by the NSF or any other agency.

George Davida issued his own minority report, rejecting even voluntary review. He dismissed the NSA's concerns outright, including its worry that research results might help foes crack our own cryptosystems. "This is not likely," he wrote, "because researchers do not engage in cryptanalysis." His conclusion was "the NSA's effort to control cryptography [is] unnecessary, divisive, wasteful, and chilling. The NSA can perform its mission the old-fashioned way: STAY AHEAD OF OTHERS."

Nonetheless, the policy worked quite well from the point of view of researchers, since this meant that there was a way to deal with the NSA—or ignore it—without having to worry about getting their work deemed a government secret. The two-year trial period of this policy passed peacefully, after which the NSA quietly dropped any pretense of demanding a presubmission of anything produced by an American academic. It faithfully read papers in the field submitted voluntarily, and one of its scientists would occasionally address a question to an author, even pointing out a mistake here and there. It was all done cordially, because the NSA had no authority to go further than that.

As the 1980s began, the first decade in the NSA's existence when it had private competition, no one understood the challenge better than Bobby Inman, whose agency was charged with routinely intercepting foreign communications concerning the Iran hostage crisis and the Russian war in Afghanistan. He was haunted by the idea that one day Fort Meade would not be able to deliver such high-quality intelligence—because cryptosystems conceived and developed in the United States would be put into widespread commercial use. "I began to appreciate the export concern much more strongly," he says. In a world where the basic concepts behind sophisticated encryption were found in public libraries and articles in *Scientific American*, and where a cryptosystem endorsed by the government itself—DES—was turning out to be more popular than the NSA expected, it was more important than ever to stop crypto at the border. The NSA director had it pegged: *the whole issue is export.*

Diffie, Hellman, and the MIT trio might have broken the NSA monopoly, but Inman and his successors were not without their weapons. In a way, the war over crypto was only beginning.

selling crypto

for the next few years, tensions seemed to ease between the government and the newly emerging independent forces in the world of crypto. After Bobby Inman's unsuccessful campaign to censor crypto researchers legislatively, the agency seemed willing to coexist with academics treading on turf it once had owned exclusively. There might have been some wishful thinking in all of this, a sense at the NSA that all of these greenhorn academics were unlikely to turn up anything that might truly threaten The Fort's mission. If the bureaucrats behind the Triple Fence believed that, though, they were in deep denial. The seminal breakthroughs at Stanford and MIT had turned a beacon upon the imaginary crossroads of crypto, where mathematics, computer science, and data security met. In 1971, when Whit Diffie wanted to talk to someone about crypto, he had to travel miles for morsels. A decade later, over a hundred members of the new crypto community were spending days together on a Pacific beach, discussing everything from cutting-edge algorithms to cryptanalysis.

The "Crypto" conferences began in 1981, when a University of California at Santa Barbara electrical engineering professor named Alan Gersho invited about 120 potential attendees to his campus, a sprawling collection of modest structures on a bluff overlooking the ocean. He'd gotten the names from a list Len Adleman had compiled of people who'd shown an interest in nongovernmental cryptography. Gersho had wheedled a grant from the National Science Foundation to stage the event. About one hundred people showed up, including Diffie, Rivest, Merkle, and other newly minted luminaries in Cipher Land. They delivered papers—many of them offering refinements on the new public key schemes like knapsacks and RSA—gave talks, and schmoozed at cafeteria lunches and a barbeque on the beach. Gersho had planned the conclave as a one-time gathering, and despite the excitement, there were no immediate plans for a follow-up. Not long afterward, some European cryptographers held an invitation-only meeting in Germany, but that was also designed to be a stand-alone event.

It was a then-minor player in the Santa Barbara shindig, a mere graduate student, who actually took the lead in making sure that such meetings would be held regularly. His name was David Chaum, and he would not be a minor player in the field for long. Working with no support, he got a copy of Adleman's list of crypto academics and began organizing a return to the beachfront campus. Chaum also felt that the overseas event should be repeated, but under a different group of leaders. He hadn't been invited to the German meeting but had gotten the impression that its organizers were "a little off to the right." So he talked to some European cryptographers about organizing an annual spring "Eurocrypt." Finally, Chaum thought that both yearly shebangs should be under the care of an actual organization of independent cryptographic researchers. He quietly made plans to form such a group. His inspiration was a speech by Martin Luther King Jr. he'd once heard that emphasized the word "organization" as a path to liberation.

Concerned about possible pressure from the NSA to smother his plans in the bassinet, Chaum kept his communications to a minimum. You never know who's listening, especially in a government of snoops. He took care to compartmentalize the information he discussed with people: while he landed Ron Rivest to chair the Santa Barbara conference program, for instance, he didn't share his plans for the crypto society with Rivest. He avoided the telephone, instead arranging face-to-face meetings with those he wanted to reach. He typeset the conference notices himself, and got them printed at the same small Berkeley type shop that produced *Covert Information Bulletin*, a well-known newsletter critical of U.S. intelligence activities.

His efforts paid off: the second conference, Crypto '82, turned out to be even more exciting than the first. Serendipitous events, like the freewheeling "rump session" held toward the end of the week, solidified into traditions. The rump sessions, usually hosted by Diffie, mixed frivolous parodies of mathematics papers with serious, last-minute cryptological developments, but the tone was often raucous and irreverent. One year, speakers were required to speak in a code that replaced certain words with silly alternatives (for instance, instead of "Diffie-Hellman," you had to say "Coke bottle"). Missed cues were greeted with a shower of water. Another year, some foreign visitors took too literally Diffie's announcement that there would be a special session before breakfast the following morning with ninety minutes of Belgian jokes.

One well-anticipated session at Crypto '82 was the presentation of a collection of papers on cryptanalysis, chaired by Whit Diffie. The very inclusion of the topic on the agenda couldn't have pleased the NSA: in its view, any knowledge of codebreaking outside the Triple Fence represented a possible threat to its own codes. Diffie himself had been worried that the session would be a bust. Over the winter he had arranged for the presentations. But one by one, for various reasons, his presenters dropped out. By late spring only one survived—a talk entitled "The Bombe at Bletchley Park," by one of the original World War II codebreakers.

It was Adi Shamir who came to the rescue. Shamir had been studying Ralph Merkle's knapsack scheme for public key cryptography. And now, several weeks before the conference, he thought he had broken it, at least the weaker variation of the system known as the single-iteration knapsack. In the days following his announcement, others figured out a way to use his techniques—which themselves were based on mathematical innovations discovered by Hendrick Lenstra—to launch wider attacks. Diffie's panel would be the ideal time to test these ideas. So by the time the cryptographers met in Santa Barbara that summer, Diffie's program was filled with would-be assaults on knapsacks.

The most interesting one would be Len Adleman's. He not only had come up with a variation on Shamir's ideas, but had also actually programmed the technique on his Apple II personal computer. The cryptographers in Santa Barbara decided to try a little experiment. During the first night of the conference, a gauntlet was tossed to Adleman—an encrypted knapsack message. Could he use his little machine to decode it? (If so, he would presumably collect the $100 reward Merkle had offered some years earlier.) The answer would come a couple of days later, right there in Diffie's session, when Adleman's attack would either bring him new glory—or leave him mortified in front of his crypto contemporaries.

Adleman was scheduled to speak last. "The hour passed," Diffie later recounted. "Various techniques for attacking knapsack systems with different characteristics were heard; and the Apple II sat on the table waiting to reveal the results of its labors." When Adleman came forward to speak, he appeared anything but confident. He said he'd give "the theory first, the public humiliation later." (He subsequently would explain that the humiliation he referred to was not Merkle's but his own, if "the numbers didn't turn out right.") Then he proceeded with a description of his methods. While he talked, Carl Nicolai (the inventor whose crypto device had been temporarily suppressed by an NSA secrecy order in 1978), fiddled with the Apple II, which had been working away for the past few days, using Adleman's formula to crack the encrypted message. Before long, Nicolai began painstakingly copying a screenful of numbers from the Apple's monitor onto an overhead-projector transparency sheet.

Finally, Adleman finished describing *how* his attack worked. It was time to see *whether* it worked. Nicolai gave the transparency to Adleman, who handed it to Adi Shamir. He also gave Shamir the sealed envelope with the numerical message encrypted earlier in the conference. Shamir placed the sheets side by side in the overhead, beaming the results on the screen. They matched precisely.

Diffie would later write that "the public humiliation was not Adleman's—it was the knapsack's." Indeed, this crack was the penultimate blow in what would turn out to be the utter destruction of the groundbreaking, clever, yet ultimately useless Merkle knapsack public key cryptosystem. The coup de grâce was instigated by Merkle himself. Paying the $100 to Adleman had not been particularly traumatic; Merkle had half expected someone to break the single-iteration knapsack scheme, which was the much weaker cousin of the real thing, the multiple-iteration version. In fact, Merkle felt secure enough to cast another challenge. In November of that year, he wrote a letter to *Time* magazine, offering $1000 to the first intrepid cryptanalyst who successfully decoded a multiple-iteration knapsack. Two years later, Merkle had to write a check for a cool grand to a researcher from Sandia National Laboratory named Ernie Brickell, who used a government Cray supercomputer to rip open a 40-iteration knapsack. When later asked what the problem was with the knapsack scheme, Merkle was succinct: "It didn't work."

The significance of the knapsack attacks went far beyond the destruction of Merkle's system. In fact, the moment at which Len Adleman's Apple publicly destroyed a potentially valuable cryptosystem could be seen as a symbolic turning point in the still uneasy balance between the NSA-affiliated crypto spooks and the swelling ranks of outsiders who independently studied the protocols of crypto and routinely published their results. It was now clear that simply by sending scientists to a conference and subscribing to a few journals, a foreign government could get the kind of training in cryptology that was previously limited only to a sanctioned elite. It meant that codebreakers everywhere would be more resourceful. Only months before, government critic George Davida had mocked the NSA's calls for prepublication review by asserting that the agency's biggest worry—that the outsiders would circulate codebreaking methods—was ridiculous. "Researchers do not engage in cryptanalysis," he wrote. But clearly, they did.

Some at the NSA understood the threat that an independent crypto community represented: one of them approached Diffie and glumly observed, "It's not that we haven't seen this territory before, but you are covering it very quickly."

The only thing worse for the NSA would be watching the work of these academic cryptographers put to practical use. If an *industry* could be built on selling cryptography, and masses of people started using coding technologies, then the clear unencrypted signals intercepted by the NSA's listening devices—whether cell phone calls or computer e-mail and files—would change to a dense white noise, a chaotic fugue that the agency's computers might, with some effort, decipher. Or might not.

Could crypto be commercialized? Although the common use of personal computers, and, later, the Internet, demanded a way to protect information and verify who was sending it, the means of getting there was at best a rutted path. The bumps and potholes in that road are best illustrated by the fortunes (or lack of them) of the company founded by Ron Rivest, Adi Shamir, and Len Adleman. As with their landmark algorithm, the firm bore their initials. But while the RSA algorithm quickly reached an enthusiastic audience, the trajectory of their commercial operation initially threatened to resemble a busted missile launch.

In fact, despite the rosy predictions of a crypto Renaissance in the seminal Diffie-Hellman and Rivest-Shamir-Adleman papers, there was little reason in the early 1980s to believe that serious bucks would ever be earned with the technology. Who would get venture capital to manufacture crypto products? How would those products be built into systems so that one could reasonably be assured that a scrambled document could actually be unscrambled by its recipient, or that the person receiving a digital signature would have the wherewithal to verify it? Nobody knew whether actual paying customers would be willing to put up with the difficulties that would come with having their computers crunch huge numbers for encryption and authentication. In fact, nobody knew if a substantial enough set of customers existed who were willing to pay for those things at all. "Some people said our stuff might turn out to be useful, but it wasn't clear whether this would turn out to be successful in a commercial sense," says Rivest.

Still, the universities that had employed the crypto researchers hedged their bets by patenting their public key breakthroughs. In December 1977, MIT filed for its patent on the RSA algorithm. Ironically, the very act of filing for a patent made crypto's widespread adoption potentially less likely. There was a definite Catch-22 aspect to claiming crypto as intellectual property: if algorithms were patented, then they could be used only by those who licensed them from the owners (presumably for a fee). But such tariffs might create a disincentive to universal adoption. If crypto was to be useful on a large scale, it stood to reason that everyone had to be using the same system, a convergence that would come about much more quickly if the system was free. It was a classic example of the Network Effect, a positive feedback loop in which value comes only with ubiquity. If everyone *wasn't* using the same algorithms, then communicating with others in secret would be infinitely more difficult. It would be as if Bob had to worry about what brand of phone Alice used before he could ring her up.

Not that this bothered the institutions that helped subsidize the public key research. While MIT had only the RSA system as its intellectual property, Stanford actually pursued a number of patents, ranging from a general claim for public key crypto to more specific implementations, including the Diffie-Hellman key exchange protocol and Merkle's knapsack scheme.

But the benefits of holding patents would be limited. For one thing, the largest current market for crypto—the government—didn't have to pay to exploit either the Stanford or the MIT work. Both sets of cryptographers had enjoyed the support of the National Science Foundation, and the fruits of such subsidized research were, by law, available without charge, in perpetuity, to any and all federal agencies. And if that weren't enough of a handicap, it turned out that both the Stanford and the RSA patents were valid only in the United States. In the case of both breakthroughs, the researchers had presented their findings before actually applying for the patent, an innocent mistake that didn't affect their patent rights in the States but that did (because of the way patents are treated abroad) disqualify them from such protection in Europe.

Still, once the patent filings were under way, it became clear to Rivest, Shamir, and Adleman that they still had the inside track on exploiting those patents. MIT was known to be generous in licensing its intellectual properties to the people who actually created them. (Any other stance would have risked a faculty revolt.) But the trio faced a unique situation: their crypto scheme had the potential to be a worldwide standard for privacy and commerce, but so far, the only thriving commerce in the field was in the realm of defense contractors and the relatively new market for DES-based products for financial institutions. In any case, none of the three researchers had any business experience. Nonetheless, they decided to forge ahead, hoping to transform their mathematical breakthroughs into something that actual human beings could use to communicate. Their hopes were high, and at least one of them thought that a payoff was around the corner. Len Adleman splurged on a flashy red Toyota. "It cost three or four thousand bucks, a big investment since I was making, like, thirteen thousand a year," he says. "But I thought I would soon have money to throw away."

One of the problems in the late 1970s was that the most common general-purpose computers were too weak to generate good RSA encryption. In order to efficiently perform the calculations required to generate primes for a key and do all the mathematics required in encryption, decryption, and authentication, the MIT professors essentially would have to build a little computer-within-a-computer (on a circuit board loaded with specially designed chips) dedicated to those tasks. Rivest, aided by his colleagues, began working on such a device. After months of work they came up with hardware that could crunch two 50-digit primes in less than a second.

Then reality sank in. There was no way that these relatively expensive circuit boards could become a mass-market product. It was absurd to assume that millions of people would pay several hundred dollars to install a complicated circuit board inside their computers in order to participate in a revolution that they hardly understood.

So in 1981, the MIT trio came up with a more plausible scenario. They would put the RSA algorithm *on a chip*. Semiconductor chips could be mass-produced, and when millions of them were churned out, their costs shrank. You could even put tiny chips on credit-card-sized "smart cards" for people to carry around.

The timing seemed right. Just a few years earlier, when IBM used its vast resources to make history by putting DES on a chip, it had been inconceivable that a few academics could attempt such a feat without a passel of deep-pocketed investors. Back then, such a feat would have been about as unlikely as a few grad students in some random engineering department deciding to launch a rocket to the moon. But in the interim, a Caltech professor named Carver Mead had changed all that. Mead, a veteran of the Silicon Valley semiconductor industry, was the guru of Very Large Scale Integration (VLSI), a technology that shrank what was once a huge computing machine into a thumbnail-size silicon chip. Eager to encourage research in the field, Mead had not only published a book on the subject, but helped set up a fabrication facility—known as a fab—to help academics actually build their own chips. At the time MIT was gearing up its own VLSI program, and Rivest signed up to run an experimental project that would result in getting the entire RSA process on one of those tiny chips.

Meanwhile, they continued what had become an ongoing, if unintentionally comedic, effort to interest a big business mogul—any mogul—in the world of cryptography. As math nerds unschooled in the niceties of venture capital and unsuited for poker-faced negotiations, they were at the mercy of any random suit they hooked up with. But sometimes they lucked out and met someone who actually connected with the religion of it all. One such fellow was Pat Cremen, a loquacious Irishman who worked for the big Ericsson electronics firm. But he, too, was more of a vision seeker than a deal cutter. After examining the MIT crew's algorithms, he broke into rhapsodies about the coming age of electronic wallets and virtual money. Rivest and his colleagues were transfixed by that vision, and probably wound up mentally counting the megabucks that would fill their own digital wallets when this new world came into being. They traveled to Dublin to pursue the idea. While the mutual admiration society was morale building, it turned out to be nothing more than that. Cremen ultimately failed to convince his bosses at Ericsson to put up the bucks.

Maybe the bosses were right. There is a telling anecdote from this period. To implement RSA on a chip, the MIT scientists found themselves on the cutting edge of VLSI chip design. They had to invent their own tools, which potentially became valuable intellectual property in and of themselves, stuff that corporations and foreign spies might covet. For instance, in order to keep track of the hundreds of thousands of logic gates and transistors on the chip design, Rivest wound up writing elaborate chip-simulation software to organize the project. His program made things much easier when negotiating the chaos the scientists were generating on the fifth floor of Tech Square—when they would spread out huge layouts of the chip, parts of which Adleman had designed, parts of which Rivest had modeled, and other pieces that Shamir had created—wondering where *this* wire went or what *that* transistor did. So much easier, in fact, that it began to dawn on the trio that the software they were using to create the chip might have as much commercial or military value as the RSA algorithm itself.

By creating this valuable technical property, they found themselves in the situation in which they imagined their future customers might one day be: possessing secrets worth protecting and in need of a system to protect it. So one night they sat down together and wondered whether they should protect all their precious ideas . . . by *encrypting* them. Did these pioneers of cryptography indeed use their own system to protect their ideas? "I remember our decision was, 'Naaah, it's too much trouble,' " says Adleman. "Too much work to encrypt it. And we never did." The irony was lost on them. But the reality was they were harboring big-time hopes for a technology that even its inventors considered a pain in the ass to use!

They all thought that Rivest's chip-simulation system was a masterpiece. "We didn't just throw this thing together and hope that a hundred thousand things were going to work out," says Adleman. "Ron's software simulated the chip according to Mead's rules." Because the simulation was sound, boasts Adleman, "we knew the chip would work."

But when they tested the actual chip, it *didn't* work. Instead of crunching primes and other stuff, it did nothing. Adleman blames the failure on their overreliance on Carver Mead's publications. "The rules in his book weren't complete," he says. But in fairness to Mead—who in any case wasn't working for the MIT trio—the RSA project was larger than any he had contemplated to date. While other researchers were creating little baby projects like chips that would operate streetlights, the MIT people were using advanced mathematical algorithms, with huge prime numbers and zillions of calculations, to choose keys, encrypt text, decipher scrambled missives, process public keys, and sign messages with digital signatures. So much was going on that the silicon "wires" in the chip were, by standards of microtechnology, extremely long, sort of nano-equivalents of transatlantic cable. This made it all too easy to place those silicon microthreads too close to each other, causing deadly "crosstalk" that would flip bits and ruin the calculations. That's not what you want when performing precision math.

"It had simulated perfectly." Rivest sighs. "But the fabrication process didn't return working chips. It probably just needed some little tweak in the processor design." In other words, though the experiment was a technical failure, Rivest was confident that the system could ultimately work. Still, the failure to produce a working prototype was not a great selling point.

Nonetheless the three scientists persisted. In 1983, they formally joined the world of commerce by creating RSA Data Security, Incorporated (they had originally hoped to call it simply "RSA," but that was the name of a garbage collection company in Maine). There was no product, no customers, and no evidence of demand. And not even their dreams at that point flirted with the possibility that one day hundreds of millions of people would use their new company's technology on a daily basis.

By that point, Len Adleman was getting fed up with the whole process. He felt that he was getting further away from where his talents lay, in theoretical math. All the intellectual effort expended in squeezing formulas into silicon, he thought, might be better spent trying to discover Fermat's last theorem or some similarly epochal challenge. Still, he hung in, hoping that if he and his colleagues could get their new company on a solid commercial footing, they would cash in. Then Adleman, at least, could return to his vocation, gleefully covering white-boards with intricate equations that had no discernable practical application.

As mathematicians, they knew that the principle of Occam's razor applied: the shortest solution to the problem was a straight line. But in this real-world puzzler of making a business succeed, there were endless detours in getting to point B. "We were clueless on this stuff," says Adleman. Their first CEO was the reluctant Adleman himself, a man whose head was clearest when among the clouds. "At various times I was the prime mover; other times it was Ron," he says now. (Adi Shamir, in the process of moving back to Israel to work at the Weizmann Institute, wasn't as active.) Adleman naively figured that he'd handle this moonlighting lark in the spare moments left over from his new post as an associate math professor at the University of Southern California.

They did understand they needed someone with experience to advise them. Somehow, they hooked up with a business consultant named Ted Izen, who was able to concoct one thing that the three brilliant MIT professors collectively had not managed to produce: a business plan. They also looked to Izen to come up with investors—fast.

After months of delay and revision, the government was expected to finally grant MIT the patent for the RSA work. The Stanford patents had already been granted; on April 29, 1980, U.S. Patent 4,200,770, "Cryptographic Apparatus and Method," credited Diffie, Hellman, and Merkle as the inventors of public key cryptography. And on August 19 of that year came another Stanford patent, for the work of Hellman and Merkle. Called "Public Key Cryptographic Apparatus and Method," it specifically dealt with knapsacks but more broadly claimed to cover any implementation of the public key idea.

The impending MIT patent built upon those Stanford patents to cover the RSA algorithm. If the new company was to succeed, it required the exclusive rights to that innovation; otherwise, more established competitors could simply license the RSA work from MIT and blow away the company formed by the actual R, S, and A. Here's where MIT's generosity kicked in. The university agreed to grant Rivest, Adleman, and Shamir the exclusive rights to their invention. For a price—$150,000. (Generosity goes only so far.) Where would these young math professors find that kind of cash?

Izen delivered the answer: a Reno, Nevada, physician and businessman named Jack Kelly. He had a company called Sierra Microsystems in Lake Tahoe that designed chips and which could be a potential business partner for this new company. One day Kelly flew his private plane to Burbank to meet with the RSA trio. For the researchers, the easy part turned out to be convincing him that in an emerging information age, a technology like RSA's was going to be absolutely pivotal. The harder part was forging a deal that the novice entrepreneurs would feel good about in the morning. Adleman later came to view the experience at a philosophical distance. "He was an experienced businessman, and I was an inexperienced businessman," he says. "And when that combination gets together, it is often the case that the inexperienced businessman gets some experience."

Nonetheless, Kelly provided the requisite six-figure sum— $225,000—that RSA Data Security needed to survive. And so, when, in September 1983, MIT was granted U.S. Patent 4,405,829, entitled "Cryptographic Communications System and Method," its inventors were ready. Nine days later the fledgling company paid MIT the $150,000 (plus 5 percent of all its future revenues) for exclusive rights to the patent.

With a real investment and control of its intellectual property, it was time to begin behaving like a business, creating and selling uncrackable cryptographic tools to anyone with a computer. With the remainder of Kelly's investment, they set up an office in Silicon Valley and hired a professional manager to run the company. His name was Ralph Bennett. He had an impressive résumé—he'd worked at respectable companies like Fairchild Semiconductors—and from the point of view of the MIT professors, this fifty-something businessman seemed as good as anyone else around.

With Bennett's help, the company began gathering a workforce, including a sharp young marketer named Bart O'Brien. Even to an academic like Len Adleman, O'Brien, who had worked for a Florida high-tech company called Paradyne, was impressive. He was a slick dresser and an aggressive salesman who dreamed of running his own business. One day Adleman accompanied O'Brien on a sales call and was dazzled at the deft manner with which O'Brien parried the potential customer's objections.

Having deemed the RSA-on-a-chip scheme too complicated, the team's first product was to be a software program mainly used to encrypt e-mail and stored data on personal computers. It would be called Mailsafe, a public key cryptosystem that would run on the most popular business personal computer, the IBM PC, and its clones. Adleman worked on the algorithms and Rivest concentrated on the implementation. Though Adleman did not find the work as intellectually thrilling as pure theory, he was engaged by the challenge of the alchemy of commercial programming, discovering tricks to make the math routines run more efficiently.

Since both professors were working in their spare time, Mailsafe turned out to be a long project. During the development period, of course, RSA Data Security had no revenues. And Kelly's investment was just about dried up. The situation became increasingly desperate. In theory, the company could get income from outside investors or advances paid on licensing deals. But under Ralph Bennett, not much of that was happening. Some of the people involved with the company would later claim that Bennett didn't understand the nature of high-tech start-ups, and he wasn't ideally prepared to evangelize the groundbreaking area of cryptography. In any case, the state of the young enterprise was, to say the least, precarious when Bart O'Brien called upon an old Paradyne friend of his named Jim Bidzos to help out with sales for RSA.

At the time, it seemed like just one more random call. But the entrance of Jim Bidzos not only changed the future of the company, but the technology itself. Crypto had found its first supersalesman. And the repercussions would ripple from Silicon Valley to Fort Meade.

Jim Bidzos was an unlikely savior for public key cryptography. The closest he came to processing algorithms was figuring out backgammon odds in the high-stakes Las Vegas tournaments he liked to frequent. Bidzos was then thirty-one, a Greek national born on February 20, 1955, in a mountainous region near the Albanian border: "A very, very small village in the middle of nowhere, no roads, maybe seventy people," he says. Bidzos's family had been there for ages; his father had taken a bride from a neighboring village in an arranged marriage. Bidzos was the second of four children, born in a small stone house. In the late 1950s, his father left Greece to do what Bidzos calls "the classic immigrant thing: he didn't speak the language, had no training, no education, no skills, but he joined some people from the village who had gone to Ohio." About two years later, when Bidzos was five, he and his mother and siblings followed.

Young Jim Bidzos took to America quickly. While his parents instilled some values from the old country in him, his iconoclastic nature seemed to fit the looser pace of American life. A naturally bright, though not particularly diligent, student, he breezed through school. He describes himself as a rebellious teenager: not necessarily a troublemaker but the kind of kid who made it a point to do precisely what he was told not to do. He wound up in the marines. After his military stint (though not as a U.S. citizen; he held, and still does, a Greek passport), Bidzos attended the University of Maryland. While he majored in business, he did take some courses in computer programming. He claims to have written one of the earliest computer viruses, "just to prove it could be done." After a couple of years at Maryland, he took a job at IBM and never went back to school.

In the early 1980s, he got a visit from a headhunter. Would he be interested in working for Paradyne, a Florida firm that made networking equipment for IBM mainframes? The position was in market-ing, but technical skills were required to explain products to customers. Paradyne was a fairly buttoned-down company, with almost two foot-ball teams' worth of vice presidents who had come over from IBM and had adopted some of the company's uptight culture: the black shoes, the starched white shirts, the feeling that you've screwed the pooch if you're the first one to leave on a given day. But Bidzos had learned how to play the corporate game. Indeed, he thrived at it, racking up a series of promotions. At Paradyne, he also learned how to use an expense account. During vacations he'd blow off steam: his passions included motorcycle racing, high-stakes backgammon, and women. His journals from the seventies are permeated with notations about this woman or that. Still in his late twenties, he was living a Hugh Hefner–esque bachelor existence.

This status was endangered only once, by a young woman he began dating; Bidzos sensed that she might really be the one. The matter was brought to a head by a change in his job situation. Bidzos had been getting bored at Paradyne. The white-shirt culture was making him nuts; he wanted to be in a less structured, more freewheeling environ-ment, with high risks and rewards. To strike out on his own. But when he finally cut the cord at Paradyne and began a global marketing firm with some friends, his girlfriend uttered the words every confirmed bachelor dreaded: it's now or never. She felt that if they didn't marry, this new venture would take him away. Ever the deal maker, Bidzos chafed at being handed an ultimatum. It would be submitting to *her* terms. He would never get married under pressure, even to a woman he loved. So it was over.

His girlfriend had been right about the lifestyle: his new job selling high-tech equipment to international customers and his own services to clients was all-consuming. Almost every month he'd go to Europe or the Far East—some months he'd hit both continents, a global ricochet—staying in the best hotels, dining in the best restaurants, choosing the priciest wines, and doing the deal, always doing the deal. Then he hit a wall. Was this to be his life—on the road all the time, looking for the next client? He began to ponder his lost love affair. He quit the com-pany and began working on freelance marketing projects. If he needed a few bucks, something would come up. He was bored with Florida by this time and wanted to move to California. A firm for whom he'd sold

IBM-compatible computer terminals offered him a job that would take him west, but he wasn't interested. The president of the small company came back with a counteroffer. "I know you want to come here," he said, "and I know you like my receptionist, so if you come and work for me two days a week, I'll pay for the move—just give me six months."

The guy had pegged Bidzos right—he *did* like the receptionist—so he was in California by August 1985. Then he got in touch with his friend Bart O'Brien at RSA Data Security.

O'Brien had mentioned RSA to Bidzos back in May, had even Fed-Exed him a business plan. But Bidzos, who'd been about to leave on a five-week trip to Europe, couldn't make any sense of it. He'd forgotten about it in the excitement of his travels. When he returned to his Florida apartment there were a few more envelopes waiting for him, all of which contained new and different RSA business plans, which apparently reversed course quicker than a backgammon game. Obviously, this strange new company was a work in progress.

But O'Brien kept pushing. He invited Bidzos to stop in San Francisco on his way back from a trip to the Far East. Bidzos had barely arrived when O'Brien immediately embarked on a business trip of his own, leaving Bidzos with the keys to his apartment and car and a mandate to stay for a week and have some fun. Naturally, Bidzos took to Baghdad by the Bay, and began to make frequent return visits. O'Brien used these opportunities to ask for advice on RSA's revolving business plans, and to solicit ideas on raising money. "You should come here to work," O'Brien kept saying.

Bidzos wasn't quite ready for that, but he began to spend more time doing freelance projects for RSA, writing up a marketing plan and studying the possibilities of selling the entire system to IBM. The more he learned about the company's mysterious product, the more intrigued he got. Despite being a motorcycle-racing, woman-chasing, wine-quaffing, high-risk gambler, Bidzos also had an intellectual streak, and he got a huge kick out of hanging out with the engineers, and particularly the cryptographers.

One amazing night in late 1985, he met the most brilliant guy of all: Whit Diffie. Bidzos joined a group of RSA people treating Diffie to dinner at a Mexican restaurant at the Stanford Mall. The company had long been urging the public key inventor to become its chief scientist (at one point Diffie had even accepted, but wound up holding off until the company got more funding). The group included O'Brien, Ralph Bennett, and Al Alcorn, who'd been a key figure in the early days of Atari and Apple; RSA had been wooing him to join the company as well. Bidzos was dazzled at the conversational interplay between the brainy Alcorn and the enigmatic Diffie. After some cursory discussion about RSA's future, the two minds just sort of hooked up and Bidzos grooved on the conversation like an uptown hipster wanna-be who'd sneaked into a secret jam session between Miles and Trane.

As the group broke up, Bidzos asked Diffie if he might be available for lunch sometime to talk more. "I'm always available for lunch," said Diffie. Over the next few months—years, really—Bidzos would take Diffie out for meals in Palo Alto and Berkeley for what was essentially a roaming tutorial in cryptography, public key, privacy, and politics. He eventually became quite knowledgeable on crypto's fine points. On the other hand, Ralph Bennett—at least as far as Bidzos could tell—didn't seem to be as charmed by Diffie. And vice versa. Bidzos recalls one lunch with the three of them at which Diffie began eyeing Bennett's ham-and-cheese croissant sandwich. The stare was so intense that Bidzos was sure that Diffie was about to lunge at the food. Bennett must have noticed, too, because he offered Diffie a piece. Diffie declined, but kept staring at it. Suddenly, the long-haired, bearded cryptographer pulled out a large knife he'd been carrying, pulled the plate toward him, and whacked off half the sandwich. Then he calmly ate it. God knows what Bennett thought about that. But it obviously wasn't a bonding moment.

Bidzos soon realized that this little company trying to sell a crazy product to scramble computer data was in huge trouble. They had yet to ship a product or even license an algorithm. Operating expenses were murderous. The rent alone was a huge burden. O'Brien, ever the optimist, had rented the company a huge space in Redwood City near the Bay, just across from Oracle. It was the size of a soccer field, even though layoffs had left fewer than five employees.

There was another potential land mine waiting to explode. It involved a loan from an investment banking operation run by two guys in New York. One was an Italian named Vinnie, who spoke with a profusion of *disses* and *dats*. His associate was a more soft-spoken Jewish fellow named Steve. They liked to hold meetings at Kaplan's Deli in New York City. Though everything was on the up-and-up with these two, they still seemed like escapees from an Elmore Leonard novel.

Drawing upon a list of about fifty investors (including, Bidzos says, dozens of New York doctors, dentists, and the comedian David Brenner), they had loaned RSA half a million dollars in December 1985. But RSA Data Security went through the money like a sugar-toothed eight-year-old gobbling Halloween candy. The $500,000 had barely been counted before it was almost gone, drained by accrued salaries, debt, and a bridge loan to cover operating expenses. The company was going bust.

If that wasn't enough to worry about, Bidzos then learned that Ralph Bennett, a Scientologist, had indicated that he might transfer his own considerable shares in the company to that organization. This would have made the Church of Scientology one of the biggest shareholders in the company—and the keeper of modern cryptography.

Oddly, one thing that was *not* considered a problem at the time was the possibility that RSA, by launching a new and powerful form of cryptography into the growing ether of computer communications, might alienate the National Security Agency, or provoke a response from law enforcement agencies that felt threatened by the advent of cryptography. "Bart and Ralph understood the NSA had an interest in this sort of thing," says Bidzos. "But they saw the agency as a potential customer." As far as the visible lack of interest from the NSA itself—no queries or threats had emerged from behind the Triple Fence—Bidzos came to believe (correctly, as it turned out) that the spooks had figured that the smartest course of action would be to leave RSA alone . . . because the company almost certainly was falling apart on its own.

"Bart was just lost and didn't know what was happening," says Bidzos. "He's an optimist and a very enthusiastic fellow, and he was going to do a $10 million deal with every computer company in the world. But there were no prospects of making money anywhere." Even so, drawn by the big-idea-ness of it all, Bidzos found himself more and more interested. In mid-January 1986, he agreed to accompany O'Brien to Boston to brainstorm with Rivest about the company's problems. They flew on People Express, a discount airline with all the frills of a Greyhound Bus route on the Texas plains. The night before the meeting he and O'Brien went over the numbers, which looked bleaker than ever. It appeared that the flag bearer for public key cryptography might die without ever even raising the damn flag. Some revolution.

In Rivest's office the next day, Bidzos laid out the whole mess, scrawling the specifics on his blackboard. At first Rivest's attitude was . . . professorial. After hearing the bad news, he sighed and said, "Oh, gee, I'd really hoped it would do well." Bidzos tried to tell him that he simply wasn't getting it. RSA's failure wasn't analogous to not winning some academic honor. There were *consequences*. When you take money from people, there's a different kind of accountability. They all could be sued. Finally, as Rivest began to get the picture, he began to flip out.

Then they got Adleman on the phone in Southern California. After hearing how dire the circumstances were, the mathematician once again realized why it was so much more pleasant dealing with theoretical problems in number space. So he decided to make his involvement theoretical. "I resign from the board of directors," he said, and hung up.

Years later, Adleman was philosophical about his role. "A large part of why the company wasn't working was me," he said. "In the beginning, RSA was a nonentity; it existed on paper but didn't really exist. Somebody had to pick up the ball, and there was good news and bad news in my picking it up. If I hadn't, the technology would have been picked up by someone else, and the patents would have gone to someone else. But while I gave birth to RSA to a certain extent, I didn't do a good enough job to get a baby out that didn't have some serious defects."

After O'Brien and Bidzos returned to California, they hired a management consultant who worked with them to try to find a way through the mess. As the meetings progressed, the consultant commented that Bidzos's ideas seemed both inventive and practical. A crazy idea crossed Bidzos's mind: maybe *he* should be running things.

Even now, Bidzos cannot come up with a coherent sense of the reasoning that led him to join the endangered company full time as the instrument of its salvation. Indeed, in the months to come, trying to unravel the ongoing crisis late at night before the computer screen, he would often ask himself: *Am I really here? I could be in a first-class cabin, flying to Paris to drink bordeaux at the Tour d'Argent with sweet Dominique!* Yes, there was the opportunity to finally run a business. Yes, there was the excitement of a new technology. And yes, there was the lure of San Francisco with its women, its restaurants, its hot-tub parties in Tiburon. But it still really didn't make sense. Though he went through the motions of figuring out how he might personally avoid the consequences if everything wound up in a horrid thicket of lawsuits and recriminations, deep down, he understood that he was involving himself in a potential train wreck.

For a while, he maintained to himself that his role was only temporary—he would help the company secure some funding, hire a new leader, and eventually collect some stock for his labors. Then he'd be on his way. But by the end of March, everybody else on the payroll had left or been cleared out. (Bennett technically didn't leave until mid-August, after some tough negotiations that led to a buyout and, incidentally, the end of a possible relationship between RSA and the Church of Scientology.) It was Good Friday, but Bidzos called it Black Friday. He went out to dinner that night with Rivest and Bennett, and officially took the title of vice president of sales and marketing. Later on, he realized that since he was the only official there, he might as well call himself the president.

His chief concern was the financial crisis. Some bills simply could not be paid. And, of course, no money was coming in. He called debtors and negotiated. "You call a law firm and tell them the company's winding down—we owe you $175,000 and we've got $10,000 to give you," says Bidzos. *And they'd settle for the cash!* Meanwhile, he set off to keep Vinnie and Steve happy. Fortunately, he had a good relationship with them. One day at Kaplan's Deli, Bidzos was signing the credit-card bill for the meal, and he mistakenly underpaid, writing a three instead of an eight. The waitress went ballistic, calling him a cheater. Bidzos was mortified. But Vinnie and Steve beamed. "We *like* that," they joked.

Affection aside, Vinnie and Steve had to think of their investors, and a lawsuit against RSA was still a possibility. They decided to get the opinion of a respected outsider, a guy whom they called "the Wizard of Wall Street." He was a no-nonsense cigar smoker who cut to the chase when Bidzos was brought to meet him. "What's the story?"

he asked. Bidzos drew on his own cigar and launched into a spiel about the brilliant young MIT geniuses who figured out a way to secure computer data and enable commerce in the next century. The wizard was impressed, and Vinnie and Steve decided to keep the faith.

The process that would truly save RSA, however, would be convincing large companies that they needed crypto, and then selling them the technology. While the encryption software program Mailsafe was getting closer to a finished version (it would finally ship in July), the current business plan assumed that it would not be software sales but licensing fees that brought in the bulk of RSA's revenues. Before leaving the company, Bart O'Brien had compiled a list of about thirty potential large customers, and Bidzos went through it. Discussions with AT&T, which O'Brien had figured for a $10 million contract, had stalled. Bidzos kept taking meetings, seeing executives at IBM, DEC, and Xerox. But that first major contract seemed frustratingly elusive, a siren just out of reach. If RSA didn't rope in a big score, all of Bidzos's efforts would be wasted. The debts would be due, and the lawsuits would follow. Then the MIT patent, the crown jewel of the company, would be auctioned off for peanuts. He needed money *now.* But who would buy first? Would *anyone* bite?

One potential savior stood out—a small software company called Iris Associates that was funded by the spreadsheet giant Lotus Development Corp. Iris's product, called Notes, was the first example of a new software category called groupware, a program meant to be used by dozens or even thousands of people over a network. Notes was an ideal candidate for a built-in encryption system since it assumed that users would electronically exchange virtually all their messages, even ones involving the most confidential corporate secrets. Without a means of securing that information against eavesdroppers, Lotus's potential customers—major corporations whose data were worth zillions— would be unlikely to purchase Notes.

No one understood this better than the inventor of Notes. Ray Ozzie was one of those double-threat computer geniuses who not only could code their way out of a trunk loaded with rocks dropped into the middle of the ocean, but were equally visionary in the analog world, with an instinctive sense of the marketplace. He began his career at Data General, the minicomputer company, but when he saw the IBM

PC microcomputer he realized that the future lay in these personal devices. So he moved to what was then one of the biggest PC software companies, Software Arts, creator of the original spreadsheet, Visi-Calc. But in his head Ozzie was thinking about what could happen when all these personal computers got networked together. He felt that IBM itself would eventually get into the business of writing software for that world, but in the meantime there was a total vacuum— one that he hoped to fill with a program of his own design. That was Notes, and he founded Iris Associates to produce the program. But he spent much of 1982 unsuccessfully seeking start-up funding.

In early 1983, he set out to pitch his vision to Mitch Kapor, the founder of Lotus, which had recently released a spreadsheet called 1-2-3 that immediately supplanted VisiCalc as the industry gold standard. Kapor's main concern was finding a master software wizard to write Symphony, a multifunction program for Lotus, one that melded a spreadsheet, word processor, and database. So they made an agreement: if Ozzie would create Symphony for him, Kapor would fund Iris Associates to create Notes, and Lotus would distribute it. On the day Symphony shipped, in 1984, Kapor said, "Okay, Ray, do your thing."

Ozzie knew early on that security would be a key feature in Notes, and he looked forward to developing a technology to frustrate snoops and crooks. As a kid, he'd loved the TV show *The Man from U.N.C.L.E.* and played secret agent with his friends. That took a backseat to electronics and, eventually, computer science, but he'd gotten excited when he read Martin Gardner's article about RSA in 1977. So he suspected that his product might benefit from a public key cryptosystem. Coincidentally, in early 1984, not long before he finished Symphony, he came across an article in *Dr. Dobb's Journal* (a sort of programming guide for granola-chomping hackers) with a FOR-TRAN source code for encrypting with RSA. "It was so cool," he recalls.

In 1984, though, the appearance of an early implementation of RSA in a computer hobbyist magazine was a symbol of public key's status: although the advance had made a lot of noise in the academic community, no one had seriously considered using it in a software product. But Notes *needed* something like it. In a memo Ozzie wrote about security issues, he identified the problem that his groupware product faced, both in protecting privacy and establishing authenticity:

Mitch Kapor wants to send mail to Jim Manzi [Lotus's second-in-command] about some (perhaps sensitive) subject. Mitch sends it to Jim. First, although this mail SAYS that it is from Mitch, has some hacker on the network "faked" the message and put it into Jim's mailbox? How can he be sure that this mail is really from Mitch? Second, he realized that this message passed through several intermediate machines; did anyone "take a peek" at the message as it was on its way to Jim?

Ozzie continued to describe the way a traditional computer security system would deal with the problem, that is, via a central authority that delivered passwords off-line, and became, essentially, a mandatory hub through which all traffic passed. This model was not only vulnerable in exactly the way that had made Whit Diffie so dissatisfied in the late 1960s—if the central authority screwed up, turned crooked, or turned you in, the whole system failed—but its very spirit was locked into an age that was destined for the junk heap. That system was synced with the mainframe model of computing, where some huge hulking circuit-laden beast did all the crunching, flipping computations to dozens or hundreds of users like some giant robotic blackjack dealer. Ozzie saw Notes not only as a pioneering product but also as a seminal example of the networked future, where the masses would have their *own* computers and not have to check in with some massive digital Big Brother. Like the phone system, communications would be one-to-one, people communicating directly with their peers (as opposed to some now-antiquated models where communications were funneled through a central authority). "We believe that this is a bad approach," wrote Ozzie of the central-authority model. "It changes the distributed nature of the network back into the old 'centralized data' approach of mainframes. . . . It also resurrects the problems with the 'traditional solution,' that is, trust in people and/or mechanisms that are not completely understood."

The way to deliver security in the far-preferable decentralized manner was, of course, via public key. Diffie and Hellman's landmark paper seemed almost to have Notes in mind when it outlined how Ozzie's problems could be addressed. Through use of a "global phone book," everybody in the organization would have access to everybody else's public key. Public key provided a way that Notes users could not only send messages in complete privacy but could also make sure that the message wasn't forged:

> Consider the aforementioned scenario where Mitch sends a message to Jim. . . . Mitch writes a memo. In Notes, it invokes a menu item called "Sign Message." Notes uses Mitch's private key and the message itself to attach to the original message a "Signature," a code that uniquely identifies both Mitch and the actual contents of the message. Once the message is signed, Mitch invokes the "Send Message" menu item. The message then leaves Mitch's PC, goes across the network, and ends up in Jim's PC. Jim, receiving the message, reads it and wonders if Mitch really sent him this message. He invokes a menu item called "Verify Message" (this, of course, could have been done automatically). Notes now looks at the directory of users to find Mitch's Public Key. Once found, Notes uses the message's attached "Signature" and Mitch's Public Key to do the verification. When Notes says "OK," it is indicating that the message was indeed sent by Mitch and the message is in its original form and has not been modified between Mitch and Jim.

Ozzie concluded that the only viable implementation of public key crypto was RSA. He needed a heavy-duty system. While the *Dr. Dobb's* program was a fun hack, it was many magnitudes too slow to be used in a commercial program, let alone to be used to encrypt large messages. When Ozzie and his team got serious about encryption, they decided to go with a more sophisticated use of RSA: a hybrid system, using the public key method as a way for users securely to create symmetrical keys, which would be used to encrypt messages in a conventional cryptosystem. They figured the proper combo was RSA as a key-exchange algorithm and DES to actually scramble the message content.

Around that time, Mitch Kapor got an unsolicited letter from Ron Rivest. *I don't know if you have any need for this,* the letter went, *but there's this useful algorithm called RSA, and we have the exclusive rights. . . .*

"Do you know what this is?" Kapor asked Ozzie.

"Oh, shit," said Ozzie. "RSA is subject to *licensing*?"

A meeting was arranged. On April 29, 1985, Bart O'Brien and Ron Rivest came to Iris. It was by far the most promising sales call in RSA company history. When O'Brien launched into his standard song and dance about the wonders of their system, Ozzie cut him off—the Iris people were *already* sold on the virtues of RSA. Discussion immediately switched to how the companies might work together. Ozzie was particularly excited at the prospect of having Rivest himself available for consultation: "Who can better verify an algorithm than its inventor?" he wrote in a memo.

The main sticking point turned out to be money. When it came time to give actual figures, O'Brien, offering what he called "a first-guess estimate," asked for the moon: $100 a unit for the first 15,000 customers (or "seats") with a sliding downward scale that stopped at $50 a seat after the 100,000th user. Ozzie told them those estimates were "tremendously out of line with reality." After all, the wholesale price of the entire software package was to be only a couple of hundred dollars. Ozzie promised, though, that he'd discuss pricing with Lotus, which would ultimately be paying the licensing fees. But he knew that there was no way Lotus would ever pay that kind of money.

Sometime during the discussion Bart O'Brien mentioned that Ozzie might want to check out whether including encryption in its product might affect overseas sales. Ozzie admitted that he'd never given any thought to the issue. Rivest and O'Brien suggested that he make contact with the National Security Agency on this, but first Iris or Lotus—whichever was going to export the product—should figure out a government strategy. "These are not people you want to deal with casually," they told Ozzie. "You want to understand the endgame." When the meeting was over, Ozzie quickly realized that no matter what system Notes used, this might be an issue, and in his memo he requested that Lotus's lawyers look into how the export regulations might affect the product.

The meeting ended amicably, but the sticking point remained: RSA's outrageous asking price. On the other hand, the public key algorithms were perfect for Notes. "We knew technologically what we wanted—we'd already prototyped it," says Ozzie. "I wasn't going to put all my cards on the table at the first negotiation, but they could tell we were clearly excited." But for a while it remained a stalemate. RSA regarded Lotus as one of many potential big scores, and Ozzie began what he saw as a sales job to Lotus, trying to get them to shell out for a reasonable license fee.

By the time Jim Bidzos joined the talks, almost a year had passed since the initial contact between RSA and Ozzie, with little progress made. In fact, after making some tentative inquiries with the government, the Notes people had reason to second-guess the whole idea of licensing crypto: they'd been given hints that the National Security Agency would be less than pleased at the prospect of a major software product with technology to scramble information that the supercomputers behind the Triple Fence could not easily read. But as soon as RSA's new leader came in—this fast-talking thirty-one-year-old Greek who was obviously not a hacker, not from the Silicon Valley culture at all—the Iris guys knew that negotiations had reached a new phase.

Bidzos jacked up the urgency quotient instantly. He clearly wanted to cut a deal and wasn't afraid to take the conversation in an adversarial direction. He emphatically reminded Lotus that RSA had the technology Notes needed, technology unattainable elsewhere. Without crypto, big corporations that wanted their communications protected would never use Notes. As far as he was concerned, Jim Bidzos had Ray Ozzie by the balls, and made sure he knew it. This aggressiveness unnerved Ozzie and his colleagues. Bidzos's come-on was so intense that for weeks the speculation at Iris and Lotus was whether this pushy Greek was actually some sort of intelligence agent who'd been planted at RSA to *control* crypto. Still, Bidzos's appearance broke the stalemate. He could switch from an iron glove to a velvet one. He reassured the Iris people that RSA—meaning Ron Rivest and some moonlighting MIT colleagues—could actually help to build the RSA algorithm into the product. And his financial demands were nowhere near the fantasy figures that Bart O'Brien had demanded earlier. In fact, one of his chief criticisms of his predecessors was their ridiculous financial demands.

Meanwhile, Ozzie had convinced Lotus CEO Mitch Kapor that

public key technology was essential to Notes and it was time to come in with a solid offer. Lotus dangled before the troubled crypto company something it needed desperately: a cash advance against royalties. The figure was $200,000, but Lotus wouldn't pay all of that until the development work was done. Upon signing, however, Bidzos would get a check for $50,000. At that point, $50,000 represented the difference between life and death for RSA Data Security.

The contracts were drawn that summer, to be executed in October, when Bidzos would go to Lotus's new headquarters on the Charles River in Cambridge, and he and Mitch Kapor would both sign the contract. But when the RSA contingent arrived that day they sensed a profound disarray at Lotus. Sitting in the waiting room, Bidzos reached for a copy of the *Wall Street Journal*. On the front page was one of its trademark ink-pen portraits—of Mitch Kapor. It accompanied a story that said that Kapor was resigning from Lotus to pursue those ever-compelling personal goals. Essentially, the former transcendental meditation teacher had grown intolerant of the business world's soul-battering minutiae, and he was following his muse out the door.

Before Bidzos had a chance to assess the impact of this on the still-unsigned contract, a receptionist summoned him upstairs. Kapor was there, his muse apparently still loitering in the building. "I don't work here anymore," he said. "But Ed Belove will take care of you." Belove, a vice-president who had worked on the deal, had the authority to sign the contract, and he did.

With that money, RSA was able not only to keep its doors open, but also to start distributing Mailsafe. Who was the audience for such a personal computer–based cryptography product? The RSA people really didn't have an idea. The mainstream of the American public didn't consider encrypting e-mail a pressing concern. On the other hand, there was a vast number of career paranoids who found the product immediately attractive.

One particular caller seemed to embody this arcane demographic. Around the time Mailsafe shipped, calls started coming in to RSA that began with heavy breathing. Then an anxious voice would burst out, *How big are the keys that come with Mailsafe?* And they'd tell him, "One hundred forty digits." Then, *puff puff,* he'd ask, *How hard is that to break?* and they'd say it would take a supercomputer a trillion years to find the key. *Can I set bigger keys?* he'd ask, *pant pant,* and they'd tell him yes and then hear heavy, almost frenzied wheezing on the line. *Can the government break that?* Uh-uh. *Can the NSA break that?* The next day, he'd call back, asking essentially the same questions. He became known at RSA as the Obscene Crypto Caller. "He obviously thought we were some huge company that wouldn't know it was the same guy calling," says Bidzos. "In fact, we'd all huddle around and listen to him when he called."

Would RSA sell its product to the Obscene Crypto Caller? Yes, it would. Just as the NSA had feared, here was a company that would sell to *anybody.* And as long as RSA didn't send it across the borders of the United States, the company was perfectly within its rights to do so. It wouldn't ask why people wanted to use it: that was nobody's business but the buyer's. It would even ship to post office boxes.

Sometimes Bidzos himself would talk to customers when they called. One fellow in Pittsburgh quizzed him at length on the strength of the product, particularly on whether the government was able to break it. Bidzos asked him why he wanted Mailsafe. It turned out the guy sold surveillance countermeasures, like equipment that swept rooms for electronic monitoring bugs. Bidzos immediately realized that he had something in common with the man: both of them dealt in tools that were regulated by a government with a high stake in restricting the most powerful technology in the field. The conversation would also get Bidzos wondering whether *he* was being bugged.

But Mailsafe was a sideshow; Bidzos realized that RSA's revenue stream would mainly be the big companies that licensed the RSA toolkit and built encryption directly into their own products. After the hurdle of the first big deal with Lotus was cleared, a number of large customers—including some of the most influential in the land—fell into line over the next few months. First came Motorola, which wanted public key technology for secure telephones. Then came Digital Equipment Corporation and Novell, both companies that required a means to secure computer networks.

All of these deals were closed by RSA's supersalesman Jim Bidzos. When negotiating with potential licensees, he had the ultimate weapon: the patents for the technology. Before naming a price, he would speak at length about the nature of encryption and authentication, drawing deeply on his informal tutorials from Diffie, Rivest, Adleman, and

Shamir. By then, Diffie had decided not to work for RSA formally—
"I've never had a start-up personality; I've never been able to work on
anything but what I was interested in at the moment," he later
explained. The company instead needed people like Rivest, who could
focus his attention and write thousands of lines of product code in a
few weeks.

Bidzos had himself become quite an explicator of the crypto revolution. He understood completely how what would later be called the
Network Effect was absolutely crucial when it came to public key
cryptography: its value increased exponentially by the degree to which
it spread throughout the population. For that reason, he almost always
insisted that RSA be built into the basic product, so buyers would get
crypto without specifically having to ask for it.

Only when Bidzos finished his rap would he get into the terms of
the deal. The kind of arrangements he liked the best were those that
involved getting encryption into the hands of thousands, maybe even
hundreds of thousands, of users. With a customer base that size, RSA
would demand only a few dollars per seat. A dream began to form: a
world where everybody could, and did, communicate with the privacy
that encryption provided; a world where people could not only swap
mail but sign contracts and pay bills with all the safeguards available
in the physical world. And RSA would get a piece of all that. It was the
ultimate salesman's dream. But it was also the NSA's nightmare.

For a crucial period in the mid-1980s, however, Bidzos heard little
from the government. He says that there were occasional rumors that
some officials were quietly urging some sort of action against RSA,
action that might have been devastating to the fragile young company. "Buy them, threaten them, do something—just stop them," he'd
heard they were saying. "There are a million ways to do it." But nobody
did. So, his theory went, the government simply sat back and waited
for RSA to self-destruct.

The government skeptics underestimated Jim Bidzos. By the end
of the summer of 1986, he had transformed the company and won the
trust, if not the total enthusiasm, of all three of the firm's namesakes.
Ron Rivest had become a good friend, and was the most committed
of the trio. He saw Len Adleman in Berkeley, who was amiable but
somewhat reserved—though still a shareholder, he'd apparently had
enough of the business life. Then in August Bidzos met Adi Shamir,

who had moved back to Israel but was in the Bay Area before heading to Santa Barbara for the annual Crypto conclave. Bidzos spent the day with him. He found Shamir very bright and very intense, and the businessman took pains to solicit ideas from the cryptographer—who was, after all, also a shareholder—on RSA's various opportunities for success.

Relations were not as good, though, with Marty Hellman. In the 1980s, Diffie's coinventor of public key had tried to go into business himself selling crypto solutions under the name Hellman Associates. But the venture never took off, perhaps because much of his energy in the eighties was devoted to intense involvement in an antinuclear group called Beyond War. "The importance of cryptography couldn't compare to the importance of the danger to human survival, and so I worked on the issue of making sure the human race survived," he later explained. Still, now he seemed upset, even hurt, that this company based in part on his ideas was finally beginning to make it, particularly since he disagreed with parts of RSA Data Security's approach to public key. Bidzos says he tried to bring Hellman in, and arranged a sort of reconciliation with all the other public key creators in a dorm room at Crypto '86 that August. Hellman, Bidzos recalls, was emotional as he voiced his complaints. But nothing came of the meeting, and for years there was a chill between Hellman and the others. Bidzos says he later offered Hellman stock in the company, *begged* him to take it—he'd already given shares to Diffie. But Hellman refused, claiming that he wasn't a stock guy. (He did accept a stipend to become a "distinguished associate.")

Had he taken the stock, he would have eventually cleared well over a million dollars, as Diffie did. This was in contrast to the pitifully low sum paid to them by Stanford, which held the actual patents for their breakthroughs—Diffie's own share came to only about $10,000.

In any case, RSA Data Security, Inc., was beginning to take off. But now it was triggering the NSA's radar. And the first to notice were RSA's customers.

patents and keys

To Ray Ozzie the whole thing was a no-brainer. He was creating a product by which people exchanged information that they might want to protect. Including encryption in the product was simply a means of providing them that protection. It was simple business. It was common sense. But now that Lotus was actually preparing to include RSA as an essential component of Notes, he found himself waist deep in a thicket of red tape concerning its export—almost as if he were a virtual enemy of the state. To his horror, he discovered that as far as the export rules were concerned, even a strictly commercial program that helps people run their businesses is considered a weapon. Not a handgun or a stiletto, either, but a weapon of mass destruction, like a Stinger missile or a nuclear bomb trigger.

Ozzie could have simply avoided the whole mess by not exporting his product. On a practical level, though, limiting sales to America was unthinkable. It would mean cutting potential revenues at least in half. Software for personal computers was a global market, particularly when it came to big corporations that were the prime consumers of Notes. But such a market hadn't existed when the export regulations were created. When Ozzie and the Lotus lawyers did their research, they found that crypto export licenses were generally issued only when the exporter (typically some company with ties to the military establishment) was able to identify and vouch for the friendliness and trustworthiness of the final users. The process was called an "end-user certification." But Notes was a mass-market product, sold shrink-wrapped like a cassette tape. The users would be . . . just plain people. To their dismay, the Lotus lawyers were unable to find any previous case where a crypto export license had been issued in those circumstances.

To wend one's way through the political, technical, and spookified minefield of these regulations and restrictions, you needed a white-shoed D.C. lawyer-minesweeper, so Lotus went out and got one. His name was Dave Wormser. His first piece of advice was to go directly to what would be the source of all objections: the NSA. The law didn't require this—the specified avenue was the State Department—but Wormser knew that even filling out an application would be a waste of time unless they knew what the minds behind the Triple Fence might find troublesome in the product.

So, in mid-1986, not long after inking the deal with RSA, Ray Ozzie went to Fort Meade, Maryland, to see what he was up against. He was accompanied by Wormser and Alan Eldridge, the Iris engineer who was in charge of the security components in Notes. Ozzie was thirty years old at the time, just a bit too young to have been swept up in the sixties rebellion but still old enough to have a skeptical attitude toward the military. As a heads-down engineer and product developer, though, he had little idea of what he had stumbled into.

Ray Ozzie, of course, knew nothing about the similar journey made over a decade earlier by Walt Tuchman of IBM. Tuchman, too, had been an outsider with a plan that would extend the powers of crypto beyond the area that The Fort had cordoned off for itself. The NSA, confident that a company like IBM would never defy a request made in the name of national security, had originally felt it had risen to that challenge, but in the years after the approval of the Data Encryption Standard, it had become clear that the problem had not gone away. As crypto edged its way more and more into the public sector—and DES became more and more common within U.S. borders—certain forces within the NSA now saw the approval of DES, despite IBM's extraordinary concessions, as a horrible mistake. Who knew that everybody from middle managers to grandmas were going to be using computers strong enough to do industrial-strength encryption? To some in the agency, the arrival of the Lotus team was probably the strongest indication yet that crypto was already leaching out into the mainstream. To those NSA people, Ray Ozzie's visit meant that the crypto barbarians were indeed at the gate.

Fort Meade, with its fences, its guardhouse, the long hallway with pictures of obscure generals, the generic meeting room you're ushered into with furniture that looked like it had been there since the McCarthy era, was pretty intimidating. It made Ray Ozzie think, *These people are obviously in control and they know it.*

The meeting began when several NSA officials came in. One of them, apparently the case officer on this matter, began questioning the trio. (This particular functionary—Ozzie is loath to disclose his name—wound up following the progress of Notes for more than ten years.) What was the product? When would it be ready? What sort of cryptography do you hope to use? Ozzie and his team described their hybrid crypto scheme: RSA for the key exchange and DES for the actual encryption.

But the very mention of DES made the NSA people go nuts. "I'll tell you right now," one of them said. "You're not going to export DES, no way, under no circumstances . . . you will *never* export DES." This seemed strange: hadn't the NSA put its seal of approval on DES? *Not to be exported to anyone with a couple hundred bucks to spend, baby.* The NSA functionary explained that DES was not merely a cryptosystem but a red-hot political issue at The Fort, with implications that a private-sector engineer would not understand and had no need to understand.

Ozzie didn't know it then, but the NSA was going through a period of post–Data Encryption Standard remorse. In fact, the agency was just then working on a project of its own called the Commercial COMSEC Endorsement Program, which it hoped would kill off the Lucifer-based cipher and replace it with a cryptosystem of its own, dubbed Project Overtake. The ostensible reason was that widespread use of DES "could motivate a hostile intelligence organization to mount a large scale attack" on the cipher. This in itself was sort of ironic, since it was the NSA that mandated the smaller key size for the code, thus making it vulnerable to such an attack. The real problem wasn't that DES was weak, but that it was sound, too sound for a cryptosystem used by the general public. DES now threatened to fall into much wider use than the agency had estimated—and if mass-market public key systems like Notes used DES, the problem would get far worse. So Fort Meade now viewed the cipher as a rogue element in its global mission. The solution was for the NSA to come up with its own cipher, which would be strictly under its control.

Yet Project Overtake was a doomed initiative because its potential private-sector customers weren't buying. For one thing, its technology was expensive and clunky. It involved audiocassette-sized devices built to snap into computers. The boxes cost well over $1000 each. Worse, the banks and other financial institutions asked to participate in this project were given no control over the system. The algorithms themselves were protected. The boxes would be tamperproof. Even the keys were to be generated and distributed by the NSA itself. What assurances did the NSA give that the agency would not be keeping copies of the keys for itself? In a rare public interview in the *Wall Street Journal*, an NSA representative sniffed, "We have better things to do with our time." In other words: *Trust us*. Elsewhere in that article, the NSA's neo-Stalinistic marketing tactics were examined. A banking executive described a typical Project Overtake sales call: "An NSA guy stands up and makes pronouncements. 'You guys have to do this.' It's a directive. You can imagine how far this gets them." No, thank you, said the banks. They'd stick with DES.

Though Ray Ozzie was unaware of all this, he was beginning to realize that the idea of exporting crypto was a *very* big deal for these guys. As the obstensibly amiable interrogation continued that day, it became clear that the NSA people did not even have the vocabulary to deal with a mass-marketed product with strong security like Lotus Notes. "They had dealt with people who knew their customers, and could vouch for them with end-user certifications," says Ozzie. "But we had to explain to them that our industry didn't work that way." When Ozzie tried to elaborate on this, his attorney began kicking him under the table—this wasn't the kind of thing that the NSA wanted to hear. But Ozzie felt it important to defend the crypto component in Notes, explaining that if people were going to use the product, they'd be risking their entire businesses on the security of the information. That argument didn't seem to impress the spooks.

Flying back to Boston after that first meeting, Ozzie asked himself,

Would it really be so bad to distribute Lotus Notes only within the United States, and avoid this whole battle? But that approach would be financial suicide. You simply could not compete if you wrote off the global marketplace.

So Ozzie had the lawyers arrange another meeting, this time in Cambridge. Had the National Security Agency softened its position at all? "Just to make sure you know where we stand," said one of the NSA representatives to the Lotus people, "we've long known you've had encryption in Lotus 1-2-3, and from our standpoint that's within our jurisdiction. We could stop your shipments of 1-2-3 tomorrow if we felt like it."

Lotus 1-2-3, of course, was the spreadsheet that provided the lion's share of the company's revenues. It was the most popular software product in the world and a huge percentage of its sales was overseas. What was the "encryption" to which the NSA referred? Lotus's spreadsheet program contained a simple password option that blocked access to unauthorized users. Now, it was highly unlikely that the U.S. government would dare halt all shipments of software that used passwords, an act that would cause the entire personal computer software industry to collapse. Still, the threat had its effect. Ozzie glanced over at his lawyer, and saw a look of sheer panic.

In the course of that meeting and several others over the next three years, it became very clear to Ray Ozzie that no matter how crucial Lotus Notes might be to his company or even to the U.S. economy, any approval he got for export would be on the government's terms only. On the other hand, he was relieved that no one dealing on behalf of the NSA ever made any demands on what encryption might be sold *within* the borders of the United States. (Such a demand would have been a violation of the Computer Security Act, but who knew where those guys would stop?) Whenever Ozzie indicated that export restrictions might force Lotus to release two versions of Notes, one with strong encryption for domestic use and the other for approved export, the government negotiators would shrug and say, "Well, that's your decision." At times Ozzie would wonder whether the NSA wanted Lotus to create some secret skeleton key by which the spooks could quickly unscramble messages encrypted by Notes. He once probed to see if that was the case. "What the hell do you want?" he asked his tormentors. "Are you waiting for me to offer you a back door?" The response was immediate: *No, we don't want you to compromise the security of the product.* "So what the hell *do* you want?" Ozzie would ask, and he'd get no good answer. And the stalemate would continue.

Finally, around the middle of 1987, Ozzie and his team got a concession from the NSA: If Lotus dropped DES and found a replacement cipher, the government would evaluate that cipher's strength and allow Notes to be exported, with a key length that the parties would then negotiate. Lotus immediately hired Ron Rivest to cook up a new encryption algorithm. After a few weeks of intense work, he came up with his own cipher that he named RC-2, for Rivest Cipher 2. (A first effort was shelved.) Rivest's system was similar to DES in that it was a block cipher that used complicated substitutions, but unlike DES, it had a variable key length. Lotus paid for all the development costs but allowed RSA to hold the patents. Rivest submitted the code to the NSA in 1987; not long afterward, he heard that the Triple Fence crypto wizards required a couple of tweaks.

"How do you know they're not doing something to weaken it?" Ozzie asked him.

Rivest replied that the government's comments actually made good sense, so he felt safe making their changes. That took a month or so, and the negotiations picked up again. Not that they were getting anywhere. "The content of the meetings was getting very thin," says Ozzie. "I believe we were definitely being stalled." His impression was that there was strife within the NSA itself on how to proceed. During 1987 and 1988, the lack of an export license wasn't that much of a crisis for Lotus, because Notes was one of those ambitious software efforts that were years late in production. So the encryption issue wasn't holding up the product itself. But as 1989 rolled around, it looked like the program might finally be ready to ship. Now an export solution was essential.

The only thing that Lotus had going for it, really, was perseverance. Not that Ozzie had any alternatives. Every time he'd mention the possibility of shipping a product only in the United States, the marketing people insisted such a course was just not financially viable. So he kept pressing. Kept asking for more meetings with the NSA. Kept supplying any and all information the government requested. So much information, he figured, that if he ever *did* get an export license, there wouldn't be a chance in hell that the government could come back and say, "Hold on, you didn't tell us that the system works like *this*." That would give it an opportunity to stop shipments. So Ozzie made sure that Lotus completely fulfilled even the Defense Department's most trivial requests.

While Ozzie was definitely the supplicant, he did have some leverage. "Are you telling me that I have to go to my congressman and tell him you're preventing me from shipping my product overseas?" he'd ask the export gatekeepers. "How much of an issue do I have to make of this?" Lotus may not have been a multibillion-dollar company, but it was the biggest company in the software industry at the time, and it wouldn't have looked very good to have some faceless spooks barring the door to the darling of the business press.

Suddenly, inexplicably, the ice broke in mid-1989. Ozzie is convinced that the struggle within the NSA had finally ended in a compromise. "It was clear that there were people for us and people against us," he says. "Originally they'd been meeting with us because it was their job and they were curious about what we in this new personal computer industry wanted. Then I believe there were severe internal battles, with some people in favor of letting a little crypto out, to make us go away. And others who didn't want a precedent set, and wanted nothing out." Apparently the former prevailed. An offer materialized. Verbally, of course. A written offer would be akin to a binding promise, an animal that does not exist in the export control menagerie.

Here was the offer: Lotus Notes could ship overseas with RSA and RC-2 encryption built in, with a key size of 32 bits. The NSA people thought that was a major concession on their part. After all, their job was to break codes. So they had to be very concerned about what might happen if the president or the National Security Council came and asked them to break a message encrypted in a program they'd allowed exported. Their first instinct had been to permit only a 24-bit key. But "after serious leaning on NSA senior policy people," said one of the government reps, they were willing to "go the extra mile" and allow what it considered unusually strong 32-bit keys.

Unusually strong? The Lotus team was appalled. That meant that the keys one chose to encrypt and decrypt data were limited to a universe of just over four billion keys. While you wouldn't want to try to crack this by hand, it was totally lame in the age of supercomputers. For the silicon sweathogs in the basement of Fort Meade, finding a key among four billion was a definite yawner. In the meeting, the NSA folks admitted that their supercomputers could indeed crack such keys inside of a couple of days (an estimate that seemed rather modest). But potential data thieves didn't really need supercomputers to crack a code scrambled with a 32-bit key. If they were determined enough, and had serious dollars to spend as well as time to kill, they'd be able to throw enough *personal* computing power at the problem to find the keys. According to RSA estimates, this could be accomplished within 60 days. The government officials insisted that this was plenty of security. "Who would go to the trouble to break a single corporate message or several of them at 60 days a pop?" they asked.

This seemed to ignore the guiding high-tech principle of Moore's Law, which dictated that personal computers would double in power every eighteen months or so. So, that 60 days would soon be less than a month. By 1995, the time to crack a 32-bit key would be less than a week. But all of that was almost beside the point. True, for most relatively innocuous messages sent on Lotus Notes, spending days or weeks on decryption was excessive. But some of the information transmitted by these multimillion-dollar companies was bound to be valuable. And how would Lotus be able to assure those firms if the key length was limited to 32 bits? It couldn't say that breaking the code was unimaginable—or even a challenge. Basically, getting hold of a secret message would be little more than a nuisance.

There was no legal reason, however, to stop Lotus from producing two versions of the product: an export version with 32 bits and a much more secure version for use only within the United States. The latter used Lotus's preferred key length of 64 bits, a degree of strength many times more difficult to crack than the export version. (Remember, each single bit doubles the size of the keyspace. A key that's twice as hard to guess as the 32-bit version would not be 64 bits long, but only 33 bits. The domestic version, then, was like doubling the difficulty 32 separate times, changing the time frame to crack a key from days to aeons. The bottom line was that it required no stretch of the imagination to use brute force to come up with a 32-bit key. But considering 1989 computer power, one could reasonably declare such an attack on a 64-bit key next to impossible.)

The drawbacks of producing two products of different key strengths were daunting. The obvious logistical costs—two packages, two sets of disks, two inventories of products—were only the beginning. Ozzie and his team had to make sure that both versions operated with each other. Because the target customer base for Notes included multinational companies like General Motors, the software had to be written so that companies with some users in the United States and others overseas could communicate securely. So Lotus had to have the product work in such a way that people didn't have to worry whether or not some of the recipients of an e-mail might be in Spain or Kansas City. Essentially (though none of this was apparent as one used the product), each person who used Notes was given two sets of keys— an international pair and a domestic pair. Implementing this was a programming nightmare. But, says Ozzie, "we were not going to compromise in this country," so Lotus went ahead and did the work.

The one problem that simply could not be coded around was that the government-imposed limitation made the international product much, much weaker than its American cousin. You could view it as a bug, but one that was built into the product. Would international customers reject it for that reason?

At first, they didn't—mainly because the entire idea of buying a product with built-in encryption was so novel that customers weren't attuned to the nuances of security. "We were trying to sell a product that was for uses they didn't know they had," says Ozzie. "It required a network card they didn't have, a graphical interface they didn't have. Only after we convinced them to put these things in did they ask, 'Is it secure?' And we'd tell them, 'Yeah, it's secure; not as much as the version in the U.S., but it's secure.' And they'd ask, 'Can someone break in?' And we'd go, 'Well, if you ganged together thirty or forty personal computers, maybe you could. But you'd have to write special software and all.' It was a customer education process to let them know we were trying to protect their data. It wasn't for a few years that the questions began coming about why the international version isn't as strong, and why didn't we use DES."

Lotus's hope was that by the time international customers got wise to the fact that their version of the software offered significantly weaker protection, the government would bend its restrictions and allow larger keys. Thirty-two-bit keys were just a compromise Ozzie made to get the product out the door. "Once we were shipping, and we had customers who had pull, we could [have the clout to argue for] a change to forty-eight-bit keys [in the export version]," says Ozzie. "That was what we were pushing for."

But the government seemed to be pushing in the opposite direction. The NSA believed that the export version, even with that lame key size, was still too strong because of certain design elements. These concerned the possible reencryption of already-encrypted information—something Ozzie figured that, at worst, would make decrypting messages only slightly more difficult. Without explaining its reasons, the government suggested design changes that might satisfy them. The best Ozzie could figure was that the issue probably related to the way that NSA cryptanalysts broke codes. But settling the matter took months of further negotiations, ultimately resulting in significant product redesign that made the program run more slowly in certain instances.

Ozzie couldn't help but wonder: *what was the point of all this?* Did shipping Lotus Notes overseas only in a 32-bit version really improve national security?

The struggle with Lotus over software exports was only one sign that after years of inaction, the National Security Agency had to wake up and face the challenge of a crypto revolution. After the mild panic following the first breakthroughs in the late 1970s, officials at The Fort thought things were under control. Though Bobby Ray Inman's compromise—the scheme by which crypto researchers would voluntarily submit their work to the NSA for a once-over—was not foolproof, an impressively high percentage of the top independent cryptographers actually went through the process. Because the choice was theirs, they could justify their decision to comply with the principles of academic freedom. Besides, these academics had no desire to destabilize national security. Correspondence with the spooks was also *fun,* in a way. It provided a certain frisson, not to mention an implicit validation that one's work was indeed serious. In over nine times out of ten, the NSA made no suggestions, and other times, a minor adjustment would be requested—typically, this would be when the researcher inadvertently stumbled on some issue that was related to the NSA's techniques in either its codes or its cryptanalysis.

Furthermore, in at least one case, the NSA actually appeared to have intervened *on behalf of* a researcher. This was none other than Adi Shamir. In the years since leaving MIT, Shamir had been extraordinarily productive. Using the ideas of public key as a starting point, he and various colleagues had come up with new ideas for crypto. Some of them were amazing. One that he worked on with Adleman and Rivest involved a way to play "mental poker . . . played just like ordinary poker, except there are no cards." A more significant creation was "secret sharing." Only two years after helping invent RSA, Shamir had been intrigued by what he considered to be a problem looking for a solution—how do you share a single key among several parties, particularly when mistrust and suspicion festers among them? The classic situation is an electronic equivalent of what happens in nuclear missile silos: in order to launch, multiple keys must be turned simultaneously, requiring more than one person. Could you replicate this safeguard in cyberspace? It turns out you could, and once Shamir got to thinking about it, he came up with the idea of secret sharing, a means to parcel out a decryption key among several people. If a foe got hold of any individual's share of the key (known as a "shadow"), he or she would have no advantage in an attempt to retrieve the entire key. Implementing that was the only the beginning, though. It was obvious how to do it in a way requiring the cooperation of all the participants to reconstruct the key. But then Shamir thought a little. . . . What would happen if one of those people disappeared or died or was kidnapped? This led to the idea to build tolerance, so that if you were given any predetermined subset of the keys, you would be able to reconstruct the secret. This came to be known as a "threshold scheme," and its uses were endless. A trade secret like a recipe for Coca-Cola, for instance, could be distributed among ten people, and then you could prearrange any number of complicated combinations to retrieve the key. If, say, the six least trusted people holding shadows of the key got together, they might not be able to reconstruct the key. But the *most* trusted shadow holder might be able to build the key with any two other people in the consortium.

In 1986, Shamir and two of his colleagues at the Weizmann Institute came up with another innovative and potentially valuable technique, known as "zero-knowledge proofs of identity." Using one-way functions, these allowed Alice to verify that she knew a number (typically something that identified her, like a social security or credit-card number) without revealing that number to the interrogator. Using this system, Shamir later said, "I could go to a Mafia-owned store a million successive times and they would still not be able to misrepresent themselves as me [and use that information to buy goods, etc.]." Recognizing the value of this scheme in future e-commerce transactions, Shamir and his coinventors applied for a patent. But in early 1987, the patent office informed the cryptographers that, by order of the U.S. Army, their invention was now an official secret; circulating information on it "would be detrimental to the national security." Not only were the Israeli scientists prevented from discussing it, but they were instructed to warn anyone who had seen the paper that sharing the idea could put one in jail for two years. Since they had already presented the paper at several universities as well as the Crypto '86 conference, and had submitted it to the Association of Computing Machinery for publication that May, this seemed a difficult, if not futile, task. Furthermore, since the authors weren't even Americans themselves, how could the U.S. government tell them what they could and could not talk about?

The NSA apparently wasn't involved in that secrecy order, but soon heard about it from concerned American scientists—and from the *New York Times*, which had been tipped off about the controversy. Within two days the order was quietly lifted. It was weeks before Shamir learned about the reprieve, and he became convinced that the NSA had intervened in his behalf. Why? As Susan Landau, an academic researching crypto policy, later guessed, the agency had intervened to preserve its prepublication submission program. If the perception was that submitting a good crypto idea could lead to a sudden embargo, the flow of papers to the NSA would end. And, as Landau wrote, "it is much easier to find out what the competition is doing if they send you their papers."

As the 1980s came to a close, however, it was clear that the voluntary submission system had reached the end of its usefulness. The turning point came, significantly, with a paper written by Ralph Merkle. Merkle had gone to work at the Xerox Corporation, in its famed Palo Alto Research Center (PARC). His main area of study— indeed, his passion—was nanotechnology, a new science based on molecule-sized machines. But he kept up with the crypto world. In 1989, he wrote a paper that introduced a series of algorithms that would speed up cryptographic computation, driving down the price of encryption. This in itself was threatening to the NSA's mission. But Merkle's paper was particularly worrisome to the agency because it included a discussion of the technology of S-box design. Ever since Lucifer, this had been a hot-button issue at The Fort.

Xerox sent the paper off to the NSA for a prepublication review. (Apparently, it had hopes of one day getting an export license for a product based on Merkle's research.) As usual, the NSA itself circulated it to experts both inside and outside the Triple Fence. But this time the result was not a helpful correction or gentle request for a change in wording. The agency wanted the whole paper suppressed, claiming—without explaining why, of course—that circulating Merkle's scheme would be a national security risk.

Xerox, as a huge government contractor, quietly agreed to the agency's request. Normally, that might have been the end of it. But in this case, apparently one of the outside reviewers of Merkle's paper was upset that the agency had spiked it—so upset that he or she slipped it to an independent watchdog, a computer-hacker millionaire named John Gilmore.

Gilmore had a weapon that wasn't available a decade earlier, when the prepublication process was initiated: the Internet. One of the most popular Usenet discussion groups on this global web of computers was called sci.crypt. It was sort of an all-night-diner equivalent of the yearly Crypto feasts in Santa Barbara, featuring a steady stream of new ideas, criticism of old schemes, and news briefs from the code world. Gilmore posted Merkle's paper to the group, and in an instant, it went out to readers on 8000 different computers around the world. Cyberspace had made the NSA's prepublication system irrelevant.

The agency rescinded its request to withhold publication. Anyway, by then even the bureaucrats at The Fort were getting wise to a new reality: its real challenges weren't coming from academic papers but from the marketplace. And the prime example was that once moribund public key software company, now rejuvenated by Jim Bidzos.

As the 1990s approached, Bidzos was dancing a complicated pas de deux with the National Security Agency. Though he had no real proof of it, he now imagined that behind the scenes it was working overtime to sabotage him and his company. It seemed that a lot of his potential customers showed enthusiasm at first, but then mysteriously stopped returning his calls. There were also government agencies whose interest in deploying his products suddenly evaporated. Bidzos felt in his bones that the silence resulted not from a failure of his sales prowess, but from clandestine pressure from Maryland.

He even came to wonder about the nature of a relationship he had with a woman who for some reason spontaneously began giving him inside dope on the NSA. It had seemed plausible at the time, but later he wondered whether she was being paid to feed him disinformation. "I believe in the intelligence community they call it a 'honey trap,' " he later said. It was ironic that from time to time people would still wonder whether Bidzos was some sort of double agent, putting on a charade of fighting the NSA while secretly implanting back doors in his company's technology. In his mind, he truly believed that he was the single greatest thorn in the agency's cybernetic paw.

But what really scared Jim Bidzos circa 1990 was not the National Security Agency, but a far more immediate threat to his business. It involved not the government but the public key cryptography patents that were the foundation of his technology. The problem involved a company whose products didn't compete directly with those of RSA—but whose patents threatened the company's existence.

The company was named Cylink, and its own history was considerably more placid than the roller-coaster ride of RSA. Its cofounder, Jim Omura, was a Stanford Ph.D. who became a UCLA professor in electrical engineering. His main field was information theory. Like just about everyone in computer science back then who didn't work for the NSA, he knew almost nothing about cryptography. But he knew of a young associate professor at Stanford who was interested in the subject. "I used to ask him, 'Why waste your time in cryptography?' It seemed like there was nothing there," says Omura. Fortunately for the invention of public key cryptography, the professor—Marty Hellman—didn't take Omura's advice.

By the late 1970s, Omura's views had changed, however, and he became an expert in the field. For extra money he would teach a five-day cryptography course to people in industry, mainly government contractors who wanted to develop products for the military. It covered the basic principles of crypto, and he taught it not only in the

United States but also in places like Switzerland. "We had to be careful not to include any classified knowledge," he says. Omura himself had never been briefed with classified material, but who knows what the government might consider verboten?

After a few years, Omura and a friend began tinkering with actual code, and they came up with a hardware product: a silicon-chip implementation of public key, using the Diffie-Hellman key exchange. He went to another friend, Lew Morris, who was an early participant in Sun Microsystems, and they began to explore the idea of making a business out of it. They wrote a business plan, and started making the rounds of venture capitalists.

This was in 1984, about the same time that RSA was going through its roughest period. Omura and Morris didn't find the going any easier. "The venture community then couldn't have cared less about information security," says Omura. It was only through a private referral that the business plan fell into the hands of Jim Simons, who was not only a mathematician and cryptographer (he'd been one of the early reviewers of Lucifer) but dabbled in venture capital as well. He agreed to help put the newly dubbed Cylink company on its feet.

Unlike RSA, which had a mission of getting crypto into the hands of the general public, Cylink focused on securing the communications of big companies, typically those that were government contractors. Cylink wasn't about to push the envelope of what the NSA would or would not permit. Its first product, shipped in 1986, was dubbed the CIDEC-HS (so much for sexy branding). It was a chip-stuffed metal box that scrambled telephone communications within a company, using a hybrid crypto system: Diffie-Hellman to generate keys, DES to encrypt the data. Since many of Cylink's customers were financial institutions that had already won clearance to use DES-based cryptography (including SWIFT, the international clearing-house for bank transactions, which handled over a trillion dollars on a slow day), Cylink didn't run into the export problems plaguing software companies like Lotus. It quickly became profitable.

From the start, of course, Cylink had gone to Stanford University to license the Diffie-Hellman patent. At first, the arrangement was nonexclusive. "Stanford was deliriously happy," says Robert Fougner, Cylink's general counsel. "They'd finally found someone who was going to actually use the patent, and we made a very, very good deal

with Stanford." During the mid-1980s, in fact, while RSA was struggling to establish itself, Cylink seemed to be the only company turning
a buck from public key. The relationship with Stanford flourished.
Eventually, Cylink proposed that the university give the company
additional rights to the public key patents. Essentially, it wanted to
control all the patents itself. When others sought to devise and market
potential public key crypto schemes, they would go not to Stanford for
the licensing rights, but to Cylink for *sub*licensing rights.

Stanford agreed to this, but there was a significant wrinkle: a continuing conflict over its patent rights and those of MIT, which owned
the RSA patent. Stanford believed that its patents were, essentially, *the*
public key patents, since they embodied the broad idea of split-key
cryptography. By this logic, anyone who wanted to use the RSA
scheme would also have to license the Stanford patents. MIT's
lawyers, however, believed that RSA could stand alone. This disagree-
ment triggered tension between the universities that went on for several years. It was (pardon the expression) a low-key dispute, since
there wasn't much money involved at the time.

Even so, everyone felt that a dispute between two august institutions was unseemly, and finally the parties reached a compromise.
Stanford bundled all its public key patents and sublicensed them to
MIT. MIT in turn transferred those rights to RSA Data Security, Inc.
This removed a huge cloud hanging over RSA, whose system really did
depend on the original public key idea of Whit Diffie and Marty Hellman. Now its software was not only fully covered by patent protection,
but there was no question of infringing on the Stanford patent.

While this was fine for RSA, it put Cylink at a disadvantage. Now if
someone wanted to license public key crypto, they could go *either* to
Cylink or to RSA Data Security. But only from RSA could they acquire
the rights to the public key system created by its founders. This didn't
become a problem immediately, since the two companies were pursuing different customers. While both championed public key and
were located within ten miles of each other, Cylink was, in Fougner's
words, "very insular, very inward . . . focused on our technology, on
making a good product, on selling that product to a [limited, but] nice
portfolio of customers." On the other hand, RSA's marketplace was
the broader world of personal computing, with their eyes on a mass
market.

Almost inevitably, though, the companies found themselves up against each other. Because of the way the patents were divided, each company had an interest in encouraging a certain approach to public key software—and disparaging the other approach. Because Cylink didn't have access to MIT's patents, it aggressively promoted the idea of using the Diffie-Hellman key exchange. Previously, people in the field had thought that, in a practical sense, the Stanford-derived work only provided for a way for two parties to agree upon secret keys; unlike RSA, it didn't outline the means for a full and efficient public key cryptosystem. But Cylink believed that by cleverly using the Diffie-Hellman patents, users *could* do everything that RSA did, just as elegantly: privacy, authentication, the whole works. Jim Omura had written a paper about it in 1987. "You could use the Stanford patents to do the same thing as RSA," says Omura. "I think this upset Jim Bidzos because suddenly his technology wasn't the unique technology."

"In order for RSA to succeed, it had to promote its software implementations, which were really focused on the MIT software," says Fougner. "And here was Cylink having obvious commercial success with the Stanford-type technology. There was going to be a fight, or there was going to be a business deal."

Fougner himself joined Cylink as counsel in 1989 specifically to deal with this issue. On his second day of work, he met with Jim Bidzos. He had little idea what to expect. Would Bidzos, who already had gained a reputation within the budding industry as a pressure artist, play tough? Far from it. As Fougner recalls, Bidzos took pains to appear submissive, acting as if he were almost in awe of Cylink's financial success. RSA, he told Fougner, was still struggling to keep its head above water: Cylink had nothing to worry about from RSA. On the other hand, both companies faced an uphill battle getting crypto established more widely. Both of them, Bidzos said, were evangelizing a technology that nobody understood, that nobody wanted to pay for. On top of that, here were the two top public key companies, each promoting a different implementation, and confusing the hell out of everybody!

Let's not fight each other, said Bidzos. *Why not pool all the patents, work together, agree on a public key standard, and license the hell out of it? We'll make a gazillion dollars!*

It made a lot of sense to Fougner. Why *not* join forces? For one thing, he figured, it would probably make Stanford's lawyers happy. They had long regretted granting MIT the sublicensing rights to its patents. By making RSA a one-stop shop for public key, Stanford had cut itself out of the loop! "The joke at Stanford," says Fougner, "was that the MIT deal was often used in their seminars as an example of what not to do in patent licensing." So Bidzos's idea of putting all the patents in one pot (with the promise of more fees for the public key patents) sounded very attractive to the Stanford people, and they urged Cylink to go along with it.

On October 17, 1989—the same day that an earthquake charting 7.0 on the Richter scale rocked the Bay Area—the two companies and the two universities came to an understanding. (The formal contract was signed the following April.) The patents would all belong to a new corporation jointly owned by RSA and Cylink. Control of the new entity, called Public Key Partners (PKP), would be shared equally between the two parent firms. Bidzos, arguing that the MIT rights were worth more (RSA had already gained some access to Stanford's patents whereas Cylink had no rights to use RSA's technology), negotiated a favorable revenue split: 55–45 in his company's favor. Meanwhile the universities themselves got only a fraction of the potential cash: out of every dollar paid to PKP by sublicensees for patent rights, Stanford University would get nine cents and MIT would take in a little under fourteen cents.

Omura recalls that after the partnership was established, Bidzos tried to get Cylink to downplay the idea that people could perform public key functions without the RSA algorithm. "He essentially said to me, 'Now that we're partners, I hope you'll stop promoting the Diffie-Hellman approach and support RSA.'" Omura told him that his company would still use the alternative method, but didn't see why that should be a problem. "It doesn't matter what technology we use," he said to Bidzos. "We're partners."

"In 1990, who cared?" explains Fougner. "Within a couple of years, though, a lot of people cared."

Initially, the two executives of Public Key Partners, Fougner and Bidzos, worked well together. Technically, Fougner was head of licensing and Bidzos the president. But the bylaws dictated unanimous consent on any decisions. For Fougner, an unassuming corporate lawyer, teaming up with a swashbuckling deal-maker like Bidzos, the enterprise was sort of a mad adventure. Two wild and crazy guys, try-ing to set a global standard for public key cryptography—and make tons of money for their respective companies.

So enamored was Fougner of the idea that he tended to shrug off the almost immediate signs that in many ways the interests of RSA and Cylink remained divergent. The first order of business for PKP was to send a letter to the National Institute of Standards and Technology (NIST), the government agency that acted as the ultimate referee of what protocols the marketplace should agree upon as a standard. In large part, the success of the partnership between the two companies would depend on whether NIST adopted as standards the patents now jointly controlled by Bidzos and Fougner. There were actually several different cryptographic standards that NIST would have to approve: one for digital signatures, one for encryption, one for key exchange, and so on. Once these were determined, the crypto revolution would be poised for liftoff. All the software developers would know exactly which algorithms were required for privacy and authentication, and they would build them into their programs. All the programs would then interact with each other: once this got going, a user of Lotus would be able to send encrypted mail to someone using WordPerfect, and a Microsoft Word user could stamp a digital signature on his or her Intuit account ledger. It was a crucial step for a crypto society, and NIST knew it.

The government decided to establish the digital signature technology as the first standard. Uh-oh. Cylink and RSA had different approaches to signatures, each one based on their separate public key religions: Stanford or MIT. Which one would PKP offer to the gov-ernment as its official candidate for a standard? Jim Bidzos had the answer: *Let's make this one RSA,* he said. The Cylink people were unsure; after all, they'd been working on Diffie-Hellman signatures for six years. Bidzos had an answer to that: We'll do RSA for signa-ture, and when it comes to a key-management standard (the means of handling and verifying the zillions of digital keys that a large-scale system would handle), we'll do Diffie-Hellman. The Cylink people agreed. Public Key Partnership's letter to NIST, under Fougner's sig-nature, went out on April 20, just two weeks after PKP was formally established. It urged that the agency adopt the RSA scheme as a stan-dard. "Public Key Partners," the letter said, "hereby gives its assurance that licenses to practice RSA signatures will be available under reasonable terms and conditions on a nondiscriminatory basis."

But when it came to digital signatures, the government had its own ideas.

In the midst of all that wrangling, Jim Bidzos was still concerned with keeping his company afloat. He was now working on his biggest licensing deal yet—a broad arrangement with the most powerful software company on earth: Microsoft, the White Whale of high tech. For the previous few years, its wizards had become increasingly aware that their customers might need cryptography built into Microsoft products. From the company headquarters in Redmond, Washington, its chief technical officer, Nathan Myhrvold, had begun to circulate memos on how crucial this would become. Myhrvold often invoked his grandmother, who lived in a small farm community where people left their doors unlocked: This was fine in an isolated setting where strangers were seldom seen, but simply would not do in an urban setting. It was the same with computers, he would say; they were moving from isolated, unconnected units on desktops to networked nodes in a large infrastructure. To protect everything from taxes to medical records, you needed locks, and Myhrvold understood that public key cryptography would provide those locks.

Myhrvold had been in college when Martin Gardner's *Scientific American* article about RSA appeared. "I thought it was infinitely cool," he said, and the future physicist (who would study under Stephen Hawking at Cambridge University) devoured the RSA paper as well as the Diffie-Hellman paper that inspired it. A decade later, after a software company Myhrvold had started was bought out by Microsoft, he had become one of Bill Gates's most trusted lieutenants. He was excited about his opportunity to help get public key into the mainstream. As was the case with Ray Ozzie and Lotus, he wound up dealing with the obvious person: Jim Bidzos.

The Microsoft license was crucial to Bidzos. It would make his technology a security standard for the hundreds of millions of customers who used Microsoft's DOS and Windows operating systems as well as its applications like the word-processor Word and the spreadsheet Excel. Nonetheless, Bidzos approached the negotiations with his usual aggressiveness, boasting that, as the patent holder, he was the only game in town for crypto supplicants. Myhrvold wasn't intimidated. If RSA is so great, he wanted to know, why isn't anybody else using it? He conceded that public key systems may be inevitable, but joked with Bidzos that they might not catch on until the patents ran out toward the end of the century.

Bidzos wasn't fazed, and the negotiations proceeded—two major egos, each giving as good as he got. The issues were complicated because Microsoft wanted the right to modify the code of RSA's crypto toolkits to suit their products. Inevitably, though, as Ray Ozzie had already learned, there was an even bigger hurdle facing all of them: the export laws.

Anticipating that including crypto in its products would be problematic, Microsoft had begun a dialogue with the NSA. Though cordial, the new relationship was uneasy. The first few times representatives from Fort Meade ventured to the Redmond headquarters, they wouldn't even reveal their last names; to get them building passes, Myhrvold had to go to the reception desk to approve badges with first names only. "They were reflexively secretive," says Myhrvold, half amused and half annoyed. Worse, they never seemed to be explicit about what was and was not permitted. But they were vocal about one thing: RSA Data Security. They seemed to have it in for the company.

Obviously, the NSA people did not relish the prospect of this upstart company providing a surveillance-proof shield to hundreds of millions of Microsoft customers. As Myhrvold tells it, they tried to turn him against Jim Bidzos and his company. Their method of dissuasion was interesting. Without saying it outright, they began dropping broad hints that behind the Triple Fence, the cipher devised by Rivest, Shamir, and Adleman had already been broken. Myhrvold was worried about giving his customers reasonable security—if the government could crack the code, why not a crook?—so he grilled Bidzos about the NSA's claim.

Bidzos was stunned: he'd felt the Microsoft deal was almost completed. He sprang into action to refute the charges. "We contacted every number theorist, every mathematician, every researcher in this field we knew, and within twenty-four hours had gotten back," he says. "[Microsoft was] blown away by what we had done and they said that obviously the charge isn't true."

Myhrvold's recollection is different. He says that the refutation was superfluous: he always did believe the RSA algorithm was sound. But Myhrvold does say that he teased Bidzos by noting that no system short of a one-time pad could be provably impervious to cryptanalysis. Bidzos answered, quite reasonably, that one could trust a publicly published cipher—open to challenge from anyone in the community—more than one of the NSA's secret algorithms. RSA's future was totally linked to the strength of its codes, so it had every incentive to make sure those codes were strong. "If somebody breaks it," Bidzos said, "what you've got are the remnants of a once-valuable company." In any case, Bidzos convinced Myhrvold. To Myhrvold the NSA's antipathy toward RSA was in a sense an endorsement: why would the agency want it stopped so much unless it was actually hard to break?

But the NSA wasn't through. According to Myhrvold, the agency made another eleventh-hour attempt to discourage Microsoft from licensing RSA, this time questioning the validity of the company's patents. In addition, its people speculated that future government standards would not use RSA technology, and Microsoft might have an orphaned set of algorithms. Bidzos rushed back to Redmond to orchestrate a presentation that conclusively proved the solidity and breadth of his patent rights.

According to Bidzos, the final NSA attempt at sabotaging the deal came when an agency official called Myhrvold and said, basically, "Don't do it." (Myhrvold says that he doesn't recollect those words specifically, but confirms the NSA conveyed to Microsoft that it believed licensing RSA would be a mistake: a powerful disincentive for the software giant to link up with this unproven company.)

Bidzos was furious. As he recollects now, he dialed up the highest ranking person he knew behind the Triple Fence and laid out what he had heard. Then, before his contact could utter a word in reply, he demanded that the official fix the problem and call Microsoft back to tell them that the agency had made a big mistake. "If that doesn't work, you're going to answer to the congressman in my district," he said. "If *that* doesn't work, you're going to answer to a district attorney, because I'm going to file a complaint. If *that* doesn't work, I'll try the *New York Times*. But one way or another, if you don't fix this, I'm gonna make you answer for it." Bidzos more or less expected his contact to deny everything, or at least insist that he knew nothing of the sabotage. Instead, Bidzos claims, the man said, "I'll call them." And, according to Bidzos, his contact called Microsoft and recanted.

The path was now clear for a deal. One small point holding up the arrangement had been Bidzos's insistence that Bill Gates personally sign the contract. Bidzos wanted to display that final page of the contract on his wall, and what would it look like without the John Hancock of Microsoft's famous CEO? By implying that Gates's signature might be a problem, Myhrvold brags that he was able to get a few deal sweeteners from Bidzos. (But Bidzos got a sweetener, too—Gates's presence at an RSA event.)

A few days later, over Memorial Day weekend in 1991, Bidzos called Fougner to boast about the now-completed deal. Fougner recalls being blown away. "Jim, that's amazing," he said. "You got Microsoft to license your proprietary toolkit, and they're going to put it in their operating system? That's unbelievable! How did you do that?"

"Salesmanship, Bob," said Jim Bidzos. "I'm a great salesman."

Salesmanship or not, by early 1991, the future of the public key patents was very much in doubt because of the lack of a government endorsement. Bidzos was, of course, desperate to have RSA established as the standard. Early in the process, NIST, the arbiter of the process, had been enthusiastic about doing just that. RSA, wrote a senior scientist at the agency, was "a most versatile public key system." Indeed, as late as December 1990, NIST was trying to convince Bidzos's foe, the NSA—whose voice in the process was crucial—that the system should be adopted. Not only was it commercially effective, said its representatives in meetings with the intelligence agency, but there was no reasonable technical argument for anything else.

But then progress stalled. None of the entreaties from Bidzos or Fougner to establish RSA as the standard seemed to have been effective. And on August 30, 1991, it became clear why. *The National Security Agency had devised its own scheme.*

Publishing in the *Federal Register*, NIST proposed a new set of algorithms as the prime candidate for a standard. The government's product, known as the Digital Signature Algorithm (DSA), was written by an NSA employee named David Kravitz. In many ways, it was similar to the RSA signature scheme. Both schemes employed a public-private key pair. In both, when Alice wishes to prepare a digitally signed message, she first applies an algorithm known as a hash function, which boils the content down to a compressed "message digest." (This, essentially, is the message boiled down to its essence, for easy processing.) Then, by way of a mathematical function that uses Alice's unique private key, that message digest is scrambled, or "signed." Both the original message and the digest are then sent off to Bob. When Bob—or anyone else—gets the message, he now has a way to verify that it was indeed Alice who sent it and that the message itself wasn't tampered with in transit. He uses Alice's public key to "unsign" the message and the digest. Then he uses the hash function to re-create Alice's message from the digest. Only if the letter came from Alice and only if the content was unchanged would the re-creation match the original.

The government method differed from RSA's signature scheme in one profound way: its public-private key pair could be used only for authentication, not encryption. In other words, this was a public key system that couldn't keep a secret. Thus it presented no threat to national security or law enforcement—literally, it was just what the government ordered. "Our underlying strategy," an NIST official would testify to Congress, "was to develop encryption technologies that did not do damage to national security or law enforcement capabilities in this country. And our objective . . . was to come out with a technology that did signatures and nothing else very well."

But NIST, which originally looked favorably on adopting the RSA solution, came to adopt this objective only after pressure from Fort Meade. During the last months of 1990, the NSA had been pushing hard for its system, and in February 1991, its new director, General William O. Studeman, forced the issue, urging NIST to "cut short the debate and get on with the things that need to be done to provide the necessary protection." At the next meeting of the two agencies' joint technical working group, NIST representatives raised the white flag, and indicated that their management "has accepted the NSA's proposal." But when NIST publicly signed off on the NSA-created algorithm in April, nothing was mentioned about the involvement of the secret intelligence agency.

Bidzos wasn't fooled, though, and was furious about the government's choice of the DSA as its standard. He contended that the NSA had completely subverted the Commerce Department, the agency to which NIST belonged. Instead of helping American industry, he charged, the Commerce Department was now working against it, totally in service to the spooks. (This suspicion was later bolstered by a congressional investigation that led the House Government Operations Committee to declare, "NSA is the wrong agency to be put in charge of this important program.") The next step, Bidzos warned, would be the unveiling of an encryption standard that didn't adopt the familiar algorithms—*his* algorithms!—but some new ones that the government could break.

Bidzos had a lot of ammunition for his attack. In purely technical terms, it was clear that the DSA was inferior to RSA. It was, as one observer put it, "an oddball standard," much slower to verify signatures than RSA's system (though faster to sign messages), more difficult to implement, and more complicated. And, of course, it didn't have encryption. Unlike RSA, it had no track record. The government scheme did offer one advantage over RSA, however, something that Bidzos was hard-pressed to match. It was free. Indeed, in the August 30 announcement, the government had proclaimed its intention to make its signature standard available worldwide on a royalty-free basis.

Bidzos felt he could fight the proposed standard by way of a patent challenge. But that would not be easy. Public Key Partners, of course, controlled the Stanford patents that involved the first digital signatures. But the government claimed that its scheme bypassed those patents by relying on a different implementation of digital signatures, one designed by another Stanford cryptographer named Tehar ElGamal. A former student of Hellman's, ElGamal had refined the idea of using the hash algorithm and the message digest for digital signatures. But ElGamal had made the mistake of publishing before applying for a patent (his paper had appeared in 1985), thus forfeiting his rights to a patent. So if the government's claim was correct, the DSA was free and clear of any patent claims.

Bidzos disagreed, but he understood that staking his claim would be time-consuming and costly. Still, there was one other way to accuse the government of pilfering intellectual property. It involved yet *another* patent.

This one was based on the work of a German cryptographer named Claus Schnorr, who'd patented his own digital signature scheme in February 1991. After hearing about the DSA, Schnorr insisted that it infringed upon *his* patent, and demanded $2 million from the United States. To many observers, this was overstepping: the conventional wisdom was that both Schnorr's and Kravitz's systems were variations of ElGamal's work. Nonetheless, the government was concerned. In its own patent application, it took pains to assert that the ideas behind the DSA were independent of Schnorr. Still, Schnorr had at the least a "scarecrow" patent: a claim that might not prove to be defensible in a long, drawn-out lawsuit, but one that nonetheless gave its holder a plausible reason to attack a similar concept. As long as Schnorr was unhappy, the government had a problem.

Bidzos saw this as a great opportunity. While the government dithered, he would try to add the German's patent to the Public Key Partners portfolio. It would be like landing on Park Place after already owning Boardwalk: patent monopoly! Bidzos found out that Schnorr was attending a conference in Marseilles, so he flew there with Fougner in tow. They arranged to have lunch at a one of the fanciest restaurants in town. The meal lasted for hours, with multiple bottles of fine wine delivered to the table. Schnorr was in his midforties, a conservative scientist who was proud of his most recent triumph— winning the lucrative Leipzig Prize. Bidzos quickly figured out the way to handle him. "I talked to him like a coach would to a tennis player," says Bidzos. "That he could do it himself, or he could let me negotiate his deals and manage his contracts and endorsements, so he could work on his game." Fougner was impressed at the hard sell. "Bidzos regaled him with tales of his friendship with Bill Gates and his global vision of public key cryptography and the universe," he says.

The meal finally wound down, with the waiters standing around, anxious to clear this final table. They moved to a pub by the waterfront. Fougner quickly sketched out on a piece of paper a transfer by which PKP would receive all rights from Schnorr's patent. At the pub, in the shadow of a fifteenth-century galleon, Schnorr, whether captivated by Bidzos's promises of riches, or just plain exhausted, signed the paper.

When Bidzos got back to the States, he had another in his endless series of meetings with NIST. His contacts were Dennis Branstad and Lynn McNulty, two computer scientists at the agency who were often caught between the demands of the public and those of their bosses. In hoping to resolve the government's patent problems, they had been desperately urging NIST to buy the Schnorr patent. They also wanted to pay off RSA to clear up any alleged conflict with the Stanford patents, and they assumed the meeting would focus on such an offer. Instead, Bidzos began by declaring, "I represent Claus Schnorr and you're infringing on my patent."

Bidzos was exultant. "I had never seen two guys look more tired," he later boasted.

Meanwhile, Bidzos was helping engineer opposition to the DSA on other fronts. As a response to the August 30 *Federal Register* announcement, NIST had received 109 comments on the scheme, the vast majority of them critical. Companies already using RSA, including Microsoft and Lotus, were unhappy that their investment in that scheme would be lost, and they would have to develop new software for the new standard. Other complaints dealt with the relatively laggardly computation rate of the DSA. Also, critics were concerned about the vulnerability of the scheme. Because the proposed standard used only 512-bit keys to calculate the signatures (RSA used 1024 bits), there was a question about whether the powerful computers inside the Triple Fence might be able to churn out forgeries. How could anyone assert that a signature was valid beyond question when an intelligence agency had the potential to create counterfeits? To Ron Rivest, the whole thing was symbolic of the government's policy in general: "What crypto policy should this country have?" he asked at a 1992 conference held in D.C. "Codes which are breakable or not?"

Though the controversy never caused major debate within the general public, it did ignite some civil liberties groups, which had been closely watching the relationship between the NSA and NIST. In fact, the balance of power between the two agencies was risible—one was the flagship of our multibillion-dollar intelligence operation, the other a dime-store government backwater. While the liberals and the

libertarians hoped that the latter organization would protect the interests of ordinary citizens, they had little confidence it would do so.

Their fears were justified. A look at the prior history of the two
organizations laid the blueprint for an imbalance of power. After the
Church hearings in the seventies, the entire organization of the NSA
had felt chastened. But in 1984, at the apex of Ronald Reagan's presidential power, the NSA showed signs of reentering the realm of
domestic policy. At the apparent behest of Fort Meade, Reagan issued
a National Security Decision Directive intended to monitor information in databases—both in- and outside government—that fell into
the vague category of "sensitive, but unclassified, government or
government-derived information." This caused a minor firestorm,
and eventually, the NSA's congressional nemesis, Representative Jack
Brooks of Texas, gave the agency a tongue-lashing: "The basement of
the White House and the back rooms of the Pentagon," he said in a
hearing, "are not places in which national policy should be developed." Eventually, the government backed down.

The experience led some in Congress, urged by frantic lobbying
from civil liberties groups, to create a law that would set boundaries
for the government in the computer age. In what was an unusual
act of independence from the demands of an intelligence agency,
Congress in 1987 passed the Computer Security Act, which specifically turned over the responsibility for securing the nation's computer
infrastructure—particularly in recommending the standards to which
industry would adhere—from the NSA to the National Bureau of
Standards (which was about to take on the higher-tech appellation of
National Institute for Standards and Technology).

Why did Congress flout the spooks? True, the civil liberties groups
had lobbied hard. But more to the point, says Marc Rotenberg, who
was then a staffer for Senator Patrick Leahy, "U.S. business didn't
particularly like the NSA setting the standards. The NSA's concerns
about computer security are not the concerns that businesses face—
they weren't worried about the Kremlin, they were worried about their
competitors."

Bolstered by industry support, the lawmakers moved fast and the
NSA was caught flat-footed. Not even an appearance by then–NSA
director General William E. Odom could stop the bill. His complaint
that shifting security responsibilities to the civilian agency would be an

unnecessary "duplication" of functions really missed the point: industry preferred that the Commerce Department, and not the spies, set standards for the national computer infrastructure. As one NSA official later wrote in a memo, "By the time we fully recognized the implications . . . [Brooks] had it orchestrated for a unanimous-consent voice-vote passage."

Of course, The Fort was not shut totally out of the process of securing the nation's computers. As the undisputed world capital of crypto, it had invaluable expertise in computer security, and Congress outlined an advisory role for Fort Meade to NIST. The question was, how would the two work together? In negotiations to determine that, the NSA sat across the table from the acting director of NIST, a bureaucrat named Raymond Kammer. Not only was Kammer sympathetic to the National Security Agency, he was actually the son of two of its veterans! The official Memorandum of Understanding reached between the two agencies did preserve the concept that NIST would take the lead in establishing standards, but formalized an NSA role as well. In "all matters related to cryptographic algorithms and cryptographic techniques," said the memo, NIST would solicit the NSA's help. To implement this, the two agencies would work through a "technical working group." Though NIST was supposedly in charge of the process, it would not hold a majority presence in the group, which consisted of three people from each agency.

Though both agencies insisted that NIST was really in the driver's seat, skeptics suspected otherwise. Even with its zippy new name, NIST was the nerdy Mr. Peepers of government agencies, suddenly thrust into the center of a huge political and national security battle. At least one high-ranking official of the agency later admitted that NIST not only hadn't sought the powers granted by the Security Act, but it didn't want them once the bill was passed. "It put us in charge of what we didn't want to be in charge of," he says.

The skirmishes over the digital signature standard seemed the ultimate proof that NIST was pretty much Fort Meade's stooge. In the years to follow, investigations would bear this out; one General Accounting Office report concluded that, contrary to congressional intent, "NIST follows NSA's lead in developing certain cryptographic standards." Declassified documents outlining the discussions in the monthly meetings of the two agencies' technical working group clearly illustrated this. At every step, the NIST people seemed to be waiting for the NSA's verdict on the signature issue.

Even NIST's own oversight group, the Computer System Security and Privacy Advisory Board, had serious problems with the relationship between the two agencies. In March 1992, it determined that "a national-level public review of the positive and negative implications of the widespread use of public and private key cryptography is required." But the NSA wanted no part of a discussion or review, and squelched that idea. In a classified memo, the new NSA head, Admiral Mike McConnell, put it bluntly: "The National Security Agency has serious reservations about a public debate on cryptography."

Still, the government was beginning to feel some heat. Once again, Representative Jack Brooks held hearings. They featured scorching testimony by the NSA's critics. Nathan Myhrvold of Microsoft testified that "the government's late publication of its proposed signature standard, together with its serious technical flaws . . . made it impossible for the computer industry to adopt the government standard for commercial use." Addison Fischer, an early RSA Data Security investor who used the company's algorithms in the mainframe computer products of his eponymous company, invoked a powerful metaphor that would reappear in crypto debates to come: "Cryptography, especially public key cryptography, is entering the mainstream," he said. "It is simply another of a long line of technological genies which is exceedingly useful, and which cannot be put back into the bottle—even if there may be some unpleasant side effects."

All of this criticism, of course, was music to Jim Bidzos's ears. While he had become a crusader for the free rein of crypto, his main goal had always been strengthening his company. If the pressure on the government continued—and he kept threatening to exercise the Schnorr patent to fight the government's candidate—he figured that eventually the standards process might go his way, and RSA technology would at least win approval as the official digital signature standard.

And then, astonishingly, the feds caved. Or at least seemed to.

As Bidzos tells it, the government finally concluded that its own standard would fail not on crypto grounds but on patent grounds. At a June 1993 meeting at the Commerce Department, a NIST lawyer said the words Bidzos longed to hear: "We want to work with you."

While Bidzos and his attorneys sat stunned, the official continued. "Why don't you make us a proposal for a licensing situation if you want to be compensated?".

Bidzos said he would get back to them in writing. And a negotiation began, with the government offering an amazing financial concession to Public Key Partners: an exclusive patent on the government's algorithm, the DSA. The United States would use the DSA as its standard, and would pay PKP a royalty fee. It was estimated that this could be as high as a dollar a user. Since millions of dollars would potentially come from this—every citizen would use this standard to communicate with the government, in everything from making contracts to filing IRS returns—there was a huge incentive for Bidzos to accept. So he did. In this sense, he was acting on behalf of his company's bottom line and against the interests of the general public. After all, his company would now be party to the use of the NSA's product as a standard, an algorithm Bidzos himself had gleefully trashed in public.

Some people began to question whether RSA's strategy of protecting crypto by patents was itself a path that retarded the progress of computer privacy. Maybe Bidzos *was* in league with the spooks. After all, as one observer noted, "One of the purposes of the patent system is to cause technology to be exploited. . . . Public key cryptography was invented almost twenty years ago, and yet is not yet in widespread use. A visit to the supermarket checkout counter reveals no digital signatures. Why not?"

But the deal would never be closed. In its haste to eliminate a nasty patent battle, the government underestimated the outrage that would come from its abandoning a commitment to make the algorithm royalty-free. When the government solicited comment on the deal, the criticism was withering. Critics called it a $2 billion giveaway to Public Key Partners. The Canadian government and the European Commission indicated that they wouldn't pay the royalties, and to hell with the patents claimed by the United States government. It was a revolt that the government didn't need. So NIST reneged on its offer to Bidzos, and reaffirmed that whatever standard it chose, it would be royalty free. And so, once again, it was back to square one on the digital signature standard.

Bidzos was philosophical about the turnaround. He did regret losing all that potential cash. But with the plan killed, Bidzos could once again take the side of the angels, a foe of a government that wanted to crush individual privacy, even if it meant impoverishing American software companies.

In any case, the bickering over the signature standard was to continue for another year. It wasn't until October 1994 that NIST finally made its choice. It chose to dismiss the patent issue, ignore the overwhelmingly negative public response, and endorse the DSA as its own candidate as the official standard for digital signatures. "NIST reviewed all the asserted patents and concluded that none of them would be infringed," it stated in a fact sheet. (To assure those who still had qualms, the agency took the extraordinary step of assuming liability for anyone using the standard who might later be sued for patent infringement.) While NIST made some beneficial technical changes from its original proposal, most notably extending the key length from 512 to 1024 bits, essentially the result was an authentication system created in secret by the government intelligence agency, one that virtually no one in industry had found attractive enough to adopt. This instead of a system already implemented by Microsoft, Apple, IBM, and Novell. Is it any wonder that years later, the digital signature standard would still be an orphan—and that in the midst of an electronic boom, there would exist no universal means of authenticating e-mail?

The funny thing is, as NIST scientist Lynn McNulty later said, "We thought that the digital signature would be the easy one." But as contentious as it was, the battle over signatures was only a warm-up for the main event in the cryptography war: the war over encryption.

crypto anarchy

When Phil Zimmermann began his cryptography adventure, he had no idea that he would end up both hailed as a folk hero and investigated for violations of federal law. He acted out of scientific curiosity, a hobbyist's passion, and a bit of political paranoia. Born in 1954, and raised in various Florida towns, he was a self-described nerd, "not naturally a party guy." An odd, awkward duck. His father was a truck driver; both parents were alcoholics. He wanted to be an astronomer. In the fourth grade, though, he became captivated by codes. A Saturday afternoon Miami television show called *M.T. Graves and the Dungeon* had a kids' club. Members were sold a physical "key" to unscramble a secret code. During the show, a series of numbers were flashed on the screen and club members could use the key to translate them into magical, clear messages. Zimmermann never sent in the money to buy the key, but he jotted down the numbers anyway—and managed to decode them into plaintext. To an only child in a troubled family, transforming such gibberish into something familiar gave a sense of mastery, of belonging. A sense of an organized home.

No wonder Zimmermann sought to learn more about ciphers. He found a book by children's author Herbert S. Zim called *Codes and*

Secret Writing. Published by Scholastic and directed at ten- to twelve-year-olds, this thin volume straightforwardly conveyed the excitement of cryptography, almost as if its author were a senior intelligence executive instructing a bright, though green, recruit. "The idea of this book is not to give you codes to copy but to help you invent your own codes—not one or two but, if you like, hundreds of codes," wrote Zim. "How you use your knowledge of codes is, of course, up to you."

The book became Zimmermann's Bible. He faithfully attempted all its exercises, such as making invisible ink out of lemon juice, creating original ciphers, and, of course, cracking the encoded messages presented in the book. A couple of years later, in junior high, a friend boasted of a code he'd made up and Zimmermann accepted the challenge of breaking it. "Make sure it's a long message," Zimmermann told the kid, who complied, foolishly thinking that a longer message would be harder to crack. The message was written in runic-style symbols, vaguely evocative of the languages of Tolkien's Middle Earth. Zimmermann did a frequency analysis, an elementary technique of cryptanalysis that simply involves counting how often alphabetic letters appear. This enabled him to solve it like a garden-variety cryptogram. All to the amazement of his buddy.

His interest in codes waned during his teenage years, and it wasn't until he was in college, at Florida Atlantic University, that Zimmermann realized computers could be cryptographic tools. Though he was majoring in physics, he wound up spending a lot of time in the computer room, at first doing course-related work, but eventually just drinking in the elixir of programming itself. The appeal was creating one's own world in the machine. "You could interact with something that wasn't a living thing but seemed to be like one," he says. Best of all, he was good at it, in contrast to his physics abilities. His nemesis: calculus.

Though he began programming his first week at college in 1972, he didn't actually *see* a real computer for a year, because his school only had terminals connected to distant machines. After all, Florida Atlantic wasn't MIT or Stanford. Not even a big state school. Zimmermann became a student assistant, teaching others to use the terminals. And after his second year, he dropped physics for computer science.

He rediscovered his passion for ciphers in that computer room. One of his experiments involved writing his own secret code, using the now-antiquated FORTRAN computer language. His scheme used random number functions to substitute each character in a plaintext message with a different character. The random number function was keyed with a password. Because his code couldn't be broken by frequency analysis (the randomizing function would change a "t" early in the message to one thing and subsequent "t's" to different characters), Zimmermann figured that not even the CIA could break it. He'd never imagined techniques like chosen plaintext attacks, or deconstructing random number generators. (And he'd never heard of the NSA.) As it was, years later he would encounter that same "unbreakable" cipher, presented in a student homework assignment as a cipher that could be easily broken with basic cryptanalytic techniques. "So much for my brilliant scheme," he says.

In the summer of 1977, with only one course to go before graduation and already employed at a minicomputer company in Fort Lauderdale, Zimmermann came across the Mathematical Recreations column of *Scientific American*, and found something that blew his mind. It was, of course, Martin Gardner's description of public key and the RSA algorithm. He was hungry to know more. Out of the blue, he called Ron Rivest at MIT and asked him about the possibilities of implementing the system on a computer. Rivest told him that in the course of experimenting, the MIT group had already done that in LISP, a tony computer language used for artificial intelligence work. "That's out of my reach," said a disappointed Zimmermann, who had never had access to the flashy LISP machines; they were luxury items costing $100,000 and geared for research, not practical tasks like accounting. Though high-level arithmetic wasn't his strong point, Zimmermann understood that the odds of getting a LISP box at Florida Atlantic University approached infinity to one. He wondered, however, whether he could do RSA on one of those cheap new microcomputers. That would be different. Zimmermann had a partial share in one of the clunky low-cost machines of the time—it ran on a Zylog Z-80 processor, sort of the Model A of the mid-1970s. But as he thought about implementing RSA, he realized that he had little idea of how to do some of the extended arithmetic routines explained in the MIT paper. So he didn't try.

There were other things happening in Phil Zimmermann's life then. The same year he discovered RSA, he married his girlfriend Kacie

Cavenaugh, who worked on the college switchboard. Not long afterward, the young couple visited friends in Boulder, Colorado, and fell in love with the area. Zimmermann returned to his Florida job but began planning for a move, and a year later he and Kacie packed up their Volkswagen Rabbit and drove to the Rockies. He got a job at a software company making workstation word processors, and began raising a family: their son was born in 1980. And then he heard Daniel Ellsberg speak at a nuclear freeze rally in Denver.

In high school, Phil Zimmermann had pretty much ignored Vietnam, but at Florida Atlantic he had come to adopt a passive but heartfelt antigovernment stance. The Nixon scandals had opened his eyes to how brazenly the government could lie. By the time of Ronald Reagan's presidency, he had totally soured on politics. He read Robert Scheer's *With Enough Shovels*, and worried about nuclear annihilation. Zimmermann and his wife decided to move to New Zealand, the better to avoid the coming holocaust. They went so far as to acquire passports and immigration papers. (He had yet to learn that there wasn't much of a computer industry in New Zealand.) And then he attended the 1982 rally where he heard Ellsberg, who, after his famous moment as the emancipator of the Pentagon Papers, had become a leading antinuclear activist. Zimmermann was galvanized. From that point on, he forgot about emigrating and decided to become active himself—to stay and fight.

He and some friends were starting a company they called Metamorphic Systems, and they planned to produce a circuit board for Apple computers that would run Intel-compatible programs. But Zimmermann still found time to dig into every book he could find on NATO policy, weapon systems, and the like. He would spend hundreds of dollars at a bookstore and tear through the volumes. Then he began teaching military policy at the Free University in Boulder. He spoke at nuclear freeze rallies and advised a couple of candidates for Congress. Twice he was arrested at rallies, once at the Nevada nuclear testing range, alongside his heroes Ellsberg and Carl Sagan. (Neither arrest resulted in any charges filed.)

But as the eighties moved on, the nuclear freeze movement seemed to lose steam. Metamorphic Systems wasn't doing well either: once the IBM PC became dominant, the idea of putting Intel processors into Apple II computers seemed kind of ridiculous. Zimmermann himself was a bit lost. But then, everything changed with a single phone call from a programmer in Arkansas who had a scheme few people could appreciate more than Phil Zimmermann.

The guy's name was Charlie Merritt, and it turned out that he was actually doing the thing that Zimmermann had dreamed of since reading Martin Gardner's column in 1977: he was implementing an RSA public key cryptosystem on a microcomputer. Merritt had experienced a similar reaction to Zimmermann's when he'd read about the work of the MIT researchers. Moving from his native Houston to Fayetteville, Arkansas, he started a company with several friends and they actually managed to create a public key program running on Z-80 computers. It ran very slowly, but it worked. But no one seemed to want to buy it. After a while, his friends dropped out, and Merritt, with his wife Hobbit, began selling the program themselves. Eventually news of their tiny enterprise reached the multibillion-dollar intelligence operation in Fort Meade. Periodically the NSA would send its representatives to Arkansas to warn Merritt of the dire consequences that might ensue if he sent any encryption packages out of the country. Since Merritt Software's customers were largely overseas companies that wanted encryption to circumvent the peeping thugs of corrupt regimes, this restriction virtually shut the company down. To try to get some domestic leads, Merritt was reduced to calling obscure companies he'd read about in computer magazines, hoping they would package his program with their stuff. That was how he found Metamorphic and Phil Zimmermann.

When Zimmermann heard what Merritt was up to, his excitement was so over the top that Merritt suspected a practical joke was being played on him: no one he'd ever met had been so nuts about encryption. Zimmermann told Merritt all about his own passion for crypto, about *M.T. Graves and the Dungeon* and Herbert Zim and Ron Rivest. He professed his hatred for Big Brother. But mostly, he wanted to know *everything* Merritt had learned about making RSA work on a personal computer.

Now that he knew it was possible to do so, Zimmermann became driven to write his own public key encryption program—for the people. Whereas his previous efforts in crypto had been solely performed as neat hacks, and as an expression of his passion for codes in general, he now was a sophisticated political activist who had twice been dragged off to a holding pen for asserting his opinion. He now understood that in the computer age, government had an extremely powerful tool for monitoring dissent: electronic surveillance. Not only could Big Brother types stick their collective ear into phone conversations, but they could pluck the increasingly popular e-mail messages out of the digital ether and read business plans and shameful secrets to their black, black hearts' content. While electronic mail was a terrific thing, it actually represented a step backward in privacy: even with relatively insecure physical mail, people had sealed envelopes to protect the privacy of their messages. What Zimmermann hoped to produce was the electronic equivalent to sealed envelopes. But if you gave people a crypto program to protect e-mail, you'd have something much *better* than sealed envelopes. If people all agreed to use it, he thought, it would be a form of solidarity, a mass movement to resist unwanted snooping. Right on, baby!

Understanding the speed limitations of public key, Zimmermann figured that his program should be a hybrid cryptosystem, using the slow public key RSA protocols to exchange keys and some other, speedier algorithm to perform the bulk encryption of the actual message. He was unaware of Lotus Notes, which was already implementing such a hybrid system, and was certainly in the dark about RSA Data Security, Inc., which was going to base an entire business on licensing public key for the kind of systems Zimmermann thought he was himself pioneering. (Neither did Zimmermann have a clue about the RSA patents.) In any case, neither of those firms had a shipping product in 1984.

Zimmermann did understand several things correctly: A useful program should run not just on a single brand of computer, but on all sorts of machines. To do this, it had to be written in a computer language that was amenable to all sorts of different processors, and as any programmer knew, the language that best satisfied that requirement was called C. Fortunately, Zimmermann knew C inside out. The program also had to be easy to use. And its circulation had to be so widespread that a near-ubiquity could quickly be realized. Thus it would benefit by the Network Effect.

Charlie Merritt was a holdout who still hadn't tackled C, but he was strong in an area where Zimmermann was sadly deficient: the complicated mathematics that enabled one to work with the huge numbers required by RSA. This was particularly important in implementing RSA on a personal computer, which used 8-bit "words" in its calculations: it was a challenging process to apply those relatively small numbers in a way that could process the mighty numbers that RSA demanded—512 bits, 1028 bits, and even more. If you didn't do it efficiently, the program would run so slowly that no one would ever use it.

Though no immediate business deal came of Merritt's call to Metamorphic, he and Zimmermann became constant telephone correspondents, with Zimmermann soliciting all of Merritt's knowledge of multiprecision arithmetic functions. It was such a complicated process that eventually they decided that Merritt should come to visit Zimmermann in Boulder for a sort of arithmetic boot camp, in November 1986.

It was an action-packed week, and not only because of the math that Zimmermann learned. Merritt was working on a project for the navy, producing a conventional cipher; he taught it to the younger man. The project had been subcontracted to Merritt by a company for whom he'd been consulting: RSA Data Security. Before he flew to Boulder, he'd called the company's new president to ask if they might meet in Colorado, a place that was a sight easier to get to than Fayetteville, Arkansas. Jim Bidzos agreed.

Bidzos had been looking forward to a testosterone-charged get-to-know-you dinner with Merritt—two guys in a steak house lighting cigars and swapping lies. Instead he found a third wheel was included, Zimmermann. And instead of a steak house, they wound up at The Good Earth, a brightly lit emporium of salads and grains.

The actual conversation at the restaurant would become a matter of dispute. Jim Bidzos later said he had been startled when Phil Zimmermann spoke of his plan to create a program that used RSA's proprietary protocols. In fact, RSA had a similar program, and Bidzos had brought along two copies. This was Mailsafe, written by Rivest and Adleman, two guys who by now had more math and cryptography knowledge in their little fingers than Zimmermann had managed to glean from Merritt in two years. Zimmermann, however, would claim that Bidzos was impressed with his plans, so much so that he offered the programmer a free license to the RSA algorithm. Bidzos would later vociferously deny making any such offer.

In any case, Zimmermann saw no reason to change his own plans, and he spent the next few years furthering his didactic education on cryptography so he could complete his own encryption program. He wrote up some of his ideas in a paper that was published, to his pride, in *IEEE Computer*, a well-regarded computer-science journal. Not bad for a kid from Florida Atlantic University.

Then he began working on the actual program. One crucial step was producing the bulk encryption algorithm that would perform the actual encoding of message content. Eschewing DES and the RSA-owned RC-2 standard devised by Ron Rivest, he attempted the risky course of producing his own cipher. It was based on the one that Charlie Merritt had taught him, the cipher Merritt had produced for the navy. But Zimmermann toughened the system by introducing multiple rounds of substitution. As he refined his concept, he recalled a Dan Aykroyd routine from the original *Saturday Night Live* television show. Portraying a fast-talking late-night huckster, Aykroyd hawked a blender so powerful that you could throw a fish into it: the liquefied output would be a healthy juice (yum). This was the Bass-O-Matic, a perfect name, Zimmermann figured, for an encryption algorithm. Any cryptanalyst who confronted his scrambled messages would be as ineffectual at reconstructing them, he hoped, as someone attempting to reconstitute a silvery, flopping fish from the noxious goo emerging from the Bass-O-Matic blender.

Zimmermann went on to other problems, and pieces fell into place—message digests, interface, and a range of protocols. But after months and months of work, all he really had were separate components that still weren't tied together into a working program. "It took a lot more work to put them together," he says. By 1990—six years after first talking to Charlie Merritt and four years since Merritt's visit to Boulder—Zimmermann realized that in order to finish he would have to make a total gung-ho commitment, even if it meant having to tighten his budget, cut out the consulting, and spend less time with his family. He embarked on a full-time regimen of programming.

Zimmermann had dreamed up a name for his work in progress, though not one as irreverent as Bass-O-Matic. Zimmermann had been an early devotee of the Macintosh computer, and had experimented with a simple data communications program when none had existed. Thinking of "Ralph's Pretty Good Grocery," an imaginary sponsor from Garrison Keillor's *A Prairie Home Companion* radio show, he had called it "Pretty Good Terminal." This gave him the idea for the name of his crypto program: Pretty Good Privacy. He never really considered that it might become a major brand name. But then, his marketing plans were vague. He did hope to make some money selling PGP, but figured on a modest amount using shareware rules, where people would download the program and pay him on the honor system.

For the next six months, Zimmermann worked twelve-hour days in a bedroom of his house, which he almost lost because he didn't have the money to make the mortgage payments. Maybe, he figured, if he finally finished PGP and released it, enough users would send him money to get him back on his feet. As the software got closer to completion, he called Jim Bidzos to see if they could finally clear up the intellectual property issue that the RSA chief had brought up during that ill-fated dinner. Zimmermann explained his product and asked for a go-ahead to use the RSA algorithm. Bidzos was appalled at the request: *this guy thinks we'll just give him our crown jewels?* Maybe instead of asking for handouts, he suggested, Zimmermann should develop his product for some company rich enough to get a standard RSA license.

The whole conversation was so out of line with Zimmermann's vision for his product—and the dim view he took of the high-powered business world—that he basically ignored the whole problem and went back to work.

By early 1991, Zimmermann was making progress toward a working product. Then something happened to change his course—and to make PGP famous. The unlikely agent in this shift was U.S. Senator Joseph Biden, the head of the Senate Judiciary Committee and a cosponsor of pending antiterrorist legislation, Senate Bill 266. In a draft of the bill introduced on January 24, Biden inserted some new language:

> It is the sense of Congress that providers of electronic communications services and manufacturers of electronic communications service equipment shall ensure that communications systems permit the government to obtain the *plaintext contents* of voice, data, and other communications when appropriately authorized by law. [Emphasis added.]

A poison needle in a haystack of clauses and qualifications, this passage originally escaped scrutiny. But its appearance was no accident. The language of the bill had been forged with the help of law enforcement agencies. That sentence was included at the explicit request of the FBI. And what a sentence it was! It plunged a virtual dagger into the heart of the crypto revolution. How could tech companies and services promise to deliver the *plaintext contents* of encrypted texts—the original messages meant to be read only by their intended recipients—if people scrambled them with programs like Mailsafe, Lotus Notes, and PGP? Logically, the only way that the "sense of Congress" could be satisfied would be a ban on any encryption except that equipped with "trapdoors" that the manufacturers and services could flip open at the demand of the feds.

It wasn't until April 1991, however, that the crypto community itself learned of this legislative time bomb. A consultant who had done work for the NSA revealed the offending clause on various Internet bulletin boards, along with apocalyptic commentary: "Are there readers of this list that believe that providers of electronic communications services can reserve to themselves the ability to read all the traffic and still keep the traffic 'confidential' in any meaningful sense? . . . Any assertion that all use of any such trapdoors would be only 'when appropriately authorized by law' is absurd on its face. . . . Any such mechanism would be subject to abuse." The message ended with a warning that would galvanize Phil Zimmermann: "I suggest you begin to stock up on crypto gear while you can still get it."

To Zimmermann, S. 266 was the ultimate deadline. If he didn't get PGP out into the world *now,* the government might prevent its very existence. At least for the time being, domestic crypto was legal. So Zimmermann decided to finish up the first version of PGP quickly and get it out to as many people as possible. He also gave up his financial hopes for PGP. Instead of releasing it as shareware, he designated it "freeware." This meant not only that the software didn't cost anything, but also that users could themselves distribute it far and wide to others with the blessing of its creator.

Fortunately, a medium existed that made it easier than in any time in history to circulate an encryption system like PGP: the Internet. In 1991, the formerly government-owned computer network was just beginning its meteoric rise to ubiquity. Thousands of discussion groups abounded, and millions of files were downloaded every day. The majority of users at the time did not yet reflect the public at large—most were very computer savvy, and a lot of them were outright nerds. But these were exactly the types of people who would respond to PGP, which, despite Zimmermann's best efforts, was still not as easy to use as MacWrite or Tetris.

Oddly, at that time, Zimmermann himself was not much of an Internet devotee. He hardly knew how to use e-mail. In this sense he was still the outsider looking in. But in recent months he had begun a correspondence with a fellow crypto enthusiast in California, Kelly Goen, whom he had met through Charlie Merritt. In the month after the on-line call to action about S. 266, Zimmermann apparently gave Goen a copy of his PGP software so that it could be spread on the Internet "like dandelion seeds," Zimmermann later wrote. On May 24 Goen e-mailed Jim Warren, a computer activist and columnist for *MicroTimes*, a Bay Area computer-oriented newspaper, and explained the purpose of flooding the networks with PGP. "The intent here," wrote Goen, "is to invalidate the so-called trapdoor provision of the new Senate bill coming down the pike before it makes it into law." In other words, if thousands of copies of PGP were in use, Senate Bill 266 would be rendered irrelevant; when confronted with PGP-encrypted files, the AT&Ts of the world would not be able to guarantee plaintext to G-men or spooks.

On the first weekend in June, Jim Warren got a series of calls from Goen, who told him that PGP day had arrived. Goen was obviously intoxicated with the drama of it all, taking precautions that were more from the book of Maxwell Smart than James Bond. "He was driving around the Bay Area with a laptop, acoustic coupler, and cellular phone," Warren later wrote in *MicroTimes*. "He would stop at a pay phone, upload a number of copies for a few minutes, then disconnect and rush off to another phone miles away. He said he wanted to get as many copies scattered as widely as possible around the nation before the government could get an injunction and stop him."

Apparently, Goen was also careful to upload only to Internet sites inside the United States. Of course, once a software program appears on a file server, anyone in the world can download it: Pakistani hackers, Iraqi terrorists, Bulgarian freedom fighters, Swiss adulterers, Japanese high schoolers, French businessmen, Dutch child pornographers,

Norwegian privacy nuts, or Colombian drug dealers. Though not yet a cliché, an Internet slogan was already becoming a familiar refrain: On the Information Highway, borders are just speed bumps.

How quickly did PGP leave the United States and find its way overseas, without as much as a howdy-do to the export laws? Instantly. Zimmermann would later marvel at hearing that the very next day people in other countries were encrypting messages with PGP. How could Zimmermann have avoided this potentially illegal passage of his program to distant shores? "I could have not released it at all," he later said. "But there's no law against Americans having strong cryptography." And, after all, Phil Zimmermann engineered his sudden release of PGP not to circumvent export laws, but to arm his countrymen, the people who might be affected by Senate Bill 266. His motto, as expressed in his documentation to the program, was "When crypto is outlawed, only outlaws will have crypto."

Ironically, Joseph Biden's offending language, the impetus for Zimmermann's extraordinary step, met a much less enthusiastic response than PGP did. Senator Biden had been taken by surprise at the huge expression of public outrage (fueled by civil liberties groups) at the stealth antiprivacy language he had introduced. By June, he had quietly withdrawn the clause. But the incident left an unexpected legacy: hundreds of thousands of PGP-encrypted messages circulating throughout the world. Pretty Good Privacy had escaped from Phil Zimmermann's hard drive and had now been cloned countless times. He could no more recall it than one could take back one's words after they were uttered.

Zimmermann was proud of PGP 1.0 though defensive at its shortcomings. Maybe it *didn't* introduce any mathematical innovations. And maybe the coding *was* so disorganized that he felt compelled to apologize for it in the documentation. But it was one of the first really usable personal computer solutions for a complete cryptosystem, from digital signatures to encryption. "If you look at what was available at that time, there were only laboratory petri-dish versions of RSA," he says. "One had been published in *Byte;* it took all afternoon to do an RSA calculation. Mine did that in a few seconds. I had brought together a practical implementation that had all the things you needed to do public key cryptography. It was a major event . . . it was a *watershed* event."

One person disagreed strongly: Jim Bidzos of RSA and Public Key Partners. When *he* saw PGP, he was outraged. This was no original product, he felt—*look at Mailsafe*—but a blatant rip-off of his company's technology and patents. Why didn't Zimmermann get honest and call it Pretty Good *Piracy*? Bidzos called the Colorado programmer and, literally screaming at him, demanded he remove the software from circulation. Despite all Bidzos's previous animosity, Zimmermann was actually taken aback at this response: "I thought he would be delighted," he says. He attempted to defend himself. He had done PGP for *political* reasons, not to challenge any commercial enterprises. After all, the Fortune 500 companies that were RSA's potential customers don't use freeware; they buy their software from companies that will back it up and support it. So what was the problem?

Bidzos accused him of actually playing into the NSA's hands— because anything that hurt his company was music to Fort Meade.

Not long afterward, Bidzos had his lawyer put Zimmermann on legal notice that he was infringing on PKP's patents. This worried Zimmermann, and he called Bidzos once again to try to make a deal. The basis of the agreement was simple: Zimmermann would not distribute his software with the RSA protocols, and Bidzos would not sue him. An agreement was indeed drawn up to that effect, and Zimmermann signed it. But each party had his own interpretation of that phone conversation. Bidzos felt that the deal compelled Zimmermann actually to kill PGP. Zimmermann insisted that he had only affirmed his understanding of a hypothetical agreement: *if* he stopped distribution of PGP, *then* he would not be sued. Zimmermann would also claim Bidzos gave him verbal assurances that RSA would sell licenses to PGP's end-users so they could use the software without infringing on RSA's patents. Bidzos denied those claims.

It later became clear that Zimmermann's interpretation of "distributing PGP" was somewhat narrow. By leaving the distribution to others, he felt that he was free to continue his involvement with the software. In fact, Zimmermann was supervising a second release of PGP, this one with the help of some more experienced cryptographers.

He'd realized that he needed help after a sobering experience at Crypto '91 in Santa Barbara. His main mission had been to get a reading from the wizards there on the security of PGP. (Admittedly this task was overdue, considering that thousands of people were already using the program.) Right away, he ran into Brian Snow, one of the top crypto mathematicians at the NSA. Zimmermann, of course, was curious as to whether the government was upset about PGP. "If I were you, I would be more concerned about getting heat from Jim Bidzos than from the government," said Snow.

This puzzled Zimmermann—why wasn't the government worried? Then he sought private comments on his program. After first getting a brush-off from Adi Shamir—the Israeli cryptographer told him to send the program to Israel and he'd spend ten minutes with it— Zimmermann got the attention of Shamir's colleague at Weizmann, Eli Biham. They retreated to the UCSB cafeteria, scene of many a bull session and impromptu cryptanalysis at the annual conference. For Zimmermann, it was a long lunch in more ways than one; Biham quickly embarrassed the amateur cryptographer by uncovering several fatal flaws in Bass-O-Matic. The cipher was, for instance, vulnerable to a differential cryptanalysis attack. While not exactly a dead fish, the Bass-O-Matic was far from a prize catch.

Zimmermann now realized that he could only truly improve PGP if he were to recognize his own limitations. His ultimate success at code-making would come from realizing that he wasn't really a great cryptographer. He was a knowledgeable packager and programmer who would need ace mathematicians and cryptographers to help him with the hard-core details.

Fortunately, a lot of very smart people had been excited by the release of PGP 1.0. Instead of feeling burned by its weaknesses, they were eager to pitch in and fix them. Soon Zimmermann had recruited volunteers in New Zealand, Holland, and California to be his mainstay engineers. A casual collection of kibitzers also contributed advice and small pieces. Together they began work on version 2.0. Zimmermann was the chief designer, approving every decision, every line of the code, but he hid his role so that Bidzos wouldn't think that he was abandoning his promise not to violate RSA's patents.

The result was PGP 2.0, an infinitely stronger product. Bass-O-Matic had been tossed aside ("Calling it that wasn't too good an idea, anyway," says Zimmermann. "Cryptography is something you can't joke about"). In its place, Zimmermann chose a preexisting Swiss cipher called the International Data Encryption Algorithm, or IDEA. Written in 1990 by two celebrated cryptographic mathematicians, IDEA had quickly stood up to public scrutiny. Zimmermann felt the IDEA cipher was even stronger than DES, particularly with the 128-bit keys he recommended. "This is not," he wrote in the 2.0 documentation, "a home-grown algorithm."

Another crucial improvement came in an area that Zimmermann basically had ignored with PGP 1.0: key certification, the process by which public keys are authenticated. Certification is often seen as the Achilles' heel of public key systems. The classic conundrum in such systems arises when Alice wants to send something to Bob. She scrambles it with Bob's public key, and only Bob can unscramble it. But what if Alice has never met Bob—how does she get his public key? If she asks him for it directly, she can't encode her request (obviously not, because she doesn't have his public key yet, which she would use to encrypt the message). So a potential eavesdropper, Eve, could act as "a man in the middle," and snatch that message en route. Then Eve, pretending to be Bob, could send her *own* public key to Alice, falsely representing it as Bob's key. (This deceptive masquerade is known as "spoofing.") If Alice is duped, she'll encode her secret message to Bob with the key. Alas, Bob won't be able to read anything scrambled with that key—only tricky Eve can. So much for the security of direct requests.

What about the idea of publishing something like a digital phone book full of public keys? The forging problem persists, unless you have a certifiably secure means of protecting that book and assuring that the keys really do belong to their purported owners. Yes, it would require an extravagant effort to pull off such a fraud. But it's possible, and as long as the vulnerability exists, any public key system has to figure out a way to get around this security hole.

Many people have come to think that the answer lies in a large-scale "certification authority" to distribute and verify public keys. Such a center would be able to process millions of public keys. Using the certification authority's own public key—presumably a key so well-circulated that no one could spoof it—you could securely query it to get someone's key, or verify a public key someone sent you. Of course, such an ambitious solution was impossible for Zimmermann. He didn't have the wherewithal, or money, to set up a closely monitored certification authority to distribute and verify public keys. So he had to come up with another method.

His solution was quite ingenious, especially since it reflected the outsider sensibility that generally characterized his efforts. Instead of a central key authority, he envisioned the PGP community itself as an authority. "PGP allows third parties, mutually trusted friends, to sign keys," explained Zimmermann in a 1993 interview. "That proves that they came from who they said they came from." By "signing" keys, Zimmermann was talking about a technique whereby someone in effect attached his or her own public key to someone else's, as a sort of stamp of approval. After you generated a public key, you'd get the key signed by people who knew you personally. These signings were to be performed face-to-face, to minimize the threat of spoofing. So if Alice knows Bob personally, she arranges to meet him, and physically hands him a disk with her PGP public key. Using his copy of PGP, Bob signs it with his own private key. (This is done simply by selecting a function in the software program and clicking the mouse.) He gives her back the signed key and keeps a copy for his own "public key ring," a collection of signed keys that PGP users are encouraged to keep on their hard drives. Later, a third party, Carol, might want to communicate with Alice but doesn't know her. So Carol seeks out Alice's public key, either from her directly or from a bulletin board full of public keys. In the latter case, how does she know it's really Alice's? She checks to see who has signed the key—does it have the imprimatur of anyone she knows? Since Carol knows Bob—and has earlier received a verified copy of Bob's public key—she can establish the veracity of *his* signature. If it checks out, that means that Bob has really met the person who holds this new key and is implicitly telling Carol, "Hey, it's really Alice." So Carol can be sure that Alice is who she says she is. At least to the degree she trusts Bob.

This system—known as a "web of trust"—requires some judgment on the user's part. After all, Carol can't be sure of Alice's identity unless she personally knows someone who has physically met her and signed her key. What if she doesn't know anyone who's physically signed it? Is it worth trusting a second-level verification? Maybe her friend Bob hasn't signed Alice's key, but he has signed a key of someone named Ted. And Ted has signed Alice's key. Whether you'll trust that signature depends on Ted's reputation: who are the people who have signed *his* key? As more and more people used PGP, some were bound to develop a reputation for being scrupulous in verifying the keys they sign. Seeing one of those trusted introducers on a key ring would be a strong assurance of authenticity. In any case, PGP allowed users to set what cryptographer Bruce Schneier refers to as "paranoia levels": how many levels of separation you're willing to accept, depending on the degree to which you trust various signers.

With this web of trust, a stronger encryption algorithm, a better interface, and a number of other improvements, PGP 2.0 was—unlike Zimmermann's favorite weekend comedy show—ready for prime time. The informal team of programmers had even prepared translations of the interface in several languages, so people worldwide could use it from the day of release. In September 1992, two of Zimmermann's helpers posted PGP 2.0 on the Net from their respective homes in Amsterdam and Auckland. This way, the program could be imported *into* the United States, violating no export regulations. In almost no time, the new version supplanted and exceeded the first one. "I got more mail in the month after the release than I had received the whole previous year," says Zimmermann. "It was like lighting a match to dry prairie grass."

Jim Bidzos became, if possible, even angrier. He was particularly outraged at a contention of Zimmermann's included in the documentation that came with every download of PGP. Zimmermann claimed that Public Key Partners was ripping off the American public by making people pay for technology developed on the government dime. After Zimmermann's attempts to cover himself with disclaimers ("The author of this software implementation of the RSA algorithm is providing this . . . for educational use only. . . . Licensing this algorithm from PKP is the responsibility of you, the user, not Philip Zimmermann. . . ."), he launched into a long justification of his actions, claiming that he didn't think he was infringing on any patents. He implied that by controlling the patents to public key cryptography, Public Key Partners—"essentially a litigation company," he called it—was doing the NSA's dirty work by denying crypto to the people! Finally, while not giving any assurances, he told potential users that they didn't have much to worry about by violating PKP's patent rights: "There are just too many PGP users to go after," he wrote. "And why would they single you out?"

"He's misleading people, defaming us as a way of getting support for his own agenda," said Bidzos in 1994. "There's the evil government trying to deny you your right to privacy and the evil patent holders bent on ripping you and the government off—it's not really clear who's worse, but you can put them both off by using this software. He knew it was false."

Bidzos did have a point: RSA itself had already produced Mailsafe, an implementation of the public key patents. Both parties agree that during the contentious 1986 dinner meeting, Bidzos gave Zimmermann a copy of Mailsafe, but Zimmermann claimed he never tested the software or read the documentation because he'd already figured out how his product would work. "This guy says he was blown away by the invention of RSA," says Bidzos. "We're supposed to believe that he took software written by the people who invented it, his heroes, and never was curious enough to look at it?"

Yet much of Bidzos's fury was directed not just at Zimmermann's actions but at the runaway popularity of PGP. Because it was free, available worldwide regardless of export laws, and had quickly attained a patina of coolness among the high-tech crowd, its usership quickly exceeded that of Mailsafe, and was now threatening to become an Internet standard. Despite not being an accomplished cryptographer with a Stanford or MIT pedigree, despite having virtually no sense of business or marketing, Zimmermann had done what neither the original world-class public key mathematicians nor the market-savvy Bidzos had succeeded in doing: create a bottom-up crypto phenomenon that not only won over grassroots users but was being described as the major challenge to the multibillion-dollar agency behind the Triple Fence. No wonder that by the end of 1992, Phil Zimmermann had gone from total obscurity to the hero of the crypto underground. "If I go to Europe, I'll never have to buy lunch," he said. "I have a huge number of adoring fans."

Zimmermann's do-it-yourself effort to create a crypto program and distribute it to the people—an effort consciously undertaken to circumvent government control—marked a new dimension in the ongoing battle between the NSA and the cryptographers who worked outside its reach. The agency had once felt that its voluntary prepublication compromise with academics had mitigated much of the potential damage of that community's emergence. (And with the troublesome First Amendment in play, there was little choice in the matter.) Fort Meade's minions were also fending off the commercial threat to its dominance by budging only slightly on the export situation.

But it was getting harder to convince people that it made sense to control cryptography. It was becoming increasingly clear that this was not a weapons technology but one that might fit in as a common artifact of everyday life. All those millions who used Lotus Notes were already aware of its benefits. Those with garden variety e-mail were shocked to find that basic protections just weren't there—sending mail on the Internet seemed secure but was actually one step removed from broadcasting. And as more people began using cellular phones, for instance, they wondered why it was that their calls could be so easily monitored by any wirehead who plunked down a hundred dollars for a scanner. Even the Prince of Wales had his cell calls to his mistress intercepted, with the whole world now chuckling at endearments he uttered to her, endearments that were intensely personal (OK, they involved menstruation supplies). In a world of highly evolved communications, why shouldn't everything be protected? Even the National Football League figured this out: it used crypto to encode the radio signals sent from coaches in the observation booth to quarterbacks on the field. This was something anyone could understand. Here was something as straightforward as a means to prevent the Green Bay Packers from stealing the next play from John Elway . . . and we called this *national security*?

These were tough questions for a branch of government not used to answering any questions at all. But the questioning was about to become more intense as a new force, in part inspired by Zimmermann, now came into play: cryptoactivism. Strong cryptography distributed on the Internet—and a revolutionary movement built around producing and distributing strong codes—seemed on its face a fringe activity. But with the crypto controversy heating up, it turned out that the time was ripe for a small movement to apply leverage.

So it seemed to two crypto enthusiasts who hatched an idea for a group that would be outside even the outsiders in the battle for cryptography. The concept developed spontaneously when Eric Hughes, a young mathematician living in the north Bay Area and thinking of moving down the California coast, visited his friend Tim May in Santa Cruz to do some house hunting.

Hughes and May were an interesting combination, bound by scientific passion, political libertarianism, and a slightly unnerving paranoia. (Hughes liked to joke about this, citing an unknown philosopher who supposedly said, "Cryptography is the mathematical consequence of paranoid assumptions.") Both cut striking figures, eschewing a math-nerd look for the frontier garb of the Old West: crypto cowboys. Hughes was often seen in a felt Stetson.

At forty, May was a physicist who had retired from Intel seven years earlier with a bundle of stocks. His major contribution at the semiconductor giant had been his proof that quantum events—the meanderings of subatomic particles—could affect the calculations performed by semiconductor chips. May's discovery allowed Intel's designers to devise strategies to deal with this problem, enabling the steady progress of Moore's Law. Outside of technology, May was an advocate of libertarianism, as opposed to government restrictions. "I got converted by reading Ayn Rand as a kid," he says. "I would write polemics about natural rights in class." As an adult he posted such polemics—intentionally provocative and highly entertaining rants—to Usenet groups, and his hard-core advocacy of unbridled cryptography had earned him an edgy reputation. A slim, bearded man who often wore an outback hat, he owned a small house cluttered with books, gadgets, and well-fed cats.

A semilapsed Mormon from Virginia, Eric Hughes had a long, wispy light-brown beard, aviator wire-rimmed glasses, and a cold, sarcastic wit. Not yet thirty, he was brimming with attitude. But his cocky sureness was tempered with a steady intelligence that enabled him to understand both sides of an issue. He loved cryptography. He'd studied math at Berkeley, and worked for a company overseas for a while. Now, at the dawn of the Internet, he was figuring out how he could use codes to fortify the information age. His ultimate goal was combining pure-market capitalism and freedom fighting. In his world view, governments—even allegedly benign ones like the United States—were a constant threat to the well-being of citizens. Individual privacy was a citadel constantly under attack by the state. The great miracle was that the state could be thwarted by algorithms.

"It used to be that you could get privacy by going to the physical frontier, where no one would bother you," he said. "With the right application of cryptography, you can again move out to the frontier—permanently."

As radical as Hughes's vision was, it paled in comparison to that of his Santa Cruz friend. When Tim May thought about crypto it was almost like dropping acid. In the computer age, we create "virtual regions," he would say. And the conduits and pipes of the future, the very mortar and walls of those virtual spaces, could be held up by nothing but crypto. *Oh, God,* May would burst out when speaking of this vision, *it's so profound. There's nothing else!* One-way functions like the ones exploited by Diffie, Merkle, and Rivest were the building blocks of cyberspace, he insisted, and if we don't use them we would be reduced to pathetic shivering creatures standing in the ashes of a virtual burned-out house. But with it, *everything* is imaginable. Secure conduits—untappable by the NSA!—from hackers in Los Gatos, California, to activists in St. Petersburg, Russia. Transactions beyond taxation. And an end to the nation-states. *That* was the coming revolution, according to Tim May.

Such were the topics discussed in May 1992 during Eric Hughes's house-hunting visit to Tim May. There was so much to talk about that the conversation lasted for three days. "We'd get up in the morning and just keep chatting and chatting and I wouldn't get anything done about looking for a house," says Hughes. "And we'd go out to lunch and come back and keep going. It just went on and on." By the end of the visit—not surprisingly, Hughes had made no progress in finding a house and went back to his shared crashpad in Berkeley—they agreed to organize a loose confederation of those with similar views. Not to sit around and bullshit, but to actually produce, à la Zimmermann, the tools that would arm the general public against cyberthieves, credit bureaus, and especially the government.

In the next few weeks, they enlisted the aid of some influential figures in the antigovernment crypto community. One forceful ally was thirty-seven-year-old John Gilmore, a gentle computer hacker with long thinning hair and a wispy beard (when he stood beside Eric Hughes, the two of them looked like a geeky version of the cough-drop-icon Smith Brothers). Gilmore had made a small fortune from being one of the original programmers at Sun Microsystems—he had been employee number five—but left in 1986. In 1990, along with Mitch Kapor and Grateful Dead lyricist John Perry Barlow, he'd founded the Electronic Frontier Foundation (EFF) to enforce civil liberties in the digital age, and had just started a new company called Cygnus Support, devoted to aiding users of free software. His hobby-horse was personal privacy. At a 1991 conference called "Computers, Freedom, and Privacy," he delivered a speech that anticipated the thoughts of Mays and Hughes—a people's crypto movement to stave off the government.

> What if we could build a society where the information was never collected? Where you could pay to rent a video without leaving a credit card or bank account number? Where you could prove you're certified to drive without giving your name? Where you could send and receive messages without revealing your physical location, like an electronic post office box? That's the kind of society I want to build. I want to guarantee—with physics and mathematics, not with laws—things like real privacy of personal communications . . . real privacy of personal records . . . real freedom of trade . . . real financial privacy . . . [and] real control of identification.

Gilmore was particularly interested in making sure that information about crypto found its way into the public domain. (He had been the one who had used the Internet to circulate Ralph Merkle's fast-encryption paper after the NSA had asked Xerox not to publish it.) More recently, he had been trying to liberate four early cryptanalysis textbooks by the NSA's legendary wizard William Friedman, filing Freedom of Information (FOI) requests to have the fifty-year-old works declassified. He even hired a Berkeley lawyer to help him negotiate the complicated process and file suit when government agencies did not respond within the specified legal time period.

Not long after demanding the Friedman texts, Gilmore began an extensive bibliographic search for them on the Internet, using "knowbots," which were automated intelligent search programs. The bots indicated that copies of two Friedman codebreaking works were publicly accessible, one in the Virginia Military Institute library, the other on microfilm at Boston University. Apparently at one time the government had lifted the restrictions on them, but in the Reagan era they had once again been classified. Gilmore immediately got friends to send him copies and notified the judge hearing his FOI appeal that the texts were on public library shelves. The government responded by notifying Gilmore that any further distribution of the Friedman texts would violate the Espionage Act, which mandated a possible ten-year sentence for violations. In other words, Gilmore could be sent to Leavenworth for a decade, just for taking a book out of the library and sharing it with friends. Gilmore not only notified the judge that his First Amendment rights were being violated, but told his story to a local reporter.

Two days later, the government backed down, formally declassifying the two texts. But Gilmore persisted in asking for the other works, and requested that the judge declare the Espionage Act itself an unconstitutional suppression of free speech. When a reporter asked him if his stance might not weaken national security, he was unrepentant. "We are not asking to threaten national security," he said. "We're asking to discard a Cold War bureaucratic idea of national security which is obsolete. They're abridging the freedom and privacy of all citizens, to defend us against a bogeyman that they will not explain."

Working with Gilmore (only later did Whitfield Diffie agree to participate as a sort of éminence grise), Hughes and May began planning a physical meeting of the proposed movement. Hughes was then calling the group CASI, or Cryptology Amateurs for Social Irresponsibility. Hughes and May prepared all summer, setting the invitation-only event for September 19, 1992, at Hughes's house in Berkeley. Because the nature of the enterprise involved an implicit attack on the government's most powerful spy agency, it was decided that discretion should be the watchword.

The meeting exceeded everyone's expectations. Unlike the Birkenstocked academics and rubber-necking spooks who met at the Crypto conferences, the twenty or so in attendance were people who saw cryptography totally outside the context of their own careers (if indeed they had one, as some did not). Their main concern was how people would and should use crypto tools. Their politics were heavily libertarian; more than a few were also self-proclaimed Extropians, whose philosophy merged an extremist view of individual liberties with a loopy belief that the far fringes of scientific research would soon accrue to our benefit. (Topics that made Extropians giddy included nanotechnology, cyborgs, and cryogenics; some Extropians had signed up to have their heads posthumously frozen, to be thawed and revived in some distant century.)

But it would be a mistake to misjudge this group by their peccadilloes or by the modest turnout at this first meeting. In fact, they would wind up becoming so influential that their grandiose fantasies would be vindicated. Profane, cranky, and totally in tune with the digital hip-hop of Internet rhythm, they were cryptographers with an attitude. If the government hadn't enough to worry about with industry, privacy advocates, and reform-minded policy wonks urging liberalization of encryption, the emergence of crypto rebels as popular culture heroes was a tipping point, an unexpected sign that the code wars had gone someplace new. The code rebels had arrived, brandishing a powerful intellectual weapon: *crypto anarchy.*

For this first meeting, Tim May had produced a fifty-seven-page handout, along with an elaborate agenda including discussion of "societal implications of cryptography," "voting networks," and "anonymous information markets." There were reports on digital money in virtual realities and John Gilmore's assessment of the NSA. And there was time set aside, of course, for the "reading of manifestos." Tim May had one prepared especially for the meeting, which he called the Crypto Anarchist Manifesto. It ended on a stirring note:

> Just as the technology of printing altered and reduced the power of medieval guilds and the social power structure, so too will cryptologic methods fundamentally alter the nature of corporations and of government interference in economic transactions. Combined with emerging information markets, crypto anarchy will create a liquid market for any and all material which can be put into words and pictures. And just as a seemingly minor invention like barbed wire made possible the fencing-off of vast ranches and farms, thus altering the concepts of land and property rights in the frontier West, so too will the seemingly minor discovery out of an arcane branch of mathematics come to be the wire

clippers which dismantle the barbed wire around intellectual property.

Arise, world; you have nothing to lose but your barbedwire fences!

For a couple of hours, people were invited to play "the Crypto Anarchy game," a role-playing exercise in which people imagined using exotic crypto protocols to keep surveillants in the dark about their activities, such as passing secrets or doing drug deals. Since PGP 2.0 had been released only days before—and most in attendance were huge fans of the first version—much of the meeting was spent discussing Phil Zimmermann's latest effort, and copies were distributed to all in the room. (Zimmermann himself was still in Boulder.) The event turned into a key-swapping party, as everyone exchanged PGP public keys and signed one another's key ring. PGP, after all, was the embodiment of the group's belief that cryptography was too important to be left to governments or even well-meaning companies. Only dedicated individuals, willing to suffer the consequences of government sanction, could assure that the tools got circulated into the Internet's bloodstream. After that, John Gilmore said, "It would take a pretty strong police state to suppress this technology."

One unexpected highlight was an observation made by Hughes's companion, a leather-clad writer who penned articles for the digital hippie magazine *Mondo 2000* under the name St. Jude. Listening to the visions of overturning society with modular arithmetic, she made the connection with the recent rise of so-called cyberpunks— hackers turned hipsters by linking the in-your-face iconoclasm of punk-rock rebels with the digital revolution. "Hey," she called out, "you guys are *cypher*punks!" They all loved the name.

The newly dubbed group was eager to meet again in a month. In the meantime, Eric Hughes set up what would be a much more robust and fertile cypherpunk gathering place: the Internet. Using John Gilmore's server (its Internet domain name was toad.com) as a cyberspace hub, Hughes set up what was known as a list-serv, an ongoing megadiscussion where anyone who signed up for the list would receive, unfiltered, the e-mail contributions of any other member who cared to report news, critique a cryptosystem, or unleash a rant. Within a few weeks, over 100 people would sign on to the list, an impressive number considering the mind-numbing volume of messages passed—often well over 150 a day.

After that first meeting, Eric Hughes drafted what he called "a small statement of purpose" to explain what the group was about. This "cypherpunk manifesto" envisioned a home-brewed privacy structure that the government couldn't crack:

> Cypherpunks write code. They know that someone has to write to defend privacy, and since it's their privacy, they're going to write it. Cypherpunks publish their code so that their fellow cypherpunks may practice and play with it. Cypherpunks realize that security is not built in a day and are patient with incremental progress.
>
> Cypherpunks don't care if you don't like the software they write. Cypherpunks know that software can't be destroyed. Cypherpunks know that a widely dispersed system can't be shut down.
>
> Cypherpunks will make the networks safe for privacy.

A couple of days afterward, Hughes revealed the details of the second meeting, to be held on October 10 at Cygnus's new office in Mountain View. "Attendance is transitive trust, arbitrarily deep," he wrote. "Invite who[m]ever you want. . . . Do not, however, post the announcement. Time for that will come."

As indeed it would. By the following year, the list had expanded to more than 700 participants. The group's original reluctance to ban journalists from its meetings—an ironic stance for people so enthusiastic about the spread of information in the Internet age—faded. Soon, cypherpunk lore would be a staple in publications ranging from *Wired* magazine to the *New York Times*. (Their faces, hidden by masks with scrawled PGP public key "fingerprints" on them, adorned *Wired*'s second issue.) The face of crypto had taken on a veneer of hipness.

Crypto anarchy was a fascinating concept, infecting not only the media but the well-ordered domains of corporations and government as well. Even Donn Parker, a well-known security expert who had previously specialized in assessments of computer crackers, was now weighing in on the danger of the "coming state of information anarchy if crypto is allowed to proliferate unchecked in its present form." (Parker recommended strong crypto, but with master keys in the hands of government—as it turned out, something that the government was already considering.)

But even as the crypto rebels were becoming media darlings, government threats, and civil liberties heroes, few were aware that the mathematical and philosophical basis of their efforts had come from a single man, arguably the ultimate cypherpunk. He never attended a meeting, didn't post to the list, and in fact had bitter running feuds with some of the people on it. Nonetheless, his ideas—and the patents he held on their implementations—were discussed with awe and fear both in the corporate and intelligence world. The creator himself was one of the most frustrating enigmas in the field, harder to crack than triple DES.

This was David Chaum.

Chaum, a bearded, ponytailed, Birkenstocked cryptographer and businessman, was the former Berkeley graduate student who had, on his own initiative, sustained the Santa Barbara Crypto conferences and organized the International Association for Cryptologic Research. But his legacy in the crypto world went far beyond that: for a number of years he was the privacy revolution's Don Quixote, idealistically pursuing crypto liberation from Big Brother. While at Berkeley in the late 1970s, he began building on the foundation of public key to create protocols for a world where people could perform any number of electronic functions while preserving their anonymity. If the use of public key is akin to magic, and if elaborations like secret sharing and zero-knowledge proofs are viewed as powerful examples of that magic, then David Chaum was the Houdini of crypto, inventor of mathematical tools that could deliver the impossible: all the benefits of the electronic world without the drawbacks of an electronic path that could lead crooks, corporations, and cops to one's doorstep. Magic, some believed, that potentially could make the entire concept of statehood disappear.

From a very early age, David Chaum had an interest in the hardware of privacy. "I think what's important to realize is that there is a strong driving force for me," he says. "My interest in computer security initially, and encryption later on, came because of my fascination with security technologies in general—things like locks and burglar alarms and safes." (At one point, as a graduate student, he even devised a new design for a lock and came close to selling it to a major manufacturer.) And, of course, he was completely fascinated by computers. Chaum was raised in suburban Los Angeles in a middle-class Jewish family (his birthdate is uncertain because of a characteristic refusal to divulge such specific identifying details). In high school and college—he began attending UCLA before graduating from high school, then enrolled at Sonoma State to be near a girlfriend, and finally finished up at UC San Diego—he did some garden variety computer pranking: password cracking, trash-can scrounging, and such. In math classes he hung out with a bunch of fellow malcontents: they would sit in the back of the class and every so often, when the teacher made an error, they would chime in with a counterproof. (Not exactly *The Blackboard Jungle*, but these were computer nerds.) He was also picking up a serious background in mathematics. And late in his college career, he came to cryptography, a discovery that in retrospect seems inevitable.

He had already been thinking about the means of protecting computer information, but his first serious thoughts on the subject were revealed in an English class paper. The politically radical young woman teaching the course had urged the students to write about what interested them passionately. Chaum wrote about encryption.

He chose Berkeley for graduate work, largely because of its association with the new paradigm of public key cryptography. He knew that Lance Hoffman, who taught there, had been Ralph Merkle's teacher. He was unaware that Hoffman had rejected Merkle's ideas out of hand. Still, he made good contacts at the school—he even met Whit Diffie, who was living in Berkeley then—and got the support he needed to begin his own work. Chaum's first papers, published in 1979, are indicative of the focus his work would take: devising cryptographic means of assuring privacy. His ideas built upon the concept of public key, particularly the authentication properties of digital signatures. "I got interested in those particular techniques because I wanted to make [anonymous] voting protocols," he says. "Then I realized that you could use them more generally as sort of untraceable communication protocols." The trail led to anonymous, untraceable digital cash.

For Chaum, politics and technology reinforced each other. He believed that as far as privacy was concerned, society stood at a crossroads. Proceeding in our current direction, we would arrive at a place where Orwell's worst prophecies were fulfilled. He delineated the problem in a paper called "Numbers Can Be a Better Form of Cash Than Paper":

> We are fast approaching a moment of crucial and perhaps irreversible decision, not merely between two kinds of technological systems, but between two kinds of society. Current developments in applying technology are rendering hollow both the remaining safeguards on privacy and the right to access and correct personal data. If these developments continue, their enormous surveillance potential will leave individual's lives vulnerable to an unprecedented concentration of scrutiny and authority.

In the early 1980s, David Chaum conducted a quest for the seemingly impossible answer to a problem that many people didn't consider a problem in the first place: how can the domain of electronic life be extended without further compromising our privacy? Or—even more daring—can we do this by actually *increasing* privacy? In the process he figured out how cryptography could produce an electronic version of the dollar bill.

In order to appreciate this, one must consider the obstacles to such a task. The most immediate concern of anyone attempting to produce a digital form of currency is counterfeiting. As anyone who has copied a program from a floppy disk to a hard drive knows, it is totally trivial to produce an exact copy of anything in the digital medium. What's to stop Eve from taking her one Digi-Buck and making a million, or a billion copies? If she can do this, her laptop, and every other computer, becomes a mint, and an infinite hyperinflation makes this form of currency worthless.

Chaum's way of overcoming that problem was the use of digital signatures to verify the authenticity of bills. Only one serial number would be assigned to a given "bill"—the number itself would *be* the bill—and when the unique number was presented to a merchant or a bank, it could be scanned to see if the virtual bill was authentic and had not been previously spent. This would be fairly easy to do if every electronic unit of currency was traced through the system at every point, but that process could also track the way people spent their money, down to the last penny. Exactly the kind of surveillance nightmare that gave Chaum the chills. How could you do this and unconditionally protect one's anonymity?

Chaum began his solution by coming up with something called a "blind signature." This is a process by which a bank, or any other authorizing agency, can authenticate a number so that it can act as a unit of currency. Yet, using Chaum's mathematics, the bank itself does not know who has the bill, and therefore cannot trace it. This way, when the bank issues you a stream of numbers designed to be accepted as cash, you have a way of changing the numbers (to make sure the money can't be traced) while maintaining the bank's imprimatur.

One of Chaum's most dramatic breakthroughs occurred when he managed to come up with a mathematical proof that this sort of anonymity could be provided unconditionally. The Eureka Moment came as he was driving his Volkswagen van from Berkeley to his home in Santa Barbara, where he taught computer science in the early eighties. "I was just turning this idea over and over in my head, and I went through all kinds of solutions. I kept riding through it, and finally by the time I got there I knew exactly how to do it in an elegant way."

He presented his theory with a vivid example: a scenario of three cryptographers finishing their meal at a restaurant and awaiting the check. The waiter appears. Your dinner, he tells the dining cryptographers, has been prepaid. The question is, by whom? Has one of the diners decided anonymously to treat his colleagues—or has the NSA or someone else paid for the meal? The dilemma was whether this information could be gleaned without compromising the anonymity of the cryptographer who might have paid for the dinner.

The answer to the "Dining Cryptographers" problem was surprisingly simple, involving coin tosses hidden from certain parties. For instance, Alice and Bob would flip a quarter behind a menu so Ted couldn't see it—and then each would privately write down the result and pass it to him. The key stipulation would be that if one of them was the benefactor who paid for the meal, that person would write down the *opposite* result of the coin toss. Thus if Ted received contradictory reports of the coin toss—one heads, one tails—he would know that one of his fellow diners paid for the meal. But without further collusion, he would have no way of knowing if it was Alice or Bob who paid. By a series of coin tosses and passed messages, any number of diners—in what would be called a DC-Net—could play this game. The idea could be scaled to a currency system.

"It was really important, because it meant that untraceability could be unconditional," he says—meaning mathematically bulletproof. "It doesn't matter how much computer power the NSA has to break codes—they can't figure it out, and you can prove that."

Chaum's subsequent work—as well as the patents he successfully applied for—built upon those ideas, addressing problems like preventing double-spending while preserving anonymity. In a particularly clever mathematical twist, he came up with a scheme whereby one's anonymity would always be preserved, with a single exception: if someone attempted to double-spend a unit that he or she had already spent somewhere else, at that point the second bit of information would allow a trace to be revealed. In other words, only cheaters would be identified—indeed, they would be providing evidence to law enforcement of their attempt to commit fraud.

This was exciting work, but Chaum received very little encouragement for pursuing it. "For many years it was very difficult for me to have to work on this sort of subject within the field, because people were not at all receptive to it," Chaum says. For a period of several years in the early 1980s, Chaum attempted to make personal connections with the leading lights in privacy policy and share his ideas with them.

"The uniform reaction was negative," he says. "And I couldn't understand this. It made it all the harder for me to keep pushing on this, because my academic advisors were saying, 'Oh, that's political, that's social—you're out of line.' " Even his advisor at Berkeley tried to dissuade him. "Don't work on this, because you can never tell the effects of a new idea on society," he told his stubborn student. Instead of heeding the warning, Chaum dedicated his dissertation to him, saying it was the rejection of the advisor's thinking that motivated him to finish the work.

Eventually, Chaum decided that the best way to spread his ideas would be to start his own company. By then he was living in Amsterdam; on an earlier visit with his Dutch girlfriend, he had fortuitously met up with some academics who offered him a post, which in turn led to an appointment at CWI, the Centre for Mathematics and Computer Science in Amsterdam. So, in 1990, he founded Digicash, with his own meager capital and a contract in hand from the Dutch government for a feasibility study of technology that would allow electronic toll payments on highways. Chaum developed a prototype by which smart cards holding a certain amount of verified cash value could be affixed to a windshield and high-speed scanning devices would subtract the tolls as the cars whizzed by. One could also use the cards to pay for public transportation and eventually for other items. Of course, the payments would be anonymous. To Chaum this was the most important part of the system: his fear was that a scheme that allowed officials to retrace the routes of citizens would be an Orwellian atrocity. (Systems eventually implemented in the United States, like the popular E-ZPass system, actually do track travelers.)

After completing that contract (the system was never implemented), Chaum kept his company active in smart-card applications; some of the projects focused on cash systems that would be used in a building or complex of buildings. He had a working example of it at Digicash headquarters on the outskirts of Amsterdam; visitors could sample the future by using anonymous cash cards to buy sodas and make phone calls.

But in the early 1990s, even as the world came around to the significance of the ideas Chaum had hatched in isolation—firms ranging from Microsoft to Citibank were pursuing digital cash projects—the company's operations remained relatively small scale. Digicash remained independent, without a close alliance with a large partner in banking or financial services. Chaum felt that in time these partners, at the least licensees who used Digicash technology, would emerge. They *had* to. It was now the conventional wisdom that paper money would be replaced by crypto-protected digits. When that happened, his paradigm would become a crucial factor in maintaining privacy in the age of e-money. This was an idea Chaum believed was worth holding out for.

Some people interpreted this as stubbornness, or, at least, poor business practice. "People wanted to buy David's patents but he asked for too much—he wanted control," says a former Digicash employee. Another tale making the rounds was that Chaum made a last-minute veto of a deal with Visa that would have made Digicash the standard for electronic money. A Digicash executive would later tell a reporter of similar blowups with other firms, including Microsoft. But Chaum furiously resisted the theory that his personality quirks and actions scotched realistic deals. When a reporter interviewed him about the subject, Chaum lashed out at the "malicious slander that it's hard to do deals with me." Still, frustrated by not being able to get Chaum's patents, some companies began devising their own schemes for anonymity, which may or may not have infringed on his patents.

Some cypherpunks felt that Chaum had taken the improper ideological approach by applying for patents on his work. (These idealists didn't like RSA's patents, either.) They complained that by withholding the technology from anyone who wanted to implement it—and threatening to sue anyone who tested the breadth of these patents—he was actually preventing his dream from being realized. This criticism enraged Chaum. "I really believe it's sort of my mission to do this, because I have this vision that stuff like this might be possible, and I really felt it was my responsibility to do it," he would say. "No one was working on this for a good half-dozen years while I was busily working on it and they all thought I was nuts. The patents are really helpful to our little company; we couldn't license, really, without the patents, and the whole purpose of them from my point of view is to get this stuff out there."

It was an article of faith among cypherpunks that protocols for anonymity would indeed flourish. This was not a foregone conclusion. Many tried to make their own schemes, with names like Magic Money. Meanwhile, Citibank and Visa were exploring digital cash on their own. And a well-funded new company called Cybercash was being formed outside of D.C.; one of its investors was RSA Data Security. The cypherpunks wanted to know whether this new form of money would provide an electronic trail to the user. They hoped not. The c-punk list was full of scenarios in which the Internet provided "data havens" outside the United States, places beyond the purview of the industrialized nations where people could bank funds or even gamble with digital cash. When some cypherpunks helped organize the first conference on financial cryptography, its location was a fore-gone conclusion: Anguilla, a small Caribbean island whose transactions laws were, to say the least, liberal.

One of Chaum's ideas, adopted wholeheartedly by cypherpunks, was the emergence of services called "remailers." These were sort of cyberspace information launderers . . . outposts on the information highway, independently maintained by cypherpunk activists, who stripped any identifying marks from a message, then passed it on either to its final destination or to another remailer, for another round of data scrubbing. Your message goes into the remailer (also known as an anonymous server) with a return address—and gets forwarded without one.

Just sending your anonymous message to a single remailer, though, was regarded as insufficient protection. Indeed, it imbued the person running the server with too much power. If he or she turned out to be untrustworthy, or got hacked, or was served with a subpoena, it would be all too easy for outsiders to get hold of one's return address. It was the same problem that Whit Diffie originally complained about with network administrators and passwords. The cypherpunks thought they had the solution to this problem: they helped seed a loose con-federation of remailers around the globe. In order to get real protection, you had to direct your messages through a series, or "string," or "chain," of remailers. Each remailing service would strip the return address; only the first one would have the original address. A cop or a spy trying to trace a message would then have to get the records (if they still existed, which they generally didn't) of ten or twelve or twenty remailers in order to retrace the steps. So if the authorities couldn't get the records from some remailer nerd in Tonga, they'd never find the original. (Some paranoid users—or, more likely, cypherpunks air-ing out their software—went through as many as a hundred remailers on their string; since there weren't that many anonymity servers in the world, this required multiple visits.)

To be *really* sure your anonymity was protected, you'd use PGP to encrypt the whole shebang with the public key of the final remailer on the chain. That way no remailer until the final one would be able to read the message, which by then would have its origins well buried. Want *more* security? Encrypt that final message in *another* envelope of PGP encryption, this one scrambled with the public key of the *pen-*

ultimate remailer on the chain. That would provide a double layer of encryption. And so on and so on, envelopes within envelopes, until privacy was fully assured. If at any point along the way, someone attempted to read the message, they'd get gibberish, "like getting a tape of microphone hiss," gloated Eric Hughes.

With cypherpunk encouragement—the first remailer was set up by Hughes himself, on the Berkeley server—about twenty remailers were up and humming by 1993. Of all the barn-building efforts of those on the list, creating an easier way to utilize remailer chains was the most intense. It didn't seem to bother the cypherpunks that those using the nascent system weren't doing much to improve society. Most of the messages sent through remailers were postings to Usenet discussion groups on the Internet; sadly, these were generally harassing attacks on people or simply idiotic flames. Instead of enriching cyberspace conversations, these unsigned stink bombs degraded it. You'd have sophisticated on-line colloquies about technical issues or personal matters, and some moron would chime in with foul-mouthed insults—and the serious participants in the discussion would be frustrated because there'd be no way of applying sanctions to the conversational vandal who disrupted things. On the other hand, in some groups—notably those encouraging contributions from whistle-blowers or victims of sex crimes—otherwise reluctant message posters discovered a measure of security in having their messages attributed to alternate, untraceable identities known as "nyms." It wasn't unusual in such groups to see a lot of mail from clearly cloaked correspondents at sites like "bogus@no.return.address."

The hardest part of running a remailer, it turned out, was not technical. Cypherpunk scripts made the process fairly easy for the technically competent noncryptographer to set up an anon server. The tough part was standing up to the social and legal pressures that would come when outraged targets of hate mail and pranks would demand that the anonymous traffic cease. A typical case was a cypherpunk at the University of Washington who wanted to use the school's computer system as a remailer. For a few months things went fine, "which wasn't bad when you consider that it was based on a student account with a Nazi-like administration," wrote the operator. "The death blow was a target [of e-mail attacks] complaining to me about someone sending unsolicited mail to them through my remailer." The plea to stop such mail went to the system "postmaster," the person in charge of the university's e-mail system. Of course, the postmaster didn't know anything about such a service being operated on the school's computer, and "when he looked into it, he was quite surprised." End of remailer.

More successful was the case of Julf Helsingius, a Finnish computer consultant who began a remailer in his home outside Helsinki in 1993. He wanted to provide cover to people posting in a Usenet group concerning alcoholic recovery. He set up "Penet" (a variation on his company's name, Pennitech) on a small UNIX machine running on a modest Intel 386 chip, and opened for business, relying solely on word of mouth for users. Soon thousands of people were sending messages through the machine, which would forward the messages to their destinations without the identifying header. The traffic got so intense that Julf had to install a high-speed Internet pipe in his home, which cost him a thousand dollars a month. Sometimes, users would write to Julf and ask him why he did it. The answer was complicated; Julf was part of the Swedish-speaking minority in Finland and had always felt strongly about the ability of minorities to speak up. In another sense though, he considered it a hobby. "Some people spend similar money on golf or whatever," he would say. When people complained that he was allowing creeps and perverts to express themselves, he had a reply for that too:

> I can only answer that I believe very firmly that it's not for me to dictate how other people ought to behave. But remember, anonymous postings are a privilege, and use them accordingly. I believe adult human beings can behave responsibly. Please don't let me down.

No matter what the result, the cypherpunk remailer effort generated a vital dialogue on the issue of anonymity in a digital society. One important cypherpunk text was *Ender's Game*, a science fiction novel by Orson Scott Card. Part of the plot hinged on an influential public debate between two unknown philosophers who took advantage of remailer-type technology to post treatises under the fictional nyms of Demosthenes and Locke. Since the ideas were subversive, it was absolutely necessary to keep their real identities secret; nonetheless, the force of their arguments changed the course of society in the novel. Another good reason to hide the real people behind these ideas was that the writers were children, a brother and sister who were, respectively, twelve and ten years old. "It's not my fault I'm twelve right now," the young man explained to his sister. "The world is always a democracy in times of flux, and the man with the best voice will win."

But it was not only science fiction that valued anonymity. The practice was crucial in the formation of the United States itself, and was arguably as American as apple pie. As cypherpunk historians loved to point out, the model for the *Ender's Game* debate may have been the *Federalist Papers*, with parts written by James Madison, John Jay, and Alexander Hamilton but published under the pseudonym Publius. And when Thomas Paine wrote *Common Sense*, he originally signed it "An Englishman." As the Supreme Court would note, "Anonymous pamphlets, leaflets, brochures, and even books have played an important role in the progress of mankind," a role the court has sustained in consistent rulings. In 1995, it would reaffirm the constitutionality of the concept once more, using the words of John Stuart Mill to hail anonymity as "a shield from the tyranny of the majority." Who could blame cypherpunks for producing the cryptographic tools to preserve a writer's ability to continue this vital tradition?

Plenty of people, as it turned out. Critics—among them FBI director Louis Freeh—would contend that when anonymity hit the Internet, it did not merely find a familiar niche in a new medium; it was amplified beyond recognition into something more menacing. David Chaum's invention of blind digital signatures and nontraceable anonymous cash had the potential to make cyberspace into an identity-free zone where one could go underground far more easily and effectively than in the physical world. When you spend hard currency in a store, for instance, no one asks you for ID papers—but your face marks the transaction in the cashier's mind, particularly if you're a return customer. (If you wore a bag over your head, you'd probably have trouble making the payment in the first place.) Using Chaumian protocols, you could potentially make all your purchases, send all your mail, even receive monies, with total assurance that no one would know who you are. But so could kidnappers, child pornographers, and terrorists, whose lives would be made much simpler and more secure with such tools.

Such concerns didn't faze the cypherpunks. On the contrary, they went out of their way to emphasize why the technologies of anonymity could be so controversial. A good example was Tim May's announcement of an enterprise he called "BlackNet." The group did not exist, of course. It was a thought experiment he originally figured to bring up for discussion at a cypherpunk meeting, but then decided to send it out anonymously on the Net. "I sent it through remailers so it would add a piquancy, a spiciness to it," says May, who certainly didn't mind going public with his own beliefs (he usually signed his e-mail with a hair-raising list of passions—"crypto anarchy, digital money, anonymous networks, digital pseudonyms, black markets, and collapse of governments").

BlackNet was a guerrilla theater presentation of those interests. "Your name has come to our attention," the message began. "We have reason to believe you may be interested in the products and services our new organization, BlackNet, has to offer. BlackNet is in the business of buying, selling, trading, and otherwise dealing with *information* in all its many forms." The offer went on to explain that with public key cryptography, a perfect data black market exists where one can get or sell everything from trade secrets to cruise missile plans without any risk of being identified. The parties in these transactions will not be known to each other, not even to BlackNet. Needless to say, no one would ever know who is behind BlackNet:

> Our location in physical space is unimportant. Our location in cyberspace is all that matters. Our primary address is the PGP key location "BlackNet" and we can be contacted (preferably through a chain of anonymous remailers) by encrypting a message to our public key (contained below) and depositing this message in one of the several locations in cyberspace we monitor.

BlackNet also purported to deal in money, offering to make anonymous deposits in the bank of your choice. You could deal with Black-Net using actual cash or "cryptocredits," BlackNet's own internal currency (which could be used in any sort of untraceable clandestine information transaction you chose). And BlackNet itself had no ideology of its own, save one: "We consider nation-states, export laws, patent laws, national security considerations, and the like to be relics of the pre-cyberspace era."

To May's delight, many accepted the BlackNet announcement at face value, especially as news of it leaked beyond the crypto community and into the more panic-prone world at large. Though BlackNet was fictional, May did believe that in the future we would see similar enterprises. It didn't bother him at all—people were free agents, and responsible for themselves. "If people die as a result of this . . . *eh!*" he said. "*I* didn't hurt them."

All in all, the exercise put a screaming exclamation point to cypherpunk philosophy. Crypto anarchy until then may have been the province of science fiction writers, but the tools to make it real were arriving. As those digital armaments were put to use, it was possible that a thousand BlackNets could bloom. Certainly this was something noted inside the Triple Fence—and at FBI headquarters as well. Did it portend a movement that had to be stopped? The establishment was beginning to think so.

With the powers of crypto, "we have the capability of 100 percent privacy," admitted security expert Donn Parker. "But if we use this, I don't think society can survive."

the clipper chip

The creator of the Clipper Chip was an unintentional spook. Clinton Brooks's passion was astronomy. He studied it at Yale during the late sixties, and wanted to make it his career, after fulfilling his ROTC obligations in the navy. His duty was slated for the Pacific, and he planned to move his wife and small children to Hawaii and sail as a shipboard communications officer. He didn't realize that people at a certain intelligence agency had other plans for him.

Several years earlier, Brooks had been assigned for his mandatory summer duty to a location unknown to him: Fort George Meade. He had driven to Maryland, expecting a typical military base. Instead he was intercepted by inscrutable guards outside what looked like a modern office building in the middle of nowhere who told him that only those with high security clearances could enter. To his surprise, a phone call revealed that he already had been granted such a clearance. Welcome, Clint Brooks, to the National Security Agency. He might have thought of this duty as an interlude, but his superiors had apparently taken note of his abilities, and offered him an alternative to the navy. Not only could he remain in the States, but he'd have a chance at a deeper satisfaction—an opportunity to indulge his cosmic yearnings, to a degree, by working in top-secret satellite reconnaissance. He would not, of course, be able to talk about his work to his friends, neighbors, and relatives, because even the title of the satellite organization was more closely protected than the No Such Agency itself. But it sounded good to Brooks. So he declined his commission on the USS *Pueblo*—the intelligence ship that would be captured by the North Koreans a few months later, on January 23, 1968. He would work at the agency that dared not speak its name.

Twenty-four years later, Clint Brooks was an assistant deputy director at the agency that now did speak its name in public. And he found himself at the center of a crisis that involved the very mission of the National Security Agency: the rise of public cryptography. One day in the late spring of 1992, he walked over to the office of a recently arrived general counsel of the agency to enlist the newcomer's aid in a campaign that, Brooks hoped, might help the agency get through this dangerous passage.

Traditionally, the NSA general counsel is recruited from outside, a lawyer familiar with government work with no particular experience in intelligence matters. Someone who can fit into the cloistered culture inside the Triple Fence, but who retains a sense of the real world beyond. It had been Bobby Ray Inman who first figured out that a sharp legal mind just plucked from the fray could best forward the agency's business, and provide a level of oversight that perhaps a career spook might not. Ever since Inman's lawyers helped him navigate the agency's problems with academic crypto research, a series of sharp, relatively young attorneys had filled the post for a couple of years, then each had moved on.

Stewart Baker fit the mold. Born in 1947 and raised outside Detroit, he went to law school at UCLA, clerked for a federal judge, then went into private practice for Steptoe and Johnson, one of the most prestigious firms in the nation's capital. He served for a few years in Jimmy Carter's Education Department, then returned to Steptoe. When recommended for the NSA job, he'd been unsure about it. "Should I do it?" he asked a military friend. "What better could you do for your country?" his friend replied.

Baker had occupied his new office for less than a month before Clint Brooks's visit. It was clear that the spindly, square-jawed NSA lifer was a true believer—but in what? Before he spoke, Brooks placed a large bottle of Advil on Stewart Baker's desk. "You're going to need this," he said.

Then Brooks laid out the entire story of how cryptography was going public. He told Baker about DES, the strong cipher that wound up in more common use than the NSA had expected, then about the development of public key, and RSA, and the agency's troubles with the new cryptographic community that led to the compromise of pre-publication review. And now, he said, the idea that you could control things by vetting academic papers was irrelevant: companies like RSA were selling crypto commercially. Baker was aghast. *How did you let that stuff out?* he wanted to know.

It wasn't that simple, Brooks explained. The NSA has two roles. One, of course, is cracking ciphers and providing great intelligence to the rest of the government. But the other is to provide the United States with the best possible codes. Inside the Triple Fence, this duality was referred to as "Equities," reflecting, no doubt, that both tasks were equally important. Clint Brooks was the Equities guy at the NSA. It was a thankless balancing act, because an advance in one mission was sometimes a threat to the other one. In the old days, at least, the debate was confined inside The Fort, but now it took place in the halls of Congress and in the pages of the *New York Times*. Meanwhile, the specter of widespread encryption was like a train bearing down not just on the NSA but on society in general. Like the cypherpunks, Clint Brooks looked into the future and saw crypto everywhere. But while the crypto rebels embraced the vision, Brooks understood that this new reality was a potential disaster, if the agency did not adjust.

This was gospel that Brooks had been preaching for several years, at first to deaf ears. During most of the 1980s, after director Inman's first skirmishes with the crypto academics, most people at the agency hadn't been much concerned with the possibility that public cryptography would affect them in any significant way. Strong export laws kept everything under control, assuring that nothing as strong as DES left the country without restrictions. In the chill of the Cold War, Congress always gave Fort Meade what it asked for. And though an occasional in-house Cassandra would cite some pundit's prediction that in two or three years widespread commercial crypto would take off, it never did seem to happen. So it was easy to think that it might *never* happen. Brooks knew otherwise. Beginning around 1988, he came to understand the direction the Internet was taking and realized that, this time, the threat was real. But his superiors laughed when he tried to lecture them. *What are you talking about?* they'd say. *We're the only cryptographers! This is a military technology, not something that people want to use!* Only when an Internet revolution became plausible, and companies like Lotus actually started to build crypto like RSA into their products, did the top levels of the agency come to realize that Brooks had a point. So they authorized him to find some sort of solution to this conundrum. And Brooks had indeed come up with one.

That was the reason for Clint Brooks's visit to Stewart Baker: to get him on board with the plan. There was, he explained, a possible way out . . . a solution that not only could give the unprecedented protection of strong crypto to the masses, but that would also preserve the government's ability to get hold of the original plaintext conversations and messages. In fact, for the past three years, Brooks revealed, the NSA had been creating such a scheme. It involved a technique known as key escrow.

The project had begun in 1989. Brooks, in his role as Fort Meade's Equities man, had been racking his brain to figure out how to reconcile the two seemingly incompatible demands: the need for strong public codes and the agency's need for plaintext traffic. Clearly, no solution was perfect. The idea was to strike the proper balance, giving users of nonclassified information both inside and outside the government a healthy measure of security, but not so much that the public's safety was abridged. At the time the NSA, acting in accordance with the Memorandum of Understanding, had formed the working group on cryptography with the National Institute of Standards and Technology. In NIST's acting director Ray Kammer, Brooks found a kindred soul. The two of them spent hours going over the problem, probing the technical and even philosophical aspects of a crypto policy.

In one of their early discussions, Brooks and Kammer had simultaneously had an epiphany: the use of encryption would have a profound effect on law enforcement, particularly in its ability to continue wiretapping. They began visiting people in the Justice Department and the FBI, none of whom had the slightest inkling of the troubles that lay ahead. Brooks or Kammer would tell them that all the authorizations to wiretap in the world might not help them when crooks used encryption, and their jaws would drop. *Can't you help us?* the law enforcement people would ask.

Brooks had once assumed the solution might lie in a giant deception. The agency could create a putatively strong cryptosystem, so apparently strong that companies would build it into their products and export it around the world. But the agency would have built in a "trapdoor," to allow the NSA secretly to derive plaintext from encoded transmissions. But after some clear thinking, he discarded that risky, and questionably legal, idea. Such a scheme would entail getting decrypted messages from U.S. citizens. You might be able to justify a hidden trapdoor to snoop on foreigners, but if Congress or some investigative reporter discovered that the NSA had launched a clandestine surveillance plan against Americans, the Church committee would look like a picnic.

So Brooks spent nights awake trying to conjure some other idea. On one of those nights, he had a flash. There *could* be a compromise that could satisfy everybody. In the physical world, a search warrant compelled a suspect in a crime to give authorities the combination of a safe. Why not translate that concept to the world of communications and computers? If you created a system by which special duplicate encryption keys were somehow spirited away and stored in secure facilities, you would essentially be holding lock combinations *in escrow,* unavailable to anyone but those who had authority to retrieve them. Those with that legal authority—a search warrant from a judge or an understood set of national security criteria—could get the keys from the trusted storage facility. Once that access was assured, there would be no problem in allowing the encryption itself to be as strong as anyone liked. Make it uncrackable! If the FBI or the police needed the key, and a judge concurred, then they'd have the wherewithal to decipher it, just as if they were the intended recipients.

To some people at the agency, the scheme was a heresy: *You're going to put a back door into a cryptosystem . . . and TELL people about it?* But full disclosure was a critical part of Brooks's vision. He really wanted this new scheme to kick off a national debate about cryptography. Only then, he believed, could an escrow scheme, which would require an elaborate infrastructure, be established. With the government no longer concerned about getting hold of encoded messages, the path would be free and clear toward a universal blanket of crypto, with organized public key distribution, standardized digital signatures, and automatic encryption of messages. The privacy nuts and conspiracy freaks would raise hell at the idea of escrowed keys. But if all the issues were aired, all the dangers addressed, all the benefits sketched out, surely reasonable people could see that this plan was the best way to protect our communications without sacrificing our safety. Anyway, what was the alternative?

Of course, if such a scheme were to be launched, the NSA itself would have to change, readjusting its focus so it would operate in a highly computerized—and *crypto*-ized—post–Cold War world. The intensity with which The Fort still maintained its veil of secrecy was no longer appropriate. If the people were to buy such a radical idea, the NSA would have to earn their trust. Thus it was imperative to bring the debate on cryptography to the public, treading on once forbidden areas with brutal honesty.

Brooks eventually got approval to pursue his plan, but his idea that the NSA should collaborate with the general public was received with skepticism or worse. He found himself arguing like some deranged Jeremiah. "This has *got* to be a national policy," Brooks said at one meeting of the top NSA officials. When asked by a deputy director to explain further, he replied, "This isn't a judgment that can be made by the director of the National Security Agency or a committee of deputies . . . it's a value judgment as to what's in the best interest of the country. It has to be decided by the president of the United States." The official who answered directly to the voters! His peers thought he'd gone off the deep end. *This was the National Security Agency,* their attitude was, *and we don't do that sort of thing.*

While waiting for the public debate to take shape, Brooks was working hard with other agencies to set up a structure for his ambitious key escrow plan. Because of the Memorandum of Understanding, of course, the agency would have to develop the scheme with NIST. But that was no problem. The joint technical working group had been working on the public crypto situation since the very first meeting in March 1989, particularly on the digital signature algorithm. Public crypto was known within the group as Issue One.

A third stakeholder in the discussions was the FBI. The early alert from Brooks and Kammer had indeed awakened interest at the bureau: in 1991, director William Sessions had written to defense secretary Dick Cheney about computer security, clearly indicating that his agency wanted a voice in determining policy. The FBI, it turned out, would actually assume the hardest line on the issue.

The NSA, of course, did the technical heavy lifting. By 1990, thirty of its mathematicians were working on the problem. They quickly settled on the bedrock of the system, a powerful encryption algorithm that had been kicking around Fort Meade for a couple of years. Its codename was Skipjack. It was a block cipher like DES but was deemed much stronger. Its recommended key length was 80 bits as opposed to DES's 56; it used 32 rounds of substitution instead of 16. (There appears also to have been some more subtle technical reasons for Skipjack's superiority, but of course, the NSA was loath to reveal these.) Though Brooks tried to argue that in this new era, it might be appropriate to reveal the algorithm—insisting, in fact, that to win over their critics they would probably be forced to publish it anyway—he met with staunch resistance. Never—*never*—would the agency allow its foes access to what amounted to an advanced course on the cutting edge of codemaking. Things don't work that way at The Fort.

Skipjack, though, was only a single component of what the NSA called Capstone, which was a complete public key system that would include the digital signature standard. Of course, this particular scheme had an additional complication: how would you implement the escrow? You'd have to figure out a way to isolate a copy of each key and send that information elsewhere for storage. By 1991, the NSA decided that trying to do this in software was too risky—it feared that some foe could change the code to build in a weakness—and concluded that a better method would be to put the whole shebang on a tamperproof computer chip. An experienced defense contractor in Torrance, California, called Mykotronx was hired to fabricate the chips.

The system itself worked by inserting several new components into the classic equation where Alice encrypts and Bob decrypts. One of them was the "unique chip identifier." It was a number that matched up with a "chip unique key" that was assigned to a single physical chip. Each device—a computer or perhaps a phone—would have its own unique chip identifier and chip unique key.

When two people wanted to communicate privately, they would

each have one of those devices. If, for instance, they wanted a phone conversation that an eavesdropper couldn't hear, they'd have special phones with the technology built in. Once the connection was made, the phones would zip signals to each other (via a Diffie-Hellman exchange) to calculate a new symmetrical key, called the session key. Using Skipjack, that key would actually encode the sounds of each speaker as the sounds left the phone and decrypt those sounds as they emerged from the other phone. But along with the encrypted conversation, the phones would transmit another set of bits, called the Law Enforcement Access Field (LEAF). (It was originally called the Law Enforcement *Exploitation* Field, but was changed to a somewhat less ominous term.) The LEAF would be generated by a set of calculations involving the session key, the chip unique key, and the unique chip identifier, winding up with two important components: an *encrypted* version of the session key and the unique chip identifier. All of that would be further scrambled by the family key.

So how would officials get hold of those keys? They would already be in possession of one of them, the family key—there's only one in the whole system. The tricky part of the scheme would be getting the proper chip unique key and, ultimately, the session key. This would be performed by way of the LEAF.

What if an eavesdropper captures the information on the LEAF? Even if he could isolate the chip identifier from the LEAF, it would be useless. All the identifier would do, really, is identify. It would point to a chip unique key in a vast database. But only the government wiretappers would have access to that database, stocked with every chip unique key in existence. Having that identifier *without* a way to get into the escrow facility would be like having someone's fingerprint and no access to crime records: it would be of no help whatsoever in telling you who it identifies. But a government agent would be able to take that identifier, along with a court order, to an escrow facility, and match it up with the chip unique key. And then combine it with the family key. Viola! You'd have the session key—and the fuzz of an encrypted conversation could be transformed into blessed, perhaps incriminating, plain language.

That led to another complication. Where would the escrowed keys be stored? If they were all kept in one place, it would be a potential gold mine for all sorts of crooks, spies, and even corrupt U.S. government agents—anyone with access could get hold of the means to violate the privacy of every encrypted conversation in the world. So Brooks and his colleagues decided that the escrowed keys would be split into two pieces that would be stored in different locations. This would be done in such a way that obtaining one piece of the key would provide no mathematical advantage in discovering the entire key. When a judge authorized a wiretap, the law enforcement officer would present the warrant to both escrow agents, construct the key, and then have the wherewithal to listen to the conversations.

In late July 1992, all the relevant government agencies met for an off-site meeting at the FBI's Engineering Research Facility in Quantico, Virginia, to discuss the alternatives for a national encryption policy. Clint Brooks made the opening presentation. As recorded by one official in attendance:

> He presented these within the context of a national goal that would satisfy the need for good commercial and unclassified cryptographic security while protecting the interests and responsibilities of national security and law enforcement organizations. He termed the achievement of this goal "Nirvana."

The agencies didn't reach total agreement. Notably, the FBI apparently was arguing for the ability to do its decrypting instantaneously, or in "real time," an approach that the NIST people deemed "draconian and intrusive." (The FBI approach would essentially dictate that the escrow facilities should be a phone call away at any time, and safeguards against abuse would go out the window.) But they all agreed that a system should provide encryption for the public while allowing the cops and the spooks access to the keys—essentially, the NSA solution.

Until the whole government got behind it, the escrow scheme was just another flashy technology concocted behind the Triple Fence. In order for it to work, it needed to be ubiquitous. As Brooks had anticipated—and as his superiors finally came to understand—such a sweeping change needed the imprimatur and active support of government's highest level, up to George Bush himself. But an election was approaching, not the time to air potentially controversial new ideas. In any case, the Bush people seemed unconvinced of the urgency of quick action. Brooks figured that in 1993, after Bush was returned to the White House, the reelected president would be able to tackle the problem, free from worries about what the electorate might think.

But in 1992, two unexpected events dramatically shaped the course of Clint Brooks's key escrow scheme. The first one involved an innovative product about to be introduced into the marketplace—a twenty-four ounce box that connected to the telephone. That pound and a half of technology portended tons of problems. The second development was the election of a new U.S. president.

The box's technical name was the AT&T Telephone Security Device (TSD) 3600. For several years, the telecommunications giant had been manufacturing secure phones for the government, using a special NSA-designed algorithm. In 1992, the company decided to broaden its market outside the government, and began limited sales of a voice data scrambler that used an encryption algorithm devised by AT&T's own crypto team. That autumn, it decided to follow up on an even wider scale—by launching a secure phone designed to sell by the thousands. If you were worried about snoopers listening for sensitive data involving intellectual property, trade issues, and business strategies, you'd want one of these. You didn't have to be an engineer or a nerd to use it, either. "It connects easily to desk telephones or . . . mobile cellular phones," gushed company literature. "And it's as easy to use as it is portable. To protect conversations, the user simply pushes a single button. The call is automatically encrypted and the conversation secured." AT&T also claimed that the voice quality on this device was, unlike the relatively fuzzy phones that the military used, almost as good as that of a regular telephone.

What's more, this new phone would use the most trusted encryption algorithm of all to scramble voice: DES, the cipher that was still a hot button behind the Triple Fence.

The NSA, of course, was unhappy at this new use of the problem child it had once blessed. But news of AT&T's plan was even more troubling to the FBI. The law enforcement agency had already been complaining that new telephone features like cellular service and call forwarding were making it more difficult to implement wiretaps. Its solution was to propose a new bill, known within the Beltway simply as "Digital Telephony." The law would mandate that all new telecommunications equipment be designed with wiretaps in mind; it essentially banned new devices and services that denied the government an easy way to conduct surveillance. Critics were already howling. It was bad enough that the bill would cost equipment makers hundreds of millions of dollars (presumably a cost passed on to consumers). Much worse was the central premise behind the legislation, which required the tail of wiretaps to wag the dog of telecommunications. Instead of encouraging one of the country's most innovative industries to produce the systems that would sustain America's high-tech success in the global marketplace, Congress would be locking a ball and chain on innovations. And for what? Just to keep its ears open to approximately 1000 annual federal wiretaps, to glean information that could arguably be recovered by other means, like hidden bugs or informants?

Though Digital Telephony didn't mention cryptography specifically, the specter of crypto restrictions hung over the legislation like some digital Sword of Damocles. As Brooks and Kammer had explained to the FBI, strong crypto could totally screw up the benefits of the bill. Even if Digital Telephony passed, and the industry faithfully followed its strictures, the G-men and other police agencies would be able to monitor the transmissions sent over the wires or the air—but then what? If those communications were scrambled, those precious intercepts would be no more than useless static. FBI director William Sessions got the message and made sure that G-men would be participants in the NSA–NIST effort to deal with the problem.

Now the FBI was freaking. Here was this new AT&T phone, designed to move secure-phone technology from a status item on the desks of national security advisors to a common commercial product, one used by executives, lawyers, and scientists, not to mention privacy nuts, crooks, terrorists, and God knows who else. It would be a law enforcement disaster . . . unless there was a way that the government could somehow overhear those conversations as they were before encryption. *Wasn't that what Clint Brooks had figured out?* So Brooks and his team were asked if the Capstone chip might go into the AT&T phone. As the Capstone was originally conceived, it was too demanding for the TSD 3600—with all its features, such as the digital signatures, it would require more computation than the device could handle. But maybe if the NSA carved out just the encryption algorithm and key escrow, it could come up with something that could simply be clipped into the phone in place of the DES chip.

Even while agreeing that it could be done, Brooks was wary. The Capstone chip was well designed and represented a complete solution. Coming up with something new would be riskier—and to do it in time to stave off the AT&T phone, it would have to be done very quickly. There would be no time for the national debate he felt was so essential.

But the FBI couldn't wait. On October 13, 1992, Judge Sessions himself placed a call to AT&T's chief executive officer Robert Allen. *We've got a problem,* he told him, and then outlined problem and solution: Would AT&T consider using an escrow encryption chip instead of its DES-based system? If the company agreed, the feds could offer considerable carrots. For one thing, AT&T could claim that it was actually providing mightier encryption, since Skipjack was much more difficult for outsiders to crack than DES. Furthermore, the United States would probably allow this key escrow phone to be exported. Best of all was a promise directed toward the bottom line: the federal government would buy thousands of units for its own use.

The downside, of course, would be that potential corporate buyers would have to buy into the basic compromise that escrow entailed: the encryption would be strong, but one not necessarily welcome third party would also have a copy of the key.

Sound familiar? It was the same situation that Whit Diffie had found utterly intolerable two decades earlier: the difficulty of two people seeking intimacy when someone else is in the bed. Diffie had invented public key in order to *avoid* this perversion of the cryptographic relationship. Indeed, the AT&T phone as originally conceived was an embodiment of Diffie's vision. The users of the phone would not need to exchange secret keys beforehand. Instead, the two respective phone devices would furiously perform the calculations of a Diffie-Hellman key exchange, in order to settle on a secure DES key that would encrypt, and then decrypt, the actual conversation. No need for anyone else. You wouldn't *want* anyone else.

But the bounty offered to AT&T—and the chance to avoid a government confrontation—was too juicy to turn down. The phone company signed off on a deal: if the government would adopt a plan to make key escrow its standard, AT&T would forgo its DES scheme and install a government-designed chip in the device instead. This would be the stripped-down version of Capstone, using the Skipjack algorithm and the escrow features, but without the signature or hashing algorithms. It was given a new code name: Clipper.

"We knew no decision would make everybody happy," said an AT&T spokesperson. "But frankly, the Clipper Chip offered an important law enforcement issue and increased the level of protection." More to the point, it also offered guaranteed sales, and the continued goodwill of one of AT&T's major customers, the United States government (at the time, the company was negotiating a government contract worth over $10 billion). If key escrow became government policy, AT&T would happily be on board.

But Clipper was still nowhere close to being the official government policy. Clint Brooks and the NSA needed one more big break before they could begin their journey toward Nirvana. That break came on November 3, 1992, when the United States went to the polling place and elected William Jefferson Clinton its president, with Albert Gore as his vice president.

It might appear counterintuitive to think that those election results favored the NSA. After all, Clinton was a Democrat who had spent the Vietnam years speaking against the conflict instead of fighting in it. During the campaign, Clinton had visited Silicon Valley, and while he had made no promises, he indicated that his presidency would be a friend to private crypto. "He talked about how silly it was that there were export controls on off-the-shelf software," remembers privacy advocate Marc Rotenberg. "He didn't say 'encryption' specifically, but that's clearly what he was referring to."

Another sign that Clinton might not be NSA-friendly was the nature of the people surrounding him. For instance, the head of his transition team was a former electronics lobbyist named John Podesta, who had vociferously supported the industry agenda of liberalizing export rules. Besides Podesta, Clinton's minions included a number of people who seemed tuned into the hip and crypto-friendly cyber world.

Chief among that contingent was the vice president himself—a self-

styled computer aficionado to whom Clinton would delegate the ultimate decision on the cryptography issue. In fact, Al Gore's presence
as the nation's second-in-command was often cited as proof that the
new leadership team was a nerd-friendly future squad who "got" the
new Internet paradigms. Their campaign speeches might have been
about bridges to the future, but Gore's vision was of an Information Highway to transform the country and indeed the globe. Gore
arranged to bring some of the most techno-savvy Senate staffers to the
White House to help on digital matters, people like Mike Nelson, a
former MIT geophysicist experienced in Info-Highway issues. They
were "extremely smart, conscious freedom-lovers," wrote John Perry
Barlow, who got to know them in his role as Electronic Frontier Foundation cofounder. "Hell, a lot of them are Deadheads. I was sure that
after they were fully moved in, they'd face down the National Security
Agency and the FBI."

Barlow had mistakenly assumed that because the Clinton staffers
recognized the opening chords of "Sugar Magnolia," they'd be im-
mune to top-secret doom lectures from the star-spangled crypto boys
at Fort George Meade. Behind the Triple Fence, the expectations were
just the opposite. The spooks understood that Bill Clinton and his
peach-fuzz tech squad were a godsend for the escrow idea. The Bush
administration had never warmed to the escrow plan. The problem
wasn't so much that the Bush people were specifically against this particular scheme. They were against *anything* that required a little gump-
tion. "The Bush people had spent twelve years in power, most of them
with a Democratic Congress, and they knew that everything that could
blow up, would blow up," one insider explained. "When you presented something to them, you got nothing but eyes staring out. . . .
You could sense that everyone was thinking, 'How might this end up
on my suit?' "

In contrast, the Clinton people were policy joyriders, like teenagers
finally granted their turn behind the wheel. They were totally juiced
that after twelve years of dinosaur rule, they now had their chance to
fix things. They were also detail freaks, eager to belly flop into the
huge piles of clauses, footnotes, and trivia that embodied the process
of governing. Present them with an idea and they surrounded it, tickled it, tore it apart to see its gears rattle, and wondered how they could
make it work for them. They drew confidence from a belief that their

own good intentions were obvious, and even if their efforts didn't pan out, the public would give them credit for trying to do the right thing.

The forces pushing key escrow didn't even wait until the new administration reached the White House before they hit Clinton and Gore with the encryption problem. The AT&T phone threat provided an impetus. "Suddenly this wasn't something where we could wait, do an orderly briefing of the new administration, let them get their feet under them, appoint their assistant secretaries, and make a decision in 1994," says Stewart Baker. The idea of getting George Bush to sign off before vacating the White House had been considered, but rejected. "We believe that going forward with the installation of the Clipper Chip based on the approval of the current administration has some potential pitfalls," wrote an FBI official to director Sessions in a late-1992 memo. What if the news of an "exploitable" chip leaked before the Clinton people formally approved the policy? "It might result in their being pushed toward disavowing the prior Bush administration approach in order to prevent the controversy."

Judge Sessions himself, whose fear of losing precious wiretaps had made him increasingly frantic on the issue, was the first one to hit Little Rock. "It had become his highest priority," says a government official working for key escrow. "He was fearless in going to the transition team and saying, 'You guys may be coming in January, but you've got to hear this *now*.'" In any case, the NSA was just as happy to let him lead. After all, Fort Meade's stated role in government was not promoting policy decisions but providing technical background and intelligence information from its files.

To frame the issues, the FBI, with the NSA's help, prepared a paper entitled "Encryption, Law Enforcement, and National Security." The classified document was packed with high-impact scenarios of what might happen if crypto ran free. It discussed the AT&T device as a possible trigger for this onslaught. But the coming disaster might be averted. "The solution is an encryption chip that provides extra privacy protection (at least a million times stronger than DES) but one that can be read by U.S. government officials when authorized by law. . . . This 'key escrow' system would protect U.S. citizens and companies from invasion of their privacy by hackers, competitors, and foreign governments. At the same time, it would allow law enforcement to conduct wiretaps in precisely the same circumstances as are currently permitted under the law." While the description sounded very much like a panacea to an otherwise apocalyptic problem, the paper did include one possibly annoying consequence of the policy: "This concept undoubtedly will be vigorously attacked by those who fear law enforcement abuses and thus would rather rely on technology than on the court to protect their privacy." But that seemed rather an easy trade-off to make. Which would you rather tolerate—a bit of flak from privacy nuts, or a powerful weapon in the hands of kidnappers and terrorists?

Stewart Baker was the NSA's point man on the issue, and wound up coordinating much of the effort to sell escrow to the incoming leadership. While Fort Meade was packed with geniuses, it wasn't as loaded with people who were comfortable dealing with the outside world. Baker had come a long way since Clint Brooks had come to his office and first told him about Equities. In that time, he had gotten a good view of the cryptographic landscape from the NSA point of view. He saw where it all fit together. You couldn't mandate what people inside the country used nor could you keep every copy of a program like PGP away from every geek on the globe. But realistically, not many people were going to take the trouble to find exotic encryption software like PGP and figure out how to use it. Export controls were the way you stopped good crypto—everything from DES on up—from being built into the systems people used every day, and thus, out of the hands of most bad guys.

Baker saw the Clipper scheme as a way of weaning the government from its dependence on export controls to contain crypto. There were signs that Congress might not support those regulations indefinitely. The business community was getting louder and louder in its opposition to them. The problem was, the software industry had grown up in an environment with few regulations, and was now a multibillion-dollar colossus. It felt that the natural order of things was to fight things out in the marketplace while the government remained some distant entity. The techies seemed to regard the premier crypto agency in the world as some doddering, irrelevant artifact of the Cold War. Their philosophy was *hey, technology happens.* Baker was horrified once when a Microsoft middle manager blithely told Baker that Bill Gates was going to put crypto into the Microsoft operating system, that it was going to be in all the applications. Who cares whether it would empower terrorists or rogue nations? Their attitude was, "Encryption is cool, let's put it anywhere."

The techies weren't unpatriotic, Baker thought, just clueless about the very real dangers in the world. They thought it was a joke that crypto was classified along with heavy munitions. But the ability to listen in on the world—with a vast multibillion-dollar network of secret satellites, radar installations, and ground sensors—was a pillar of U.S. defense policy. How did they think we discovered those Libyan terrorists who brought down the Pan Am jet over Lockerbie? How else to keep track of the North Korean nuke program or Iraq's use of chemical weapons against the Kurds? The public had only heard hints of the importance of those "intercepts," signals snatched from telephone conversations, digital transfers, and even walkie-talkie transmissions. Most of it was classified, deep black stuff. That's why there were no reporters when George Bush himself had ventured to The Fort to extend his personal congratulations to the codebreakers for their work during the Gulf War. Just what did the spooks do? If the public only knew. . . .

Baker and his fellow advocates of escrow thought it essential that the worldview taken by the new administration be a more realistic and tougher one. Encryption should be an important part of the Networked Society, sure, but you needed controls. You needed limits. You needed a way for the good guys to hear what the terrorists and crooks were saying to each other.

Early in the campaign to win the hearts and minds of the Clinton people, Baker and Sessions briefed Leon Fuerth, who would become Al Gore's national security advisor. Though Fuerth was cautious, the escrow advocates could see that their presentation had hit the mark. They thought they could see it in his face: the realization that the election campaign was over and now the Clinton folks were going to be wrestling with some hard, hard issues. This was one that the NSA and the FBI could win.

As December rolled on, the briefings continued. And not long after the inauguration, Al Gore himself got exposed to the religion by NSA director McConnell and Clint Brooks. It was a bull's-eye for The Fort. Because Gore loved technology, he was able to appreciate the ingenuity of the key escrow scheme. A neo-Luddite Republican might have fuzzed out on those particulars, but Gore's openness toward the idea seemed tied to his perception that these software gears and levers might actually work, providing a solution that gave something to everybody.

As the Clinton-Gore teams shifted from transition to governing, the Clipper people stepped up the meetings. Memos flew between the NSA and NIST on how best to anticipate and respond to possible objections. They knew one potential problem: Fort Meade's insistence on keeping the Clipper's workings a secret from the public. Brooks tried to convince his colleagues to open up, but failed. His fallback plan was somehow to gin up some assurances that the NSA hadn't intentionally weakened Skipjack for its own purposes. "Get a panel of academics from cryptomath/analyst community to examine classified level SKIPJACK to 'assure' it is valid/good algorithm," he scrawled on a memo to his director on January 5. "Who should it be?"

Meanwhile, in the White House, the barrage of briefings was having its effect. In their first weeks in office, Clinton and Gore hadn't signed off on Clipper. But their staffs were coming to the conclusion that there was no other alternative.

John Podesta was already on board. Maybe his personal tipping point came very early after the inauguration when some high-tech lobbyists came to visit him. At this point, civil libertarians and software industry people were still hoping that the new administration would act *against* the spooks and the cops and liberalize crypto export regulations. (If they'd known about the Clipper Chip they would have gone ballistic.) Podesta, still dazzled by the new toys in his office, showed them his STU-III phone, the standard-issue crypto phone the government had used for about five years. They sneered at it. "Typical clunky government solution," they said. "But you know what's cool? AT&T is going to make a device that's half the size, much cheaper, and will do everything that one does, but better. You should buy *those!*" Though the high-tech guys didn't know it, their comments resonated with the briefings Podesta had been getting. If the government didn't do something, those damn devices probably *would* sweep the market.

Not that the NSA/FBI Clipper cabal was relying on serendipity to bring the Clinton folks around. They were essentially stacking the deck, presenting a limited set of options to the greenhorns. *Want to do nothing, and let the marketplace take its course? Fine. If you want to trigger crypto anarchy, that is.* Doing nothing, they warned, would mean that AT&T would begin selling its phones and the next thing you knew the costs would come down and everybody would be talking on secure phones and e-mailing with crypto software. The smoke had hardly cleared from the World Trade Center bombing. What if another, maybe a worse, terrorist disaster came, and it turned out that the government failed to prevent it because the perpetrators were able to communicate with unbreakable crypto? *You want to give Saddam Hussein access to ciphers we can't break? Go ahead—do nothing. The blood will be on your hands.* This terrified the Clinton people.

The other alternative, which some law enforcement hardliners were urging, was even more extreme: ban crypto *within* the United States. In one of the FBI's presentations, illustrated by a slide show with bullet charts to underline the salient points, the G-men merged their Clipper-related goals with their Digital Telephony vision. Essentially, the show said: because the domestic use of encryption is not regulated, there is a NEED FOR A NATIONAL POLICY that allows "legitimate" users crypto strong enough to foil their adversaries but also "insures that cryptographic devices and systems are capable of real-time encryption by law enforcement." The implication was unavoidable: any cryptography that does not meet that standard should be *prohibited.* Even stuff distributed by American manufacturers for American users. Otherwise, an intolerable "electronic sanctuary" would exist. Forget about the strategy of using export controls to mitigate what people used inside the country. . . . Our nation was at risk because such tools were legally available to anyone motivated enough to find them. Just as it was illegal to have nuclear weapons lying around, it should be illegal to have codes that could fall into the hands of those who would destroy society with it. In a weird way, this sentiment echoed Phil Zimmermann: *when crypto is outlawed, only outlaws will have crypto.*

The Clinton people did manage to resist that demand, which would have started riots in Silicon Valley and probably wouldn't have survived a court challenge anyway. The Gore team in particular was sensitive to the idea that the emerging Information Highway needed privacy protections. Besides, how would you enforce such a ban? What did these guys want the government to do, go house to house and search people's hard disk drives for copies of PGP?

So, after being presented with two unpalatable alternatives, the Clinton people were offered a third way, one which, in contrast, seemed a compromise with which everyone could live. In retrospect, one administration insider came to see it as akin to the choices offered the Kennedy people on the invasion of Cuba—a cowardly evasion of the problem, a destabilizing full-scale military operation, or this other plan, a small operation at some place called the Bay of Pigs.

The scheme was presented to the Clinton people as plug-ready, poised to go into operation as soon as the president gave the word. Even temporary inaction would mean a severe and probably lingering loss of respect from the law-and-order constituency the administration needed. One of the FBI men briefing the Clinton people was a burly, street-smart assistant director named James Kallstrom. Formerly head of the bureau's technology team, he had made his bones in the bugging operation that took down John Gotti. Some people described him as the FBI's version of "Q," the gadget wizard of the James Bond films. He had an in-your-face style of briefing, making eye contact and personalizing his rap. *Are you married? Do you have a child?* he'd ask. Then he'd launch into a scenario in which someone had kidnapped one of your kids and was holding him in a fortress up in the Bronx. The bureau suspects your kid is there; they have a search warrant to find him. But the crooks have constructed the fortress out of some new metal that can't be penetrated. Your kid's potential rescuers can't get in. What a nightmare: the kidnappers, with their precious hostage, watching you and the G-men trying to get in and *laughing* at you.

"That's what the basis of this issue really is," Kallstrom would say in his New York accent. "From the standpoint of law enforcement, there's a super-big threat—this guy is gonna build this domain in the Bronx right now, because he's got a big steel door, and none of the welding torches, none of the boomerangs, nothing we have is gonna blast our way in there. Sure, we want those new steel doors ourselves, to protect our banks, to protect the American trade secrets, patent rights, technology. But do we want a digital superhighway where major criminals can operate impervious to the legal process? If we don't want that, then we have to look at Clipper."

Kallstrom, along with Baker, Brooks, McConnell, and the CIA's John Deutch, became part of the key escrow team ostensibly briefing the administration on its options, but really steering it, with one hand on the scruff of its Democratic neck, toward an inevitable embrace of

Clipper. One unexpectedly ally was commerce secretary Ron Brown; in the first briefing he attended, Brown mentioned that his army days had been spent at an NSA listening post, and he was fully aware of the vital importance of signals intelligence. By now the briefings included not only national security people but the Clinton-Gore science staffers like the Office of Science and Technology Policy's Mike Nelson, info- nauts well attuned to issues like personal privacy and the industry's need for secure systems. (Nelson got his top-secret clearance in a lightning-quick three weeks.) In a January 26 FBI briefing, Kallstrom laid out a lot of the fine points of the scheme, but Gore's senior direc- tor on intelligence programs, George Tenet, had further questions on the Clipper methodology. Who would be the key escrow agents? How would the international aspects be handled? A lengthy February 9 memo from Judge Sessions gave a detailed summary of the plan and the dire implications that would ensue if no action was taken.

So, barely a month into the Clinton administration, the pressure was intense to move on Clipper. Supposedly, AT&T would ship ten thou- sand DES-equipped phone devices by April 1 if no action was taken. But by then, the administration's crypto team—consisting of national security people and Internet specialists—had almost imperceptibly shifted from decision making to implementation. It was their first big initiative, and they wanted it done fast: the word "closure" kept pop- ping up in their correspondence. A typical internal memo, dated March 5, was from George Tenet to Gore's national security advisor Leon Fuerth and his colleague William Wise: the header read "HELP HELP HELP." Then, "Desperately need time from the VP"—for a meeting with the past and current NSA directors on the encryption issue. "I think I know what the VP wants to hear McConnell/Stude- man talk about," Tenet continued, finishing with the odd closing, "God bless you all."

All through March, the meetings continued. Meanwhile, industry and civil liberties groups were lobbying the newcomers, still hoping that the new administration would be amenable to considerable reform on crypto. "You're holding back e-commerce, you're endangering the security network, and besides, it's all out of control, anyway!" one of them shouted at Gore's people. But the Clinton people had already mentally aligned themselves with the government insiders at the NSA, the FBI, the Justice Department, and the CIA. The classified briefings had done the trick, particularly the warning that if no action was taken, *people will die. Are you willing to sacrifice human lives,* they were asked, *for a fraction of a decimal point rise in the GNP?* The tack was devastatingly effective: the dilemma was essentially resolved by framing it as a choice between thousands of people dying and Bill Gates being 10 percent richer. "That's a pretty easy decision," says an administration official.

Not that there weren't qualms within the White House. The biggest question the Clinton aides asked themselves was, "Why would anyone want Clipper?" (After all, the plan *was* supposed to be voluntary.) Another problem was the requirement that the Skipjack algorithm remain under wraps. It was inevitable that its secrecy would lead critics to charge that the scheme was a Trojan horse to bring flawed crypto into the infrastructure. But the NSA wouldn't budge on secrecy.

Finally, there was the problem of how the key escrow scheme would play overseas. If a crypto solution was not global, it would be useless. If buyers abroad did not trust U.S. products with the escrow scheme, they would eschew those products and buy instead from manufacturers in Switzerland, Germany, or even Russia. And how could you handle key escrow in other countries? Should the United States allow access to stored keys to free-speech–challenged nations like Singapore, or China? And would France, Egypt, Japan, and other countries be happy to let their citizens use products that allowed spooks in the United States to decipher conversations but not their own law enforcement and intelligence agencies? The answers to those questions were not forthcoming because the planners of Clipper never did work out a solution to its global implications—another consequence that came with rushing Clipper out of the door.

None of those objections were sufficient to sink the plan. At six in the evening on March 31, 1993, in the White House Situation Room, Vice President Gore went over the proposed directives in a meeting that included the whole gamut of law enforcement, intelligence, and national security leaders. Not long afterward, he briefed the president with his recommendation. Bill Clinton agreed.

Clipper was a go.

From that point the operation shifted to what one participant calls "White House Marketing." Press releases were drafted. Mike Nelson set about writing an explanation of the proposal in question-and-answer form. Then on the eve of the announcement itself, the White House prebriefed a number of representatives from Congress, industry, and the civil liberties groups on the issue, not so much to collect feedback as to forestall charges that the Clinton people had blindsided them with the abrupt change in course.

Still, no one at the White House anticipated a major clamor over Clipper. But Clint Brooks saw trouble coming—this issue had the potential to leak outside the Beltway, to make real enemies out of potential sympathizers. *They just don't get it,* he complained to Stew Baker on one drive between Fort Meade and the White House. At one meeting, he asked, "Who's going to handle this on *Larry King Live*?" His question was ignored. A few minutes later, he repeated it. A senior administration official sternly told him, "Clint, we appreciate your sense of humor but this is really serious—you handle the technical stuff and we'll handle the political stuff." (Some months later, when Al Gore appeared on *Larry King Live* to talk about the Information Highway, the first question posed to him was about . . . the Clipper Chip.)

The briefings with Congress and industry went pretty much as expected: the proposal was received cautiously, even skeptically, but not dismissed out of hand. One legislative staffer complained that when the Clinton people were challenged, they went on the offensive. "Do you want to be responsible for kidnappers?" the Clintonistas would ask, and the legislators would crumble. The sessions with civil liberties groups weren't so cordial. John Perry Barlow of the Electronic Frontier Foundation got one of those last-minute briefings and couldn't believe his ears. He felt that his new friends in the White House had been "drinking the Kool-Aid," a national security version of Jonestown. What particularly offended him was Mike Nelson's invocation of the classified information he had heard and Barlow had not. "If only I could tell you what I know, you'd feel the same way I do," Nelson said. *Thousands* could die, he confided. Barlow felt he was hearing the same phony music that had been sung by the Vietnam warmongers. What Clipper *really* represented, he felt, was a plan that would "initiate a process that might end freedom in America."

Then there was Clint Brooks's effort to get outside experts the information necessary to explain the benign nature of the system to the public. The night before the announcement, Brooks himself ventured through a driving rain to brief Georgetown computer science professor Dorothy Denning, his first choice to lead the panel to vet the classified Skipjack algorithm. It would be an inspired choice. Denning was an expert on crypto and computer security but her demeanor was as benign as Betty Crocker's. (Science fiction writer Bruce Sterling once described the diminutive woman as "something like a Pilgrim maiden behind leaden glass.") She was already on the record as supporting the regulation of cryptography, and coincidentally at the time of Brooks's visit had just experienced an awkward situation in which she'd been unable to get into her locker after a swim in the university's indoor pool; only helpful maintenance men with heavy-duty cutters (the equivalent of escrow agents!) saved her from venturing into forty-degree weather in her wet bathing suit. Not only was she ready to defend key escrow, she came to feel it was her destiny.

On April 16, President Clinton unveiled the new initiative. In his press secretary's announcement of the plan, the issue was presented to the public as a middle ground between two dreadful extremes—much as the situation had been presented to the administration by the NSA. Seen through that filter, the Clipper Chip was to be regarded as a godsend:

> The chip is an important step in addressing the problem of encryption's dual-edged sword: encryption helps the privacy of individuals and industry, but it can also shield criminals and terrorists. We need the "Clipper Chip" and other approaches that can both provide law-abiding citizens with access to the encryption they need and prevent criminals from using it to hide their illegal activities.

The actual announcement did not establish Clipper as a standard, but it did affirm that the government itself was committed to buying thousands of the AT&T Clipper-inside devices for its own agencies. The hope was that while Clipper was designed to be a voluntary standard, its adoption and endorsement by the government would tip the marketplace to make it ubiquitous. The ultimate recommendation would come after Clinton received the results of a widespread blue-ribbon review on the national crypto policy that would look at the escrow initiative and reevaluate the export laws.

With that announcement, Bill Clinton and his people felt that they had made a big step toward avoiding what seemed like a disastrous collision in the crypto world, one that had seemed predestined since the day that Whit Diffie figured out how to split the cryptographic key. In fact, the Clipper Chip *did* mark the turning point in the battle, but not at all in the way the Clinton administration had intended. By promoting Clipper as its key escrow flagship, the government profoundly erred. Instead of a nuanced debate on encryption, from that point on the merits—and drawbacks—of this particular scheme would become the main crypto battleground. Clipper itself was the issue, and Clipper as proposed was vulnerable. And Clint Brooks, who was more than anyone its architect, saw what was happening, but was powerless to prevent it.

At first, things didn't look so bad. From the vantage point of the White House and Fort Meade, it appeared that what relatively little public attention the Clipper Chip had garnered was fairly balanced. The *New York Times* article, published on the day of the announcement, had set a reasonable tone, right from its lead. The Clinton administration was "about to announce a plan to preserve privacy in electronic communications . . . while also insuring the government's right to eavesdrop for law enforcement and national security reasons." Balance. Of course, the article did quote one industry representative as saying, "The government is creating a monster."

In the days following, there was no rush to embrace the plan by the various stakeholders who might be affected by it. The feds took succor, though, in the lack of a widespread outcry against it. The Internet, of course, was buzzing with fears of police-state tactics, but on the other hand, Dorothy Denning had almost immediately posted a clear-headed description of the system itself and was already serving as an example that the crypto community was not universally anti-Clipper. Better yet, an unexpectedly friendly description of the plan came from Marty Hellman, whom Brooks had briefed by phone on the eve of the announcement. Hellman's explanation of the scheme was cautiously neutral (though he did warn that there should be safeguards in the legal process leading to key retrieval), and was posted on the influential "Interesting People" mailing list run by Net gadfly David Farber.

On April 20, Clint Brooks wrote a memo reflecting his optimism. "The reactions I am getting from academic and industry people is that this may succeed," he wrote. So much so, these people were telling him, that the government may have not allocated enough digits in the chip identification fields to handle all the Clippers that would come into use. A hundred million would not be enough!

But that initial success was illusory, like a second-rate baseball team sitting in first place after a lucky string of April wins. The first serious rumbles came from the crucial information industries. After going over the plan, they concluded that the opportunity it offered to build strong exportable crypto into their systems was more than canceled out by the presence of the Law Enforcement Access Field, which provided keys to government snoops with warrants. The point of exporting crypto, after all, was to serve customers overseas. But what foreign companies wanted to buy a security system where the keys were stored in United States government escrow facilities? The business leaders joined with the already skeptical civil liberties people and fed on the energy of the grassroots Internet folk, who'd hated it from the get-go. Then they all took their case to the media. Though the reaction took a few months to build, the Clipper coverage eventually exceeded all the publicity that any previous cryptological development had ever received.

Little of it was favorable. All the time the government was planning its key escrow initiative, its creators had implicitly believed that only an isolated few would question their motives. They saw the selling of Clipper as a process by which responsible people would have a number of concerns, and the government would respond to those. One prime concern, they figured, would be a fear that the mechanics of the escrow scheme would somehow compromise the security of the encryption itself, making it easier for crooks and spies from other countries to do the unscrambling. Another would be that the key escrow facilities themselves might be vulnerable. What this thinking didn't account for was that *the very basis for the scheme*—a government means by which to flip the "descramble" switch for its own purposes—was offensive to most people. All opponents had to do was use a simple analogy—What if you had to leave a copy of your front door key at the police station?—and even a Joe Sixpack who didn't know encryption from a forward pass would be an anti-Clipper convert. "The idea that government holds the keys to all our locks, even before anyone has been accused of committing a crime, doesn't parse with the public," explained Jerry Berman of the EFF. "It's not America."

Others didn't need such analogies. One of the basic reasons many people wanted to use crypto was to keep information from the government itself. Not that they were necessarily lawbreakers. They simply didn't trust the government. The bureaucrats who made the plan were a generation removed from Watergate, but anyone who had been around in the seventies might have known better.

Former NSA director Bobby Inman, for instance, got an early briefing on the Clipper Chip and he sensed right away that it was doomed. Who wanted to give the government a direct pipeline to your information? The cypherpunks understood this, and immediately initiated a guerrilla campaign to infect the media and the general population with the anti-Clipper message. At their monthly meeting, Eric Hughes solicited an agenda of possible actions including everything from advocacy press kits to stumping for a procrypto constitutional amendment. Tim May suggested active sabotage of Clipper, or a boycott of AT&T. One effective prank they did pull off was distributing a little decal to stick on your laptop. Designed to resemble the famous Intel Inside logo, it read, "Big Brother Inside." That pretty much said it all. (Intel quickly threatened to sue for trademark infringement, and the offending cypherpunks stopped distributing the stickers.)

Opposition came from all quarters. The ACLU found itself agreeing with Rush Limbaugh, who attacked Clipper on his radio show. Digital hippies savored the William Safire column "Sink the Clipper Chip," where he noted that the solution's name was well chosen, "as it clips the wings of individual liberty."

Tim May often expounded a theory that Americans are of two minds when it comes to privacy. One involves the public interest and was essentially anticrypto: "What do you have to hide?" The other expresses the individual ethic of the Bill of Rights, and is proprivacy: "None of your business." Any successful policy has to walk down the middle of those opposing sentiments. But Clipper, in its insistence that nothing should be hidden from the government, never established that balance. Once people began calling it the Big Brother Chip, the game was over.

The government did its best to defend the scheme. Stewart Baker briefed industry figures including crypto advocate Bill Gates, to little avail. He went into the lion's den, speaking at procrypto events like the Computers, Freedom, and Privacy conference—where he belittled the anti-Clipper forces to their faces, calling their actions, "the revenge of people who couldn't go to Woodstock because they had too much trig homework." He taunted them with the "If you knew what I know" argument. Your view of privacy, he told them, reflects a hopelessly naive view of the world. "By insisting on having a claim to privacy that is beyond social regulation, we are creating a world in which [crooks and terrorists] will flourish and be able to do more than they can do today," Baker warned.

Not all the news was bad for the government. In the summer of 1993, the Skipjack algorithm was deemed strong by the team of "independent experts" led by Dorothy Denning and including Walt Tuchman (who had led IBM's DES team) and Ernie Brickell (who had picked up the $1000 reward for cracking Merkle's multi-iteration knapsack cipher). Denning had become so fierce in her defense of the government, clearly articulating a position that posited the dangers of crypto anarchy, that critics were calling her "Clipper Chick." Her disinterested status made her more effective in public forums than the administration's battered tech squad, which was beginning to regard its appearances at Internet-related conferences with all the enthusiasm of dental surgery. Who could blame them, as question after question drilled in the reality that their natural constituency of tech-savvy "Netizens" now saw them as virtual brownshirts? The White House's Mike Nelson came to refer to crypto as "the Bosnia of telecommunications."

Still, Clipper seemed cursed. At every turn a new problem cropped up. For example, not long after the announcement of the plan, the government heard from an MIT professor named Silvio Micali. Micali, who worked in MIT's mathematics and cryptography group (led by Ron Rivest), had devised some mathematical protocols he called "Fair Cryptosystems" that seemed similar to the government's key escrow scheme. He had published a paper on them in 1992 and had gotten a patent for them. The government quietly paid Micali a million dollars to license his patent.

Even the chip's name proved to be a problem. "Clipper was our cover name, *a la* NSA normal operations," Brooks wrote in an early

1992 memo. "I tried to get people *not* to use this outside the agency, but the policy makers and their staffs found it so convenient to use that it stuck." Unfortunately, a company named Intergraph was already selling a microprocessor it called Clipper, and the United States had to pay a considerable sum to buy the rights to a moniker that was well on its way to what marketers call a brand disaster.

Other problems were purely technical. The chipmaker Mykotronx was a government and commercial contractor unaccustomed to the demands of the consumer marketplace, and its chip wasn't built to accommodate high-bandwidth data rates. In its haste to get the Clipper Chip into the AT&T phones, the NSA had created a product that might have been adequate for the communications technology of 1993 but was woefully inefficient for the high speed of information flow in the glistening future that would arrive, oh, two years or so later. In other words, as critics noted with withering irony, by the time a security company took the fifteen to eighteen months to build a product around Clipper, the hardware would be obsolete.

Did *anyone* like Clipper? As part of the process, NIST had been required to solicit public comment on the plan. Three hundred and twenty individuals and organizations responded; of those, only two agreed with Clipper. "This is not a Hall of Fame batting average," conceded NIST official Lynn McNulty.

But the Clinton people would not budge. On February 4, 1994, the president formally endorsed Clipper—known as the Escrow Encryption Standard—as a Federal Information Processing Standard. The government would immediately start buying Clipper-equipped AT&T phones for its own use, escrowing keys with NIST and the Treasury Department. (This despite the fact that the technology did not yet actually exist to perform decryption of keys retrieved from the as-yet-nonexistent escrow facilities.)

"The War is upon us," wrote Tim May. "Clinton and Gore folks have shown themselves to be enthusiastic supporters of Big Brother."

In the Senate, Patrick Leahy, among others, vowed to fight Clipper, insisting that without congressional approval the project could not be funded (setting up the program would cost $14 million, with an annual $16 million budgeted for the escrow facilities). In May 1994 he held hearings. In rare public appearances, Clint Brooks and Mike McConnell presented the view from behind the Triple Fence, essentially congratulating the administration for taking the right approach. "There are, to be sure, issues to be ironed out," concluded McConnell. "But I am confident we will work out the wrinkles."

Then a panel of opponents showed those "wrinkles" to be approximately the size of the Colorado River basin.

One tough question they posed: *Who would want to use Clipper, when there were already programs like PGP readily available?* The government's response had been the "stupid crook theory," best explained by the FBI's Jim Kallstrom, who professed to have himself heard mobsters on wiretaps make jokes about being wiretapped—and then engage in incriminating conversations, simply because it was too awkward to go outside and use a pay phone. "If in five years this catches on and people put Clipper in their devices, a high percentage of criminals will go to a Radio Shack or some other place like that to buy some sort of encryptor," he said. "They're not going to remember that in 1994 some article [appeared] in the *Wall Street Journal* [about key escrow]. Maybe in the fine print somewhere it'll say Clipper something. But it's not going to be readily apparent—it'll be part of the landscape. That's what would be our desire."

OK, so stupid crooks might use it. But the antigovernment witnesses noted that if *smart* criminals eschewed Clipper, so would the overseas customers who were crucial to its adoption. What was in it for France or Japan or Indonesia to sign on to a plan where the keys to their citizen's private conversations—possibly involving invaluable business secrets—were held jointly by two branches of the United States government?

Perhaps the most persuasive witness was Whit Diffie. He testified not only as one of the inventors of public key but as a representative of one of the ad hoc organizations lobbying against Clipper, the Digital Privacy and Security Working Group. Diffie tried to put the issue into historical perspective. Governments had been similarly concerned with previous revolutions in telecommunications, like the transatlantic cable and the advent of radio. Despite fears that governments would lose sovereignty, these developments turned out to prove tremendously useful to governments. Computer communications, too, would probably, on the whole, increase government power. But the United States seemed loath to allow any of that power to accrue to its citizens. While the government claimed only the desire to retain its current ability to wiretap, the fact was that during the time of the founding fathers, privacy was easily obtained simply by walking out of the earshot of others. "It seems that the right . . . of the participants to take measures to guarantee the right to speak privately can hardly have been in doubt, despite the fact that the right to speak privately could be abused in the service of a crime," said Diffie. Today, of course, people communicate largely by electronic means, from the telephone to the computer. Could it be that the government has the right to deny the possibility of privacy in those conversations? "The legitimacy of laws in a democracy grows out of the democratic process," Diffie told the senators. "Unless the people are free to discuss the issues—and privacy is an essential component of many of those discussions—that process cannot take place."

Not long after the Senate hearings, Clipper suffered perhaps the worst blow of all. It came not as a tirade in Congress, an attack by an industry representative, or a screed from a cypherpunk. It was the result of a scientific experiment conducted by a formerly obscure research scientist named Matthew Blaze. Essentially, he made the Clipper Chip look stupid.

Blaze was a New York kid, a classic science nerd. He'd dropped out of a preppy private school, worked for a while as a paramedic (the first person hired by the city's emergency medical service without a driver's license), then drifted back to college, earning a degree in two seemingly incompatible sciences: computer and political. At graduate school at Columbia, he began seriously thinking about crypto. Talking to his officemate, a guy named Stuart Haber, who had devised a way to use public key to time-stamp documents digitally (providing an electronic equivalent to the old trick of postmarking a letter to affirm its age), he realized that crypto was both a way to tackle important mathematical problems and a practical lever to change society. Blaze was also a big believer in privacy rights.

After switching to Princeton and getting a Ph.D., he went to work for the small crypto group at AT&T's Bell Labs research facility. Blaze began working in areas of encryption other than algorithms. His group was more concerned with basic research than AT&T's secure system group in North Carolina, which had produced the TSD 3600 device that was slated to be the Clipper phone. In fact, he found out about Clipper by reading the newspaper like everyone else.

But as the Clinton administration was readying its February 1994 endorsement of the escrow standard, it had initiated a series of technical briefings that included the Bell Labs crypto group. Several NSA scientists came to New Jersey for a briefing. Though the group could generally be described as anti-Clipper—besides the privacy implications, as cryptographers they were offended at the security risks of sending a key to a third party—"we managed to be on our best behavior," says Blaze, "not letting the meeting degenerate into whether this is a good idea." Afterward, he asked if he could post a summary of the meeting to the Internet, and Blaze stuck to the facts in that as well.

This impressed people behind the Triple Fence, who apparently thought Blaze could be another valuable outside tester of Clipper technology. They invited him and a colleague to Fort Meade to get a prototype of Tessera, the smart-card-based version of the escrow system. (Tessera was to be a portable version of the whole-enchilada Capstone cryptosystem that Clint Brooks favored over the limited Clipper Chip.) Never having been there, Blaze was excited. He was given the standard visitor's badge with a sensor that tracked him through the building: when his host took him through he had to keep facing security cameras and assuring some unseen guard that Blaze was with him, and a disembodied voice said, "Okay, thank you." Even between the briefing room and the bathroom this happened a couple of times. "They didn't actually follow me into the bathroom," Blaze says. When the Bell researchers left, they were given Tessera cards, a stack of manuals, and NSA coffee mugs.

Blaze immediately began testing the system, focusing on the Clipper aspects of the device. Unlike Dorothy Denning's team, which had focused on Skipjack, Blaze wondered whether there was a way to actually use the strong encryption while defeating the escrow feature. In other words, could a crook, terrorist, or someone just wanting privacy use Clipper's crypto without being identified? He focused his efforts on studying the Law Enforcement Access Field. "I wasn't even thinking of it as a potential weakness," he says. "But it turned out that the obvious way of defeating the LEAF was pretty much the first thing you would initially think of."

Using a card reader and a little program that simulated a wiretap, he began testing. The simplest things—altering the code so you wouldn't send the identifier, or sending some other number in place of the identifier—didn't work. But it took only a bit of thought to come up with slightly more complicated ways that *did* work. The breakthrough came when Blaze, poring over the manuals, noted that the "checksum" in the LEAF was only 16 bits long. (The checksum is the way to verify that the proper LEAF, including the chip identifier and session key that encoded the conversation, was indeed sent off to the authorities. The proper number in the checksum is like an "all's clear" that says everything is OK. If there was some way of creating a counterfeit LEAF with a legitimate checksum, in effect you would have defeated the Clipper system. The encryption would work, but the wiretappers wouldn't have the proper session key to decrypt the conversation.)

"Sixteen bits isn't a very big number these days, computationally," Blaze says. Within a few hours he hacked up a "LEAF-blower," a quick program that could send out every possible combination (2 to the 16th power) of checksum numbers, then hooked it to his test system. He really didn't expect it to work—it seemed so easy. But it did work, each time he tried it. In no more than forty-two minutes, he was able to send out a checksum that spoofed the escrow system into mistakenly assuming he was sending out the data that could lead investigators to the escrowed key—when in fact that data would lead them nowhere. Instead, the wiretapper would be faced with a conversation encrypted by the powerful Skipjack algorithm, deemed uncrackable by the NSA itself. (He also found a way in which two people conspiring to defeat the LEAF system could do so even more quickly.)

What Blaze did not know was that the small checksum space was no accident but an artifact of the haste with which Clipper was prepared. During the hurried design process the NSA engineers consulted with various technical experts at telephone companies, and were warned that with wireless phones, any system that required transmission of too many bits would be deemed impractical. So the LEAF field was limited to 128 bits. Of that, 32 bits had to be used for the chip identifiers, leaving only 96 bits for an actual encryption key and the checksum. The NSA wanted a large checksum, but the FBI insisted on using 80 bits so the full session key would be transmitted. (An alternative may have been to leave off some of the key bits and allow the FBI to complete the decoding by a brute-force attack. If, for instance, eight bits had been diverted from the keyspace to the checksum, the FBI could have run through a mere 256 different alternatives to find its key—but Blaze's attempt to crack the checksum would have taken not 42 minutes, but more than a week. That's a long time on hold.)

In a few days, Blaze sent a draft paper of his findings to his colleagues at Bell Labs. Most of them couldn't believe it. "Are you sure about this?" they asked, suggesting he recheck his work. He did. Then he began the more delicate process of checking it with outsiders. One morning Blaze girded himself and sent a fax of his draft to Fort Meade. Right after lunch he got a call back, affirming his results were technically correct.

"What are you planning on doing with this?" asked his NSA contact.

Blaze took a deep breath. "I'd like to publish it."

To his surprise, no objection was raised. His NSA reader did point out a couple of errors in numerical transcription and one grammatical error. Now all Blaze had to do was get an okay from his employer— who had millions of dollars riding on its Clipper phones. Though there were some who wanted to bury the paper, eventually Blaze managed to convince his bosses that it would be impossible to keep his findings secret, so they shouldn't even try. In any case, John Markoff of the *New York Times* had already gotten wind of the work. Blaze got permission to send him a draft, so that whatever story ran would be accurate. Markoff called back for some clarification and a few hours later called back again and asked Blaze a strange question: how newsworthy did he consider the story? Blaze felt that it was indeed a story—it showed how rushed the NSA was to get its system out, and emphasized how dangerous it was to foist something half baked on the public—but not a front-page story or anything like that. Not long afterward, Markoff called again, almost apologetically, and said that it had been a slow news day so the story was going to be more prominently placed. Blaze figured that meant it would lead the business section.

He'd heard that you could get the next day's paper at 9 P.M. if you went to the Times Building, and he was curious enough to do so. After opening the paper, he went through it and was disappointed to find nothing. "It hadn't occurred to me to even look on the front page until

I had gotten out of the building." But there it was—leading the entire paper on the sweet spot in the rightmost column of page one, head-lined "FLAW DISCOVERED IN FEDERAL PLAN FOR WIRETAPPING."

This was significant in several ways. First, though the flaw itself could be fixed—and arguably didn't compromise security much—the very fact that such a weakness existed put a permanent taint on a system dependent on public trust. But perhaps more important was that the former backwater, mumbo-jumbo subject of crypto had raised its profile so high that even a moderate development like Blaze's crack could be seen by the *Times* editors as the most important story in the world that day. What made this dry topic sexy was the whiff of a Big Brother who couldn't even program correctly. The government unintentionally played into that role when an imperious NSA official insisted that Blaze's attack, while feasible, was unlikely in practice—not a particularly comforting assurance for the nation's cryptographic caretaker. Much stronger was Marty Hellman's assertion, "The government is fighting an uphill battle."

Meanwhile, after some initial supply problems, the government was already starting to use Clipper phones. (The more comprehensive Capstone chips, designed to escrow computer communications, were late in entering the pipeline.) Approximately once a week, four couriers with security clearance—two each from NIST and the Treasury Department—flew from Washington, D.C., to Torrance, California, to the so-called programming facility at Mykotronx headquarters. (The redundancy was intentional, conforming to the Two-Person Integrity Protocol also used for nuclear weapon controls.) Once inside they waited while a Sun workstation did its work, first generating the unique cryptographic keys that would be blown into the MYK-78 (Clipper) chips, then splitting the keys into two parts and creating two stacks of floppy disks, each one with a set of partial keys. To reconstruct the full keys inside the chips required both sets of disks.

Backup sets were produced by the same method. Then the disks were separated, each one going with a pair of couriers. A plastic seal went over the disks. When the couriers returned to their respective agencies, the disks were placed in double-walled safes meeting government standards for classified materials. A set of the backups went in another safe. And there they waited, about 20,000 key splits by May 1994, sitting undisturbed while the war over Clipper continued.

In late January 1994, the Computer Professionals for Social Responsibility had written a letter to the president urging that he rescind the Clipper proposal. It was cosigned by privacy experts, industry figures, academics, and cryptographers, and supplemented by signatures gathered over the Internet. Within a few months, the petition—one of the first Internet political protests—boasted over 47,000 endorsers. While a skeptic might dismiss this as a result of overheated Net-heads, a *New York Times*/CNN poll showed that the government had clearly suffered a Custer-sized rout in the public relations arena. *Eighty percent* of the American public now opposed Clipper.

Not that it did any good. The administration was betting that the export regulations would prevent strong crypto from being built into products that people routinely used, and key escrow would be the only game in town. But Congress had the power to change those regulations. And pushing hardest on the issue was a thirty-eight-year-old single woman in her first term in Congress.

Maria Cantwell was a daughter of an Indiana politician. She'd moved to Washington State in her twenties, served in the legislature there, and in 1992 pulled off a successful run for the House. Her district, consisting of part of Seattle and the towns east of Lake Washington, was loaded with high-tech companies, from Nintendo to Microsoft. So when choosing a committee to serve on she focused on one of the software industry's main concerns, exports, and requested the Foreign Affairs Committee—specifically, its subcommittee on economic policy, trade, and environment.

She'd hardly gotten familiar enough with the House to find the cloakroom when the Clipper announcement hit. It infuriated her big high-tech constituents, and she began to look more deeply into the problem, particularly at the export regulations. She worked closely with the affected software companies, not only those in her district like Microsoft but others like Lotus. The more she learned about the export regulations of crypto, the more absurd they seemed in the computer age. *They can't be so myopic to think cryptography is a munition,* she'd say to Sam Gejdenson, the subcommittee chair and one of her legislative mentors. *If they continue, you won't be able to get protection on the Internet.*

Meanwhile, the export situation was at a standstill. In 1992, some of the leaders of the new industry, like Lotus's Ray Ozzie and Microsoft's Nathan Myhrvold, had spent an incredible amount of energy negotiating a deal with the NSA. The talks were a classic culture clash. The software guys thought it absurd that government was attempting to contain bits of code within national borders, when algorithms with the same ciphers were openly published in countries from Germany to Russia. It was the worst sin among nerds: illogical behavior. *Or was it?* "Don't you realize," Myhrvold once asked one of the spooks in a briefing session, "that you're like the little Dutch boy, trying to use your fingers to plug the dike against a sea of strong crypto?"

His tormentor smiled. "Every day the dike doesn't break," he said softly, "is a victory." And it was true. Sure, the crypto genie had escaped the bottle. But if you throw enough obstacles in the genie's way, it'll take him a long time to perform any magic.

Finally, all that energy resulted in a temporary compromise. Working with an industry group called the Software Publishers Association, the companies got an agreement for "expedited consideration" when they exported software programs sold in shrink-wrap to retail customers. The requirement was that the encryption in those products would be Ron Rivest's ciphers RC-2 or RC-4, using keys of no more than 40 bits. This would allegedly be increased in subsequent years to keep pace with faster computers. In exchange, the NSA got some restrictions of its own. The regulation would not be formalized in an explicit standard. RSA and the companies using the cipher had to agree to keep the details of its design a secret.

But no one particularly liked that deal. Companies had two choices. They could, like Lotus, offer American customers a version with strong (64-bit) encryption, and a weaker version for export. Then foreign customers would wonder why their software had second-class crypto— and sometimes, buy other products. Ray Ozzie claimed that it was already happening with Lotus. (He called the 40-bit limit *espionage-enabled encryption.*) Or, like Microsoft, they could avoid the hassle of manufacturing and shipping two versions and give *everyone* weak encryption. Meanwhile, hard-liners in the government felt that by green-lighting an export exemption, no matter what the key length, they were on a slippery slope toward strong crypto. Give the Lotuses and the Microsofts 40 bits now, and tomorrow they're at your door demanding 48 bits, and more.

But when Cantwell and Gejdenson went to the White House to urge movement toward export of stronger crypto, they hit a brick wall. The Clinton people held firm.

In October 1993 Gejdenson and Cantwell held a subcommittee hearing to draw attention to the problem. "This hearing is about the well-intentioned attempts of the National Security Agency to control that which is uncontrollable," said Gejdenson. He was talking about export regulations, but he might have been talking about something else—the support from Congress that Fort Meade once took for granted. While the majority of legislators accepted the NSA's contentions at face value, a cognitive dissonance was emerging between its arguments and what appeared to be a more compelling view of reality. Cantwell put it clearly in her own opening statement: "We are here to discuss, really, competing visions of the future." On one hand was a mind-set so locked into Cold War posturing that it ignored the inevitable. On the other were the techno-visionaries who powered our future, eager to fortify American ascendancy in a global marketplace.

The hearing's first witness was Ray Ozzie, who had come prepared with a software demo. He had a screen connected by phone line to his computer in Massachusetts, which he used to venture onto the Internet and download one of "hundreds of thousands" of copies of implementations of DES available overseas. He chose one in German, and downloaded it into his machine within seconds, as anyone in the world could do. But, he noted, if he were then to send the same software back to Germany, he would be guilty of the federal offense of exporting strong crypto.

Next was Steve Walker, a former NSA official who now headed Trusted Information Systems, a consulting firm helping businesses implement crypto. He presented the results of a Software Publishers Association study that identified 264 cryptographic products produced overseas, 123 of which employed DES. Foreign individuals and companies could buy any of these, but not similar products created by American firms because the NSA would not permit their export. "It cannot be clearer," he said. "The existence of widespread and affordable cryptographic products overseas is an indisputable fact . . . the U.S. government is succeeding only in crippling a vital American industry's exporting ability." He then cited specific examples of business lost by American companies, like one firm that lost half of its European customers because it could not provide them strong cryptographic security.

Phil Zimmermann gave testimony that trying to restrict cryptography is like attempting to "regulate the tides and the weather." Don Harbert, an executive of Digital Equipment Corporation, insisted that "U.S. export controls on encryption must be brought into line with reality."

One of the committee members who had not been previously vocal in challenging the government, a conservative Californian named Dana Rohrbacher, noted for the record that if it were five years earlier, he would have chastised the witnesses for seeking profit at the potential loss of national security. But now, he said, "the Cold War is over. It is time for us to get on."

After the public session, security experts swept the room for bugs before the inevitable follow-up hearings involving the interests of the National Security Agency: The Briefing, "where the NSA answers all those questions in secret," said Gejdenson. NSA briefings were notorious in Congress. They involved a dramatic presentation by the NSA on why our international eavesdropping abilities were so vital, typically including a litany of victories achieved by clandestine snooping (victories that would have been unthinkable without billions of dollars in funding), and perilous international situations that required continued vigilance and support. Perfected by Bobby Ray Inman in his days as NSA director, they initiated legislators into the society of Top Secret, implicitly shifting their alliance from the citizenry to the intelligence agencies. A newly cleared congressperson would get a presumably unvarnished and reportedly terrifying dose of global reality, after which he or she thereafter could be assumed to dutifully support any demands of the National Security Agency, lest the Huns gain a purchase on our liberty. Representatives and senators had been known to venture into the bug-swept room and emerge grim faced, stunning their go-go staffers by remarking, "Well, maybe we should reconsider."

Not Maria Cantwell. She was among a growing number of legislators who found The Briefing impressive but not persuasive. The issue for these skeptics wasn't just how important crypto was, or what successes we'd had breaking codes, but whether maintaining export rules was actually productive. If the genie was out of the bottle, so what if American companies couldn't export? Crooks would get crypto elsewhere!

Cantwell began to prepare a legislative remedy. In 1994 the Foreign Affairs Committee was already planning its periodic overhaul of the export regulations. She prepared H.R. 3627, "Legislation to Amend the Export Administration Act of 1979," a bill adding a new subsection to the old rules, with specific implications for software exports, including encryption. It would move the decision-making process from the Department of Defense to Commerce, and would essentially make shrink-wrapped or public-domain software exempt from export regulations. It would put an end to the NSA's game of controlling American crypto by use of the export laws.

Naturally, the administration could not let that stand. When Cantwell was ready to introduce the bill, her staff notified her of an incoming phone call—from the vice president. The only previous time she had engaged Al Gore in a one-on-one had been during the budget battle, when Cantwell, despite severe reservations, had supported the administration (and would eventually wind up losing her reelection campaign in part because of it). What did he want this time?

"I want you to stop this bill," he said. He reiterated the stuff from the briefings about national security and all that.

Cantwell held firm. "I'm sorry, Mr. Vice President," she said. "I respect your opinion but I'm not changing my mind."

In a way, that was a turning point for Maria Cantwell. She got the bill through the subcommittee and kept pressing, even though fellow committee members were already trying to get her to drop the thing. Even before she left the hearing room after the vote—she hadn't even gotten up from her chair—one representative came up to her and said outright, "If you don't stop this it's going to get very ugly." And Maria Cantwell said to herself, "I'm not stopping."

On November 24, 1993, Cantwell introduced H.R. 3627 on the House floor. Her comments were blunt. "The United States' export control system is broken," she said. "It was designed as a tool of the Cold War, to help fight against enemies that no longer exist. The myriad federal agencies responsible for controlling the flow of exports from our country must have a new charter, recognizing today's realities."

The pressure continued, though most members were collegial in their attempts at persuasion. There was one instance in which a fellow Democrat came up to her on the floor and began berating her for ignoring national security issues. She felt intimidated but more than ever was convinced she should go on. With all the forces lined up to bolster these bizarre export laws and the silly Clipper Chip, it struck her as an exercise in unchecked power—against consumers.

Still, she knew that on this issue she was *out there*. Though she was doing yeoman service for the techies she represented, most of her constituents in Washington State's First Congressional District preferred her to be concentrating on issues such as health care, and here she was, locked in meetings with National Security Advisor Tony Lake. One day she heard that Bill Gates would be in town. So she asked the people at Microsoft who had been working with her—Nathan Myhrvold and company counsel Bill Neukom—if they could convince the world's most famous techno-geek to lobby her colleagues on the matter. *I'm out on a political limb here,* she pleaded. Without publicity, she had Bill Gates address the intelligence committee. The National Security stooges started to explain to the billionaire how important the export laws were, but the icon of the New Economy had little patience for being lectured. Gates let them know that was a *bullshit* reason. The committee members didn't get offended—it was kind of a kick, getting snapped at by the world's richest guy. You certainly had to take him seriously when he talked about what was good for business.

Cantwell dug in her heels with the White House, too. She asked them not to fight her bill, but to let it take its course in Congress. The response was unexpected, and it came two days before the vote. It was a deal. *If we change our position,* the Gore people wanted to know, *would you drop the bill?* They suggested that instead of forcing the Clipper Chip on people, they would instead advocate a different voluntary key escrow scheme. And maybe it could be based on more flexible software implementations than that already antiquated chip. And maybe, instead of only government escrow facilities, some could be in the more-trusted private sector, like banks or security companies.

A significant retreat, but it was still an escrow scheme, not at all the ultimate solution that Cantwell and her constituents wanted. On the other hand, the chances of her bill passing were equivalent to that of Microsoft's shipping an operating system without bugs. (Even then it would face a near-certain veto.) Cantwell went back to the people who had been fighting the battle long before she switched Washingtons. Bruce Heiman of the industry group called the Business Software Alliance was encouraged that the administration was giving a framework for a compromise. Nathan Myhrvold straight out celebrated. "They blinked," he later said. All of Cantwell's advisors agreed, though, that before she stood down, she should get promises in writing.

On July 20, 1994, the afternoon before the vote, the letter from Al Gore arrived. After the usual flatulence ("I write to express my sincere appreciation for your efforts to move the national debate forward . . .") Gore got to the point.

> The administration understands the concerns that industry has regarding the Clipper Chip. We welcome the opportunity to work with industry to design a versatile, less expensive system. Such a key escrow system would be implementable in software, firmware, hardware, or any combination thereof, would not rely on a classified algorithm, would be voluntary, and would be exportable. . . .
> We also recognize that a new key escrow encryption system must permit the use of private-sector key escrow agents as one option.

Apparently, the White House figured that the exercise was simply a way to quiet a potential firestorm. (Later in the summer, a Defense Department official seeking clarification on the implications of the policy shift was told that the letter was intended "to placate Rep. Cantwell and avoid a national debate.") But when the contents of Gore's missive found their way to the front page of the *Washington Post* the next day (a slight embarrassment for Cantwell, who didn't want to look like she was showboating), the Gore people rediscovered that the Bosnia of telecommunications was as thorny as ever. The White House had made its promises without clearing them with the NSA or the FBI. (The first Clint Brooks had heard about it was the day it ran in the *Washington Post*.) Cantwell got a call from a Gore person. *Do you mind,* he asked, *if we, um, rescind the letter?*

"Do you know how silly you'd look?" she replied. It was, after all, Gore's letter, Gore's words. She promised that she wasn't out to milk the incident with the press, but the news was out there, and she didn't have the authority to let him rescind the agreement. So the deal stood. Cantwell dropped her bill, though in the next few years it would be only the first of a number of increasingly popular congressional initiatives to reform the export rules. Meanwhile, the Gore letter, whether intentional or not, was essentially a blueprint for the direction that the administration would take in tinkering with their ill-fated Clipper Chip. A step backward. A rejection. Another step backward. Stalling and confusion, while the great honest debate that Clint Brooks had envisioned about a national crypto policy never did come to the forefront. Meanwhile, the platform that Brooks considered absolutely essential—a full encryption solution to protect privacy, a policy that would generate a pervasive digital signature policy to empower electronic commerce and prevent electronic forgeries, *and* access for law enforcement—never did get straightened out.

Clint Brooks himself wanted out of the struggle. After a couple of years of driving back and forth from Maryland to D.C., having the same arguments with the same people, he asked the new NSA director if he could work on something that utilized his talents more effectively. His request was granted. Nirvana was lost.

slouching toward crypto

by 1995, it was clear that the field of cryptography—as well as its reach—had dramatically changed, despite the government's best efforts. Crypto, propelled by computer power and new discoveries by the Whit Diffies of the world, was moving at a turbocharged pace, shifting from Pony Express to Internet time. But the basic principles remained. Despite the increasingly invoked specter of crypto anarchy—where codes would proliferate unchecked, to the point where no government or institution could even hope to get a handle on digital commerce or law—the ancient clash of measure and countermeasure persisted. Only now the outsiders had a hand in the game.

Over a century before, Edgar Allan Poe, who had been nearly obsessive on the subject of cryptology, wrote, "It may roundly be asserted . . . that human ingenuity cannot concoct a cipher which human ingenuity cannot resolve." Mathematically, of course, Poe was wrong; the verifiably impenetrable one-time pad was a firm "nevermore" to his claim. But implementing a one-time pad was demanding; certainly it was inappropriate in large-scale settings. So on a practical basis, was the poet's claim correct? When Martin Gardner had cited Poe's quote in his famous *Scientific American* article about RSA, he had thought not.

The question certainly bugged Phil Zimmermann. In his heart, he felt that the encryption algorithm at the center of his PGP software was sound. In naming his program, he felt that "pretty good" was an understatement: users should be able to count on its imperviousness to codebreakers. The government, at least publicly, hinted that PGP was strong, too. In the spring of 1995, Louis Freeh of the FBI and William Crowell of the National Security Agency had testified in a classified congressional briefing about the difficulty of breaking crypto with long key sizes. Freeh complained, "We don't have the technology or the brute-force capability to get to this information." Crowell went even further. Citing current personal computer technology, he said that to crack "128-bit cryptography, which is what PGP is . . . would [take] 8.6 trillion times the age of the universe."

But Zimmermann knew that a brute-force attack on IDEA (International Data Encryption Algorithm) was not the only way to gut his cipher into something that could be called "Pretty Good Try at Privacy." There were countless ways to crack a code. Maybe through stronger factoring algorithms and dedicated hardware a supercomputer could make much faster work of the public key part of the program. Or, even more likely, there could be quirks in the details of PGP's implementation that would provide a cryptanalyst with a precious shortcut to plaintext.

As it happened, one evening at the 1995 crypto conference at Santa Barbara, there was a cocktail party alfresco, and late in the evening a few cryptographers, decked in traditional garb of T-shirts and sandals, gathered around one of the event's keynote speakers. He was Robert Morris, Sr., and until recently the only crowds he'd addressed were those authorized to receive U.S. government secrets. He had just retired as a top scientist at Fort George Meade. Morris's reputation—enhanced by the unknowable feats he may have accomplished in the service of spookdom—drew a small crowd to his table. And when Morris mentioned that he wouldn't mind meeting Phil Zimmermann, the neatly bearded forty-one-year-old was quickly called over.

"Phil, let me ask you a question," said the former intelligence man, puffing aggressively on a cigarette. "Say that someone used PGP for very bad stuff. How much would it cost us to break it?"

Zimmermann seemed flustered. "Well, I've been asked that before," he said. "It could be done."

"But how much would it cost us?"

It was far from Zimmermann's favorite subject, but he played along. He conjectured that the best attacks on PGP would not be on its key size but on other weaknesses. Its data structure could be troublesome, he admitted, its error correction poor.

Morris nodded and said nothing. He'd been playing with Zimmermann. Who the hell knew if the NSA had already unearthed some elementary flaw that enabled the acres of silicon in its vaunted basement instantly to cough up the plaintext of the freedom fighters who allegedly used Zimmermann's program? But the next day in his talk, Morris implicitly provided a commentary on the new cryptographers and their crypto-anarchist visions. He revealed no trade secrets. But somewhat in the spirit of the Eastern masters, Morris did present a pair of truisms—koans of the crypto faith—that pointed toward an eventual rapprochement between the Equities, one beyond the current political struggles. A glimpse of a post-Clipper society in the century to come.

Koan One (for codemakers): *never underestimate the time and expense your opponent will take to break your code.* The inner text of the Morris speech was that cryptography is best left to those of a paranoid mind-set, those who believe beyond question that their opponents just may be very rich, very clever, and very dedicated—hellhounds on the trail. They will launch powerful frontal assaults on your codes. And, often, they will win.

Koan Two (for codebreakers): *look for plaintext.* This was reassurance to the crowd that no matter how baffling the task of codebreaking might seem, the fact is that very fallible human beings are the ones who must employ these sophisticated systems. So sometimes, when one least expects it, a seemingly impenetrable code—the jumble of ASCII confetti one must hammer into human language—might have a passage, or an entire message, somehow unencoded. In that case, you could read it as easily as a fortune cookie.

To the crypto anarchists, Morris was saying, "Hey, it's not that easy to create a cipher utopia." The ancient game would go on. But by imparting the lesson to outsiders he was also tacitly acknowledging that the future belonged not just to the NSA illuminati, but to these T-shirted longhairs at Santa Barbara as well.

Morris's statements came at a time when the tension between public and government crypto was at its height. Further, a novel twist had recently been introduced. Some of the emerging crypto forces were now well beyond code making and deeply into cryptanalysis. While this had been undertaken by the crypto crowd before—most famously in the attacks on Merkle's knapsack scheme—there was now a new sort of effort. It did not conform to the traditional rules forged in the world of William Friedman or Alan Turing. . . . It was an *aggregate* code breaking, a mass effort powered by the amplifying abilities of the Net. Its practitioners were, of course, cypherpunks. This breed of codebreaker was not interested in crime and espionage, but in making a political point and reaping big fun in the process.

One of the first efforts began with Phil Zimmermann's PGP software. Long before Morris brought up the question of PGP's strength at Crypto '95, its users had been plagued by nagging questions of its resilience. Their angst reflected the key dilemma of guerrilla cryptography: could you trust software developed without the imprimatur of an organization known for secure codes? This was the question that Derek Atkins, then a twenty-year-old electrical engineering student at MIT, was asking himself in 1992. His initial reaction to Zimmermann's program was to join the crusade, and he became part of the impromptu development team creating new versions of the software. But then Atkins came to wonder what attacks might work against it.

As Bob Morris indicated in his talk, there are two general ways to crack a cryptosystem. The first way is brute force—to try all possible solutions until you hit on the right one. The second method involves seeking a shortcut, an unintended weakness, which may enable you to break the codes. As Atkins spoke to his friends—including Michael Graff at Iowa State University and Paul Leyland of Oxford University— he decided on the former style of attack. Trying to find a subtle flaw was a task beyond his abilities and experience. (Though, as Morris implied, it was a route that the NSA had probably attempted.) On the other hand, everybody seemed to agree that a direct, and perhaps feasible, route to cracking PGP would be one that worked against *any* RSA-based program: factoring.

Rivest, Shamir, and Adleman had understood, of course, that if someone figured out a quick way to factor—to determine two original primes from the key based on the product of those numbers—their system was dead meat. But even though they had expected somewhat better factoring algorithms to come, they figured that nothing on the horizon would make it feasible to break RSA. Atkins and his friends, however, wanted to test that proposition. They suspected that by relying on a previously unavailable resource—the thousands of computers accessible to people on the Internet—they might be able to make factoring history. This was a fascinating premise, regarding the aggregate computing power of Internet users as sort of a giant super-computer, perhaps a kludged cousin to the ones that supposedly existed in the basement of Fort Meade. They ran the idea past Arjen Lenstra, the renowned mathematical expert at Bellcore in New Jersey. He told them that the large prime numbers commonly used in PGP (as well as the commercial versions of RSA) would be too formidable to attack. Then he suggested another challenge: RSA 129.

Lenstra's idea cut to the heart of the issue of whether or not cryptography could ever assure perfect security. The RSA 129 challenge was the one offered in Martin Gardner's *Scientific American* column in 1977—the column that began by declaring moot Poe's dictum that no code was impervious to cracking. The challenge still had not been met in all these years. The estimate of time it would take a dedicated supercomputer to factor a number that size was forty *quadrillion* years. But even if you did not accept that number (Rivest now says it was a miscalculation) even a much, much smaller number—a billion years, say, or a measly few million—would indicate that anyone breathing today's air would have been long rendered into a dust ball before the secret of the RSA message encoded with a 129-digit key would be revealed.

Yet fifteen years later, Atkins, Graff, Leyland, and Lenstra joined forces with the Internet to attempt to collect that hundred dollars—in a matter of months.

The first, and probably most important, thing they needed was a good factoring algorithm. There had been some conceptual advances in this area since Gardner's column had been published. Specifically, someone had devised the "double large prime multiple polynomial variation of the quadratic sieve." This involves searching in a numbers realm called vector space for numbers known as univectors. These can be combined to chart mathematical relations in a way that yields the two original primes. "You don't have to search the full space of possibilities, but only a small finite portion of the space," says Atkins. "One way of looking at it is that we were looking for eight million needles in a haystack full of countless needles. You're not looking for any particular needle—you just find enough of them and combine them in a special mathematical means to actually factor the number." That technique was perfect for a distributed Internet attack, where literally hundreds of people would join forces to solve the problem.

During the summer of 1993, the software was ready—Atkins had been running some of it on the MIT Media Lab computers—and they could now recruit volunteers with computers. The response was terrific: over 1600 machines worked on the problem, all over the world, every continent except Antarctica. The computers ranged from garden variety PCs to the 16,000-processor Maspar supercomputer at Bell Labs.

A standard measurement of computer power is a MIPS year—one year of constant use of a Million Instructions per Second machine. From September 1993 to April 1994, the RSA 129 experiment used about five thousand of those MIPS years. It was then that Atkins and the others guessed that they finally had enough univectors to do the final calculations. As planned, they sent it to Lenstra at Bell Labs, who would then do the final "matrix reduction." Atkins sent Lenstra a tape with 400 megabytes worth of univectors, via U.S. mail. He also sent a backup by FedEx. Lenstra fed it to his machines, and for two days they matrix-reduced. On April 24, 1994, Atkins posted the following message on the Net:

> We are happy to announce that
>
> RSA-129 =
> 1143816257578888676692357799761466120102182967212423625625618429 \3
> 57069352457338978305971235639587050589890751475992900268795435441 =
> 3490529510847650949147849619903898133417764638493387843990820577*3
> 2769132993266709549961988190834461413177642967992942539798288533

Applying that key to the number that represented the enciphered message text, they were able to transform it into a similarly long number. This was easily converted to English by one of the oldest decoding schemes in history: 01 = A, 02 = B, and so on. That yielded the secret that supposedly would last for a quadrillion years:

THE MAGIC WORDS ARE SQUEAMISH OSSIFRAGE

Did this discovery rock Ron Rivest's world? Not really. In the years since Gardner's article, he had kept track of developments in factoring, and had concluded it wasn't impossible that one day he might have to write out a check for $100 to someone. (Amazingly, he had forgotten the actual message.) He even defends Gardner's prediction that a break in our lifetime was extremely remote. "It was probably accurate for the analysis of the fastest algorithm we knew about at the time, but technology was moving fast on the factoring frontier."

But the very idea of a "factoring frontier" was enough to throw some doubt into the security of the most popular public key cryptosystem. After all, if factoring was easy, RSA was, well, worthless. Of course, breaking RSA 129 was nowhere near as challenging as cracking RSA codes set at commercial strength. When the RSA system uses 129 digits, the key turns out to be 425 bits long. But the standard RSA key—the one used by the company's actual software—was 1024 bits long. Had the Atkins team attempted the same task with that key length, their computers would still be working on the problem—for a few million more years.

Yet that degree of futility had once been predicted for RSA 129. Might new techniques to factor numbers melt down even the fattest RSA keys? There may well be mathematical breakthroughs to speed up factoring, but an even greater threat to the strength of the cryptosystems was the development of what are called quantum computers, machines that take advantage of subatomic physics to run much faster than our current models. (Think of the speed differential between turtles and laser beams.) While these machines still existed only in theory, scientists had been taking the first difficult steps toward implementation. Once the journey toward quantum computers was completed, you could stick a fork into the RSA cryptosystem. "I think that I shall see a special-purpose quantum factorization device in my lifetime," cryptographer Giles Brassard wrote in 1996. "If this happens, RSA will have to be abandoned." This was published, of all places, in *CryptoBytes,* the technical newsletter of RSA Data Security.

But that remained speculation. The reality is that Derek Atkins and his colleagues took what seemed to be an invincible problem and, working informally, with an ad hoc collection of computers, managed to crack it. "What we learned is that a bunch of amateurs can get together and do this," he says. And that all claims of invincibility should be regarded with skepticism.

The next target was an irresistible one: the 40-bit crypto allowed by the government for export. The point this time would be purely political. If the barn-raising style of cryptanalysis used in the RSA crack was directed against the puny key lengths negotiated by the Software Publishers Association in 1992 (and, despite government promises, not adjusted in subsequent years), those keys would surely fall, and the need for stronger crypto would be obvious.

After one cypherpunk suggested a "Key Cracking Ring," Tim May urged action, guessing that the "CPU horsepower of this list could be quite impressively applied" to crack the key in six months, making a strong statement against U.S. export standards. (Six months was a guess. But comparing the computation effort to the RSA's crack was somewhat like apples and oranges—keyspace search versus factoring.)

"Heh, I was already working on it . . . ," wrote Adam Back, a twenty-five-year-old computer science student at Exeter College in England. Immediately after seeing the first posting, he'd begun writing scripts to allow people to participate in a group crack. He knew what he was doing, since he had been recently playing around with Rivest's RC-4 algorithm—the actual cipher that performed the 40-bit encryption permitted for export by the government in programs by Microsoft and Lotus.

A brute-force attack on a bulk encryption cipher like RC-4 or DES requires the codebreaker to try out every possible key combination. Finding a key requires searching through the entire space of possibilities; in the case of a 40-bit key there are about a trillion actual possibilities, enough to keep a pack of computers busy for days. That's what Adam Back had in mind: a mass effort with each attacker claiming some portion of keyspace, testing it, and then requesting another. The process would continue until someone found the key. Back posted his scripts to his Web page, and a group of conspirators from various corners of the world quickly gathered. Eventually, eighty-nine cypherpunks participated in trying to find a 40-bit key in Microsoft's database program Access.

But the Microsoft Access crack was doomed. After the entire keyspace was "swept," none of the millions of potential keys unlocked the message. It turned out that the would-be crackers were stuck on a technical point that kept them from actually getting the plaintext. ("The problem was a lack of specifications," says Back. "We didn't know what format the file was in.")

Still, the cypherpunks emerged from the failed Microsoft attack with some group-cracking software, a loose yet dedicated organization, and a continuing desire to expose what they believed was the pitiful sham of export-level crypto. And then the cypherpunks hit upon an even better target for a brute-force attack: Netscape.

In 1993, two students at the University of Illinois had engaged in a coffeehouse conversation that would not only change the course of the twenty-two-year-old international network called the Internet but would profoundly affect the adoption of crypto. One of them, a chunky undergrad named Marc Andreessen, had recently been learning about a new system on the Internet brashly named the World Wide Web by its inventor, Tim Berners-Lee, a British computer scientist working in Switzerland. The Web was an ingenious way to publish and get access to information on the Net, but only a few in the technical community had adopted the system. Andreessen saw a wider potential. If someone created a slick "browser" to surf through the information space created by a multitude of people who shared text, pictures, and sounds on the Web, he said to his colleague Eric Bina, the Internet itself would be easier to use and a better way to get information. The pair, both of whom worked at the Supercomputing Center at the university, created Mosaic, the first great Web browser. Instead of being forced to use arcane commands and tackle a baffling alphabet soup of acronyms, people could now get all sorts of wonderful stuff from handmade Web "pages"—at the click of a mouse! It was an instant phenomenon; to use Mosaic was to swoon with the excitement of participating in a vast experiment with the future of information sharing. Soon a team at Illinois had churned out versions of the program for virtually every computing platform. Millions of people downloaded them, and thousands of Web sites sprang up to take advantage of the audience.

In 1994, Andreessen had another famous cup of coffee, this time with Silicon Valley entrepreneur Jim Clark. The just-departed CEO of Silicon Graphics was casting about for a big new idea for a start-up company, and with this college kid he hit one of the richest pay dirts in history. Clark, who'd been unaware of the Web boom up till then, quickly realized that there were untapped commercial possibilities for the Web, and grabbed not only Andreessen but most of the Illinois team to start Mosaic Communications. (When the university objected to the name, Clark changed it to Netscape.) The idea was to develop an improved browser called the Navigator, along with software for "servers" that would allow businesses to go on-line. The one missing component was security. If companies were going to sell products and make transactions over the Internet, surely customers would demand protection. It was the perfect job for encryption technology.

Fortunately Clark knew someone in the field—Jim Bidzos. By the time negotiations were completed, Netscape had a license for RSA and the company's help in developing a security standard for the Web: a public key–based protocol known as Secure Sockets Layer. Netscape would build this into its software, ensuring that its estimated millions of users would automatically get the benefits of crypto as envisioned by Merkle, Diffie, and Hellman, and implemented by Rivest, Shamir, and Adleman. A click of a mouse would send Netscape users into crypto mode: a message would appear informing them that all information entered from that point was secure. Meanwhile, RSA's encryption and authentication would be running behind the scenes.

Jim Bidzos drove his usual hard bargain with Netscape: in exchange for its algorithms, RSA was given 1 percent of the new company. In mid-1995, Netscape ran the most successful public offering in Wall Street's history to date, making RSA's share of the company worth over $20 million. (Not bad, Bidzos realized, for a company that was just about flatlining until Lotus's $100,000 advance for the Notes license.)

It was just after that eye-opening IPO that a cypherpunk named Hal Finney began looking at Netscape's security. Finney, a Santa Barbara–based programmer who had participated in PGP development, was particularly interested in how cryptography would be used with electronic commerce, and had become familiar with Netscape's Secure Sockets Layer. In adhering to the export regulations, Netscape had released two versions of the browser: a domestic version with a 128-bit key for its RC-4 encryption function, and a 40-bit version for export.

Finney set up a challenge to break a message encrypted with that weaker key. He would make a dummy Netscape transaction—just as if he were a customer—then use the encryption in the export version. "I basically connected to Netscape in one of their secure pages and typed in some random data where I was supposed to be ordering a T-shirt or something," he says. Then he captured the encrypted data and included it in his challenge:

Date: Mon, 10 Jul 1995 16:13:52-0700
From: Hal <hfinney@shell.portal.com>
To: cypherpunks@toad.com
Subject: Let's try breaking an SSL RC4 key

Since this whole Microsoft Access thing turned out to be a dud, maybe an alternative would be to try breaking the 40-bit RC4 used in Netscape's SSL (Secure Sockets Layer) exportable encryption . . .

From England, Adam Back's group accepted the challenge. Though Back's original intent seems to have been to apportion the keyspace among many people, he wound up accepting the offer of an Australian programmer to organize half the search. The rest of the keyspace was to be swept by volunteers who were assigned slices. But there was some confusion between the two groups that slowed down the effort for some days.

It was during this lull in the action that Damien Doligez began to wonder what was taking so long. Doligez was a twenty-seven-year-old computer scientist who had just gotten his Ph.D. a few months before and was working as a researcher at INRIA, the French government computer lab. His office was in one of a cluster of shacks in what was once a NATO base a few miles outside of Versailles. Doligez had a personal interest in crypto. He shared the sense of disgust at the way governments attempt to suppress their citizens' ability to communicate privately with each other, and he believed that if someone cracked one of those artificially lame 40-bit cryptosystems, it would be a blow against the powers that be. He also guessed that after the successful RSA 129 crack, a two- or three-week effort should do the job. So as time passed between Finney's challenge and its solution, he wondered what the hell had happened.

As a researcher at INRIA Doligez had access not only to the workstation in his small office, but also to an entire network of computers, including a Maspar supercomputer. Doligez studied the SSL specifications and concocted a small program to allow a computer quickly to test out a potential key, then adapted the program so it would work on the various machines on the INRIA network, as well as on some machines at the nearby universities, L'École Polytechnique and L'École Normale Supérieure.

Then he began his own multiple-computer attack. Whenever an INRIA worker would stray from his or her computer, within five minutes, Doligez's program would take over the machine, crunching perhaps 10,000 keys a second. Simply by touching the keyboard, a user could regain control over the machine. No one complained.

Doligez figured that his odds of finding the key would be better if he started from the end of the keyspace and worked backward. "I figured the cypherpunks would start from the start, so I started from the end." He set his network into action on Friday, August 4, and left for the weekend. On Monday, he returned and discovered a bug in his program. He restarted the process. From that point, the number crunching ran perfectly, but he wound up writing ten new versions of the software over the next few days to address glitches in the communications between machines. The program was working fine when Doligez left work on Friday, August 11. Due to a national midsummer holiday that next Tuesday, on August 15, it would be a four-day weekend, but checking on his home computer before the holiday ended, his software gave him the message he was waiting for.

"I saw it found the key," he says. SSL had been cracked!

The following day, Damien Doligez drove to work from his home outside Paris and recovered the key from his workstation, then successfully decrypted the message. He posted a message to cypherpunks with the heading "SSL challenge—broken!" As proof, he displayed the plaintext. Those familiar with the RSA 129 crack appreciated the significance of the address of the fictional character that Hal Finney had created in his coded message. Mr. Cosmic Kumquat, of SSL Trusters, Inc., lived at 1234 Squeamish Ossifrage Road.

Though technically it was anything but shocking—the mathematics of cryptography dictated that a weak key *should* fall to a concentrated effort—the very idea of cracking Netscape's crypto captured the imagination of the popular press. The media descended on Damien Doligez. Because the break occurred only a week after Netscape enjoyed perhaps the most successful IPO in history, some journalists played the crack as if it spoke to the nature of the browser's overall security, and not as an example of the way the government export rules weaken software in general. In a message that Netscape posted on its site later that week, the company noted that Doligez had simply broken one message—and that it took about 64 MIPS years to do so. Netscape also estimated that the cost of breaking the message had been $10,000. But as Doligez pointed out in his own response, he had used idle computer time, and paid nothing to do so. Netscape was on firmer ground when it noted that the domestic version of Navigator used a much sounder 128-bit key. "The computer power required to decrypt such a message would be more than a thousand trillion trillion times greater than that which was used to decrypt the RC-4-40 message," wrote Netscape.

Which as far as the cypherpunks were concerned was exactly the point: export-level crypto was needlessly weak.

But the cypherpunks were not through with Netscape. At Berkeley, two first-year graduate students were inspired by group cryptanalysis. They were twenty-two-year-old Ian Goldberg and twenty-two-year-old Dave Wagner. They, too, thought it would be a good idea to hack Netscape, the new flagship for Internet security. But they had missed out on the obvious brute-force attacks—Goldberg had been moving to California from his native Canada and Wagner had just arrived after getting his undergraduate degree at Princeton. So they began to explore a different mode of attack, more akin to the second of Robert Morris's recommendations: *look for plaintext*. Could it be possible that the Netscape security team made some simple yet egregious error in implementing their software, thus exposing what might be millions of electronic commerce transactions to eavesdroppers? Not likely. But, as Morris had suggested, you never know unless you look.

And that's when Wagner saw it. Buried in the code were the instructions for Netscape's Random Number Generator (RNG). This is an important part of any sophisticated cryptosystem—the piece of code crucial to scrambling the letters so that the encoded text offers no tell-tale patterns that would help a cryptanalyst. It is well known that a lack of true randomness is a weakness smart codebreakers can eventually exploit. So it is important to have a solid RNG—something that spins the alphabetic roulette wheel thoroughly.

An important part of a good RNG is the use of an unpredictable "seed"—a number that begins the randomization process. Since, unlike dice, computers do the same thing each time they run, it is essential to begin the process with a seed that a potential opponent cannot possibly guess. Methods of doing this often include using some off-the-wall statistics from the real world—the position of the mouse, for instance. Anything that an enemy could not possibly know.

Netscape, as it turns out, had ignored this wisdom. When Dave Wagner looked closely at the code, the error jumped out at him. Netscape derived the seed of its RNG from three elements: the time of day and two forms of user identification called the Process ID and the Parent ID. A disaster. A foe would burn few computer cycles and even fewer brain cells finding the first part of the seed: it is easy to run through the limited number of times of day. And in many cases, both kinds of identification numbers were also easy to find, particularly if someone is sharing a server with a number of people—as often happens in an Internet environment. "If an attacker has an account on your machine, it's trivial," says Goldberg. "Here at Berkeley, there are thousands of users. If anyone uses Netscape, you can discover the IDs." But even without that advantage, it would be fairly trivial for attackers to calculate out those IDs. The identification numbers in question were only fifteen bits long, easily susceptible to brute-force attacks.

Over the course of a weekend, Wagner and Goldberg wrote a program to exploit the weakness. On Sunday night, they tested it. By zeroing in on the huge flaw in Netscape's implementation, they were able to find a secret key in less than a minute. *Hasta la vista,* Netscape security. Goldberg posted the result on the cypherpunks' mailing list that night. "We didn't expect lots of press," he said. Silly boy. Among the readers was a *New York Times* reporter. When the story ran in the

Paper of Record, the two grad students were deluged with curiosity seekers and journalists. Of the things that the two grad students had to say, perhaps the most sobering was Goldberg's observation, "We're good guys—but we don't know if this flaw has been discovered by bad guys."

Unlike the first Netscape crack, where the company could quite rightfully claim that their otherwise strong crypto was crippled by government restrictions, this was a total flub. You didn't need to tap a multi-workstation network, or get access to a supercomputer. In certain circumstances all you needed was a minute's worth of crunching on a vanilla Pentium machine. "Our engineers made an implementation mistake," admitted Mike Homer, Netscape's vice president of marketing.

The error cast a shadow on the security of the leading Internet software company. "If Netscape did this wrong, what else did they do wrong?" asked cryptographer Bruce Schneier. But the more pressing question was, if Netscape was unsafe, what *was* safe? Netscape, after all, was making a concerted effort to protect its users. If the Navigator could be cracked so easily, what hope was there for the others?

There *was* a bright side to the event: you could argue that things worked properly because the cypherpunks publicly exposed a weakness, which Netscape immediately moved to fix. But the lasting lesson was somewhat darker. As the Internet proliferated, the public was beginning to become truly dependent on networked computers for financial transactions and storing private information—everything from buying books to making stock trades to paying bills. New businesses were planning to put *medical* records on-line. But security was still haphazard at best. And more and more, it was becoming clear that one big reason for this failing was the United States government's long-term stalling action. While it tried to push Clipper and key escrow as its pet solution to the problem, the Internet kept going—without an organized effort to provide the protections it needed.

During the mid-1990s, though, those trying hardest to bring to fruition a new era of cipher protection—one that would finally secure the Internet and other electronic means of communication—found themselves under increasing fire. It seemed that those in charge of the

laws and institutions of society, while not able to shut down mathematical and engineering progress, could do plenty to make crypto
innovators know that their actions had consequences. The question
became how far was the government willing to go to invoke those
consequences.

For Ray Ozzie of Lotus such a lesson in power would have seemed
unnecessary: he was committed to working within the system.
(Besides, in 1993, Lotus had officially joined the Establishment when
it was bought by IBM for $3 billion.) In the years since his early adop-
tion of RSA, Ozzie had become a vocal figure in the crypto battles, tes-
tifying in Congress and visiting key administration figures. Though his
procrypto bias was plain, Ozzie's easy manner and willingness to consider the opposing view earned him the respect of even export hard-
liners. He was a realist. Unable to wait for the government to liberalize
its rules, he was constantly brainstorming for innovative ways around
the export impasse.

After the Netscape crack, overseas buyers of Lotus Notes became
increasingly uneasy using the 40-bit encryption IBM was permitted to
ship overseas. They wanted to know why it was that American customers were sold a version with 64-bit keys, millions of times more
difficult to break—while their version could be cracked by some random postdoc outside Paris. (Meanwhile, companies like Microsoft,
which didn't want the hassles of making two flavors of the same product, gave *all* their customers weaker crypto. This made the whole
product line less valuable to those who wanted encryption, and some
of those customers began buying from foreign companies that could
legally sell them strong crypto.)

In 1995, Ozzie came up with what seemed a preferable compromise, at least in the short term: a mathematical fix devised to satisfy
the NSA's requirements. Though Ozzie hated Clipper, his scheme was
sort of a less onerous version of it. Lotus would still sell two versions
of Notes, but unlike prior versions, *both* would have 64-bit encryption.
But the international version would have a little gift for the NSA:
something called the National Security Access Field (NSAF). This
consisted of 24 bits of the encrypted data that the NSA, and only the
NSA, could decode. It was to be encrypted by the NSA's public key,
so only the folks at The Fort could exclusively decrypt that field. After
the NSA used its private key to unscramble the 24-bit NSAF, the

Notes-encrypted messages would have shrunk from 64-bit cipher-text to 40-bit ciphertext. Cracking the remaining code would require precisely the same work factor as messages encrypted with 40-bit keys shipped under the old system. But since the overall encryption was stronger against all attackers other than the NSA—and it was those other attackers most users were worried about, like vandals or industrial spies—Ozzie figured that this solution might help in the short run.

Lotus filed two patents for its innovation, called "Differential Work-factor Cryptography Method and System," in December 1995, and included the innovation in the new version of its software, Notes Release 4. He first spoke about it publicly in January 1996, at the RSA Data Security Conference in San Francisco. The conference was another of Jim Bidzos's marketing brainstorms. Since 1990, the RSA Data Security honcho had been gathering commercial crypto cus-tomers in the Bay Area, sponsoring a few days of seminars and a small trade show where vendors could show their wares. From a gathering of a few dozen geeks at the Sofitel Hotel near RSA's Redwood City offices, the conclave had grown to thousands and was now held at a large hotel near Union Square. Ozzie's speech drew a lot of attention, and not a little hand-wringing: some wondered whether the dynamic designer behind Notes had given up the fight.

No, he hadn't. Ozzie was just pursuing a more subtle agenda. "I wanted to stir things up," he said. The idea was to knock a wedge between the administration and the NSA. Once Al Gore had backed down from the idea of government-controlled escrow facilities, the NSA found little to like in those post-Clipper ideas. If people stored keys in private facilities, authorities would need a warrant to get hold of them. But the NSA operated in secret and was banned from domes-tic surveillance. So the agency might prefer Ozzie's scheme—which gave it a head start in cryptanalysis. (It wouldn't need a warrant to get those 24-bits' worth of decryption.) Thus, Ozzie's scheme was far from a sellout—it was a subversive strategy to get the NSA and the administration arguing for different approaches. In the confusion, he hoped that his industry could sneak through its own solution.

Before Ozzie could congratulate himself on his cleverness, he dis-covered that the government was not without its own means for deal-ing with such strategies. On December 30, 1996, both Ozzie and his coinventor Charles Kaufman were sent letters labeled in boldface: SECRECY ORDER. Their patent application, read the letters, "contains subject matter the unauthorized disclosure of which would, in the opinion of the sponsoring defense agency, be detrimental to the national security." (In the space where the government patent officer could check off which agency that was, there was an X next to "ARMY.") Disclosing the subject matter to anyone without authorization, they were warned, would subject the inventors and IBM to a penalty, including a jail term. Finally, they were instructed, any copies of the subject matter "should be destroyed by a method that will prevent disclosure of the contents or reconstruction of the document."

Ozzie, who received the order on January 7, 1997, immediately understood that complying with that order presented something of a problem. Not only had he spoken in detail about the scheme numerous times, but the "subject matter" had also already been distributed to almost six million Lotus Notes users, about half of whom were outside the United States. He quickly informed his bosses at Lotus, who immediately began pondering the consequences of having one of the most popular software programs in the world deemed a government secret.

Perhaps the best thing Ozzie did was to have a friend call the deputy director of the NSA, Bill Crowell, who reportedly laughed when he heard of the news, and told the friend he'd look into it. On January 9, Crowell called Ozzie. It was all a mistake, he said. Everything would be fixed. Indeed, the next day, when IBM attorneys got in touch with the Patent Office, they got a verbal confirmation that the order had been rescinded, and later got a fax to that effect. No longer were Ray Ozzie, his coinventor, and IBM liable for about six million violations of the patent secrecy act. But after everyone had some time to breathe, questions remained. If this was the fate that welcomed someone trying to serve his customers *in the spirit* of key escrow, what would happen to those who outright challenged the government?

Jim Bidzos could answer that question. As he took the most public stance possible in opposition to the government—he even distributed posters urging people to "Sink Clipper"—the relationship between his company and the NSA had gotten more contentious. Though Bidzos had no hard evidence of having been wiretapped, he assumed that he was under surveillance. Perhaps the most egregious confrontation came in April 1994, during a meeting with three NSA export officers, all of whom Bidzos had been grappling with for years. Two were women he'd come to trust to some degree, but the third was a man who clearly despised Bidzos and his company.

Since the NSA reps didn't open the meeting with any specific issues, Bidzos used the opportunity to lecture them about Clipper: no one would use it, it was a flawed system, yadda yadda. Bidzos noticed the man from the NSA getting more and more agitated. Finally the official spoke. *If I see you in the parking lot,* he said, *I'll run your ass over.*

Bidzos recalls being stunned but finally he replied. "I'll give you an opportunity to retract that or apologize," he said. But the man kept pressing. *I'm serious,* he raged. *You don't understand me, do you?*

Was Bidzos getting an official warning, sort of a Triple Fence equivalent of a Mafia kiss on the lips? Should he avoid parking lots? Bidzos felt that most likely the guy was probably just venting, but he didn't want to let the threat go unchallenged. He told a newspaper reporter, and the story found its way into the local paper. Not long afterward Bidzos received a phone call from the NSA guy's boss. Bidzos got an apology. Even if his life wasn't at risk, though, Bidzos felt that the agency wanted him out of business.

But at least Bidzos wasn't under the threat of indictment. That fate was reserved for his sometime nemesis Phil Zimmermann.

Ever since the release of Pretty Good Privacy, Zimmermann had assumed that his biggest problem was the intellectual property dispute with RSA. Jim Bidzos thought nothing of publicly attacking Zimmermann, and at the drop of a fax button, he would zip journalists a copy of Zimmermann's (ambiguously) written promise to stop distributing PGP, a vow apparently not kept in spirit. But Zimmermann never thought that he would find himself under criminal investigation. So when two women from the U.S. Customs Service in northern California came to visit him in 1993, he assumed that they were there at Jim Bidzos's bidding. Indeed, though the investigators wanted to know how PGP was distributed, many of the questions dealt with PGP's similarity to RSA's products. As far as technological expertise, the investigators seemed clueless. Zimmermann had to explain to them the very basic ideas of crypto and software distribution. When they left he felt that he had little to worry about. The whole thing was some

Bidzos harassment, he figured. "I don't think that there will be action against me," he said at the time. "They raised questions about the [export regulations], but I diffused that."

Not quite. United States Attorney William Keane was indeed concerned about a possible export violation. After all, within hours of PGP's release on the Internet, the strong crypto program had found its way overseas. It's unclear whether pressure from Washington had anything to do with it, but some weeks later, Keane informed Zimmermann that he was under investigation for illegally exporting munitions. (Kelly Goen, who had identified himself to *MicroTimes* columnist Jim Warren as a Johnny Appleseed of PGP, was also a potential target.)

For the next three years, Zimmermann was in legal purgatory, investigated by a grand jury but unindicted. His lawyers advised him to lie low. But PGP's fame had given Phil Zimmermann a taste for speaking out loud. Besides, he felt that his best chance lay in taking the case to the public. Whenever he had talked to just plain folks about PGP and crypto issues, they had become outraged at the prospect of the government's limiting the ability of people to communicate privately. He suspected, with good reason, that even techno virgins would be equally indignant at this new atrocity: here was Big Brother himself, contemplating a prison cell for someone who freely distributed privacy software to freedom fighters, lovers, and those who simply felt that their secrets were nobody's business. What's more, the case against Zimmermann himself was weak; he wasn't even the one who'd posted his program to the Net. The guy who had had told Jim Warren that he scrupulously limited the uploads to American sites. Was the Justice Department actually asserting that export restrictions prohibited U.S. citizens from distributing legal materials to other U.S. citizens?

Oh, the export regulations. The more you looked at them, the weirder they appeared. One recent controversy involved Bruce Schneier's 1994 book, *Applied Cryptography*. It was a technical cornucopia of cryptological mathematical theory, explanations of popular cryptosystems, and all the algorithms that a security specialist or cypherpunk would ever need. *The Millennium Whole Earth Catalog* called it "the Bible of code hackers." But while anyone could ship the physical book overseas, the crypto restrictions seemed to ban the export of those same contents in digital form. At least that's what cypherpunk Phil Karn found out when he applied for a "commodities jurisdiction" (or CJ) to export the book, along with an accompanying floppy disk with the same contents on it. Officials confirmed that the book could be exported, but not the floppy. It seemed absurd.

So Zimmermann talked, and generated publicity. He seldom failed to note that Burmese rebels reportedly used PGP to avoid the deadly consequences of being discovered in antigovernment activities; in testimony to a congressional hearing in 1993 he also noted that he'd received an effusive thank-you from a Latvian patriot who claimed, "your PGP is widespread from Baltic to Far East and will help democratic people if necessary." When confronted with the charges from law enforcement agencies that PGP was particularly useful to criminals—in one Sacramento case, the cops couldn't read a pedophile's diary encrypted with Zimmermann's software—he argued that all technology has trade-offs.

Perhaps the highlight of Zimmermann's odd celebrity came one day in San Francisco when some businesspeople decided to take him for an evening on the town that wound up at a North Beach strip club. The young lady lap dancing in proximity to Zimmermann asked casually what he did. "I'm a cryptographer," he said. "I wrote a program called PGP."

The lap dance stopped in midgyration. "You're *Phil Zimmermann*?" she asked in awe. "I know all about PGP!"

True, cypherpunk sex workers were not everyday occurrences. But PGP's audience was beginning to extend beyond techies and privacy nuts. The *Wall Street Journal* described how PGP was used by lawyers maintaining electronic confidentiality with clients, authors protecting their works in progress from copyright infringers, and an astronomer staking his claims to his celestial discoveries.

In order to entice commercial audiences, Zimmermann had licensed the code to a company called ViaCrypt. Since ViaCrypt already had paid a licensing fee to RSA, it could sell PGP to business customers without fear of a lawsuit. (Supposedly paying two license fees was worth it, since PGP had become, by virtue of its underground following, a wonderful brand.) Beginning in 1994, the main distribution point for the much more popular freeware version was an unexpectedly mainstream ally, the Massachusetts Institute of Technology. Some there, notably professor Hal Abelson and network manager Jeff Schiller, believed that the Institute should be allowed to provide Americans with programs that they were legally permitted to use—and do it on the Internet, which was by far the most expedient method of software distribution. So MIT stored the latest versions of PGP on its Internet server and allowed anyone to download it—after asserting that they were, indeed, Americans.

The honor system obviously wasn't what the government had in mind when establishing the export laws. So flimsy was the MIT protection against export that copies of PGP downloaded from its site were spotted outside the country two days after the program was made available. Still, the citizenship restriction apparently was sufficient for MIT to avoid official complaints, let alone a criminal investigation. Not that the government officially approved of the arrangement. In one memorable session at a 1995 conference, MIT's Jeff Schiller and NSA counsel Ronald Lee (who replaced Stewart Baker in 1994) faced off. Despite repeated pleas to make some sort of statement about whether MIT's restrictions were sufficient, Lee refused to draw even the vaguest guidelines for what was permissible and what could land you in jail. Meanwhile, the MIT Press published a book (those analog dead-tree artifacts were still around) that contained nothing but hundreds of pages of C source code—the entire PGP program, formatted so that computer scanners and character recognition software could easily transform the printed hard copy into a real-life industrial-strength crypto product. It seemed almost surreal that such a scheme could be legal while a grand jury still contemplated indicting Phil Zimmermann, but that was the shaky state of crypto export policy in 1995.

Another crypto rebel faced with intrusions from the nasty real world was Julf Helsingius, the Finnish programmer who ran one of the first, and certainly the most popular, remailers in the world. By 1995, his operation called Penet was a shining example of crypto anarchy, stripping identification from thousands of messages each week, and sending them off on their merry anonymous way. Its operator was himself becoming well known in certain circles—and reviled by government doomsayers who warned that such services would prove the end of civilized society itself. But when the real trouble came it was not instigated by a government, but a private group: the Church of Scientology.

Scientologists had been routinely incensed by the criticisms of unhappy former members on Internet discussion groups. In some cases, these apostates had obtained church documents and were posting them on the Net. Scientology officials wanted to charge these people with violating the church's copyright and trade secrets. But since the addresses of the critics were laundered through the cypherpunk remailer system—very often on Penet, as it turned out—there was no easy way to find who was responsible for the messages.

Then it turned out there *was* a way. Penet—unlike many of the cypherpunk remailers—was "two way," enabling people to respond directly to anonymous postings. This required a means for Julf's system to keep track of who was sending messages. First, church lawyers wrote a letter to Helsingius, formally notifying him that his service was forwarding mail that violated their copyright. Julf politely replied that his policy was to keep hands off the traffic going through his computers. *Didn't they "get" remailers?* The lawyers wrote back, threatening legal action. Helsingius, in Finland, figured that the chances were slight that these faceless attorneys in California could do any such thing. Then Julf Helsingius's phone rang. It was a representative of the Church of Scientology, in person. In Finland.

Would Julf like to be taken out for dinner?

No sense in turning down a meal, Julf figured. He suggested a Thai joint. The man was friendly, saying that he was a retired policeman, and that all he wanted was two things: for the messages to stop, and for Helsingius to let him know who was sending them.

"I'm sorry," said Helsingius, "I can't do that."

But the Scientologists were not relying on Julf Helsingius's good will to cough up a name. They filed a complaint with the Los Angeles police, charging that their stolen property was being shipped over the Internet, and fingered Julf as someone willfully withholding the identity of the thieves. In Finland, that's a grave crime, sufficient to get a search and seizure warrant.

About a week after apologetically turning down the retired cop, Julf Helsingius got another call—from the Helsinki police. *We have a court order,* they told him, *and must take your computer away so it can be searched.* Helsingius's heart sank—he knew that he had to comply. (Ironically, if Helsingius had used readily available crypto software to encrypt his data and protect his customers, such a search would have proven useless. But because of "performance reasons"—"the database is huge," he explains—he did not encrypt the contents of his disk.)

But while Helsingius knew that he had to give up the single customer whom the Scientologists wanted, he didn't want to put thousands of others at risk. Fortunately, in keeping with the cordial relations Finns have with their police, he was able to negotiate a transfer that would not require him to turn over the contents of his entire database. Helsingius simply copied the e-mail address of the offending party onto a floppy disk, and set it on the table, allowing the police to take possession of that disk. "I was not too happy, but it *was* a compromise," he says.

Helsingius's troubles were not over, however, because another institution of the real world was about to rain on his crypto anarchy parade: the media. The same day he handed over the disk to the police, a story ran in a Swedish newspaper claiming that the majority of all child pornography on the Internet was routed through a server in Finland. Obviously it was referring to Penet. But Julf knew that his service did not distribute such materials, since he blocked "binaries" (digital photographs). Not that people cared to check. When he tracked down the source of the information, it turned out that some child pornography ring had forged the headers on porno binaries, making it look as if the stuff came from his site when it actually was posted from a location in the United Kingdom. Still, the publicity was damaging, and became worse when a British newspaper repeated the charge, this time citing Helsingius personally as the evil middleman of Internet kiddie porn.

Meanwhile, the Scientology civil case wasn't going away; Helsingius was called to a Finnish court to explain why he shouldn't turn his names over. By then he had taken measures to protect the security of the 700,000 e-mail addresses on his server. The names still weren't encrypted, but hidden: he'd moved the computer out of his home to a storage room at a secret location. And he'd hired lawyers, though God knows he didn't have the money for that sort of thing. He claimed to the Finnish court that those who used his services were entitled to privacy. But to his dismay, the judge ruled that e-mail shouldn't have the same protections as physical mail. The whole thing had taken cyberspace a step *backward,* at least in Finland.

That was it for Julf Helsingius. "The decision was quite clear," he said. "There's no way you can run a server like mine in Finland." So on August 30, 1996, he shut down Penet. The ineluctable lesson was that while technology can provide crypto freedom, the real people who use it must live in the real world—where governments and regulators have the means to track them down. The real world can make things very, very complicated.

But David Chaum could have told you that, too.

The maverick inventor of anonymous digital cash—and the holder of important patents on electronic money—was having a difficult time keeping his company Digicash afloat. Though he had assembled a terrific staff of enthusiastic programmers and cryptographers at his Amsterdam headquarters, there was increasing unrest within the team. Chaum wasn't completing the important alliances he needed to get his ideas into the mainstream. The intrigue in his little group intensified when one of his former students, Stefan Brands, claimed to have devised an alternative means to produce anonymous cash, and began exploring ways to license these ideas. Chaum insisted that Brands's work was dependent on his. (Brands obtained valid patents.) Meanwhile, Digicash was still looking for the big deal.

Digicash had begun an experimental pilot program on the Internet called E-Cash. It used a form of scrip, digital Monopoly money. But it really was a test run for the prospect of true digital cash on the Net, a form of currency that would one day usurp folding bills and metal coins. For now, though, a user could get 100 "cyberbucks" simply by asking. The digital tokens could be e-mailed to friends or used to "buy" things from any merchants who decided, in the spirit of experimentation, to accept cyberbucks. All of this was done anonymously. Though one participating merchant was the *Encyclopedia Britannica*, which took Chaum's pretend money in exchange for its articles, most of the extremely limited universe of E-Cash merchants was ad hoc operations like "Big Mac's Monty Python Archive Shop," which offered unauthorized transcriptions of that comedy group's routines for various increments of cyberbucks.

When Chaum finally did break some news, it was with a Midwestern institution with a name more familiar to literature students than international financiers: the Mark Twain Bank. The idea was to deliver a version of E-Cash where the units finally could be exchanged for *real* money, backed by Mark Twain. Then, perhaps, larger institutions would jump in. At that point Chaum's critics—one of whom dismissed his ideas as Walden Pond meets the Internet—might shut up. But the Mark Twain scheme never took off.

It wasn't just Chaum who was having difficulties establishing crypto cash as an Internet standard. Electronic commerce hadn't taken off quickly enough, and the still-evolving standards of the Net made any sort of crypto-cash scheme relatively hard to use. Chaum's competitors were unfettered by the moral obligation to provide anonymity to their digital money—they generally felt that people really didn't demand it. But those companies were falling short of expectations as well, among them the well-funded start-up Cybercash and Mondex, which allowed consumers to download money on credit-card-sized smart cards (think of a bank cash machine on your personal computer). But those disappointments paled beside Chaum's. It was Chaum who had the patents for anonymous digital cash. And when Digicash finally filed for bankruptcy in 1998, it was Chaum who lost the patents.

Yet despite the problems and harassments suffered by the crypto revolutionaries in the mid-1990s, their larger cause kept advancing. Skirmishes and setbacks to the contrary, it was the government that was on the run. After Al Gore first retreated by promising to amend the Clipper scheme in the letter to Representative Cantwell, the administration offered to negotiate a compromise with industry, and several meetings were held at NIST's Maryland headquarters to try and reach a consensus. Hopes were high that some scheme would be reached whereby export standards were liberalized and any key escrow would be truly optional. Some of the things that the government was saying seemed quite reasonable. But when the administration's officials unveiled the final rules, there were devils in the details. Bottom line: the export restrictions would continue as they always had and Clipper's rules were only partially relaxed (for instance, users would be offered a choice of escrow agencies). The plan earned its sobriquet of Clipper II.

Inevitably, it was followed by Clipper III, in 1996. That plan had a new angle. The idea was to give cooperating companies a carrot—if companies promised to build escrow into their future products, they'd be allowed to export unescrowed DES-strength crypto now. But in practice, this proved no more attractive than the earlier versions. The obvious relief would have been a blanket export exemption of reasonably strong crypto. Instead the government tinkered with variations of its same old policy.

One continuing problem for the administration was that foreign countries regarded any American escrow scheme with suspicion. At one point, a "crypto ambassador" was sent off to try to convince the world community that such a global solution could work for all. But since he could offer no implementation where all countries had equal access to keys, his failure was a foregone conclusion. Some members of the administration considered this shortcoming the death blow to the entire policy.

Meanwhile, spurred by complaints that American industry was losing business to foreign firms selling crypto software, Congress was reconsidering a legislative solution. In 1996, Senator Conrad Burns of Montana introduced the Security and Freedom through Encryption (SAFE) bill, designed to lift export restrictions on programs that offered a "generally available" level of crypto. (Presumably, this included DES and domestic-strength RSA.) The bill also addressed fears that the government might one day declare that Clipper technology would be the only permissible crypto: SAFE would specifically forbid mandatory key escrow. Burns, a crusty Westerner who felt more comfortable seated on a saddle than in front of a computer screen, was tickled at his new reputation as a high-tech privacy crusader. But the bill itself sat bottled in committee, as legislators still swayed by NSA's well-orchestrated briefing stifled what the spooks continued to warn them was a threat to national security. "Some people here fully understand the issue," complained Senator Patrick Leahy, an early SAFE supporter. "But with others, they're talking like it was ten years ago, about an industry where ten days is an eternity."

If the government's goal was simply to stall—*each day the dike doesn't crack, we win*—then its approach could be considered a success. But as the cypherpunk attacks against export-strength crypto demonstrated—and the interception of unencrypted cell phone conversations, including the House Republican leadership, dramatized—

such a policy had its perils. The country lacked a strong electronic security system, a vulnerability that became more serious as the Internet wound itself more deeply into the fabric of American life.

That, at least, was a key conclusion of a major study by the National Research Council (NRC). That organization, the research arm of Congress, undertook a comprehensive examination of the national crypto policy, and recruited a panel of experts from all sides of the issue, including former cabinet members, officials from the NSA, and critics from business and academia like Ray Ozzie and Marty Hellman. Their report, "Cryptography's Role in Securing the Information Society," was a surprisingly strong criticism of government policy, and recommended continued freedom for domestic encryption, relaxed export controls, and, above all, "a mechanism to promote information security in the private sector." In other words, *more* crypto.

Perhaps the most interesting observation of the study came as a result of the classified briefings its members had received. (Three of the sixteen members declined clearances and did not attend.) Though they could not of course reveal what they had heard in the briefings, they could—and did—evaluate the importance of that secret knowledge in determining national policy. Answer: not much. "Those [classified] details . . . ," the report stated, "are not particularly relevant to the larger issues of why policy has the shape and texture that it does today nor to the general outline of how technology will and policy should evolve in the future." So much for the "If you only knew what we know" argument.

Some people in the administration chafed at that conclusion. (In the NSA, there was even some unhappiness that the title of the report could be read as an acronym, CRISIS.) They conceded that the classified briefings given the NRC participants were thorough, but contended that to really understand the issue, you have to live and breathe intelligence. Sure, Marty Hellman or Ray Ozzie understood in theory that it was important to wiretap a crook or intercept a terrorist's call on a cell phone. But every morning the president and the vice president got nice thick books that zeroed in on the world's pressure points—everything from cracked diplomatic dispatches to the carphone conversations of Russian mafiosi. The Clinton people knew damn well that if crypto was universal, significant hunks of those books would disappear.

But that fine point was lost on the general public—and indeed on much of Congress, which commissioned the study. Instead, the NRC report stood as a call to arms to drop the silly restrictions against crypto and start using it to strengthen our *own* systems. After all, it argued, *the genie's out of the bottle*. And quietly, some of the staunchest defenders of government's control of crypto were themselves admitting it, too.

Then another front opened in the crypto wars. For the first time, export regulations were facing a serious challenge in the courts. A decade earlier, the NSA's Bobby Ray Inman felt that he had successfully fended off the 1978 opinion of a Justice Department lawyer that the export regulations violated the First Amendment. But no judge had ever addressed the issue. Many legal experts thought that if a ruling did come on the question, it might not be to the liking of the crypto community. Indeed, a recent decision involving cypherpunk Phil Karn's legal challenge to export the floppy disk version of *Applied Cryptography* ended in flames. Rejecting the idea that the same information permitted for export in hard copy should be provided the same privilege in digital form, a federal judge had not only denied the request but also delivered a withering opinion on Phil Karn's request, virtually accusing him of an immoral attack on national security. But that was a sideshow to a more important suit: that of Daniel Bernstein.

Bernstein was a graduate student at Berkeley. He'd become interested in crypto and security after someone hacked his own computer account in 1987, and thereafter wanted to include crypto algorithms in his course work. As a reflection of how times had changed, courses focusing on cryptography were now almost mainstream. Technically, though, regulations seemed to forbid anyone from placing a crypto concoction somewhere a foreigner might see it. Which was exactly what Bernstein wanted to do.

Bernstein's project was inspired, coincidentally, by something Ralph Merkle had produced at Xerox PARC in 1989: a hash function called Snefru. Written in 1990 when he was an undergraduate at

NYU, Bernstein's addition to Snefru playfully tweaked the illogic of the export codes. He knew that while encryption programs were subject to restrictions, hash functions like Merkle's (which don't scramble information per se) were not. So Bernstein wrote a program that transformed the hash function Snefru into something that could perform encryption and decryption. (Think of Snefru as a banned automatic weapon shipped through customs without a trigger, and the new program as a kit that installs the missing part.) "It takes *any* good hash function and turns it into a good encryption function," he later explained of his creation. He called his crypto package Snuffle and wrote a paper to describe what he'd done. But he was worried about publishing it, figuring, he later said, that "the government might not be too happy about me pointing this out." So he put Snuffle on the shelf.

But at Berkeley in 1992, he reconsidered. Why *not* publish Snuffle? After all, it was not a commercial product but an academic exercise. Since the actual encryption relied on an already-published hash algorithm—he introduced no original encryption algorithms of his own—it presented no threat to the republic, so why would publishing it be a problem? The obvious place to release it was the sci.crypt discussion group on the Internet. But before uploading Snuffle to sci.crypt, he decided to take one final precaution to make sure he wasn't violating any laws. He would ask someone in the government if such a step was permissible.

That little step kept Snuffle off the Internet for the rest of the twentieth century.

Bernstein's first problem was identifying the proper government office to handle his request. After a series of queries he finally wound up at something called the Office of Defense Trade Controls. He sent his letter off in June 1992. To his dismay, the reply, signed by William B. Robinson, the director of that mysterious office, asserted that distributing Snuffle without a license would indeed put Bernstein in legal jeopardy.

Okay, Bernstein figured, I'll go through the formality of getting the commodities jurisdiction—the "CJ." First, though, he hoped that the Office of Defense Trade Controls would clarify what his rights were, and what appeals he might have if he disagreed with a government decision. It took him until March 1993 to get someone to talk to him.

Finally he got Charles Ray, the special assistant to William B. Robinson, on the horn. (Bernstein taped his conversations, with permission.) Basically, Ray told him that his rights were, well, nonexistent. If he posted Snuffle on the Net without clearance, and some foe of the United States downloaded his program from a terrorist base in Afghanistan or an apartment in Paris, Bernstein might have to scope out a jail cell for his next home. "There are no exempt groups," Ray told him. "If you've got something considered technical information covered by the Munitions List . . . then being a member of the press [or an academic] does not provide you with any sanctuary. . . . You can still be prosecuted." *But what about the First Amendment?* he asked.

"That freedom carries with it a responsibility to comply with the existing legislation and regulations" was Charles Ray's interpretation of the U.S. Constitution.

A month later, Bernstein finally reached Ray's boss, William Robinson, who confirmed that a CJ would be required before Bernstein could distribute his work. Subsequent conversations with government officials were even more frustrating. Not only was Internet posting forbidden, but Bernstein might be prosecuted even if he placed a copy of his paper in a public library. Of course, the National Security Agency became involved, as it always does in export cases of new crypto systems. Eventually, Bernstein managed to have some conversations with NSA representatives, learning that behind the Triple Fence some people considered Snuffle "strategic." This meant, he inferred, that it was not trivial to break. "They offered to help me rewrite it to make it *not* strategic," says Bernstein, but he deemed such a move counterproductive.

So he'd play the game. In September 1992, Bernstein filed for five separate CJs. He'd broken the problem up into different versions—ranging from English-language descriptions of the system to mathematical formulas—"to see where they'd draw the line." Could the government consider each one a "defense article"? He still maintained a belief that at some point the fog would clear from a bureaucrat's eyes and he would finally realize that Snuffle was simply one graduate student's academic work, not a weapon. But in October 1993, the government replied that yes, each one of his mathematical formulas *was* a weapon, "subject to the licensing jurisdiction of the Department of State."

Bernstein hadn't begun the process as a rabble-rouser, but now he was himself thoroughly roused. He continued to pursue the case with a methodical patience that would prove devastating to the U.S. government's eventual defense of its export regulations as they applied to Snuffle. He appealed the first CJ. When months passed without a response, he decided that he needed help.

His benefactor was John Gilmore, no stranger to court battles against the government. The senior cypherpunk already had accumulated a file cabinet's worth of documents with Freedom of Information requests originally withheld but later kicked loose by legal appeals. Gilmore referred Bernstein to a lawyer named Cindy Cohn, who took the case pro bono (the Electronic Frontier Foundation helped with the costs and coordinated the effort with supplementary counsel). In early 1995, Bernstein and the EFF filed a complaint against the State Department, charging that the export laws were unconstitutional. At the center of the case was the contention that Bernstein's computer source code was a form of speech, and that by preventing its publication, the government was denying Bernstein's right to express himself.

That 1978 opinion—that the regulations might flout the First Amendment—was finally about to be tested. But few thought that a judge would resist the government's inevitable claim that the export laws were crucial to national security, and that striking them down would unleash the modern-day version of the Four Horsemen of the Apocalypse: drug dealers, kidnappers, child pornographers, and terrorists.

The case was tried before Judge Marilyn Patel in the Northern California District Court. One of her first acts did not seem promising for the plaintiff: she ordered the trial exhibits sealed, since the export rules forbade their distribution. But as the case progressed, Judge Patel proved to be more than sympathetic to Bernstein's claims. Perhaps sensing this, the government tried a number of tactics to get the suit out of her court. It reversed itself on two of the five CJ determinations, admitting that those particular mathematical decisions were simply "technical data." It argued that Judge Patel's court had no jurisdiction in matters involving export law. It filed for immediate dismissal. But on April 27, 1996, Patel decided the case should proceed. The reason was enough to make a government regulator's blood run cold: Judge Marilyn Patel had determined that at least part of the encryption export control rules was indeed unconstitutional. Furthermore, she accepted the Bernstein team's assertion that computer source code could be considered a form of speech. Which meant that the much stricter First Amendment rules regarding prior restraint applied to Snuffle. As far as Judge Patel was concerned, this wasn't about keeping a weapon within our borders. It was about illegally suppressing an opinion. That summer, Patel officially affirmed her preliminary decision.

The government appealed to the higher Ninth Circuit court. By then Bernstein had received his doctorate and was teaching at the University of Chicago. He wanted to teach a course involving cryptography, but because of the continuing case, he required a government waiver to do so. It took another judicial ruling before he was finally permitted to distribute materials about his work—and then only to his students. The course was taught without discernible damage to the nation.

But still the case dragged on. Oral arguments before a three-judge panel were scheduled for December 1997. Conventional wisdom had it that the appeals court would strike down what was seen as an impudent ruling from a judge who, after all, sat on the bench in wacky San Francisco. But in the packed courtroom, a rather harried government lawyer, a man of baby-boom vintage with experience before higher courts, was questioned harshly by the judges. The panel seemed more impressed with Bernstein's advocate, Cindy Cohn, a diminutive woman in her early thirties, who, despite an occasional wavering in her voice, presented her arguments forcefully. One unexpected point she made was that by preventing publication on the Internet, the government was failing to heed the recent Supreme Court decision that struck down a law known as the Communications Decency Act: the court had ruled that the Net was a beacon of democracy entitled to the highest level of First Amendment protection. Cohn also urged the judges to consider the implications of not allowing crypto to thrive: was it proper for the government to deny the tools that citizens might use to safeguard their privacy?

The three-judge panel pondered the case for more than a year, not handing down their ruling until May 1999. For Daniel Bernstein, it was worth the wait. By a two to one margin, they issued a broad opinion that not only affirmed Patel, but also went even further in celebrating cryptography itself as a vital component of democracy. Crypto should not be merely a state secret, they wrote, but also a protector of the people's privacy. Somehow these two technologically unschooled jurists had *gotten it*. "Government attempts to control encryption . . . may well implicate not only First Amendment rights of cryptographers," wrote Judge Betty Fletcher, "but also the constitutional rights of each of us as potential recipients of encryption's bounty."

Encryption's bounty? Judge Fletcher was a cypherpunk in robes!

The afternoon that the decision came down, Bernstein was proctoring a calculus exam in Chicago. Only afterward, when he checked his e-mail, did he learn that he had clobbered the government.

The government appealed of course—but the export rules it was defending were looking less and less likely to survive. For years, the crypto dike had held admirably. But now it was crumbling.

It was endgame for the government.

Oddly, the NSA no longer appeared to be the prime obstacle to a solution—behind the Triple Fence one could discern a sense of resigned acceptance of the new crypto reality. Clint Brooks himself was no longer on the front lines, but ultimately the institution he served had come to accept his idea of change. Maybe its leaders recognized that instead of trying to hold back progress, their efforts might be better spent trying to prepare for the inevitable. Probably, when the NSA cipher wizards had really thought about it, the putative nightmare of crypto everywhere was something they felt they could handle—if they were granted more funding, of course. Perhaps, as Robert Morris hinted in his Crypto '95 speech, and the cypherpunk-cracking effort had indicated, these shiny, "uncrackable" programs created by the private sector really weren't so uncrackable after all, and the NSA was satisfied at its ability to get plaintext when it needed to. One caper funded by the Electronic Frontier Foundation had been particularly telling: a team of engineers led by John Gilmore and Paul Kocher had built a DES-cracking machine for $210,000. (DES, of course, was still deemed a munition too hazardous to send abroad in normal circumstances.) In a demonstration at a 1998 crypto conference, the device produced the plaintext to a DES message in less than twenty-four hours. Obviously, if such machines were produced in bulk, obtaining such keys would be dirt cheap. One had to assume that the NSA had plenty of similar units in its basement.

In any case, it was the FBI, particularly its director Louis Freeh, that kept urging a hard line—even to the point of continuing to insist that the bureau should have access to plaintext even at the cost of regulating crypto within U.S. borders. Freeh had finally managed to get a version of the Digital Telephony bill passed, presumably forcing the telecommunications industry to design its products to be wiretap friendly. (Congressional opponents of the concept, however, had foiled its intent by refusing to budget the hundreds of millions of dollars needed to implement the effort.) But Freeh continued to fear that crypto would be the death of wiretapping. Since 1994, he had been demanding publicly that if his agents were unable to get plaintext from their wiretaps, Congress should institute a new era of prohibition by banning unescrowed strong encryption. "The objective is to get those conversations, whether they're [conducted] by alligator clips or [by] ones and zeros," he said. "Whoever they are, whatever they are, I need them." But Freeh was no longer a Clinton administration favorite, and White House officials shrugged off his remarks.

Not that the administration had given up its hopes of stemming the cipher tide. It's just that with each iteration, its anticrypto vision got flimsier and flimsier. White House apparatchiks insisted that the changes were all in the spirit of Al Gore's willingness to work with stakeholders in the crypto world to find the proper balance between codes and snoops. But the only direction that Clinton's people were going was backward. "The boat was getting shelled," Mike Nelson admits. The surest sign that a policy is in big trouble is when the words used to describe it are so discredited that they require euphemisms. By 1997, the word "escrow" became *verbum non gratum*, despite the fact that thousands of Clipper-equipped phones had now been purchased, their keys gathering digital dust in the prescribed escrow facilities. Now the stated goal was called key recovery. A policy that began with the firm controls of Clipper—secret algorithms in tamperproof hardware, government-controlled escrow facilities—had been modified to a software-based scheme where users could choose their own, privately run escrow facilities. Another compromise: the formerly top-secret Skipjack algorithm was finally made public. "We're not stupid," one administration official later explained. "We listened to the marketplace." But the marketplace—meaning real people trying to buy, sell, and use crypto—didn't want *any* part of an escrow scheme.

Meanwhile, Congress was discovering the confidence to follow that market, rather than fall prey to the administration's doomsday scenarios. Probably the most important factor was the rise of a well-organized lobbying effort by the computer industry. Since (now former) Representative Maria Cantwell's kamikaze run at the export laws, the high-tech crowd had learned a lot about what the white-shoe contingent could do for them. Regulatory warriors like Bruce Heiman of the Business Software Alliance had made crypto their cause célèbre. Their alliances with civil liberties groups like the Electronic Privacy Information Center, EFF, and the Center for Democracy and Technology gave them populist street cred. The lobbyists met with crucial administration officials so often that either side could flawlessly complete the other's sentences. And they cleverly identified the legislators who would promote procrypto bills, not so much in anticipation of actually passing them, but to increase the already considerable pressure for strong-crypto détente. The lobbyists' prize converts were a conservative Republican from Virginia, Robert Goodlatte, and a new-economy Democrat representing Silicon Valley, Zoe Lofgren. Goodlatte in particular was a firebrand on the issue, a newly born crypto head in pinstripes. "The first thing we did was have him spend time with the NSA on this, so he could hear the point of view from the other side," says Heiman. After being inoculated by a full-contact classified briefing, Goodlatte then was served the alternative reality: crypto was already abroad, industry was in danger of losing billions, and so on. Once the congressman adopted the outsider's vision, he appeared so often with Internet industry leaders that it was a shame he was ineligible for stock options.

Helped by a newly formed industry group called Americans for Computer Privacy (those "Americans" were thirteen corporations including RSA, IBM, Novell, Sun, and Microsoft), Goodlatte and Lofgren educated their colleagues on the political benefits of supporting strong crypto. In the Senate, the unlikely crypto crusader Conrad Burns of Montana took on the administration, backed by privacy-savant Patrick Leahy and the senator from Microsoft, Washington's Patty Murray.

A dramatically different variation on The Briefing was coming into vogue in congressional hearing rooms. Instead of shrouded conversations about maintaining our successes in codebreaking, witnesses were warning of potential disasters caused by outsiders screwing up our *own* systems—which were vulnerable, in part, because the world's most advanced technological nation had failed to adopt strong crypto to protect those systems. Every corruption of a Web site and theft of on-line credit-card numbers seemed to reinforce those fears; the conclusions of the National Research Council were finally resonating. Even *the FBI's* Web site got hacked! Capitol Hill was suddenly abuzz with the prospects of a "digital Pearl Harbor," where hackers, terrorists, and hostile nations would grind our society to a halt by shutting down computer-controlled functions like the electrical grid or weapons systems. And though there was no magic bullet that might shore up our defenses, we did have a powerful tool to protect ourselves: strong crypto, the very thing that the administration had been trying to suppress!

By 1999, an emboldened Congress was finally rallying around the SAFE bill, the three-year-old proposed legislation to relax the export rules. In fact, a majority of the House—258 members—had signed on as cosponsors. In the Senate, the news for the administration was no better. Its leader in the fight against relaxed export controls had been John McCain, the former Vietnam prisoner of war whose credibility on such matters was unimpeachable. A bill McCain and Senator Bob Kerry had introduced in June 1997 would deny the services of any future government-sponsored "certificate authorities" (agencies to distribute and authenticate public keys, a necessary component in a full-blown crypto infrastructure) to those who refused to escrow their keys—potentially giving citizens the choice of either using Clipper-type schemes or losing their ability to participate in the electronic society. But by 1999, McCain had looked more closely at the issue (and perhaps its impact on his pending presidential run). In a stunning switcheroo, McCain suddenly turned into Mr. Crypto, a vocal supporter of the SAFE bill.

Was it time for the administration to finally toss its export forms in the air and yell "ciphertext"? Apparently so. Even though the administration never really believed that Congress would pass a bill demanding liberalized exports—the system was too convoluted to tackle, the risk of compromising national security too dicey, and in any case there was always the promised presidential veto—the White House was distressed and anxious that votes in the subcommittees kept the issue alive. More to the point, the Clinton people began pondering the potential consequences of a national disaster resulting from a *lack* of crypto—for which they could be blamed. Sure, allowing crypto exports could be dangerous, they figured, *people may die . . .* but on the other hand, if someone attacked an unprotected digital infrastructure . . . *people may die!* As one White House policy maker later explained, it came down to *how* they would die: "Do you want them shot out of the sky with a surface-to-air missile, or do you want the floodgates on the Grand Coulee Dam to be rewired?" If the whole issue boiled down to six of one against half a dozen of the other, what was the sense of fighting such a thankless, uphill battle?

In September 1999, Al Gore—himself preparing for a run at the White House—announced that a new set of regulations would be unveiled in December: the net result of which would be permission to export consumer-directed crypto products in any key length. So drastic a change was this that upon being briefed on the policy, Curt Weldon, a Pennsylvania congressman who had carried serious water for the administration in fending off the SAFE bill, could not contain himself. *How can you be implementing this policy?* he shouted. *For years, you've been telling us that exports of strong crypto will compromise security and empower criminals. And now you're telling us you've changed your minds?*

"It's over," concluded Stewart Baker, who since leaving the NSA in 1994 had returned to his law firm to practice cyberlaw. Some suspected that the whole thing was yet another government stalling tactic; at the last moment, the regulators would unveil a plan loaded with fine print that represented very little change. Just like Lucy snatching away the football when Charlie Brown was ready to boot it, they imagined, the NSA and the FBI would once again deny the crypto community the ability to export strong keys. But by now it was clear that the game could have fewer and fewer iterations before Charlie would finally, inevitably put toe to pigskin.

This time, in fact, the government made good. The first draft of the regulations seemed to dictate an alarming amount of red tape before strong crypto could be granted an "automatic" exemption—but tactful yet firm opposition from the Goodlatte-Lofgren faction and the industry led to a more commodious second draft. Not perfect, but sufficiently straightforward to assure even the paranoid that this time the good stuff could be sent abroad. No longer was a 56-bit DES key, or even keys of 64, 80, 128, or more bits, regarded as a deadly weapon.

If was official: public crypto was our friend.

A few days into the new millennium, it was time for the tenth-anniversary gathering of RSA's annual cryptography conference. The gathering now had outgrown San Francisco's largest hotels and was held at the mammoth San Jose Convention Center. It had become a huge crypto bazaar with a conference program with five separate tracks of seminars and over ten thousand people in attendance.

Almost every year at the show, one of the keynote sessions tracked the progress, or lack of progress, of cryptography in the political realm. It would play out almost like Kabuki theater, with aggrieved representatives from the commercial, academic, or civil liberties world griping about the intransigence of the government. Then some unlucky emissary from the administration—an assistant attorney general, an NSA lawyer, a White House techno-policy wonk—would lecture an unforgiving crowd about the ineffable balance between privacy and national security, perhaps inflaming the gathering by an ill-placed "If you knew what we know" reply to one of the inevitably hostile questions. But this year it was different. Jim Bidzos came to the podium with a bottle of champagne, offering it to the people from Justice and the NSA on the panel. *The fight is over,* he was saying, *and our guys won.*

Bidzos himself was no longer working full time, partly as a consequence of the June 1996 acquisition of RSA Data Security by an East Coast computer security firm called Security Dynamics. (Weeks before the January conference, the purchasing company decided to change its name and was now called RSA Security, Inc.) The price tag was around $300 million, of which Bidzos himself took in $40 million. Some think that the sum might have been even higher—or RSA might have been able to pull off its own billion-buck Internet IPO—had it not been for the acrimonious breakup of Public Key Partners, when lawsuits flared between RSA Data Security and its partner Cylink. The people at Cylink had become unhappy with the arrangement, and also frustrated that the original agreement did not allow them to exploit

RSA technology freely in their own products; they went so far as to challenge the validity of the MIT patent on the breakthroughs of Rivest, et al. (A remarkable action, since Cylink, through PKP, received a share of the royalties from that patent.) Bidzos and his colleagues, meanwhile, were livid that Cylink had developed an RSA-based product for the global transaction clearinghouse SWIFT. The suits were finally settled in late 1996, with the assistance of a federal judge. Both sides claimed victory at the complicated settlement (Bidzos noted that there were no findings that RSA had acted improperly) but valuable energies had been expended—while the patents themselves inched closer to their expiration dates.

Not long after the sale, Bidzos figured he'd be happier with less involvement in the firm. He'd moved into a Marin County mansion, owned a sleek posse of BMW motorcycles, sampled exotic bottles of wine, practiced classical guitar, flew his minifleet of airplanes, and checked on his impressive stock portfolio. Investments had made him a millionaire many, many times over—his personal stake in the VeriSign digital certificate company alone (which he cofounded) was worth more than the money he cleared in the RSA sale (a stake that had itself now grown to over $100 million). His main job was now as a quasi-ambassador of the commercial crypto cause, and his main visibility came at the annual conference.

Diffie was there, of course. Still unrepentantly longhaired and strikingly bearded, he cut a startling figure in one of his bespoke suits. Though not wealthy by Silicon Valley standards, the few million dollars he had received from his patents and RSA stock made him quite comfortable. He and Mary Fischer were still together, still very much in love, though their one-time petting zoo was now down to two Tibetan mastiffs.

Rivest, Shamir, and Adleman attended as well. Rivest was now a well-respected graybeard, still on the MIT faculty but wealthy from his RSA holdings. He was still doing original crypto research. Shamir was even more active in the field, brainstorming everything from systems for digital cash micropayments to a new computer that could factor huge numbers. But Len Adleman was pretty much out of crypto, working instead on schemes that combined mathematics with organic chemicals, like DNA computers.

Some key cryptographers and figures in the struggle didn't make it to San Jose for the event. Ralph Merkle, too busy with his work at Xerox PARC in the field of nanotechnology, couldn't find the time to accept an award bestowed by RSA for significant contributions in the field. And Ray Ozzie was immersed in the development of his first major project since Notes: within weeks he would receive—fifteen years after his first frustrating contacts with the NSA—export clearance to ship 2048-bit RSA keys, 256-byte RC-4 (yes, byte—eight times more than bits!) keys, and, by the way, clearance for plain old DES as well.

Another unfortunate no-show was David Chaum. Had he attended, he might have seen plenty of things he liked. Anonymous crypto solutions like Chaum's were increasingly cited as an antidote to the unwanted transmission of personal data. One start-up prominently displaying at the conference trade show was a Canadian company called Zero Knowledge that sucked up millions in venture capital to launch its "Anonymizer," a Web site that allowed people to surf the Net without leaving their digital footprints behind.

And though Julf Helsingius didn't venture from Finland for the conference, his ideas still flourished. At the monthly cypherpunks meeting held the weekend before the event, there was the usual discussion of a new generation of remailers called "mixmasters," which used an improved technology to make encrypted anonymous Internet messaging easy to use and devilishly difficult for governments to unravel.

Phil Zimmermann, however, did manage to attend the conference. On January 11, 1996, the government had officially dropped its investigation of him and his co-target, Kelly Goen. To celebrate, Zimmermann's wife had tossed a "Phil Got Off the Hook" party at the Rocky Mountain Peace Center. Not long afterward, Zimmermann decided to move to Silicon Valley and start a company, Pretty Good Privacy, Inc., to produce the software commercially. (An RSA lawsuit filed against the new company for copyright infringement was eventually settled, with PGP paying normal royalties for public key protocols.) But PGP, Inc. was short-lived. Admittedly the kind of guy who couldn't balance his own checkbook, Zimmermann turned over the operations of his company to businesspeople who went through millions of dollars in barely the time it takes to calculate a long prime. The new company acquired other firms, had splashy displays at trade shows, and pursued an overly ambitious plan of transforming itself into a full-service security giant. Finally, the nearly broke company was sold to an established personal computer security firm, Network Associates. Zimmermann was kept on as the official head of PGP, but his contribution came not so much as a software developer but as a living symbol of strong cryptography. It was in that iconic role that Phil Zimmermann attended the 2000 RSA conference; his best moment came at a Network Associates party on the event's second night. Standing at a computer keyboard, he made a big show of mouse clicking a file transfer that launched a copy of commercial PGP abroad. Only a few years earlier, the government wanted to throw him in jail for the same alleged act.

Later in the conference came a series of sessions focused on a so-called crypto bakeoff run by NIST to choose a successor to the now-ancient Data Encryption Standard. In contrast to the selection of DES, which was made after closed-door meetings with its creators and agreements to keep its design principles secret, the Advanced Encryption Standard was being run as an open competition, with the winner to be chosen by 2001. Not only the algorithms themselves but also the design considerations were completely public. All, as required by NIST, were much stronger than DES, with minimum 128-bit keys. It would have been difficult to argue for strong restrictions against the export of the algorithm in any case, since more than half of the contenders were written by cryptographers outside the United States.

It had taken more than twenty years since Whit Diffie's discovery—so long, in fact, that in just a few months into the new century, the suite of patents covering public key and RSA would one by one reach their expiration dates—but the era that Diffie had dreamed of was finally beginning. In a keynote speech following Bidzos, a vice president at Microsoft announced that its new operating system, Windows 2000—variations of which would undoubtedly find their way into almost every personal computer sold in the new century—would have 128-bit crypto built in, with government clearance to export it. And Apple Computer was *already* shipping strong crypto in its new operating system.

And, of course, crypto was already a component in every Web browser, enabling the secure transfer of credit-card numbers and financial information. In 2000, there would be over $80 billion worth of e-commerce transactions—a number that was estimated to eventually shoot into the trillions; virtually all of that was protected by RSA crypto. And later that year, a national digital signature bill would be passed, finally clearing the way out of the logjam caused by the administration's foot-dragging back in 1992. President Clinton would sign the bill electronically.

The once-forbidden technology was suddenly the new panacea. It was envisioned that the solution to the pirated, downloading of music and films would be . . . crypto. In addition, crypto was the secret sauce of protected corporate discussions used in "virtual private networks," a hot business trend that allowed snoop-proof conferencing. The movement of medical records to the on-line world would be possible only with crypto. And crypto was expected to be an essential component in the next generation of the Internet, where all of us would communicate with non-personal-computer "devices" ranging from palmtops to phones to kitchen appliances. We would be wired and wirelessed up the wazoo, and crypto would be our privacy safety net.

To be sure, its revolutionary impact would be stealthy. The hundreds of millions already using it in browsers and operating systems, for instance, knew nothing of Whit Diffie and the others, even as their machines silently made key exchanges and scrambled, unscrambled, and successfully completed transactions with secrecy that would stagger the medieval occultist Trithemius, stun autokey wizard Vigenère, and perhaps bring a wistful smile to Lucifer's creator, Horst Feistel. Why didn't it happen sooner, as Diffie had expected? Because it wasn't until the Internet that it *had* to happen.

So there was reason to celebrate at the 2000 RSA conference. But those wondering why the turnaround had come so quickly would have found a succinct answer one year earlier—same season, same place, at the 1999 conference. That event had opened with the soaring vocalists of the Oakland Interfaith Gospel Choir. Decked out in electric blue robes, they filed onstage, booming out a holy-roller version of the rock song "I Still Haven't Found What I'm Looking For." The lyrics had been changed to refer to the long struggle for widespread, strong encryption. But when Jim Bidzos himself hit the stage, similarly berobed, his preacherlike testimony presciently claimed that the clouds were parting, the rainbow just ahead. If not crypto anarchy, he knew, crypto ubiquity was on the way. He realized that for all those years he'd been flogging the public key dream, he'd been pushing a boulder uphill. But the problem hadn't been only the government or the export regulations, but the product itself. Public key cryptography was a mathematical marvel, but it had actually been born too soon. Twenty years ago, it was a solution whose problem hadn't fully materialized.

No more. Not when every desktop had a computer on it and was connected to the Internet. Not when nearly every lap had one of the things, too. Not when phones were beginning to get hooked to the World Wide Web, along with set-top television boxes, and even videogame consoles. Certainly not when all those Net-connection devices were being used to shuttle everyone's private information, and even their credit cards. *Especially* their credit cards.

Jim Bidzos looked at his audience and made his own joyful gospel sound: "We've found the problem to the solution," he said, ". . . and it's e-commerce!"

epilogue: the open secret

flashback to 1969. Whitfield Diffie is just beginning to cogitate on cryptography. Marty Hellman isn't working at Stanford yet. Ralph Merkle is still in high school. The world of high-level codes is owned and operated by intelligence agencies. And would be, until the invention of public key by Diffie, Hellman, and Merkle, and its implementation by Rivest, Shamir, and Adleman. Their mind-blowing ideas that would smash the monopoly of the spooks were years away.

James Ellis wasn't the type to call himself a spook. True, he worked for General Communication Headquarters (GCHQ), the British counterpart to the National Security Agency. But he preferred to describe his agency, along with its NSA cousin, as "the closed community." He was a member of a clan driven by patriotism, pride, and the simple need to bring home a paycheck. If brilliant work was done, it would be acknowledged privately, within the bounds of the secret society. James Ellis's brush with brilliance was a prime example. He was the real inventor of public key cryptography. And for almost thirty years, virtually no one knew it.

Ellis's colleagues would never have pegged him as a likely candidate for a breakthrough that could change the very rules of their science. He was seen as capable of good ideas but at heart more of a dreamer.

Some thought him a borderline wacko. He was an Australian-born orphan who had been raised by grandparents in the East End of London. He'd joined GCHQ, located in the Cotswolds town of Cheltenham, in the 1950s, after attending Imperial College. Ellis understood that he was entering a world where communication about one's work with the outside was strictly forbidden, now and forever. The job was to work for one's country; dreams of personal ambition and public recognition were to be put aside. "The fullest value of cryptography is realized by minimizing the information available to potential adversaries," Ellis would write. "Professional cryptographers normally work in closed communities to provide sufficient professional interaction to ensure quality while maintaining secrecy for outsiders."

This sounds rather lofty, but in truth Ellis's assignment did not place him in the white-hot center of international intrigue. "I think in some ways," says Malcolm Williamson, who as a future colleague would have his own role in this story, "he was sort of sidetracked. At least my impression was that he was working on not really critical stuff and not really slated to be in charge of big projects or anything like that."

"He was an almost classic English eccentric: nice, disorganized, shambling around," says Nick Patterson, who arrived at GCHQ in the late 1960s. "Some managers wrote him off as a nutcase, but he was full of ideas. Half of them were ridiculous, but half could be brilliant."

Most people, though, saw only the strange fellow who habitually spooned instant coffee from a hand-mixed jar containing Nescafé and sugar—he thought it was less efficient to add the sweetener every time he made a cup. Another obstacle to the recognition of his talents was an inability to express some of his insights clearly. "He was the worst technical public speaker I'd ever seen," says one colleague. "Listeners would consider his talks an absolute ordeal. Ellis would typically begin a talk by apologizing that he'd been asked to give a presentation on something he knew nothing about, then he'd go on for twenty minutes in some bizarre direction. But then—and this is why his talks were attended at all—without fanfare, he'd slip in something amazing."

Ellis himself was somewhat bitter that one of the best ideas he'd ever had had been wasted. A longtime fanatic of radio design, he had come up with a certain kind of audio circuit that would provide better reception. He actually patented his idea, and a company offered to try building it into its radios. But apparently the company's engineers, under orders to save money by cutting down on components, butchered his design. As a result, the radio reception was unexceptional. The fiasco was always a sore point with Ellis.

In 1969, Ellis, then in his forties, was working in the part of the agency called Communications Electronics Security Group (CESG), in what was probably the most appropriate position for him: a group of maybe a half dozen researchers working on long-range projects. Blue sky stuff. He had just rejoined CESG as a senior scientist after a stint at the post office, presumably helping on security issues. And now he found himself working on a problem that most people believed was unsolvable.

In the 1960s, the intelligence establishment was just beginning to consider the revolution in computers and wireless technologies, and the subsequent huge demand to provide protection for government communications that went over these channels. But while devices to perform encryption had gotten cheaper, one part of the process hadn't changed fundamentally since World War II. This was the means of distributing and holding cryptographic keys. The restrictions needed to protect those keys acted as a bottleneck: for every two people wishing to communicate securely, a brand-new secret key had to be generated for that particular conversation. Thousands of people were in the classified loop; that meant literally millions of keys to move securely and protect. The problem was essentially the same one that would soon bother Whit Diffie: the hair-pulling complexity, and the security risks, that came from managing this vast number of keys.

It was a tough problem, and of course no one expected James Ellis to solve it. After all, certain rules of cryptography seemed as firm as the laws of physics. And what law was more certain than the one which assumed that secret keys used to encrypt communications should never be placed in a position where outsiders could intercept them? But Ellis, according to another colleague, Clifford Cocks, "was the sort of person who, whatever the problem you'd give him, would always start by challenging the basic assumptions, coming up often with questions that pointed to the invalidity of the assumptions you were working on—assumptions that maybe were stopping you from getting the solution." In attempting to crack the key management problem, almost any cryptographer would rule out of hand any solution that involved sending secure messages when not only the method of encipherment is known to the potential interceptor, but every transmission is assumed to be as equally accessible to the snoop as to the intended recipient. Including the transmission of key material. Even Ellis doubted that it could be done. "It was obvious to everyone, including me," he later wrote, "that no secure communication was possible without a secret key, some other secret knowledge, or at least some way in which the recipient was in a different position from an interceptor. After all, if they were in identical situations, how could one possibly be able to receive what the other could not? Thus there was no incentive to look for something so clearly impossible."

Ellis would soon get that incentive. It was an unsigned paper that had long been buried in the mountain of secret material accumulated inside the boundaries of the shadow world. It described a project conceived by Bell Telephone during the final days of World War II, one that had been quickly classified and forgotten. The scheme was part of something called Project C43, a primitive yet ingenious experiment in analog voice scrambling. Say you want to send a message over a phone line and suspect that someone is listening. How can you keep the message secure? The anonymous Bell scientist postulated that the person who wants to receive the message should simply add noise to the line. When the message gets sent, it will be intermingled with the noise so that an eavesdropper will hear only garbage. But the recipient, who knows precisely how that noise was generated, may be able to subtract that noise from the transmission—and wind up with the original, unscrambled message.

For purposes of modern cryptography, Project C43 was useless. For one thing, it was an analog model and now everyone used digital communications. But Ellis found it exciting: here was a system where the sender of a message didn't have to worry about whether a potential enemy was listening, even if the foe knew how the system worked. What made this possible, Ellis realized, was that, in contrast to conventional cryptography, the recipient is actually a collaborator in the process of encryption. "Secure communication," Ellis would write, "was at least theoretically possible if the recipient took part in the encipherment."

Could such a system work with real-life digital cryptography? Ellis decided that the heart of the matter was a heretical issue: whether a secure, digitally encrypted message could actually be sent without any keys being exchanged in advance. According to his later account, that actual question popped into his head one night after he had gone to bed. And only a few minutes later, he had his answer.

Yes.

Sitting there in the dark in his Cheltenham bedroom, he came up with an existence proof for the question. And his name for it would embody the contradiction: Non-Secret Encryption.

Ellis's scheme was centered around a set of three mathematical transformations. A recipient, Alice, would use two of these and a sender (hello again, Bob) would use a third. A third, unwelcome party, Eve, is a potential interceptor who also has access to these functions, since they are, in this scenario, public knowledge. The process begins by a crucial act suggested to Ellis by Project C43: the potential message *recipient* gets involved in the scrambling process. Alice starts by generating a large number chosen at random—this, in effect, is a secret key that only she holds. She does this by performing a certain mathematical function to transform the key to a different number. Then she sends that number to Bob.

This new number is analogous to what Diffie and Hellman would later call a public key. Since an important property of the mathematical function is that it cannot be calculated in reverse, even those who have this second, nonsecret number, and also know what function produced it, cannot do an inverse calculation to retrieve the first, secret number. This is something that will remain known only to the recipient, Alice.

Now that Bob has this nonsecret number, he uses it with a second function to scramble the private message he has for Alice. Then he sends the scrambled message to Alice. How does Alice restore the message back to its original plaintext form? With the third mathematical function, she uses her original, secret key essentially to strip the encryption from the message. Alice can now read it, and Eve can do nothing but gnash her teeth.

In effect, the nonsecret key acts like the line noise in Project C43: although any eavesdropper can hear the noise on the line, only the recipient knows how the noise was generated (this information being the equivalent of a secret key), and thus only the recipient can strip out the noise (or, in this case, perform the proper function) to restore the scrambled message to its original, clear form. By figuring out a scheme that adapted the principles of that project to the digital age, Ellis had potentially changed the rules of cryptography. Since these non-secret keys did not have to be protected, it was possible to have secure communications without prior arrangement. This meant that field personnel would not have to be provided with symmetrical keys beforehand, keys that then had to be fanatically protected. It was now possible to conceive of protected communications on a much vaster scale.

It had not been Ellis's specific assignment to create a revolution in cryptography, but now he had to deal with the possibility that he had done just that. Certainly, the very basis of the idea—its "nonsecret" element—was so seemingly antithetical to the practice of cryptography that, to some GCHQ muckety-mucks, striking down Ellis's thesis was a blow for the natural order.

In any case, the idea had to be vetted. In July 1969, a draft of Ellis's paper was sent to the GCHQ chief mathematician, Shawn Wylie. If God was in His Heaven, surely the mathematics staff, or perhaps the chief himself, would find a fatal flaw in this system. It took months for their results to be reported, but just before Christmas that year, Wylie wrote his summation. "Unfortunately," he wrote, "I can't see anything wrong with this."

But, the mathematician noted, Ellis had come up only with a proof that such a system *could* exist—not the system itself. What was missing was the means to assure that there was a secure way of generating a "nonsecret" key from the original private key. You needed to be sure that the Eves of the world, who after all would have free access to the nonsecret key, could not reverse that first process and discover the secret key. Ellis had conjectured a set of look-up tables that would perform the various scrambling and descrambling calculations, but had not come up with the specific functions themselves. Until they were discovered—and skepticism ran rampant that this was even possible—nonsecret encryption could only be seen as a curious theoretical anomaly. And nothing more.

"The conclusion," says Clifford Cocks, "was 'This is really wonderful, this is ingenious, it's really clever, but how will we ever be able to make use of it?' "

Ellis did not sugarcoat this problem when he formally wrote up the scheme in January 1970. But neither did he shy away from the implications of his idea. The internally published—and of course, classified—paper was entitled "The *Possibility* of Secure Non-Secret Encryption" (emphasis added). "It is necessary to distinguish carefully between fact and opinion, i.e., between that which has been actually proved and that which seems likely," he wrote in the conclusion. "It is particularly difficult to do this in this case because we have established something which, to most people, seems inherently impossible." In fact, he continues, the concept is *not* impossible because he had "rigorously" proven that his scheme was "theoretically plausible."

Only one step was required, then, to produce a revolutionary means of encryption, and that was finding the proper mathematical functions. Not so easy. Ellis's concern, even as he set about the search, was that his mathematical skills were not up to the task. (He was an engineer by training.) And despite the apparent advantages that a nonsecret system would offer, GCHQ didn't think it worthwhile to assign much brainpower to aid him in the quest. Still, at various times over the next few years, some CESG cryptographers would come across the paper and work on possible solutions. In 1971, a new chief scientist took an interest in the problem and did assign some people to spend a bit of time seeking a solution. But while those looking for the mystery functions developed an understanding of what the characteristics of such things might be, nothing they tried was successful. The high ground seemed to belong to those insisting that the whole concept was preposterous.

It is unknown to what degree, if any, the NSA participated in this process. Dating from the collaboration of their respective predecessors in the days of Bletchley, GCHQ has shared confidential secrets with its so-called cousins in America. Yet there is no evidence that NSA efforts were being expended on nonsecret encryption at this point. The papers released by GCHQ indicate that the work in this field was limited to those few CESG cryptographers who had access to the project and interest in playing with it. And as a solution seemed less likely, those were becoming fewer.

That is where Clifford Cocks plays his role in the story. In 1973, Cocks was a recent CESG hire. Born of middle-class parents—his father was an accountant—Cocks had been bright enough to pass the exams for Manchester Grammar School, a competitive independent school with a solid academic reputation. From there, he had gone to Kings College, Cambridge, for an undergraduate degree in math.

Then he took a year of graduate study at Oxford, working on number theory. "I wasn't making real progress," he admits. So, where to work? Though he didn't know much about GCHQ, and really hadn't thought about cryptography as a focus for his work, he knew that the secret agency needed mathematicians. Also, one of his childhood friends, Malcolm Williamson, was already working for GCHQ. (When the government investigated Cocks's application, they took special notice of this, presumably fearing that there might have been something sinister in the coincidence.) So, at age twenty-two, in September 1973, Cocks entered the closed community.

The prospect of not having papers distributed publicly did not bother Cocks. "I was happy about it," he says. There would be no pressure to compete with the geniuses of academia. The lack of results in his student research led him to think that his contribution would lie more in the practical efforts he would devote to his government.

When people arrived at GCHQ, they were given a mentor, "to teach you the ropes and tell you what you need to know," says Cocks. His was Nick Patterson, another former Cambridge mathematician. Patterson, who had been a chess prodigy in his native Ireland, was himself only a few years older than Cocks. But he had been identified as an up-and-comer. One day at teatime, about two months after Cocks's arrival, Patterson mentioned Ellis's idea. He presented it to the younger man not as a challenge to implement a new form of cryptography, but as more of a puzzle. "Nick explained it to me very mathematically, in terms of wanting a nonreversible function, with a property where you could encrypt and decrypt with the input of this function," says Cocks, who thinks that it was an advantage that he didn't actually see Ellis's paper. This way he could approach the problem with no preconceptions. Since he had done his research the previous year in number theory—working with large primes and multiplication—it made sense to him to use that knowledge to, he hoped, implement Ellis's theory.

"I suppose it was actually also helpful that I wasn't doing anything that evening," he adds. Because that night he walked back to the modest room he rented in Cheltenham, ate the dinner cooked by the woman who let him the room in her family home, and sat down to think. Because of the secrecy imposed by GCHQ in all things concerned with his work, he had certain limitations. He could not bring anything home from his office, and if he pondered a work-related problem "in digs," he was not permitted to write anything down, not even notes on wastepaper. The only material he had was his brain. "Happily," he said, "the first idea seemed to work just fine."

The idea was more than just fine—it was elegant. "If you wanted a function that couldn't be inverted," he says, "it seemed very natural to me to think of the concept of multiplying quite large numbers together." Cocks figured that the secret "key" in his implementation would be two huge primes, generated on the spot by the recipient, Alice. The product would be the nonsecret key, the number given to the sender, Bob. (Bob could also find this number in a publicly distributed directory.) Cocks then figured out a simple mathematical formula in which Bob could use that nonsecret number to encrypt the message in such a way that it could only be decrypted by a person who knew the original primes.

The formula was virtually the same as what we now call the RSA algorithm. Clifford Cocks, in one evening, had produced what, three years later, would be rediscovered by three soon-to-be famous MIT mathematicians after a four-month period of intense trial and error.

Clifford Cocks recalls that it was probably around seven or eight o'clock when the first public key implementation in the world was discovered. "This is very interesting," he thought to himself. Then, after he had mapped it out in his head, he went to sleep. "I went back to work the next morning and wrote it down," he said.

He put the short paper on Nick Patterson's desk and waited for his mentor's reaction. Patterson, admitting to "an Irish excitability," reports that "I went kind of crazy." He literally dashed down the corridor to the office of the Communications Security specialists forty yards away, flung open the door, and shouted, to the astonishment of the stodgy bureaucrats planted behind their desks, "This is the most important cryptographic discovery of the century!"

That, however, was a minority opinion. Even Cocks at that time felt that it was more a clever solution to a math puzzle than a practical landmark. Certainly, as word began to get around CESG that someone had found a way to implement James Ellis's strange idea, no one treated it like the Second Coming or anything. "People said, 'Ha, ha, now here's a method,'" Cocks recalls.

No one seems to remember the moment James Ellis heard about

Cocks's discovery. "I think it would have happened that morning," Patterson guesses. "He was very happy." But Ellis was also cautious—fearful, perhaps, that GCHQ would still not treat the idea with the seriousness it deserved. Cocks himself does not remember his first meeting with Ellis, whom he would come to know in the coming months.

Cocks got a go-ahead to write a paper on his idea, and he mentioned this to his friend Malcolm Williamson. (Even though Williamson was at the time living in the same house as Cocks, the conversation had to take place at work, since work-related exchanges were verboten outside GCHQ walls.) This was sort of a one-up move, since it was fairly unusual for a young recruit to be circulating a paper so quickly after arriving. The announcement got Williamson's attention, and he listened closely as Cocks explained the problem he had tackled and how he had solved it.

Williamson had known Cocks ever since he was twelve—he also had attended Manchester Grammar. Williamson, too, was of the middle class; his father was a salesman for a textile company. Since both Cocks and Williamson excelled at math, there had been a friendly, though unspoken competition between the two. Williamson also went to Cambridge—Trinity College, which boasted Newton among its alumni—then took some graduate work in topology at Liverpool University. One day he had an epiphany: if he did get his doctorate, he would be a math instructor all his life. He was currently teaching a class of engineers and was discouraged that none of his students could prove that the square root of 3 was irrational. "I couldn't explain to them why they should care," he says, "and I didn't care that much myself. So I thought, 'Why am I doing this?' " Around that time he saw an ad for mathematicians posted by GCHQ. Without knowing much about the agency, he replied, and found himself assigned to problems of cryptography.

Williamson had not heard of the Ellis problem before, but it struck him as rather nonsensical. How could you do cryptography when you passed the key in the open? So he set about to shoot down the concept—to "disprove Cliff's idea," Williamson says.

It was after dinner, in *his* room, that Williamson began his debunking effort. "You try to reduce a problem to very basic general kinds of concepts, just sort of probe it," he explains. "I didn't manage to prove that there were any flaws in what he had."

But in the process, Williamson began considering different ways that two collaborating parties could pass numbers back and forth to arrive at a key—a shared key that would be secure even if an eavesdropper (some evil Eve) was monitoring every bit of the exchange. It was late at night when he finally got it—eight or twelve hours after he sat down to think, he reckons—but eventually he had a scheme of his own. It involved a complex set of exchanges in which each party would pick a random number, perform a calculation on it by a difficult-to-reverse formula, and finally arrive at a shared key. That Williamson was legally forbidden to write it down while at home—for, of course, as soon as it sprang out of his head it was instantly a state secret— did not bother him. "When you've got a concept that is right, you can't forget it," he says. "Everything follows logically." Still, as his friend Cocks later recalls wryly, the next morning was the first within memory that Williamson arrived at work early.

Williamson says that one of the first people he told about his breakthrough was Ellis himself, whom he knew only slightly at that time. He doesn't remember much of the conversation, but does recall that in the weeks that followed, "James made me see it more clearly." Still, it is indicative of the project's relative unimportance in GCHQ's view of things that Williamson didn't actually write up his work for a couple of months. (He finished his memo in January 1974; Cocks's work had been dated November 1973.) Not long after that, and after more conversations with Ellis, he came up with another idea that further streamlined the original concept. This is almost the precise formulation for what would later be known as the Diffie-Hellman key exchange. As far as Williamson is concerned, though, it was pretty much a consequence of the first paper, so obvious that he felt in no hurry to circulate it. "It's slightly easier," he says. "It really didn't feel like such a big step."

Now GCHQ had not one but two means of implementing James Ellis's heresy. But just as the agency had been suspicious of Ellis's initial plan, it moved ultra-cautiously with these two schemes. "First of all, we wanted to make sure it was secure," says Cocks.

Oddly, one factor ruling against nonsecret encryption was the pure beauty of Cocks's scheme and Williamson's second implementation. "It's enticing and nice," says Williamson, "but elegance is not what we've looked for before in cipher systems. There's a basic principle that neat and tidy problems have neat and tidy solutions, and messy problems don't have neat and tidy solutions. Now, most of cipher design is essentially messy; it's not neat and tidy and mathematical. So we're pretty comfortable that people are not going to be able to break those things, because even if you hack away at it, you're not going to suddenly find a little magic screw that if you unscrew it, everything falls to pieces. But in all this stuff with public key, there absolutely may be a magic screw. Some graduate student mathematician could really cause a disaster."

So concerned was GCHQ with this issue that it not only looked at the schemes internally—finding no inherent flaws—but also took the unusual step of going to a renowned outsider, professor R. F. Churchhouse, giving him the mathematics of Cocks's idea and asking if it was secure. Churchhouse concluded that as long as no one figured out a fast way of factoring large numbers—something that no mathematician had ever come close to—the scheme *was* secure.

The agency ultimately figured that of the two methods, Williamson's was preferable because its particular functions were easier to work with than the huge numbers that came with Cocks's multiplication-based scheme. Even so, the system was judged to be impractical. "The machines that would be used were expensive and very slow," explains Cocks. "It took minutes to generate [a key]. We looked at the circumstances under which you would find it useful to have a machine that took that long to produce [keys] and immediately thought the applications were too limited to make it worth floating."

Inside GCHQ, the conventional wisdom had shifted from *It's impossible* to *It's impractical*. And too many people were still terrified by the method's "nonsecret" aspect. Perhaps, went the thinking, such a radically new kind of cryptography might have weaknesses too subtle to detect, weaknesses that an enemy might use to break the system.

Even Malcolm Williamson believed that the whole venture was too risky. When he finally wrote up the revised version of his key scheme, he cited these reservations as the reason for the two-year delay. "I find myself in an embarrassing position," he wrote. "Having written [my first paper], I have come to doubt the whole theory of nonsecret encryption. The trouble is that I have no proof that the method . . . is genuinely secure." Later in the paper, however, he complains that "I feel that there should be a flaw in the security of the method. But I cannot find anything wrong with it and would be grateful if anyone else can."

No one did. But by then it had tacitly been concluded at GCHQ that it wasn't worth the effort to implement a public key cryptosystem.

In 1976, of course, Diffie and Hellman presented their findings, first in January (after circulating drafts informally even before that), then in their November revision, "New Directions in Cryptography." This was followed in 1977 by the RSA paper. The authors won fame if not instant fortune. But by ethics and law, the GCHQ scientists could not let a word slip of the real truth.

According to Cocks, James Ellis read the first paper, which outlined the idea but suggested no implementation, and said, "They're where I was in 1969." The Stanford team's second paper, of course, did suggest a means of implementation—one identical to the Malcolm Williamson solution. (It is unclear whether the Diffie-Hellman papers led him to write up his second, "small step" in implementing it, but the paper is dated August 1976, some months after Diffie and Hellman's first publication.) Cocks himself had temporarily left GCHQ for a stint at the ministry of defense, and first learned of the American discoveries in Martin Gardner's column in mid-1977—the one that described the RSA algorithm that he had first discovered three years earlier. "I was surprised," he says.

Certainly by then, the British cryptographers were keeping track of their counterparts outside the shadow world. And later in 1977, it obviously caused them consternation when they learned that both Stanford University and MIT were, respectively, planning to patent the Diffie-Hellman and RSA algorithms—both of which were originally conceived at CESG. Williamson in particular was outraged.

"I tried to get [GCHQ] to block the U.S. patent," he says. "We could have done that, but in fact the people higher up didn't want to. Patents are complicated." Specifically there was a question as to whether one could obtain a patent under British law for what was essentially a mathematical algorithm. And of course, there were security issues. It wouldn't do for the GCHQ to let outsiders know what its people were thinking. "The advice we received was 'Don't bother,' " says Cocks. Williamson, who still believes that his bosses erred in this case, recalls the chief scientist eventually coming to him and saying, "No, we're not going to block the patent."

So the shadow world kept quiet.

Thus, the timidity and isolation of what Ellis called the "closed community" led to a creative failure: despite its head start, it essentially ceded the public key idea to the outsiders who used it to build not only an alternative community, but also an entire industry. (The first product known to have used public key technology coming out of the NSA or GCHQ was the former's STU-III secure telephone, which rolled out in 1987, long after the Diffie-Hellman paper was published. By then RSA Data Security was on its way toward offering easy-to-use crypto solutions.)

Also, by shunting the idea of public key cryptography aside, the government people were unable to see some of the most important aspects of their own discovery. Chief among them was the idea that public key cryptography was as valuable for its ability to authenticate message senders (the digital signature aspect) as it was for its encryption properties. What's more, in rejecting nonsecret encryption as impracticably slow, the agencies missed what turned out to be a simple solution to that problem: using the nonsecret algorithms in conjunction with conventional, symmetrical-key systems. Once Diffie and Hellman published their work, it didn't take long for creative minds in the private sector to figure out that these "hybrid" systems were the future of privacy technologies.

This was only one of the public key–based innovations that were to arise from the freewheeling exchanges that occurred in an atmosphere of openness. There would be digital cash (anonymous or traceable), secret sharing, digital certificates, digital time stamping, electronic receipts, remote gambling . . . any number of amazing variations by academics, commercial scientists, and cypherpunks. As a result of these efforts, public key became ubiquitous, on every copy of Netscape and Lotus Notes, embedded in Windows and Macintosh, and, inevitably, in everyone's wallet—with no thanks to the closed community and owing everything to the open one.

Should GCHQ and its partners have worked harder to make the ideas viable? Could they have come up with some of those innovations? Perhaps. But while it's easy to fault the intelligence community for not implementing their original ideas, there's another side to the story.

Looking at it from a national security point of view, prudence made sense. It was one thing to implement a totally new system in the private sector, where using any kind of crypto to secure data was a novelty in itself. But doing so for government secrets, where reliable systems were already providing protection in life-and-death situations, posed a different kind of risk. "The government has to be very cautious," says Williamson. "It's much more important to secure some of this stuff than, say, banking transactions or Internet communications, or what the next model Ford is going to look like. If I were on the top of the pyramid then, would I have dared to implement it? What was the chance that somebody would find that magic screw that unlocks everything?"

Williamson also makes no apologies for the intelligence community's failure to discovery any of the marvelous innovations that sprang from the original concept of the split-key system. GCHQ, the argument goes, was essentially a spy and security agency, and had no interest in developing the sort of technologies that would provide benefits to the public at large (even if the public does pay their salaries). "There's a basic core of things the government has to do," Williamson says, "and the rest is probably better done by private industry." The only reason for the agency to keep working on the technologies was to see whether it could improve the sorts of activities that GCHQ was already performing.

But by not exploiting nonsecret encryption, the intelligence people were quite possibly missing an important opportunity to do just that. In 1982, years after GCHQ had all the information it needed to implement a public key system, the British agency suffered one of its worst scandals when an employee named Geoffrey Prime sold crucial information to the Russians. During that general time period, the NSA also had huge security failures, in infamous cases involving the Walker family, and Christopher Boyce and Andrew Lee. These involved the transfer of invaluable key material that wouldn't have existed in a public key system. It wasn't really surprising that the agencies could be compromised in this manner—after all, the difficulty in protecting these keys was a well-identified problem. The problem, in fact, that James Ellis had set out to solve.

So why hadn't the agencies moved decisively in exploring nonsecret encryption–based alternatives to their systems? In the final reckoning, nonsecret encryption was too much a departure from the norm. It was radical and risky—appealing traits to an entrepreneur but terrifying ones to a bureaucrat. "You've got to remember," says Malcolm Williamson, "this is the civil service. I mean, this is something new and different. 'Let's ignore it. Let's sweep it under the carpet.' "

Do the GCHQ scientists feel shortchanged at seeing others win acclaim for what they originally discovered? They claim not to, and believe they also speak for James Ellis on this point. "Ellis got internal recognition," says Cocks, who himself feels perfectly comfortable with the situation. "You accept that [when you work for GCHQ]. Internal recognition is all you get."

Williamson also rejects the idea that their silence was the raw end of a Faustian bargain cut when they entered the shadow world. To the contrary, he says that the disadvantaged ones are crypto people who *don't* work for the government. "I sometimes wonder why people on the outside work on cryptography," he says. "What's their reason for it? Clearly, governments have good reason for this—they want to secure their own communications, they want to read communications of other countries. Those are important jobs. Who would want to sit in a university and do that sort of thing? It's sort of like being a shipbuilder and insisting on living in Iowa." (Williamson himself, after some years working in the private sector, is now an American citizen—and is back in the shadow world, working for a nonprofit think tank that does classified defense work.)

But James Ellis apparently had thoughts of his place in posterity. "His career wasn't going anywhere," says Nick Patterson. "I would guess he was frustrated and viewed it as he did his previous disappointment with the radio invention." In 1985, he wrote a paper specifically to set the general public straight on just who invented public key cryptography. In the opening paragraphs, he explains that while secrecy is utterly crucial in his business, there are circumstances when it can be put aside "in the interests of historical accuracy after it has been demonstrated clearly that no further benefit can be obtained from continued secrecy." Given that, he continued, "it is now appropriate to tell the story."

Clearly, he hoped to establish his claim. The paper itself ends by emphasizing, for anyone thick enough to have missed the point, that it was "some time after the basic work was done" that Diffie and Hellman made what he called the rediscovery of the nonsecret encryption techniques. But if Ellis hoped that his account would quickly find its way outside the closed community, he was to be bitterly disappointed. Year after year went by and his attempt to set the record straight remained classified. His superiors felt it was not time yet. Nor was it time five years after he wrote it. Or ten years.

So why did they finally allow the papers to see daylight in December 1997, twelve years after Ellis compiled the history and almost twenty years after a brainstorm that would shake cryptography itself? Cliff Cocks says that the impetus was a speech he was scheduled to give around that time, on a variation of what will always be called the RSA algorithm. But Malcolm Williamson is more frank on the issue. The papers were all ready to go, he says, but could not be published "until a certain person retired."

That retirement apparently occurred before December 23, 1997, when GCHQ finally posted the original papers of Ellis, Cocks, and Williamson on its Web site, along with the "History of Non-Secret Encryption" that Ellis had written in 1985. But the release came too late for Ellis. Barely a month before the world learned of his crowning achievement, James H. Ellis died.

But not before he got to meet his counterpart in the "open community." For years Whit Diffie had been wondering about rumors that public key cryptography had indeed been discovered by the spooks. In the late 1970s NSA director Bobby Inman made a point of informing cryptographer Gus Simmons, who was writing the cryptography entry for the *Encyclopedia Britannica*, that it was an NSA invention. Diffie once pressed NSA deputy director Howard Rosenblum on the matter and was surprised that Rosenblum referred him not to anyone behind the Triple Fence but to a British GCHQ engineer he'd never heard of. Without stating his motivation—he hoped it would be obvious—he called Ellis, who indicated he might also like a meeting.

It was September 1982. Diffie had a trip planned to Paris, and his itinerary allowed a visit to Cheltenham. Diffie and his wife Mary Fischer left Paris to the sound of Gregorian chants blaring from every radio and television: it was the funeral of Princess Grace of Monaco. Diffie and Fischer flew to Heathrow and went to Salisbury for the weekend. Then he drove alone to Cheltenham.

Ellis lived on the outskirts of town; from the back of the house the ground fell off steeply, and one had a beautiful view of the town below.

He called it the Dilkusha House, which means "little delight" in Persian. In the backyard he raised bees. Ellis in his late fifties was a tall man, going gray. His wife was friendly; they had a daughter bound to attend the London School of Economics. After some small talk with Ellis's wife, Diffie and Ellis headed to a pub.

Diffie turned to Ellis as they pulled out of the driveway. "Tell me," he said, "how you invented nonsecret encryption."

"Who says I did?" asked James Ellis.

Diffie gave him the NSA official's name.

"Do you work for him?" asked Ellis. Diffie said no. He was not part of the closed community.

After a bit more of this back-and-forth, Diffie realized that Ellis wasn't going to talk about it. Indeed, Diffie would meet Ellis several times more, and while they would come closer to discussing the subject, Ellis would never really lay out the story of nonsecret encryption as clearly as he did in his papers. But the two scientists would become friends. Diffie's wife, after getting to know Ellis, would come to see a clear connection between Ellis and her husband. "They're both mystics," says Mary Fischer.

Who knows what was going through James Ellis's head that day? He was a man who came across a revolutionary idea and lived to see others win fame for its reinvention; who took pains to write a paper outlining his contribution and waited, in vain, for it to be published in his lifetime; who saw his idea, when presented by others, not only flourish but create a new industry and a new community and a virtual transformation of the subject—so thorough a shift that even the shadow world would never be the same. But he could not, and would not, break the rules and share his secrets—not even to his private-sector doppelgänger.

Later at the pub, Ellis would get Diffie tipsy on hard cider while they spoke of anything but the matter that had drawn them together and permanently bound them. But before leaving the subject, Ellis couldn't resist a tacit acknowledgment, one that spoke volumes about the world he lived in and the new world of cryptography that Diffie was helping to create.

"You did more with it than we did," said the father of nonsecret encryption to the father of public key cryptography. And thereafter kept his secret.

The core of this book is a series of personal interviews conducted between 1992 and 2000. Throughout that period, I attended conferences, visited key sites, and performed my own version of Signals Intelligence, using the Internet's vast resources to gather information. (Monitoring discussions on sci.crypt or cypher punks@toad.com was almost a full-time job.) Besides published texts, sources include government and court documents and memos, as well as corporate memos and reports.

The Loner

Besides personal interviews and communications, the Diffie material is supplemented by unpublished autobiographical notes, "Personal Memories on the Discovery of Public Key Cryptography," July 1981.

Page

7 **classical cryptographic systems** Sources for background on conventional cryptography include Kahn's *The Codebreakers* as well as Dorothy Denning's *Cryptography and Data Security*, Gaines's *Cryptanalysis*, Wrixton's *Codes and Ciphers*, and Gustavus J. Simmons's "Cryptology" entry in the *Encyclopaedia Britannica*.

7 **all things** *The Codebreakers*, p. 146.

11 **Enigma** Explained thoroughly in Hodge's *Turing: The Enigma*. There is a working Enigma unit at the National Cryptologic Museum in Maryland.

13 **National Security Agency** Bamford's *The Puzzle Palace* is the definitive study of the NSA. The *Baltimore Sun* did a well-researched series of articles by Scott Shane and Tom Bowman, "America's Fortress of Spies," December 3–15, 1995.

14 **By joining** "NSA Employees Security Manual," reprinted in *Phrack*, No. 45, March 30, 1994.

15 **Triple Fence** Bamford, *The Puzzle Palace*, p. 88. "The entire complex is surrounded by a ten-foot Cyclone fence crowned with multiple rows of barbed wire. . . . Inside this is another fence, consisting of five thin strands of high-voltage electrified wire attached to wooden posts planted around the building in a bed of green asphalt pebbles. Finally there is another tall Cyclone fence reinforcing the others."

17 **Shannon** His complete work can be found in N.J.A. Sloane and Aaron D. Wyner, *Shannon: Collected Papers*, Los Alamitos, CA, IEEE Press, 1993.

23 **attempt to sandbag** Bamford, *The Puzzle Palace*, p. 168. Bamford drew upon the papers of Lt. Gen. Marshall S. Carter to verify the NSA's attempts to quash Kahn's book.

25 **low on the hog** Whit Diffie e-mail to Eric Jungbluth, April 25, 1999.

27 **Friedman** The Friedman information was drawn from Kahn's *The Code-breakers* and Lambros D. Callimahos, "The Legendary William F. Friedman," *Cryptologia*, Vol. 15, No. 3, July 1991, p. 219.

28 **dinner plate** Bruce Schneier, *Applied Cryptography*, p. 29.

The Standard

For all that has been written about DES, there has never been a fully developed account of its development. Walt Tuchman gave a speech revised as "A Brief History of the Data Encryption Standard," in *Internet Besieged*, pp. 275–280. There are helpful sections about DES in Bamford's *The Puzzle Palace*, Diffie's *Privacy on the Line*, *Kahn on Codes*, Schneier and Banisar's *The Electronic Privacy Papers*, and Schneier's *Applied Cryptography*. A number of internal IBM memos helped me sort out the dates and provided detail.

Page

38 **key size** Whitfield Diffie, "Preliminary Remarks on the National Bureau of Standards Proposed Standard Encryption Algorithm for Computer Data Protection," May 1975.

39 **Feistel** Biographical information on this seminal figure is sparse. Diffie's *Privacy on the Line* does the best job.

40   **during the war**   David Kahn, unpublished notes on an interview with Feistel, March 29, 1976.

40   **told Whit Diffie**   Diffie, *Privacy on the Line*, p. 57.

40   **a co-worker**   Alan Konheim

41   **Computers now constitute**   Horst Feistel, "Cryptography and Computer Privacy," *Scientific American*, Vol. 228, No. 5, May 1973, pp. 15–23.

41   **IBM colleague**   Feistel told Diffie that the Watson Labs researcher John Lynn Smith came up with the name.

49   **his report**   "A Study of the Lucifer Crypto-Algorithm," August 18, IBM Memorandum, 1973.

52   **dez**   While the Kingston engineers commonly used this single syllable, the mathematicians at Watson fussily referred to it as *Dee-Ee-Ess*.

55   **technical article**   "The Data Encryption Standard and Its Strength Against Attacks," *IBM Research Journal*, Vol. 38, No. 3, May 1994.

63   **summary**   U.S. Senate, Select Committee on Intelligence, Unclassified Summary: *Involvement of the NSA in the Development of the Data Encryption Standard* (1978).

64   **differential cryptanalysis**   E. Biham and A. Shamir, *Differential Cryptanalysis of the Data Encryption Standard*, New York, Springer-Verlag, 1993.

64   **linear cryptanalysis**   M. Matsui, "Linear Cryptanalysis Method for DES Cipher," *Advances in Cryptology: Proceedings of Eurocrypt '93*, New York: Springer-Verlag, 1994.

Public Key

The key papers are Diffie and Hellman's "New Directions in Cryptography" (*IEEE Transactions on Information Theory*, Vol. IT-22, No. 6, November 1976) and Merkle's "Secure Communications Under Insecure Channels" (*Communications of the ACM*, Vol. 21, No. 4, 1978). Diffie recounts some history in "The First Ten Years of Public Key Cryptography" (in Simmons's *Contemporary Cryptography*) and "Personal Memories." More technical descriptions on how the actual algorithms work are found in Bruce Schneier's *Applied Cryptography* and Garfinkel's *PGP*.

Page

75   **the result**   Diffie, Whitfield, and Martin Hellman, "Multiuser Cryptographic Techniques," *Proceedings of the AFIPS National Computer Conference*, 1976, pp. 109–12.

84   **problems**   Diffie, "First Ten Years of Public Key Cryptography," op. cit.

Prime Time

Page
96 **going downhill ... extremely lucky** Adi Shamir, "Cryptography: Myths and Realities," ICAR Distinguished Lecture, delivered at Crypto '95, August 30, 1995.

97 **factoring** Len Adleman, "Algorithmic Number Theory—The Complexity Contribution." Unpublished paper.

98 **The problem of distinguishing** Ibid.

101 **Technical Memo** Later revised and published as R. A. Rivest, A. Shamir, and L. Adleman, "A Method for Obtaining Digital Signatures and Public Key Cryptosystems," *Communications of the ACM*, Vol. 21 (2), pp. 120–26, February 1978.

104 **Gardner's column** "A New Kind of Cipher That Would Take Millions of Years to Break," *Scientific American*, Vol. 237, No. 2, August 1977.

106 **Church** U.S. Senate, Select Committee on Intelligence, Subcommittee on Intelligence and the Rights of Americans, Foreign Intelligence Surveillance Act of 1978, Hearings, Ninety-fifth Cong. Second Sess. (1978). Bamford's *The Puzzle Palace* offers a concise summary of Shamrock and Church's investigation.

107 **National Science Foundation** The NSF events were revealed in U.S. House of Representatives, Committee of Government Operations, Government Information, and Individual Rights Subcommittee, *The Government's Classification of Private Ideas*, Ninety-sixth Cong., Second Sess. (1980). Bamford, Diffie and Landau and Gina Bari Kolata, "Computer Encryption and the National Security Agency Connection," *Science*, Vol. 97, July 29, 1977, pp. 438–40 also describes the activities.

110 **J. A. Meyer** The article was "Crime Deterrent Transponder System," *Transactions on Aerospace and Electronics Systems* Vol. 7, No. 1, January 1971.

110 **Confirmed the rumors** Deborah Shapley and Gina Kolata, "Cryptology: Scientists Puzzle over Threat to Open Research, Publication," *Science*, Vol. 197, September 30, 1977, pp. 1345–349.

113 **I have tenure** Malcolm Browne, "Scientists Accuse Security Agency of Harassment Over Code Studies," *New York Times*, October 18, 1977.

114 **As usual with NSA** A. Shamir, "Cryptography: Myths and Realities," op. cit.

115 **Davida** Deborah Shapley, "DOD Vacillates on Wisconsin Cryptography Work," *Science*, Vol. 201, July 14, 1978, p. 141. Louis Kruh, "Cryptology and the Law—VII," *Cryptologia*, Vol. 10, No. 4, October 1986, p. 248. Also Bamford's *The Puzzle Palace*, pp. 449–50.

116 **Nocolai** Deborah Shapley, "NSA Slaps Secrecy Order on Inventors' Communications Patent," *Science*, Vol., 201, September 8, 1978, pp. 891–94.

Also Louis Kruh "Cryptology and the Law—VII," *Science*, "DOD Vacillates . . ." and Bamford's *The Puzzle Palace*, pp. 446–51.

117 **soft sell** Statement given in U.S. House of Representatives, Committee of Government Operations, Government Information, and Individual Rights Subcommittee, *The Government's Classification of Private Ideas*, hearing cited above. Ninety-sixth Cong., Second Sess. (1980)

119 **bombshell** John M. Harmon, "Constitutionality Under the First Amendment of ITAR Restrictions of Public Cryptography," memo to Dr. Frank Press, science advisor to the president, May 11, 1978. Reprinted in Hoffman's *Building in Big Brother*.

119 **brilliant new lawyer** His name was Dan Silver.

121 **went public** Deborah Shapley, "Intelligence Agency Chief Seeks 'Dialogue' with Academics," *Science*, Vol. 202, October 27, 1978, pp. 407–9.

121 **public speech** Inman's address to the Armed Forces Communication and Electronics Association is reprinted as "The NSA Perspective on Telecommunications Protection in the Nongovernmental Sector" in Schneier and Banisar's *The Electronic Privacy Papers*, p. 347.

124 **minority report** "The Case Against Restraints on Non-governmental Research in Cryptography," reprinted in *Cryptologia*, Vol. 5, No. 3, July 1981, p. 143.

Selling Crypto

Some of this material was drawn from taped journals and documents of early RSA provided by Jim Bidzos. There is also a good account of RSA's origins in Garfinkel's *PGP*.

Page

128 **Diffie later recounted** Diffie, "The First Ten Years of Public Key Cryptography," op. cit.

129 **seen this territory** Diffie, *Privacy on the Line*, p. 283.

Patents and Keys

Page

157 **Project Overtake** Bob Davis, "A Supersecret Agency Finds Selling Secrecy to Others Isn't Easy," *Wall Street Journal*, March 28, 1988.

158 **public interview** The official was David McMais, chief of staff for information security.

165 **"mental poker"** A. Shamir, R. A. Rivest, and L. Adleman, "Mental Poker," MIT/LCS Technical Memo 125, February 1979.

165 **"secret sharing"** A. Shamir, "How to Share a Secret," *Communications of the ACM*, Vol. 24, No. 11, November 1979, pp. 612–13. Shamir and G. R. Blakley are generally granted shared credit for the innovation.

166 **Mafia-owned store** A. Shamir, lecture at Securicom '89, quoted in Schneier's *Applied Cryptography*, p. 92.

166 **Landau** "Zero Knowledge and the Department of Defense," *Notices of the American Mathematical Society* (Special Article Series), Vol. 35, No. 1 (1988), pp. 5–12.

166 **Merkle** John Markoff, "Paper on Codes Is Sent Despite U.S. Objections," *New York Times*, August 9, 1989.

177 **NIST,** "A Proposed Federal Information Processing Standard for the Digital Signature Standard (DSS)," *Federal Register*, Vo. 56, August 1991, p. 169.

178 **white flag** NIST memo, "Twenty-third Meeting of the NIST/NSA Technical Working Group," March 18, 1991.

179 **the wrong agency** Diffie, *Privacy on the Line*, p. 74.

181 **"What crypto policy"** Rivest's remarks were made at the 1992 Computers, Freedom, and Privacy Conference.

182 **National Security Decision Directive** Background on NSDD 145 can be found in Diffie's *Privacy on the Line*, Schneier and Banisar's *The Electronic Privacy Papers*, and Tom Athanasiou, "Encryption: Technology, Privacy, and National Security," *Technology Review*, August–September 1986.

183 **orchestrated** Clinton Brooks, Memo, April 28, 1992.

183 **Memorandum of Understanding** The MOU between the directors of NIST and the NSA "concerning the implementation of Public Law 100-235" is reprinted in Schneier and Banisar's *The Electronic Privacy Papers*, pp. 401–4.

183 **General Accounting Office** "Communications Privacy: Federal Policy and Actions," GAO/OSI-92-2-3 (November 1993).

184 **hearings** U.S. House of Representatives, Economic and Commercial Law Subcommittee of the Judiciary Committee, *The Threat of Foreign Economic Espionage to U.S. Corporations*, April 29 and May 7, 1992, 102d Congress, Second Sess.

Crypto Anarchy

Some portions of this chapter draw on my previous articles, "Crypto Rebels," *Wired*, May/June 1993, and "E-Money (That's What I Want)," *Wired*, December 1994.

Page

191 **Merritt** Background on Charlie Merritt was drawn in part from Garfinkel's *PGP* and Maureen Harrington, "Cyber Rebel," *Denver Post*, March 3, 1996.

196 **consultant** Identified as W. H. Murray in Jim Warren, "Is Phil Zimmermann Being Persecuted? Why? By Whom? Who's Next?" *MicroTimes*, April 1995.

197 **Goen** Ibid.

202 **1993 interview** Jon Lebkowsky, "The Internet Code Ring," *Fringeware Review*, No. 9, January 1995.

205 **Prince of Wales** Salley Bedell Smith, *Diana in Search of Herself*, New York, Signet, 2000, p. 247.

205 **Quarterbacks** Gordon Forbes, "Helmet Radios Give Scrambling New Meaning," *USA Today*," April 7, 1994.

208 **a speech** Gilmore's talk is reprinted as "Preserving Privacy in America," *Intertek*, Vol. 3, No. 2, Summer, 1991.

210 **Crypto Anarchist Manifesto** Reprinted in Ludlow's *High Noon on the Electronic Frontier*, pp. 237–39.

212 **Cypherpunk Manifesto** Posted to cypherpunk listserv October 5, 1992.

213 **Parker** "Crypto and Avoidance of Business Information Anarchy," speech to the ACM Conference on Computer and Communication Security, November 1993.

215 **Numbers** In David Chaum, editor, *Smart Card 2000*, North Holland, 1991.

216 **Dining** David Chaum, "The Dining Cryptographer's Problem: Unconditional Sender and Receiver Untraceability," *Journal of Cryptology*, Vol. 1, No. 1, 1988, pp. 65–75.

221 **University of Washington** Matt Thomlinson, posting to cypherpunk listserv, January 30, 1994.

223 **Anonymity** A good discussion is found in Jonathan D. Wallace, "Nameless in Cyberspace: Anonymity on the Internet," *Cato Briefing Papers*, No. 54, December 8, 1999.

224 **BlackNet** May's posting is reprinted in Ludlow's *High Noon on the Electronic Frontier*, pp. 241–44.

225 **Parker** "Crypto and Avoidance," op. cit.

The Clipper Chip

The bulk of this chapter was derived from personal interviews and a wealth of declassified documents supplied to me by EPIC or John Gilmore. My contemporary account of the Clipper battle was "The Cypherpunks vs. Uncle Sam," *Sunday*

New York Times Magazine, June 12, 1994. Another helpful article was Bob Davis, "Clipper Chip Is Your Friend," *Wall Street Journal*, March 22, 1994.

Page

231 **Issue One** Meetings of the "TWG" were summarized in (now partially declassified) memoranda. In the first meeting, held at Fort Meade on May 5, 1989, NIST called public key "TWG Issue Number One."

232 **Capstone** The workings of Capstone and Clipper are described in more detail in Dorothy Denning, "The Clipper Encryption System," *American Scientist*, Vol. 81, July–August 1993.

234 **presented these . . . draconian and invasive** Lynn McNulty, NIST Memo, "Summary of 7/23-24/92 Off-Site Meeting," July 27, 1992.

237 **Sessions call** David Stipp, "Techno-Hero or Public Enemy," *Fortune*, November 11, 1996.

239 **Barlow** "Jackboots on the Infobahn," reprinted in Ludlow's *High Noon on the Electronic Frontier*, pp. 207–13.

240 **going forward** J. R. Davis, "Use of Clipper Chip in AT&T TSD 3600 During Phase of Production," memo to Sessions, December 23, 1992.

240 **Encryption, Law Enforcement** Briefing document sent to Tenet, February 19, 1993.

244 **slide show** "Telecommunications Overview" prepared by the FBI's Advanced Telephony Unit.

248 **Barlow** "Jackboots on the Infobahn," reprinted in Ludlow's *High Noon on the Electronic Frontier*, pp. 207–13.

249 **Denning** See Steven Levy, "Clipper Chick," *Wired*, September 1996.

249 **Pilgrim maiden** Sterling, *The Hacker Crackdown*, p. 299.

249 **important step** "Statement by the Press Secretary," The White House, April 16, 1993.

250 ***Times* article** John Markoff, "New Communication System Stirs Talk of Privacy vs. Eavesdropping," April 16, 1993.

252 **It's not America** Steven Levy, "Uncle Sam."

252 **Safire** "Sink the Clipper," *New York Times*, February 4, 1994.

253 **lion's den** Baker's speech was adapted as "Don't Worry Be Happy: Why Clipper Is Good for You," in *Wired*, June 1994.

253 **Skipjack** E. F. Brickell, D. E. Denning, S. T. Kent, D. P. Maher, and W. Tuchman, "Skipjack Review—Interim Report," unpublished, July 28, 1993.

253 **Micali** Silvio Micali, "Fair Cryptosystems," Technical Memo, Laboratory for Computer Science, MIT, August 21, 1992.

254 **Hall of Fame** Levy, "Uncle Sam . . . ,"

254 **War** Tim May, "The Coming Police State," posting to cypherpunk listserv March 9, 1994.

254 **hearings**   U.S. Senate, Committee on the Judiciary, Subcommittee on Technology and the Law, *Clipper Chip Key Escrow Encryption Program*, hearings, May 3, 1994, 103d Congress, Second Sess.

260 **there it was**   John Markoff, "Flaw Discovered in Federal Plan for Wire-tapping," *New York Times*, June 2, 1994. Blaze's paper on the Clipper flaw is "Protocol Failure in the Escrowed Encryption Standard," *Proceedings of the Second ACM Conference on Computer and Communications Security*, November, 1994.

261 **poll**   Philip Elmer-Dewitt, "Who Should Keep the Keys?" *Time*, March 14, 1994.

263 **Gejdenson and Cantwell**   U.S. House of Representatives, Committee on Foreign Affairs, Subcommittee on Economic Policy, Trade, and Environment, *Export Controls on Mass Market Software*, Hearings, October 12, 1993, 103d Congress, First Sess.

267 **Gore's letter**   Reprinted in Schneier and Banisar's *The Electronic Privacy Papers*, p. 692.

Slouching Toward Crypto

Some of this chapter was drawn from my article "Wisecrackers," *Wired*, April 1996.

Page

271 **his talk**   Robert Morris, "Ways of Losing Information," Invited Lecture at Crypto '95, August 29, 1995.

275 **quantum factorization**   Giles Brassard, *CryptoBytes*, Vol. 1, No. 1, Spring, 1995.

287 **the local paper**   David Bank, "The Keys to the Kingdom," *San Jose Mercury News*, June 27, 1994.

289 **hearing**   *Export Controls on Mass Market Software.*

291 **filed a complaint**   Accounts of the search warrant are told in Wendy M. Grossman, "alt.scientology.war," *Wired*, December 1995 and Wallace and Morgan's *Sex, Laws, and Cyberspace*.

294 **lost the patents**   The story is most completely recounted in "How Digicash Blew Everything," originally published in Dutch-language *Next! Magazine*.

296 **classified details**   In Dam and Lin's *Cryptography's Role in Securing the Information Society*,

297 **ended in flames**   Judge Charles R. Richey, Memorandum Opinion, *Karn* v. *State*, CA-95-1812 (D.C.C), March 22, 1996.

297 **Bernstein**   Besides personal interviews and court documents, additional background on Bernstein was drawn from Peter Cassidy, "Reluctant Hero," *Wired*, June 1996.

299 **no exempt groups**   Tapes Bernstein made of this and other conversations are included in the court record.

302 **DES-cracking machine**   The project is described in great detail in the Electronic Frontier Foundation's *Cracking DES*.

303 **the objective**   Freeh's remarks were made at the Conference on Global Cryptography, September 26, 1994.

306 **Weldon**   Mike Godwin, "The New Cryptographic Landscape," *E-Commerce Law Weekly*, Vol. 1, No. 1, October 19, 1999.

307 **price tag**   Don Clark, "Bidzos Holds Key to Guarding Internet Secrets," *Wall Street Journal*, April 16, 1996.

307 **lawsuits**   Though much of the case is sealed, some documents in *RSA Data Security, Inc.* vs. *Cylink Corporation and Caro-Kann Corporation* are public.

311 **expiration date**   In fact, two of the Stanford patents, covering Diffie-Hellman key exchange and knapsacks (and arguably the concept of public key itself) had expired in 1997. The MIT patent covering RSA expired September 20, 2000.

Epilogue: The Open Secret

Some of the information here first appeared in *Wired*, April 1999, "The Open Secret," which was the first complete account of the Communications-Electronics Security Group (CESG) advances. (Simon Singh's account in *The Code Book* was to follow.) Ellis's paper "The Story of Non-Secret Encryption" lays the outline for the discoveries and, like the other CESG papers, is available on its Web site. Some of Clifford Cocks's remarks here were drawn from "The Invention of Non-Secret Encryption," a talk given at Bletchley Park on June 20, 1998, at a "History of Cryptography" seminar hosted by the British Society for the History of Mathematics.

Page

316 **Project C43**   The paper is still not available. It is unclear whether this research was related to speech-encryption work known as "Project X" in Bell Labs. In *Turing: The Enigma*, Andrew Hodges describes Alan Turing's participation in that project, which also benefited from the input of Claude Shannon (also at Bell Labs then) and William Friedman. If there was any cross-influence of those projects, that means that public key's heritage directly flows from the century's major prepublic key cryptographic figures.

323 **finished his memo**   M. J. Williamson, "Non-Secret Encryption Using a Finite Field," CESG Report, January 21, 1974. Cocks's scheme was "A Note on Non-Secret Encryption," CESG Report, November, 20, 1973.

325   **small step**   M. J. Williamson, "Thoughts on Cheaper Non-Secret Encryption," CESG Report, August 10, 1976.

327   **Prime**   Prime's story is told in the afterword of Bamford's *The Puzzle Palace*.

327   **Walker family**   The Walker tale is nicely laid out in Howard Blum's *I Pledge Allegiance . . .* New York, Simon & Schuster, 1987.

327   **Boyce and Lee**   Boyce and Lee are the protagonists in Robert Lindsey's *The Falcon and the Snowman*, New York, Simon & Schuster, 1979.

bibliography

Bamford, James. *The Puzzle Palace*. New York: Penguin, 1983.

Boyer, Carl B. revised by Uta C. Merzbach. *A History of Mathematics*. Wiley, 1989.

Burham, David. *The Rise of the Computer State*. New York: Random House, 1983.

Campbell, Jeremy. *Grammatical Man: Information, Entropy, Language and Life*. New York: Simon & Schuster, 1982.

Card, Orson Scott. *Ender's Game*. New York: Tor Books, 1985.

Computer Professionals for Social Responsibility. *Cryptography and Privacy Sourcebook*, Years 1991–1993.

Dam, Kenneth, and Herbert Lin, eds., National Research Council. *Cryptography's Role in Securing the Information Society*. National Academy Press, 1996.

Denning, Dorothy E. *Cryptography and Data Security*. Reading, MA: Addison-Wesley, 1982.

———. *Information Warfare and Security*. Reading, MA: Addison-Wesley, 1999.

———, and Peter J. Denning. *Internet Besieged*, ACM Press, 1998.

Diffie, Whitfield, and Susan Landau. *Privacy on the Line*. Boston: MIT Press, 1998.

Electronic Frontier Foundation. *Cracking DES: Secrets of Encryption Research, Wiretap Politics & Chip Design*. Sebastopol, CA: O'Reilly, 1998.

Electronic Privacy Information Center. *Cryptography and Privacy Sourcebook*. Years 1994–1998.

Gaines, Helen Fouche. *Cryptanalysis*. New York: Dover, 1939.

Gardner, Martin. *Penrose Tiles to Trapdoor Ciphers*. New York: Freeman, 1989.

Garfinkcl, Simpson. *PGP: Pretty Good Privacy*. Sebastopol, CA: O'Reilly, 1995.

Godwin, Mike. *Cyber Rights*. New York: Times Books, 1998.

Hodges, Andrew. *Turing: The Enigma*. New York: Simon & Schuster, 1983.

Hoffman, Lance, ed. *Building Big Brother*. New York: Springer-Verlag, 1995.

Kahn, David. *The Codebreakers: The Story of Secret Writing*. New York: Macmillan, 1967.

———. *Kahn on Codes: Secrets of the New Cryptology*. New York: Macmillan, 1983.

Kelly, Kevin. *Out of Control*. Reading, MA: Addison Wesley, 1994.

Lessig, Lawrence. *Code and Other Laws of Cyberspace*. New York: Basic Books, 1999.

Levy, Steven. *Hackers: Heroes of the Computer Revolution*. New York: Doubleday, 1984.

Ludlow, Peter, ed. *High Noon on the Electronic Frontier: Conceptual Issues in Cyberspace*. Boston: MIT Press, 1996.

Rosenheim, Shawn James. *The Cryptographic Imagination: Secret Writing from Edgar Poe to the Internet*. Baltimore, MD: Johns Hopkins University Press, 1997.

Schneier, Bruce. *Applied Cryptography*, second edition. New York: Wiley, 1996.

———, and David Banisar, eds. *The Electronic Privacy Papers: Documents on the Battle for Privacy in the Age of Surveillance*. New York: Wiley Computer Publishing, 1997.

Simmons, Gustavus J., ed. *Contemporary Cryptography: The Science of Information Integrity*. New York: IEEE Press, 1992.

Singh, Simon. *The Code Book: The Evolution of Secrecy from Mary Queen of Scots to Quantum Cryptography*. New York: Doubleday, 1999.

Sterling, Bruce. *The Hacker Crackdown*. New York: Bantam, 1993.

Wallace, Jonathan D., and Mark Mangan. *Sex, Laws, and Cyberspace*. New York: Holt, 1996.

Wrixon, Fred B. *Codes and Ciphers*. Englewood Cliffs, NJ: Prentice-Hall, 1992.

Zim, Herbert T. *Codes and Secret Writing*. New York: Morrow, 1948.

glossary

Capstone A National Security Agency–designed chip with capabilities for strong encryption and digital signatures, but with key escrow so authorities can read encrypted messages.

Cipher Also known as a cryptographic algorithm, it is the mathematical function used to scramble and unscramble messages.

Ciphertext The (presumably unreadable) state of a message after it has been encrypted.

Clipper Chip The NSA-designed key escrow system earmarked for telephone devices. The tamperproof chip offered only the encryption and escrow features of the Capstone's system.

Communications Security (COMSEC) The practice of ensuring that codes are strong and well implemented. (This is half of the NSA's mission, along with SIGINT.)

Cryptanalysis Codebreaking—the black art of turning ciphertext back into plaintext without using the key.

Cryptography The use of secret codes and ciphers.

Cryptology The study and mathematics of secret codes and ciphers. Sometimes used interchangeably with cryptography.

Cryptosystem A means of encrypting data and performing other cryptographic functions, often synonymous with the algorithm that performs the actual scrambling.

Data Encryption Standard (DES) A cryptosystem developed by IBM, evolved from the earlier Lucifer. Though originally questioned by critics, this conventional cipher has proved secure, vulnerable only by what critics consider a weak provision for the length of its keys.

Diffie-Hellman Key Exchange The algorithm devised by Whit Diffie and Marty Hellman that allows two people to generate a secret key in such a way that each will possess it, but an eavesdropper listening to the entire exchange won't be able to construct it himself.

Digital Signature Mathematically generated cryptographic data that undeniably identify a message with its sender.

Digital Signature Algorithm (DSA) An algorithm, produced by the NSA, that the government endorsed as the Digital Signature Standard. It differs from the RSA signature scheme in that it does not encrypt information.

Encryption The act of scrambling information (into ciphertext) so that intercepted messages cannot be read.

Factoring The mathematical feat of taking a number produced by the multiplication of two smaller numbers and finding the original figures. This one-way function is the basis of the RSA algorithm.

Hash Function A cryptographic means of compressing a message so that it provides a compact "fingerprint" of the original.

IDEA A conventional cipher used by later versions of PGP, replacing the original "Bass-O-Matic."

Key The component of a cryptosystem that determines how the message will be scrambled. A key applied to a plaintext message becomes ciphertext; the same key (or in a public key system, a matching half of a key pair) will change it back.

Key Escrow A shortcut, or trapdoor, intentionally built into cryptosystems that allows authorities to quickly decrypt messages, ostensibly without otherwise compromising security.

Key Length The longer the key, the more difficult a cipher is to break by "brute force" (testing each different possibility until plaintext emerges). The range of all possible keys is called a keyspace. The amount of effort it takes to conduct a brute-force attack is the workfactor.

Knapsack Early public key cryptosystem, devised by Ralph Merkle, and subsequently broken.

Lucifer Conventional cryptosystem devised by Horst Feistel at IBM in the early 1970s. It was the basis for the 1975 Data Encryption Standard.

One-Time Pad The only mathematically unbreakable form of cipher; unwieldy as it requires a key length as long as the message itself and can never be reused.

One-Way Function A mathematical operation that is easy to calculate, but many times harder to reverse. A trapdoor one-way function has an additional feature in that someone with the proper information *can* reverse the calculation.

Plaintext The original, preencrypted form of a message.

Pretty Good Privacy (PGP) Phil Zimmermann's popular home-grown public key cryptosystem, distributed for free on the Internet beginning in 1991.

Private Key In a public key system, the private key is the component of the key pair that must be closely held: only by the use of it can one unscramble messages created by the holder's public key and "sign" messages to verify that the holder actually sent them.

Public Key The component of a key pair that allows others to send private messages to its holder. It is also used to verify digitial signatures. It can be widely distributed with no compromise in security.

Public Key Cryptography The breakthrough system devised by Diffie and Hellman in 1975 that eschews symmetric keys for a key pair.

Random Number Generator (RNG) A part of a computer-based cryptosystem that adds unpredictability to the way keys scramble the message.

RC2, RC4 Conventional ciphers created by Ron Rivest (the RC stands for Rivest cipher).

Remailer An Internet service that allows people to send electronic messages without revealing their identities.

RSA Algorithm The most popular public key cryptosystem, devised by Rivest, Shamir, and Adleman in 1977.

Signals Intelligence (SIGINT) The means of intercepting communications and, when necessary, breaking codes.

Skipjack A strong conventional encryption cipher, produced by the NSA, that was at the heart of the Capstone and Clipper schemes.

Symmetric Key Used in conventional cryptography, a single one of these is used by the sender of a message to scramble the text and by the receiver to unscramble it.

index

Abelson, Hal, 290
Access, 277
Adleman, Leonard, 93–101, 104,
    105, 112, 117–18, 126–37, 143,
    152, 153, 165, 193, 272, 308,
    313
Advanced Encryption Standard, 310
Albert, A. Adrian, 40–41
Alcorn, Al, 141
Allen, Lewis, 111
Allen, Robert, 237
Ambler, Ernest, 61
Andreessen, Marc, 277, 278
anonymity, 223–24
Anonymizer, 309
anonymous servers, *see* remailers
Apple Computer, 310
Applied Cryptography (Schneier),
    288–89, 297
ARPAnet, 20
AT&T Telephone Security Device,
    235–38, 240, 243–44, 246, 249,
    252, 254, 256–57
Atkins, Derek, 272, 273–76

Back, Adam, 276–77, 279
Baker, Stewart, 227–28, 229, 240,
    241–42, 245, 248, 252–53, 290,
    306
Bamford, James, 23, 116
Barlow, John Perry, 208, 239, 248
Bass-O-Matic, 194, 200
Bell Telephone, 316
Belove, Ed, 151
Bennett, Ralph, 137, 141, 142, 144
Berman, Jerry, 252
Berners-Lee, Tim, 277
Bernstein, Daniel, 297–302
Biden, Joseph, 195–96, 198
Bidzos, Jim, 138–45, 150–54,
    167–68, 171–77, 179–80,
    184–86, 193–94, 285–87, 307,
    308, 311–12
    Netscape and, 278
    PGP and, 195, 199, 200, 203–4,
    287–88
Biham, Eli, 200
Bina, Eric, 277
black box, 11

BlackNet, 224–25
Blatman, Peter, 67–68, 76
Blaze, Matthew, 256–60
block ciphers, 40
Brands, Stefan, 293
Branscombe, Lewis, 49, 51–52, 62
Branstad, Dennis, 181
Brassard, Giles, 275
Brickell, Ernie, 129, 253
Broken Seal, The (Farago), 17
Brooks, Clinton, 226–32, 234–38,
    241–43, 245, 248–51, 253–55,
    257, 267–68, 302
Brooks, Jack, 182, 183, 184
Brown, Ron, 246
browsers, 277–78, 279, 310
Bruce, Anni, 98
brute-force attacks, 38, 41–42, 57, 58,
    62, 63, 64, 87, 104, 259, 270,
    272, 276, 277, 281, 282
Burns, Conrad, 295, 304
Bush, George, 234–35, 239, 240, 242

Cantwell, Maria, 261, 263, 264–68,
    294, 304
Capstone, 232, 236–37, 238, 257, 260
Card, Orson Scott, 222–23
Carter, Marshall S., 23
cash-issuing machines, 43, 44, 45, 48
CASI (Cryptology Amateurs for Social
    Irresponsibility), 209–10
cellular phones, 205
Chaum, David, 126–27, 213–19, 220,
    223, 293–94, 309
checksum, 258–59
Cheney, Dick, 232
child pornography, 292
chips, 132–33, 134, 137
    escrow system and, 232–33; *see
    also* Clipper Chip
chip simulation, 133–35
Church, Frank, 106, 182, 230
Churchhouse, R. F., 324
Church of Scientology, 142, 144,
    290–92
Clark, Jim, 278

Clinton, Bill, 238–40, 242–48,
    249–50, 254, 257, 263, 296,
    303, 306, 311
Clipper Chip, 226, 238, 240, 241–68,
    283, 284, 286, 287, 294, 303, 305
Clipper III, 294–95
Cocks, Clifford, 315, 318, 319–25,
    328, 329
Codebreakers, The (Kahn), 6, 17, 21,
    22–24, 29
Cohn, Cindy, 300, 301
Collins, Mary, 5, 6–7
commodities jurisdiction (CJ),
    298–300
Communications Electronics Security
    Group (CESG), 315, 319, 321,
    325
Computer Professionals for Social
    Responsibility, 261
Computer Security Act, 182
Computer System Security and
    Privacy Advisory Board, 184
Coppersmith, Don, 55–56
Corry, Cecil C., 107, 108
Cremen, Pat, 133
Crowell, William, 270, 286
Cryptanalysis (Gaines), 7
cryptoactivism, 205–13
crypto anarchy, 210–13, 225
Crypto conferences, 125–28, 154,
    270–71
Cryptography Study Group, 123
currency, digital, 215–20, 223–25,
    293–94
Cybercash, 219, 294
Cygnus Support, 208, 212
Cylink, 168–73, 307–8
cypherpunks, 211–12, 213, 219–20,
    221–22, 223, 224, 225, 228, 252
    code breaking by, 272–77, 280,
    281–83, 302

Data Encryption Standard (DES),
    37–39, 52–66, 85, 122, 124, 132,
    148, 156–60, 163, 169, 201, 228,
    232, 263, 295, 302, 307, 309, 310

in AT&T device, 235, 237, 238, 246
key size of, 38–39, 57–64, 65, 157,
    160, 310
NSA and, 38–39, 52–57, 59–65,
    66, 122, 124, 156–60, 228, 232
triple, 62
Davida, George, 115–17, 123, 124,
    129
Davis, Ruth, 52
Demon. *See* Lucifer
Denning, Dorothy, 249, 250, 253, 257
Deutch, John, 245
differential cryptanalysis (T attack),
    55–56, 64, 200
Diffie, Whitfield, 3–13, 15–21, 24–31,
    33–36, 40, 53, 66–77, 82–95,
    97–100, 102, 107, 113, 114,
    136, 209, 214, 220, 237, 308,
    310, 313, 315, 325, 326, 328
    Clipper and, 255–56
    Crypto conferences and, 125, 126,
        127, 128, 129
    DES and, 38–39, 56, 59, 61, 66, 85
    Ellis and, 329–30
    RSA Data Security and, 140–41,
        152–53, 154
Diffie-Hellman algorithm, 84–86, 104,
    106, 131, 169–73, 237, 323, 325
Digicash, 218–19, 293, 294
Digital Privacy and Security Working
    Group, 255
Digital Signature Algorithm (DSA),
    178–81, 185, 186
digital signatures, *see* signatures, digital
Digital Telephony bill, 236, 244, 303
"Dining Cryptographers" problem,
    216–17
discrete exponentiation, 84
Doligez, Damien, 279–81
DSD-1, 45, 47, 51–52
Dwivedi, Narenda P., 111–12

E-Cash, 293–94
Edwards, Dan, 16
Eldridge, Alan, 156
ElGamal, Tehar, 179, 180

Elias, Peter, 32
Ellis, James, 313–19, 320–23, 325,
    326, 327–30
e-mail, 101–2, 137, 151–52, 186,
    192, 205, 244
Ender's Game (Card), 222–23
Enigma, 11, 89
escrow system, 229, 230–35, 236–38,
    239, 240–68, 283, 286, 294–95,
    303, 305
Espionage Act, 209
Euler, Leonhard, 99
export regulations, 109, 111–14,
    118–20, 123, 124, 175, 238,
    241, 243, 262–68, 279, 281,
    288–90, 294–95, 297–98, 302,
    305–7, 310
    Applied Cryptography and, 288–89,
        297
    key escrow and, 237, 241, 249, 267,
        294–95
    legislation to amend, 265–68
    Lotus Notes and, 149, 155–64,
        262–63, 284
    PGP and, 198, 203, 204
    Snuffle and, 300–302
E-ZPass, 218

Fabry, Robert, 80
factoring, 97–100, 102–3, 272–76
Fair Cryptosystems, 253
Farber, David, 250
FBI, 223, 225, 229, 231–32, 234,
    235–36, 239, 240, 242–46,
    258–59, 267, 303, 305, 306
Feistel, Horst, 30, 32, 39–43, 44–46,
    47–48, 54, 57, 59, 74–75
Finney, Hal, 278–79, 280, 281
Fischer, Addison, 184
Fischer, Mary, 3–5, 8, 24–27, 29, 31,
    33, 35–36, 67, 68, 69, 74, 308,
    329, 330
Fletcher, Betty, 302
Fougner, Robert, 169–70, 171–73,
    177, 180
Freeh, Louis, 223, 270, 303

freeware, 196, 204
Friedman, William, 27, 33, 208
Fuerth, Leon, 242, 246

Gaines, Helen Forché, 7
Gannett, E. K., 109, 111
Gardner, Martin, 103–5, 114, 174,
    189, 269, 273, 275, 325
Gates, Bill, 174, 177, 180, 241, 247,
    253, 266
Gauss, Carl Friedrich, 93, 94, 97–98,
    99
Gejdenson, Sam, 261, 263, 264
General Communication
    Headquarters (GCHQ), 313,
    314, 318–20, 322–29
Gersho, Alan, 125–26
Gill, John, 84
Gilmore, John, 167, 207–9, 210, 211,
    300, 302
Glaser, Edward, 48
Goen, Kelly, 197–98, 288, 309
Goldberg, Ian, 281, 282–83
Goodlatte, Robert, 304, 306
Gore, Al, 238–39, 240, 242–44, 246,
    247, 248, 254, 265–68, 285,
    294, 303, 306
Graff, Michael, 272, 273
Graham, Sue, 81
groupware, 145

Haber, Stuart, 256
Hammond, Larry, 119
Harbert, Don, 264
Harmon, John, 119, 120
Heiman, Bruce, 267, 304
Hellman, Martin, 31–39, 56, 59–67,
    74–77, 80, 82–84, 86–95,
    97–100, 102, 107, 109, 111–13,
    117, 123, 136, 154, 168, 250,
    260, 296, 313, 325, 326, 328
    Diffie-Hellman algorithm, 84–86,
    104, 106, 131, 169–73, 237,
    323, 325
Helsingius, Julf, 222, 290, 291–93,
    309

heuristic qualifiers, 47
Hoffman, Lance, 77, 78, 80, 214
Homer, Mike, 283
Hughes, Eric, 205–7, 208, 209,
    211–12, 221, 252
hybrid system, 86

IBM, 29, 30, 32, 37, 39–56, 58,
    59–64, 66, 138–40, 145–46,
    156, 186, 284, 286
Identification Friend or Foe (IFF),
    29–30, 39, 40, 68
identity proofs:
    digital signatures, see signatures,
        digital
    zero-knowledge, 165–66
Ingram, Tim, 120
Inman, Bobby Ray, 110–11, 115, 117,
    118–23, 124, 125, 164, 227,
    228, 252, 264, 297, 329
Intergraph, 254
International Data Encryption
    Algorithm (IDEA), 200–201, 270
Internet, 167, 196–98, 203, 204, 205,
    208, 229, 239, 261, 283, 311,
    312
    anonymity and, 223–24
    browsers and, 277–78, 279, 310
    factoring and, 273, 274
Iris Associates, 145, 146, 149, 150
ITAR, see export regulations
Izen, Ted, 135–36

Jefferson, Thomas, 89

Kahn, David, 6, 15, 17, 21–24, 27,
    29, 32, 40, 117
Kallstrom, James, 245, 246, 255
Kammer, Raymond, 183, 229–31,
    236
Kapor, Mitch, 146, 147, 148–49,
    150–51, 208
Karn, Phil, 289, 297
Kaufman, Charles, 286
Keane, William, 288
Kelly, Jack, 136, 137

Kerckhoffs, Auguste, 75
Kerry, Bob, 305
keys, 11, 34
  escrow system and, 229, 230–35,
    236–38, 239, 240–68, 283, 286,
    294–95, 303, 305
  nonsecret, 317–30
  pairs of, 69–71, 74, 93, 178
  public, see public key cryptography
  secret sharing of, 165
  size of, 38–39, 41–42, 57–64, 65,
    157, 160, 161–64, 186, 232,
    270, 275, 310
  symmetrical, 69–70, 77, 78, 148,
    318, 326
knapsacks, 86–88, 93, 127, 128–29,
  131, 136
  multiple-iteration, 129
  single-iteration, 127
  superincreasing, 87
Knuth, Donald, 83, 92, 102, 103
Kocher, Paul, 302
Kolata, Gina, 118
Konheim, Alan, 30–31, 41, 42, 44–45,
  46, 48, 59, 65
Kravitz, David, 178, 180
Kreps, Juanita, 117

Landau, Susan, 166
Larry King Live, 248
law enforcement, 229–30, 238, 240,
  241, 244, 245
Law Enforcement Access Field
  (LEAF), 233, 257–58
Leahy, Patrick, 254, 295, 304
Lee, Ronald, 290
Lenstra, Arjen, 273, 274
Lenstra, Hendrick, 127
Leyland, Paul, 272, 273
Limbaugh, Rush, 252
linear cryptanalysis, 64
Lloyds of London, 43, 45, 48
Lofgren, Zoe, 304, 306
Lotus, 145, 146, 149–52, 155–64,
  169, 173, 181, 192, 205, 229,
  262–63, 276, 284–86

Lucifer, 41–43, 44–45, 46–50, 57
  DSD-1, 45, 47, 51–52
  see also Data Encryption Standard

McCain, John, 305
McCarthy, John, 19–20, 31, 34, 36,
  67, 69
McConnell, Mike, 184, 242, 245, 246,
  254–55
McNulty, Lynn, 181, 186, 254
Mailsafe, 137, 145, 151–52, 193, 204
Mann, Bill, 28, 29, 69
Manzi, Jim, 147
Markoff, John, 259
May, Tim, 206, 207, 208, 209,
  210–11, 252, 254, 276
  BlackNet, 224–25
Mead, Carver, 132, 134
Merkle, Ralph C., 68, 76–83, 85–88,
  93, 113, 126–29, 131, 136,
  166–67, 208, 214, 253, 297–98,
  309, 313
Merritt, Charlie, 191, 192–93, 194,
  197
Metamorphic Systems, 190, 191
Meyer, Joseph A., 110–11, 112, 113,
  115
Meyer, Karl, 45, 59, 62
Micali, Silvio, 253
Microsoft, 174–77, 181, 186, 219,
  241, 262–63, 276, 284, 304, 310
  Access, 277
Moore's Law, 162, 206
Morris, Lew, 169
Morris, Robert, Sr., 270–72, 281, 302
Mosaic, 277–78
"Multiuser Cryptographic Techniques"
  (Diffie and Hellman), 75–76, 82,
  86
Murray, Patty, 304
Myhrvold, Nathan, 174–76, 177, 184,
  262, 266, 267
Mykotronx, 232, 254, 260

National Bureau of Standards (NBS),
  37, 38, 50–52, 57, 59, 60–61, 63

National Institute of Standards and
Technology (NIST), 173,
177–79, 181–86, 229, 231, 234,
236, 243, 254, 294, 310
National Research Council (NRC),
296–97, 305
National Science Foundation (NSF),
34, 107, 108, 117–18, 123, 126,
131
National Security Access Field
(NSAF), 284–85
National Security Agency (NSA),
13–16, 20, 26, 32, 34, 40, 42,
46, 106–8, 110–24, 125–29,
142, 152–54, 164–69, 175–85,
196, 199, 200, 203–5, 208,
226–32, 234–38, 265, 267, 268,
272, 284–87, 290, 302, 304,
306, 326, 329
    Clipper and, 238, 240–43, 246,
    253–55, 257, 258, 259, 260,
    262, 263, 264
    DES and, 38–39, 52–57, 59–65,
    66, 122, 124, 156–60, 228, 232
    Diffie and, 13, 26, 27–28, 33, 34,
    40, 66, 106, 107, 114
    dual roles of, 228
    GCHQ and, 313, 319
    Kahn and, 22–23, 27
    Lotus Notes and, 149, 150, 164,
    284–85
    NRC report and, 296
    NSAF and, 284–85
    Project Overtake of, 157–58
    security failures at, 327
    Snuffle and, 299
National Security Decision Directive,
182
Nelson, Mike, 239, 246, 247–48, 248,
253, 303
Netscape, 277, 278–83, 284
Neukom, Bill, 266
"New Directions in Cryptography"
(Diffie and Hellman), 86, 88–89,
90–94, 102, 147, 325, 326
New York Times, 259–60, 282–83

Nicolai, Carl, 116, 128
nonrepudiation feature, 73
nonsecret encryption, 317–30
Notes, 145, 146, 147–51, 155–64,
192, 205, 284–85, 286
NP-complete functions, 84, 86

O'Brien, Bart, 137–38, 140, 141,
142–43, 145, 149, 150
Odom, William E., 182–83
Omura, Jim, 168–69, 171
one-time pads, 12, 176, 269
one-way functions, 28, 29, 30, 35,
68–69, 70, 71, 84, 93, 165, 276
    factoring, 97–100, 102–3, 272–76
    knapsacks, 86–88, 93, 127,
    128–29, 131, 136
    trapdoor, 28, 69, 71, 75
Ozzie, Ray, 145–51, 155–64, 262,
263, 284–86, 296, 309

paranoia levels, 203
Parker, Donn, 213, 225
passwords, 16–17, 30, 68, 69, 147,
159, 220
Pasta, John R., 208
Patel, Marilyn, 300–301
patents, 131, 136, 145, 152, 160, 166,
168–73, 175–77, 179–81,
184–86, 199, 200, 203–4, 213,
217, 219, 286, 293, 294, 308,
310, 325
Patterson, Nick, 314, 320, 321–22,
328
Penet, 222, 290, 291, 292, 293
Phasorphone, 116
Podesta, John, 238, 243
Poe, Edgar Allan, 104, 269, 273
pornography, 292
Press, Frank, 119
Pretty Good Privacy (PGP), 195,
196–204, 211, 212, 220–21,
241, 244, 255, 270, 287–88,
289–90, 309–10
    breaking of, 270–71, 272
Prime, Geoffrey, 327

prime numbers, 97, 98, 99, 102, 272–74, 320, 321
Project C43, 316, 317
Project Overtake, 157–58
public key cryptography, 3, 5, 69–89, 93, 94–114, 117, 119, 127, 136, 146, 148–50, 165, 168–73, 175, 177, 178, 184–85, 191, 192, 203–4, 227–29, 310, 312, 317, 321, 326
  certification of, 201–3
  escrow and, 229, 230–35, 236–38, 239, 240–68, 283, 286, 294–95, 303, 305
  nonsecret encryption and, 317–30
  Secure Sockets Layer, 278, 279, 280–81
  security failures and, 327
Public Key Partners (PKP), 172–74, 179–80, 185, 199, 203, 307–8
Puzzle Palace, The (Bamford), 23, 116

quantum computers, 275

Random Number Generator (RNG), 282
Ray, Charles, 299
RC-2, 160, 161, 262
RC-4, 262, 276, 279, 309
Reagan, Ronald, 182, 209
Reeds, Jim, 28
remailers (anonymous servers), 220–23, 224, 290, 291, 309
  Penet, 222, 290, 291, 292, 293
Richardson, Elliot, 60–61
Ritner, Peter, 22, 23
Rivest, Ron, 90–107, 109, 112, 126, 130–37, 142–44, 148–50, 152, 153, 160, 165, 181, 189, 193, 262, 272, 273, 275, 308, 313
Rizzo, Paul, 51
Roberts, Larry, 20
Robinson, William B., 298, 299
Rohrbacher, Dana, 264
Rosenblum, Howard, 65, 329
Rotenberg, Marc, 182, 238

RSA, 101–5, 107, 112, 114, 117–18, 130–34, 138, 143, 146, 148–50, 152–53, 155, 157, 161–62, 172, 175–79, 181, 184, 189, 192, 195, 198–200, 203, 204, 228, 272, 295, 309, 311, 321, 325
  Netscape and, 278
  patents for, 131, 136, 152, 170, 176, 179–81, 199, 200, 203–4, 310, 325
  personal computers and, 191, 192–93
RSA Data Security, Inc., 135, 136–38, 140–54, 168–77, 181, 184–85, 192–93, 199, 204, 219, 228, 262, 287, 289, 307–9, 326
  conference of, 307, 308–9, 310, 311

Sacco, Luigi, 33
Safire, William, 252
S-boxes (substitution boxes), 42, 47, 55, 56, 58, 61, 167
Schiller, Jeff, 290
Schneier, Bruce, 203, 283, 288–89
Schnorr, Claus, 180–81, 184
Schroeppel, Richard, 28–29, 34, 102–3, 104
Schwartz, John J., 113
Science, 112, 117, 118, 121
Scientific American, 41, 46, 103–5, 112, 174, 189, 269, 273
Scientologists, 142, 144, 290–92
search warrants, 230, 251, 285, 291–92
secret sharing, 165
Secure Sockets Layer (SSL), 278, 279, 280–81
Security and Freedom through Encryption (SAFE) bill, 295, 305, 306
Security Dynamics, 307
Senate Bill 266, 195–96, 197, 198
servers, 278, 282
  anonymous, *see* remailers
Sessions, William, 232, 236, 237, 240, 242, 246

Shamir, Adi, 94–101, 104, 105, 112, 114, 127–28, 130, 131, 133, 135, 136, 153–54, 165–66, 200, 272, 308, 313
Shannon, Claude, 17–18, 32, 33, 45, 46–47
shareware, 195, 196
signals intelligence, 65
signatures, digital, 19–20, 72–73, 85, 88, 93, 100, 148, 173–74, 178–81, 185–86, 215–16, 311, 326
  blind, 216, 223
  DSA, 178–81, 185, 186
Silver, Roland, 9, 10–12, 13, 21
Simmons, Gus, 329
Simons, Jim, 49, 169
Skipjack, 232, 233, 237, 238, 243, 247, 249, 253, 257, 258, 303
Snefru, 297–98
Snow, Brian, 200
Snuffle, 298–302
stream ciphers, 40
Studeman, William O., 178, 246
substitution boxes (S-boxes), 42, 47, 55, 56, 58, 61, 167
SWIFT, 308

T Attack (differential cryptanalysis), 55–56, 64, 200
telephones:
  cellular, 205
  security devices for, 235–38, 240, 243–44, 246, 249, 252, 254, 256–57, 303, 326
Tempest technology, 43
Tenet, George, 246
Tessera, 257
threshold scheme, 165
Time, 129
time-sharing, 16, 19
toll payments, 218
trapdoors, 60–61, 62–63, 66–67, 68, 70, 72, 84, 122, 230
  knapsacks, 86–88, 93, 127, 128–29, 131, 136

one-way function, 28, 69, 71, 75
  Senate bill and, 195–96, 197, 198
Tritter, Alan, 29–30, 48, 49, 50
Tuchman, Walter, 43–46, 47, 50, 51, 52–54, 55, 58–59, 61–64, 156, 253

univectors, 273, 274
Usenet, 221, 222

vector space, 273
VeriSign, 308
Very Large Scale Integration (VLSI), 132–33
ViaCrypt, 289
virtual private networks, 311

Wagner, Dave, 281–83
Walker, Steve, 263–64
Wall Street Journal, 158, 289
Warren, Jim, 197, 288
Washington Post, 267–68
web of trust, 202–3
Weingarten, Fred, 107–8
Weldon, Curt, 306
Williamson, Malcolm, 314, 320, 322–25, 327, 328, 329
Windows, 310
wiretapping, 229–30, 234, 235–36, 240, 255–56, 257–58, 303
Wise, William, 246
World Wide Web, 277–78, 312
  browsers for, 277–78, 279, 310
Wormser, Dave, 156
Wylie, Shawn, 318

Xerox Corporation, 166–67, 208
xor operations, 11–12

Zero Knowledge, 309
zero-knowledge proofs of identity, 165–66
Zimmermann, Kacie, 189–90
Zimmermann, Phil, 187–204, 205, 211, 244, 264, 270–71, 272, 287–88, 289, 290, 309–10